TOM SCHEERER
MORE DECORATING

TOM SCHEERER
MORE DECORATING

PHOTOGRAPHS BY
FRANCESCO LAGNESE

VENDOME
NEW YORK · LONDON

 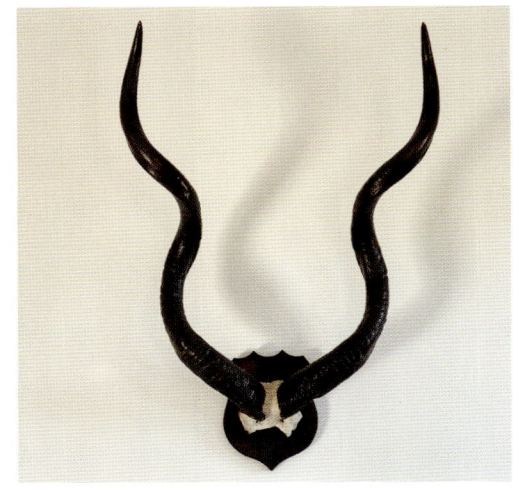  

Contents

INTRODUCTION *13*

TOWN
AMERICANS IN PARIS *25* • BREAD AND BUTTER *43*
SHOCK AND AWE *53* • HOME AGAIN *69*
GENTLEMAN'S AGREEMENT *79* • CAMPING *97*
PLAY IT AGAIN *109*

SUMMER
HEDGES *125* • PINK STRING *143*
OLD EAST HAMPTON *157* • HOUSEKEEPING *169*

THE TROPICS
HARBOUR ISLAND *183* • HAPPY, ALIVE AND WELL *201*
SUNRISE AND SUNSET *217* • FRENCH LEAVE *251*
ZANZIBAR *269*

SOURCES *292*
ACKNOWLEDGMENTS *294*

Introduction

I'LL NEVER BE ACCUSED OF JUMPING ON DECORATING bandwagons. There's a house on these pages that's pretty much unchanged since I decorated it twenty-three years ago. My first New York apartment may very well be the most like my most recent. I am more apt to fall into step with the way things were done when I was growing up.

My paternal grandmother had a knack for good-looking and comfortable houses without any apparent help from a decorator. She was lucky to be given a good head start with a fine 1920s Georgian-style Marion Sims Wyeth house in New Jersey and a shingled summer house of the same vintage that my family still has today. In that East Hampton house especially, there was no deliberate or serious decorating. She used paint and wallpaper liberally and fresh chintzes on the furniture that had come with the house. It turned out well enough that my twin-bedded room has barely changed in my sixty-three summers there.

After our multi-generational summer idylls, my sisters and I were returned to the suburbs, but not to a "decorated" house. That house and the New York apartment that followed it were primarily concocted from hand-me-downs and other offerings from my house-happy grandmother, and here and there advice from amateur (some talented) decorators who always seemed to be at the periphery of my parents' social life.

One such friend, a young-ish widow from St Louis, plucked me from childhood and gave me my first summer job at age thirteen. You guessed it—as a decorator. She

OPPOSITE The doors of the nine-foot storage cabinet in my Union Square office were inspired by Josef Frank. The inset panels are papered in 1901 prints by Brazilian botanist João Barbosa Rodrigues. They also form the endpapers of this book.
ABOVE A Florence Knoll conference table doubles as my desk.

My first New York apartment at 83rd Street and Park Avenue, as photographed for the *New York Times Magazine* in 1990. The design was inspired by Ward Bennett, Joseph D'Urso, and Benjamin Baldwin. The architectural drawing over the sofa is by Aldo Rossi, one of my professors at The Cooper Union. The custom-made bamboo bookcases flanking the sofa became one of my standbys.

arrived in East Hampton to "do up" a house —a generous and trusting offer long before anyone thought of calling it "grief therapy." The house, newly bought by her friends (they were my parents' friends too) had to be ready for their August arrival.

The utterly picturesque, slightly dilapidated Cotswolds-style cottage at the far end of an enormous privet-edged lawn was widely admired and already coveted by a thirteen-year-old. I was enchanted before we started.

Queen Anne (yes, that's what they called her), known for her arch and undeniable glamour, had ordered the entire house interior painted bright white before her arrival—the floors and the wood ceilings glossy and the rusticated walls matte. I'm pretty sure the bolts of summery fabric fanned out, selvages flapping, from the back seat of a convertible when she drove up. Her hands were flying and flashing with chunky rings of semiprecious stones. Tourmalines. That's the way I remember it anyway, and only much later in life did I recognize that those bolts of fabric were Dek Tillett.

It was all very rushed and fun—the decorator version of summer stock. My stagehand tasks may have been

The *objet trouvé* resting on the mantel was found in a Park Avenue dumpster. It can now be seen in a recent project (see page 61). The lacquered-plywood furniture made for the apartment remains with me to this day.

OPPOSITE The dining veranda of my first house in the Bahamas, originally a nineteenth-century convent, as photographed for *Elle Decor* in 1996. Purple has long been a favorite color for outdoor upholstery. ABOVE My most recent Paris apartment is on the Île Saint-Louis. The dining room table came from my mother's New York apartment. The wicker chairs are contemporary re-editions of a design by Robert Wengler, wicker maker to the Danish Crown.

menial, but they were eye opening. I scraped and painted the rusty iron terrace furniture that we found in the cellar (to this day I can't abide noisy and cold-to-the-touch metal furniture), and I sponged faux lichen onto terra-cotta pots from the hardware store.

I watched the colorful fabrics being cut into table drops with pinking shears and her improvisatory (in retrospect amateurish) painting of broad faux-bois planks onto the plain Parsons-style dining table ordered from New York.

Color-coding the bathrooms by coating the claw-foot-tub bottoms in pastel tints might have even been my own idea. At home, our bedrooms were (and are still) always called out by their color.

Fifty years later, minus the manual labor, I'm doing things in this same spirit whenever I'm allowed. And as a further prognostication and irony, I've decorated houses for several of the children who arrived there with their parents that August.

My history as an "adult" decorator is curious in that I didn't purposefully educate myself for it. I was going to be an architect. I entered school with a fascination for houses and the intricate and accurate house plans I could draw from memory and imagination. It was a skill I hoped would propel me.

It turned out that there was little about the designing of houses at The Cooper Union, let alone the kind I found

ABOVE I recently redecorated my office to last through a renewed lease. The chairs were designed by Josef Hoffmann in 1925 and are my Thonet favorites. OPPOSITE A triad of French aquarelle prints from a 1789 series on Captain Cook in Fiji by John Cleveley makes a fitting subject for tropical and nautical decorative schemes. I have adapted them into wall panels for a yacht and into a folding screen.

The Florence Knoll conference table was bleached and refinished for the freshly decorated office. The paper-cone pendant lights were made to order by Blanche P. Field, New York. Cécile carpet tiles by Studio Four form a subtle checkerboard and serve as practical flooring for an office. The curtain fabric is Quadrille's Saya Gata pattern.

interesting. Domesticity in general was frowned upon in favor of large and rigorous philosophical concepts. Le Corbusier's Villa Savoye may have been revered but mostly as a crucible of ideas for "social housing."

When I graduated from this long and challenging stopover in the world of academe, I was broadly educated but not inculcated. Luckily, those five years were not entirely wasted—I found my way into decorating almost immediately. My skills were handy and my sense for space, proportion, and materiality had been fine-tuned.

Not incidentally, I did not take a job with one of New York's pantheon of venerable decorators. I did not sully myself with the defining style and the burden of professionalism required by any particular boss. This was not a deliberate plan; when my education re-started, I "learned by doing."

My first apartment was a wonderful high-ceilinged room at 83rd Street and Park Avenue. It had served as a "bedsit" and studio for five years, drafting table by the window, yellow tracing paper taped to the walls in layers.

The place was elegant, though, and the rent had been low enough to justify living uptown. As soon as I was finished with school, the building "went co-op" and the apartment came at good price.

Throughout my school years I had been looking wistfully (and surreptitiously) at "interior design" magazines, and my head was full of Joe D'Urso, Ward Bennett, and Benjamin Baldwin (the decorator Billy Baldwin revealed himself later as an equal master).

I flanked the chimneybreast with mirror, installed wall-to-wall sisal, and made a series of modernist upholstered pieces, including a bed, and a suite of Bauhaus-inspired plywood desks and tables. The decorated version of the apartment, which you can see on these pages, became my calling card and the first rung of my climb up the "property ladder."

Several years later there was a rash and eye-opening sub-urban and semitropical adventure to Charleston, South Carolina. There I bought my first "proper" house, paid for entirely with the proceeds from my one-bedroom apartment on 87th Street. The palm trees offered hope—false as it turned out—that Charleston winters would be sunny and warm, and the stock of wonderful old and not-yet-fixed-up houses offered a possibility that business there would burgeon. It did not, but that's another story. Social and fun though it was, it gave me a hankering to seek a watering hole further south.

A house for a client on Harbour Island precipitated (again rashly) the purchase and renovation of a derelict convent. What followed was an entire, and adjunct, career of making tropical houses for myself and various clients in the Bahamas and elsewhere in the Caribbean. Being asked to decorate the Lyford Cay Club in Nassau was likely the pivotal moment in my career.

The tropics have always been on the frontlines of my own night and daydreams of sensual and domestic opulence. Even at a young age, the houses I drew for myself were most often open-air—with swimming pools surrounded by palm trees. The restraint and asceticism for which I am sometimes known (as far as decorating goes) came later.

The Harbour Island life I engineered for myself as a self-anointed and wishful "slacker" was not destined to last. As it turns out, I am naturally restless and surprisingly (to me anyway) prone to work. A Gramercy Park pied-à-terre morphed into something larger, with an adjacent studio apartment as an office, and then into a full-fledged decorating operation in the Union Square office, where I still am today.

What I called the "property ladder" is really a euphemism. "Real estate junkie" is probably a better term. Mind you, the houses are all relatively modest, and some are shared with siblings. I still have more of them at the moment than I'd recommend. A four-story house in Paris's Marais and an apartment less than a mile away is clearly excessive.

But as they say, "Decorators do not have children—they have houses." Evidently, I am a "family man." And a house always has a story to tell about its *two* parents, the decorator and the client. A biographical narrative—whether a fiction, a memoir, or a roman à clef (and it's often subliminal)—is what makes for strong decorating. Without a compelling story to animate a house, it's all just real estate and shopping.

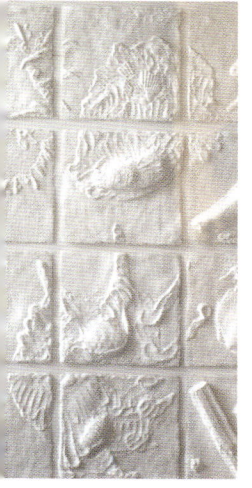

TOWN

Americans in Paris

THE FRENCH HAVE A SOMEWHAT IMPRECISE but useful term: *appartement de réception*—an apartment of stature, not quite a large family apartment, yet larger than what one might call a pied-à-terre. An apartment used by its owners when in town, for guests, and for entertainments.

The players here are a seasonally peripatetic American lady, a couple with business and recreational interests that bring them through Paris a few times a year, and lastly, a certain New York decorator, the leaseholder of the apartment, and his Oklahoman partner, the only one who speaks French. "Overlap" is assiduously avoided but sometimes inevitable—the perfect formula for a Feydeau farce.

A central entrance gallery opens to a series of rooms through tall, paned doors, allowing the light to bounce off the Seine deep into the apartment. These doors are opened or closed, shades up or down, depending on the current residents and their need for privacy or lack thereof.

Happily, there are two water closets, the nicer, windowed one in the zigzagging bedroom hall and a large, communal, hammam-like room with a deep tub and a huge stall shower—the scene of potential tension and comedy. The decorator has provided robes; the guests may fashion their own turbans.

A shallow balcony runs the width of the apartment and overlooks the quay. The long row of south-facing windows can be shaded by the landlord's ingenious bright orange, rope-rigged awnings. These are especially useful on gloomy days, when they are lowered to give a sunny glow that enlivens the interior and distracts from the predictably gray Parisian sky shrouding the Pantheon in the near distance.

The decorator is justified in saying that the apartment decorated itself. The grandiose niche in the hall merely needed dramatizing dark paint, then a mitigating and apt object to fill it.

By landlord edict, the early nineteenth-century scenic mural in the main room, like a theater drop, could not be touched. Its surrounding walls and frame cried out, however, for more hospitable paint. A deep green crisped up the white, quasi-rococo overdoors and moldings, and the pastoral scene is now well settled in the expanded verdancy.

The kitchen came bare boned but with the "prompter" of an eccentric, magenta-lacquered monolith housing a sink, a cooktop, and the requisite plumbing. Plenty of room was left for the addition of workaday marble countertops and walls, a fridge, an oven, and a curtained-off laundry area. Americans require these things, whereas the French may not, apparently.

Otherwise, the mandate was to make the rooms as French as American interlopers might dare, cautious of the gaffes. French taste, past and present, always correct, if a bit formulaic, was skirted but not entirely embraced. A vaguely Proustian *jardin d'hiver* was evoked in the dining room with a new iteration of the decorator's signature lattice wallpaper from 1970s WASP America. The requirement of a balanced pair of armoires for the guest room was resolved with "post-modern" ones crafted for the apartment in India. In a last theatrical gesture, a television set (a comely one, to be sure) was placed center stage in front of the scenic scrim—another American character in the French play.

OPPOSITE Dark brown paint deepens the niche at the end of the entrance gallery. The seat of a Louis XVI-style bench was covered in a needlepoint version of a Rousseau painting found at the Marché aux Puces and cut to fit. The suspended book sculpture was found at Modernity in Stockholm. The charming and surreal carved-wood lamp has appeared in several of my dwellings over the years. **OVERLEAF** Matching slipcovered sofas face each other in the living room. The orange canvas awnings are rolled out to shade the afternoon sun.

ABOVE The nineteenth-century pastoral scene on canvas came with the apartment, and the well-designed television is by Samsung. OPPOSITE The potted *Alocasia zebrina* is one of my preferred house plants. OVERLEAF LEFT This view toward the guest room reveals the series of tall doors facing south over the Seine. OVERLEAF RIGHT A collection of brass objects on the mantel echoes the 1950s brass cube coffee tables in the living room.

OPPOSITE In the dining room, a winter garden atmosphere was achieved with an adapted version of Lyford Trellis wallpaper. The chairs against the wall are early twentieth-century reproductions of the iconic Georges Jacob Klismos chair. ABOVE The dining room is open to the kitchen, which still has the apartment's original 1860s encaustic floor tiles.

ABOVE A framed linen dish towel printed with a Louise Bourgeois drawing is surrounded by an arrangement of patinaed "shipwreck" Ming dynasty plates. OPPOSITE The magenta-lacquered unit came with the apartment. The traditional "butcher's shop" Carrara marble and the stainless-steel cabinetry were added by the decorator, picking up the gray in the floor tiles.

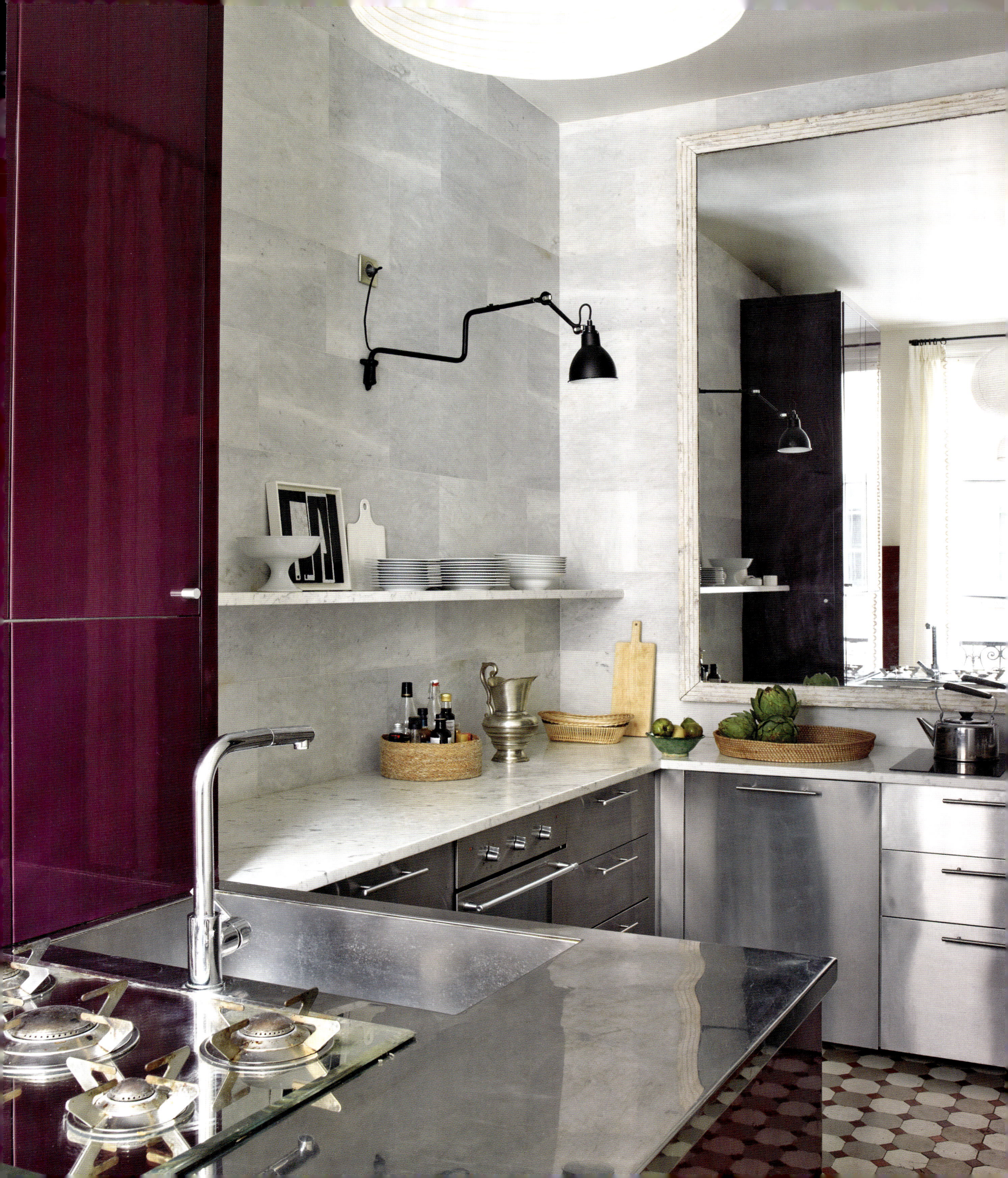

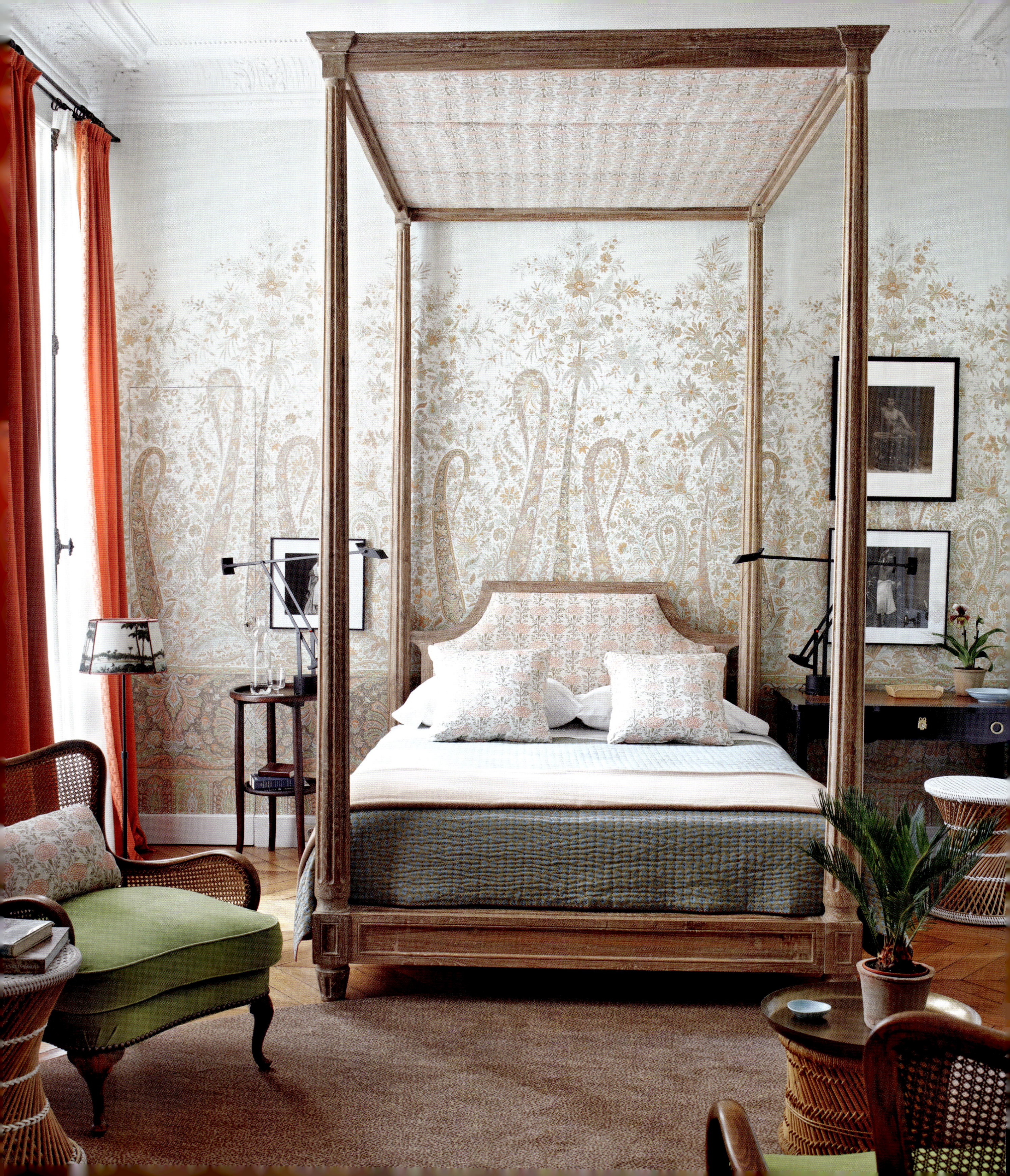

OPPOSITE AND ABOVE The attenuated four-poster was made for this bedroom in India. In form it references Louis XVI-style furniture of the 1930s. The caned and bentwood suite of furniture is vintage and covered in cotton velvet. Marcus Leatherdale's photographs of India add to the exotic atmosphere. The wall covering was adapted from a Kashmiri shawl. Printed linen in the Samode pattern from Lisa Fine Textiles adds another touch of the Subcontinent, as do the Indian straw hassocks-cum-occasional tables. The finely woven straw fan was bought on a summer trip to Hydra.

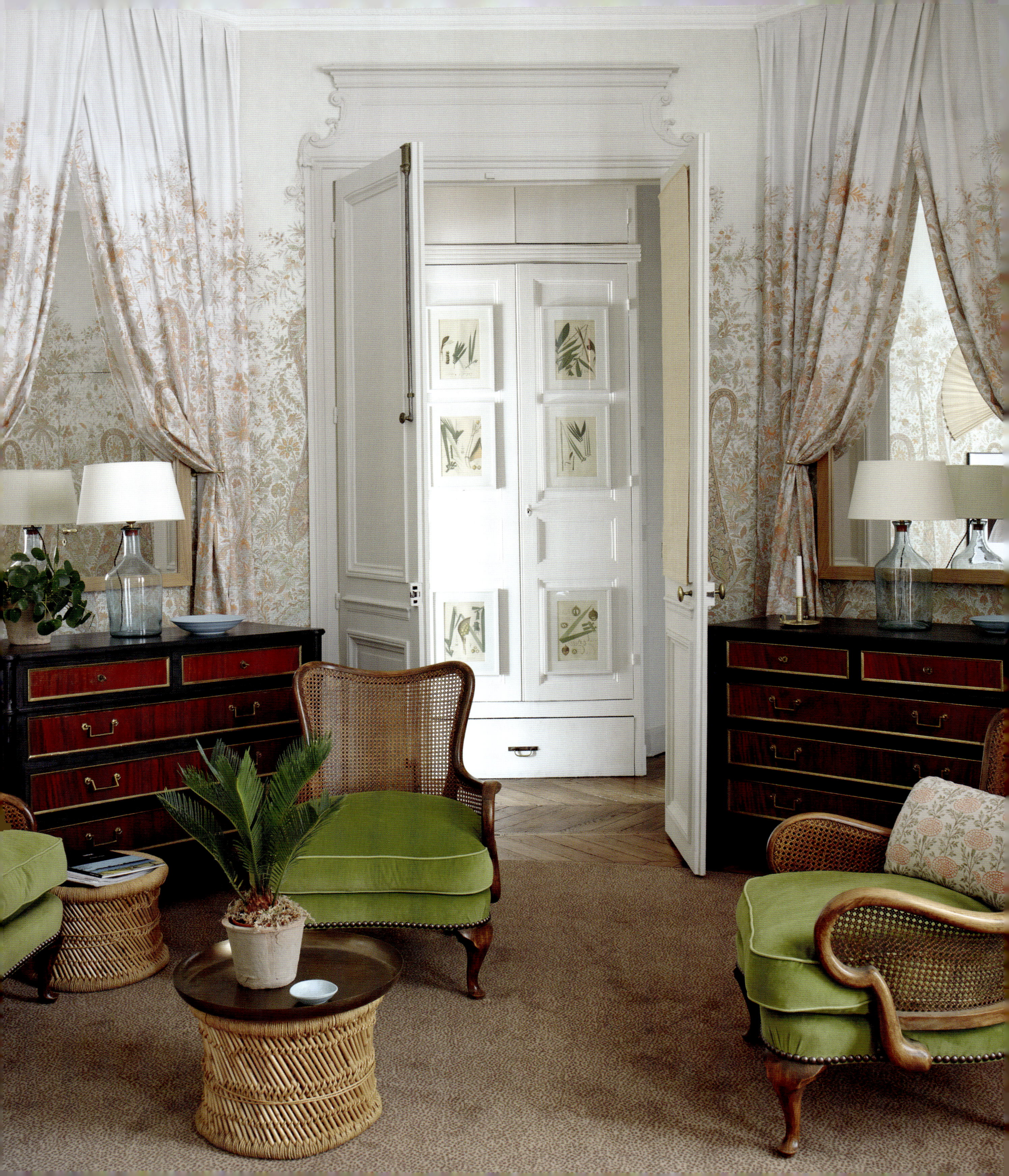

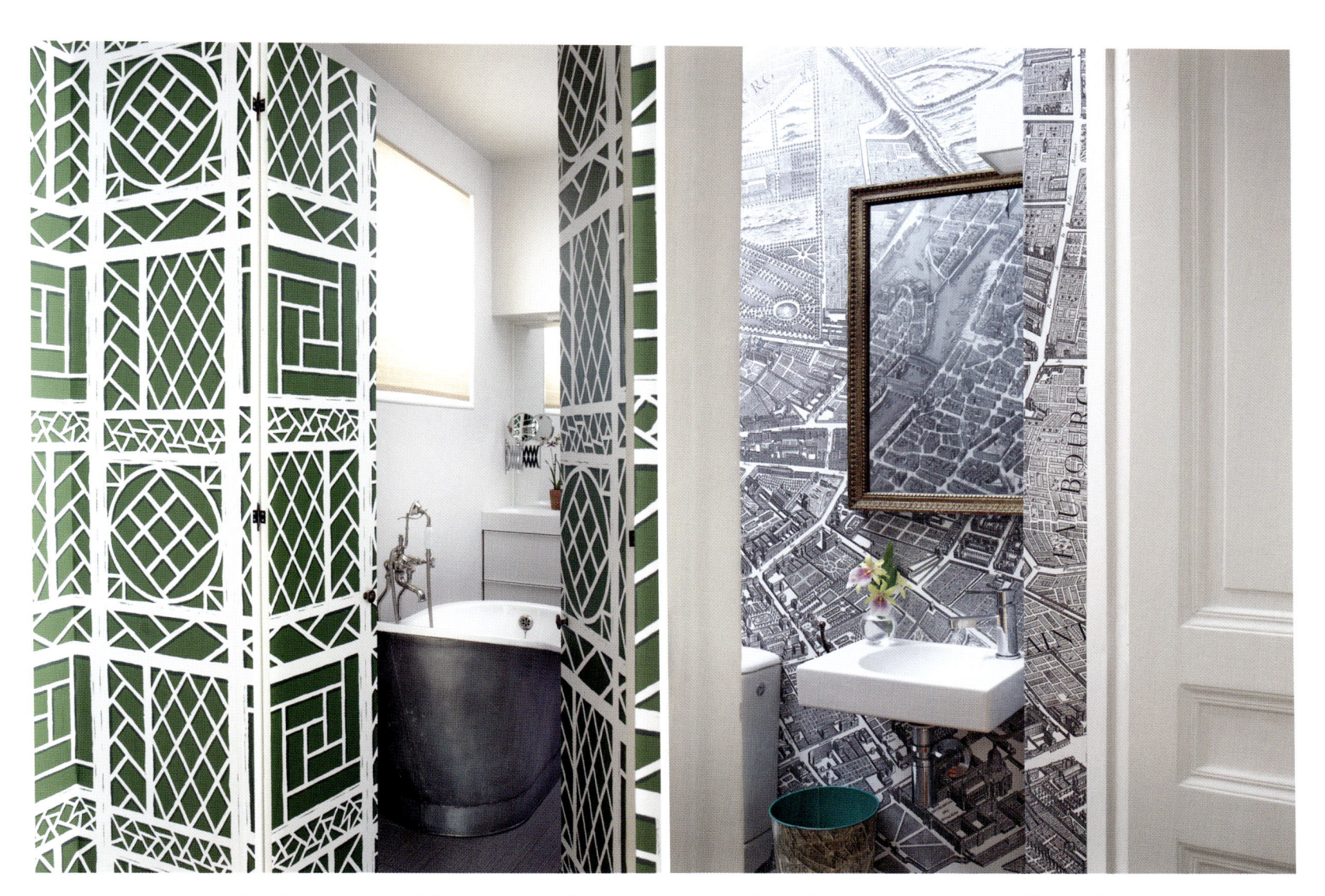

OPPOSITE Twentieth-century Louis XVI-style commodes flank the doors to the corridor and linen cupboard. **ABOVE LEFT** The principal bathroom houses a "Marat"-style soaking tub and a stall shower. **ABOVE RIGHT** A separate water closet is papered in an enlargement of the widely known and exceedingly accurate Turgot map of Paris, originally published in 1739.

ABOVE I designed the armoires and the pair of twin beds in the guest room and had them made in India. The vintage Jansen fauteuils are covered in green linen. The reading lamps are from Galerie des Lampes. The tobacco velvet curtains are unlined.

ABOVE RIGHT The cotton bedspreads are from Les Indiennes. The wall assemblage was made by the decorator out of Ikea picture frames and leftover paint from the adjacent room. RIGHT The painting resting on the mantel is by the American artist Peter Dayton.

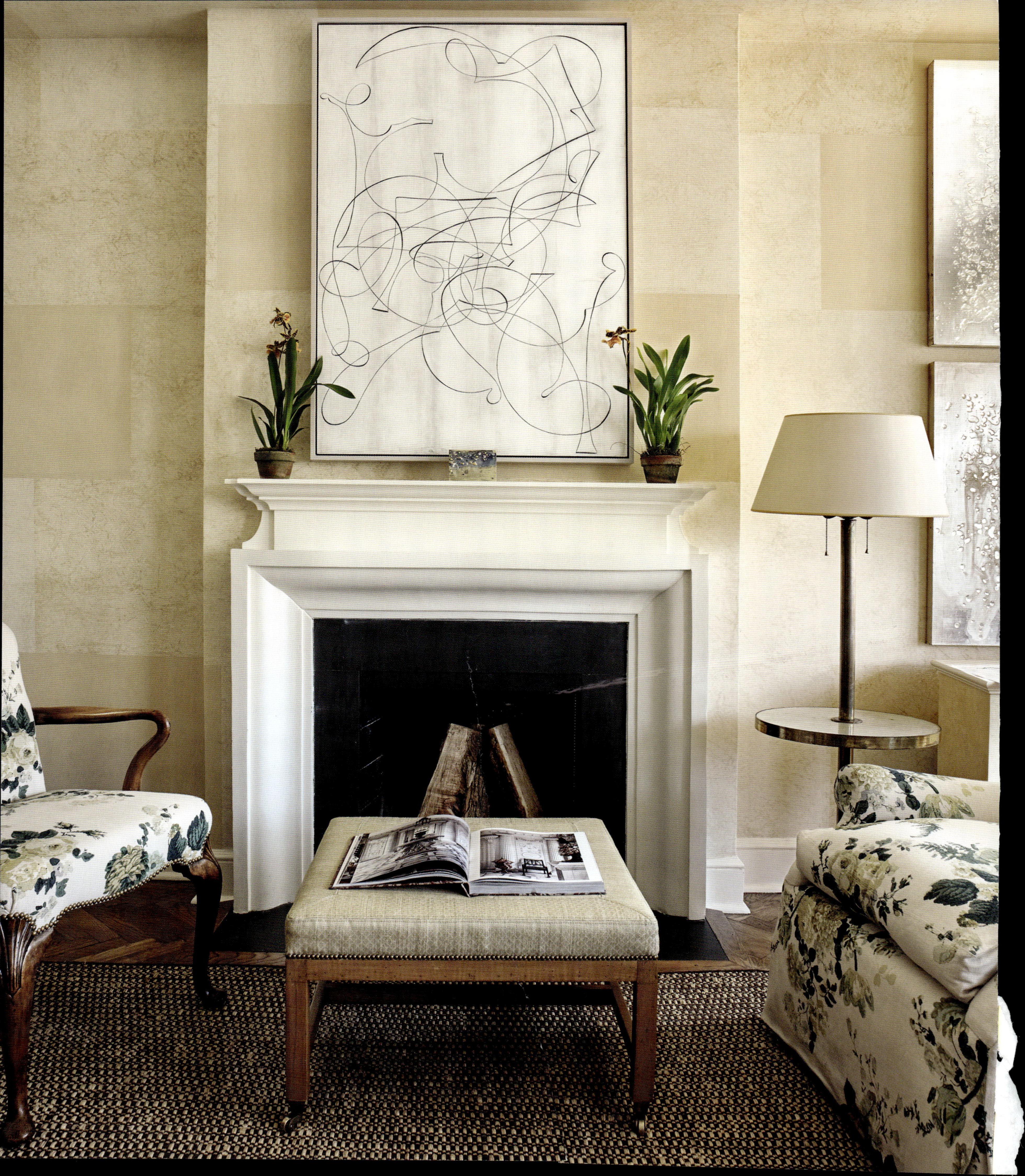

Bread and Butter

There was not much about their former apartment that they didn't like. It was their third in Brooklyn Heights in a mere seventeen years—a larger apartment suitable for their three growing children and in the very same building as their first.

Those beautifully arranged and decorated rooms (by yours truly) overlooked Pierrepont Park, the bustling harbor, and the Financial District beyond. Alas, it was deemed profligate for their by then college-bound, shrinking family and too far from all their daytime avocations and social pastimes in Manhattan.

The lady of the house pleads restlessness and "real estate dysfunction" but is widely admired for her sensibleness and her instinctively good, if impulsive, real estate choices. The decorator's suggestion and enthusiastic endorsement of this Fifth Avenue building was all it took. The apartment was the only one she considered.

Trusting and loyal clients (and empty nesters) are the bread and butter of the decorating business. After three New York apartments, a Pennsylvania country house, three consecutively up-ticked Maine summer houses, and ultimately the conjuring of this recent apartment, the term "lifestyle guru" (bestowed by the lady and her husband) for the decorator may actually be appropriate. The word ought to be avoided, but a "lifestyle" it nevertheless is.

The building is "full service" in the best and most extreme sense. The back-of-house staff is genuinely helpful. The doormen and ever-present concierge are welcoming to tenants and their guests alike. Lunches and dinners, when sent up by the classically trained resident chef, are served on one's own crockery by uniformed and charmingly behaved butlers. Butterballs are iced. The detritus is whisked away but not before the dishwasher is loaded. The toting of firewood and setting of the hearths in winter by these same men was an added and unexpected bonus, as was the Central Park–adjacent dog-washing room worthy of the Westminster Kennel Club.

The couple is so deliriously happy in this *comme il faut* and thoroughly pampering nest that the decorating is almost beside the point. Objects and furnishings, refined and whittled from the former apartment, arrived to a setting very familiar, decorated for the ongoing roundelay. The Italianate scenic paper was not to be parted with so was eagerly reordered. After installation it was glazed with the same "tobacco smoke" patina as before.

The brass Cole Porter étagères were resized to fit the family's ever reoccurring Red Room. It's now a compact and hybridized library/dining room. The son's avid collection of Napoleon memorabilia was augmented (only a tad) by the decorator to fill out a campaign-style "tented" guest room.

Luckily, there were still a few things for the decorator to do to earn his keep: fresh fabrics for reupholstery, and new carpets and wall coverings, of course, but also the imposing tester bed ordered from India to work around the high ceiling's upholstered soffit without diminishing the bed's overall height. Again from India, a Georgian-style, pagoda-roofed bookcase/secretaire that required a very precise height and width. A charming Russian chandelier/lantern was found in London for the entrance hall's high ceiling. An extravagant and impulsive purchase for the lady, but one not regretted for a minute.

OPPOSITE Over the newly installed mantel in the living room is a painting by Elliott Puckette. Green horsehair covers the ottoman below it.
OVERLEAF One of a pair of 1960s tub chairs functions as a modern note in an otherwise very proper living room. The walls are covered in squares of bark paper by the Caba Company. Over the tufted corner banquette is a landscape painting by Stephen Hannock.

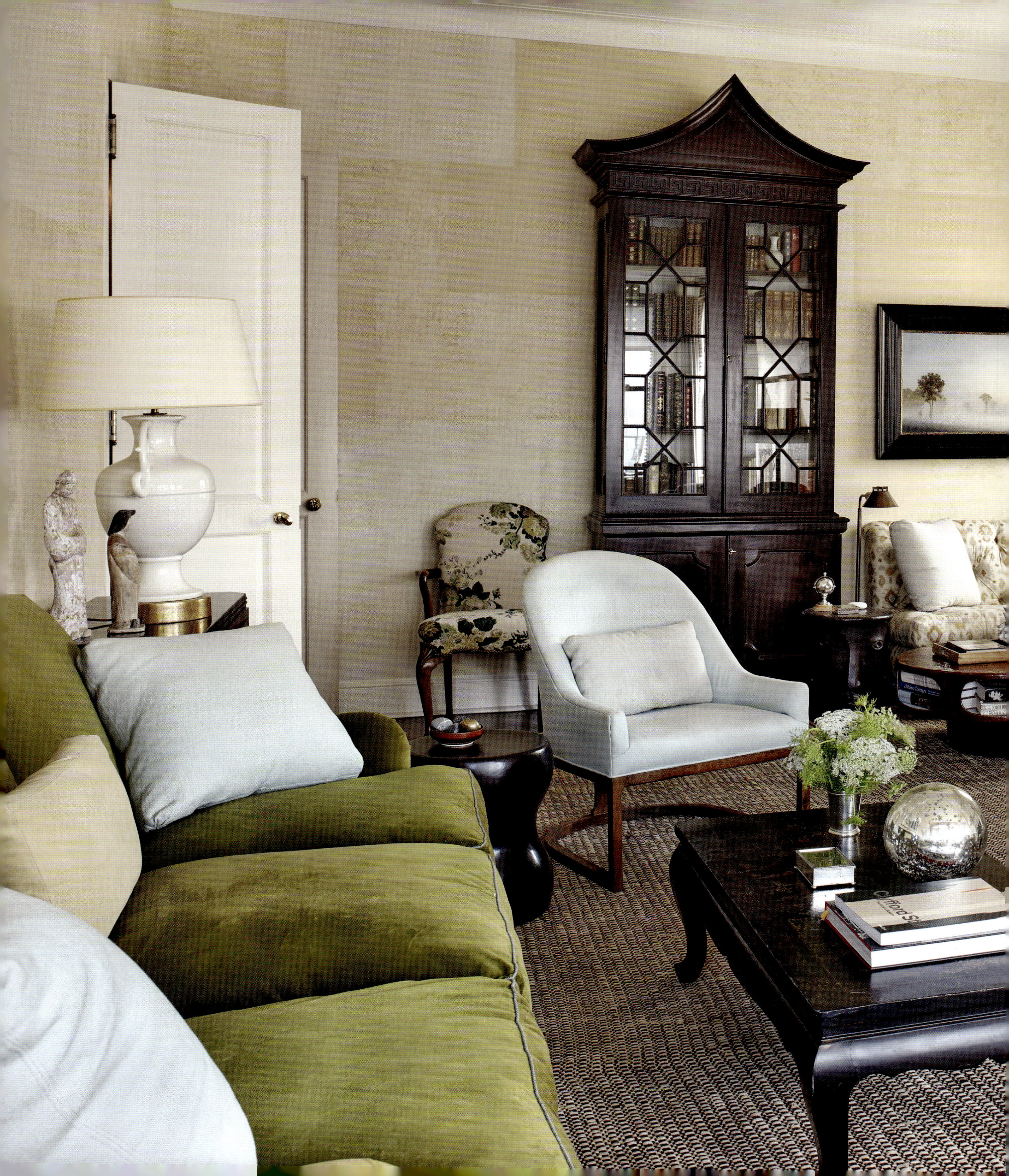

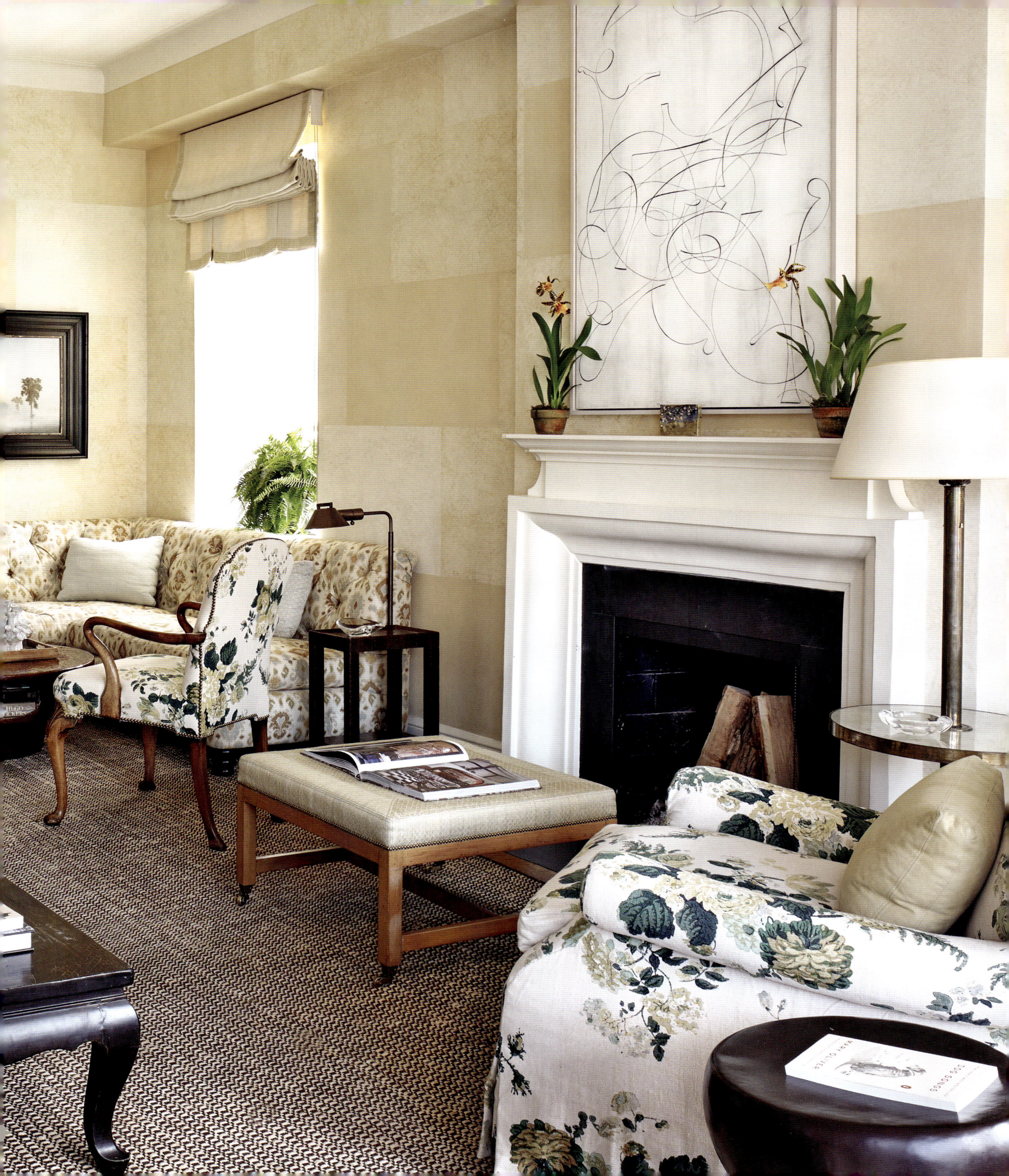
MARY OLIVER
DOG SONGS

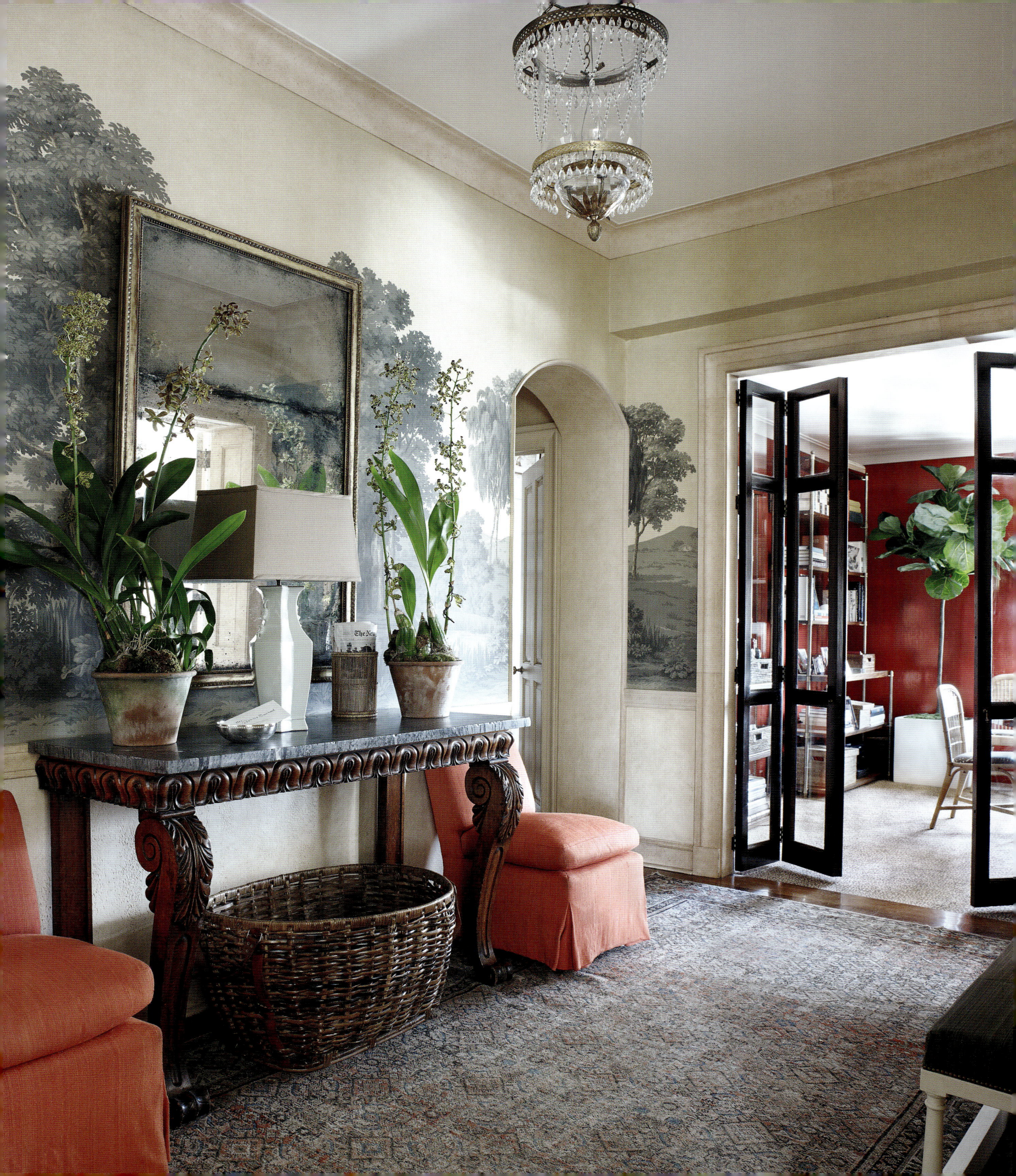

OPPOSITE In the entrance hall, Zuber's Paysage Italien wallpaper panels are overglazed with a protective coat of sepia-tinted varnish. The slipper chairs came from an apartment decorated by Billy Baldwin and were re-covered for the clients' previous one. ABOVE A painting by Jane Wilson presides over the dining table, which is surrounded by rattan-and-wicker chairs by Vittorio Bonacina. The seat cushions are covered in Penny Morrison's Luma print, which is reminiscent of African mud cloth.

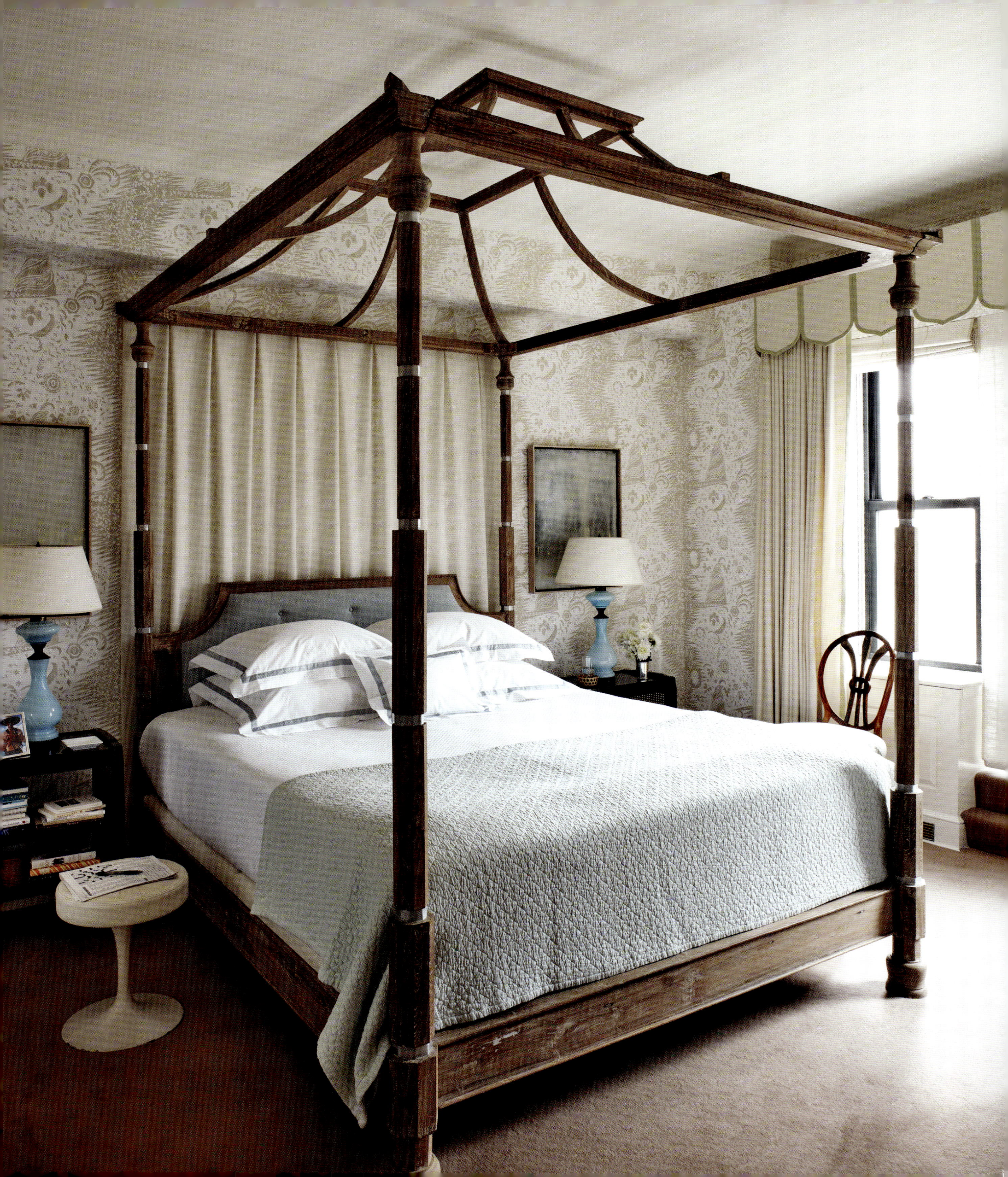

OPPOSITE Quadrille's Riviere Enchantee printed cotton covers the walls of the master bedroom. The tester bed with silver-leaf accents was made for the apartment by the Raj Company. The bed is flanked by a pair of New York winter scenes by Kathryn Lynch.
ABOVE The exuberantly curvaceous walnut chest of drawers is French Régence, ca. 1720, and came from Cove Landing in New York.

ABOVE The guest bedroom houses a collection of Napoleon memorabilia and was decorated in campaign style to suit. The cashmere throws with embroidered monograms on the beds are from Loro Piana. OPPOSITE, CLOCKWISE FROM TOP LEFT The Swedish Grace–period chair is still covered in its original leather. A very fine George III mirror faces the twin beds. The pebbled-leather and brass-trimmed semainier greets the guest and announces the room's theme. Every surface of the bathroom was faux-painted to match the marble shower stall, floor, and sink top.

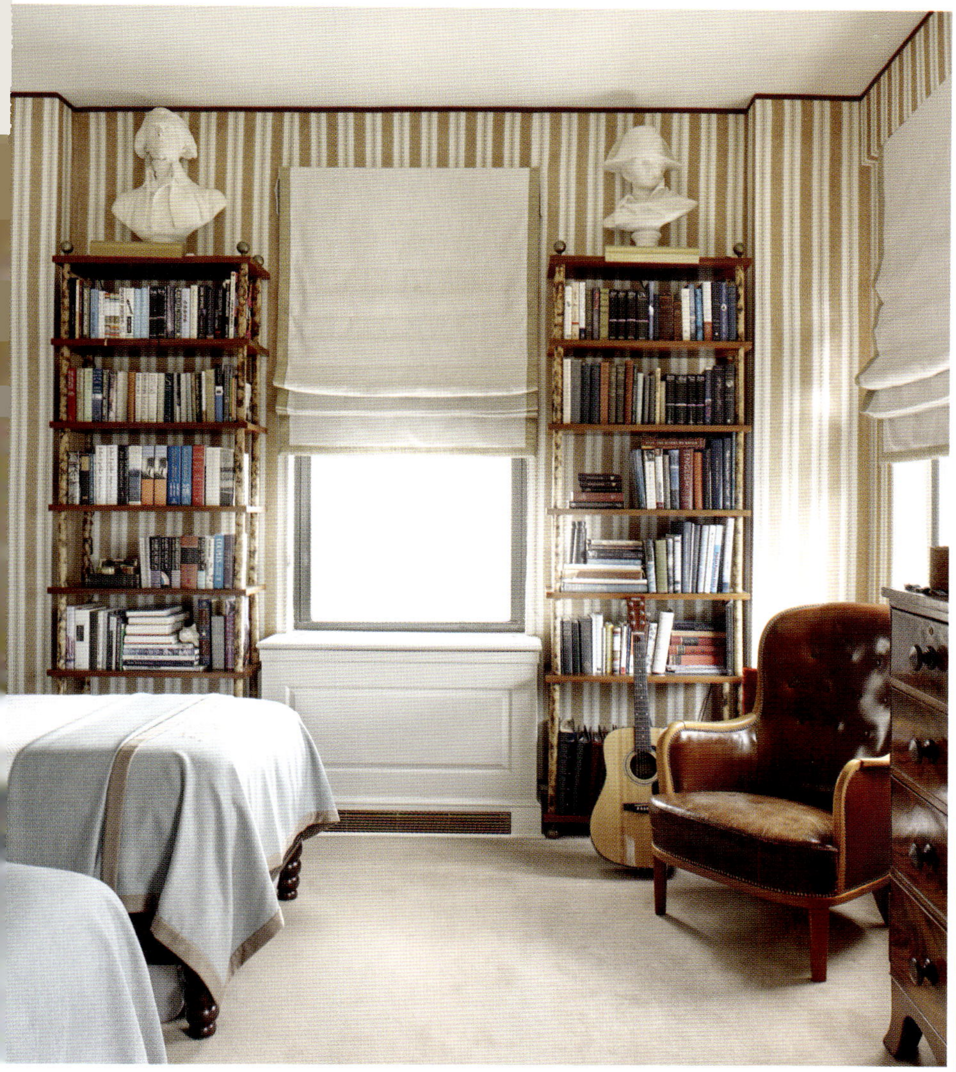

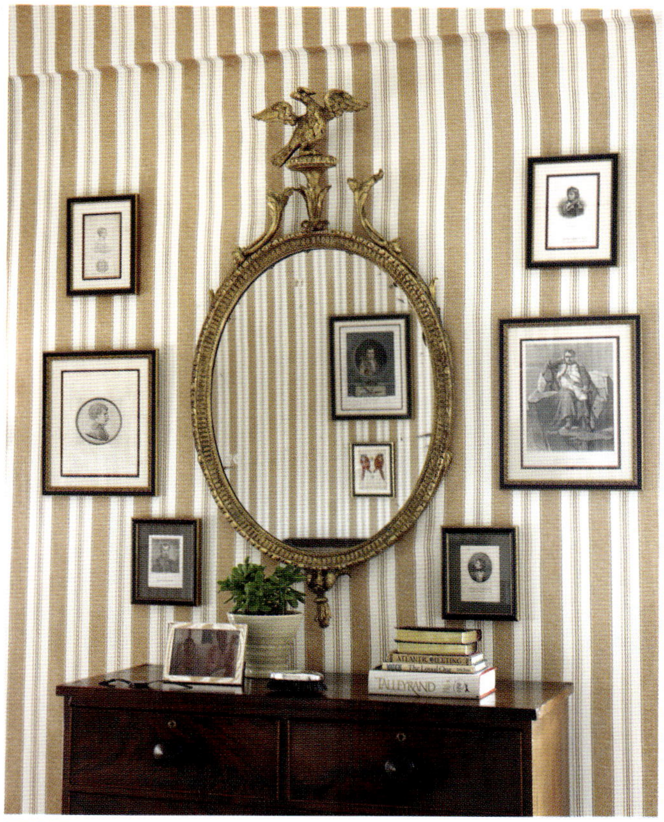

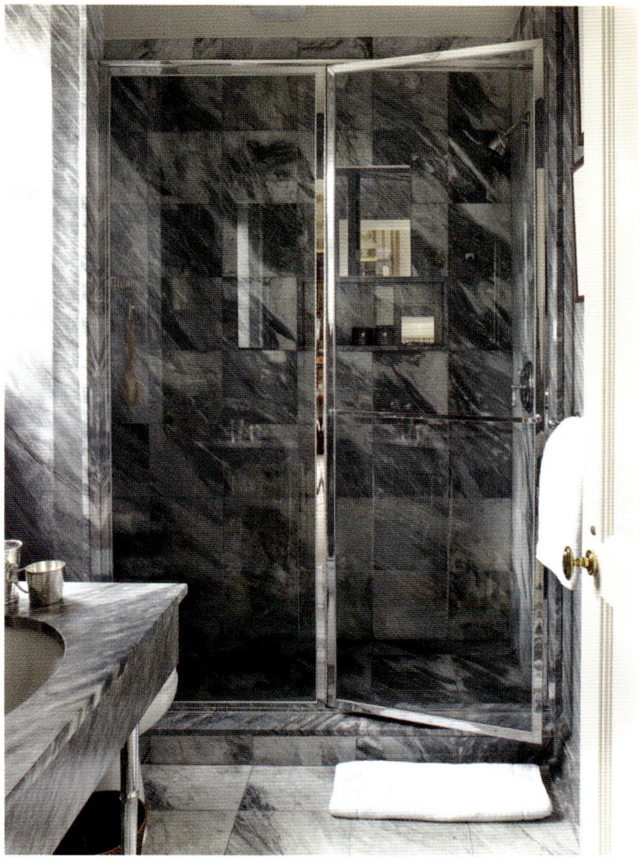

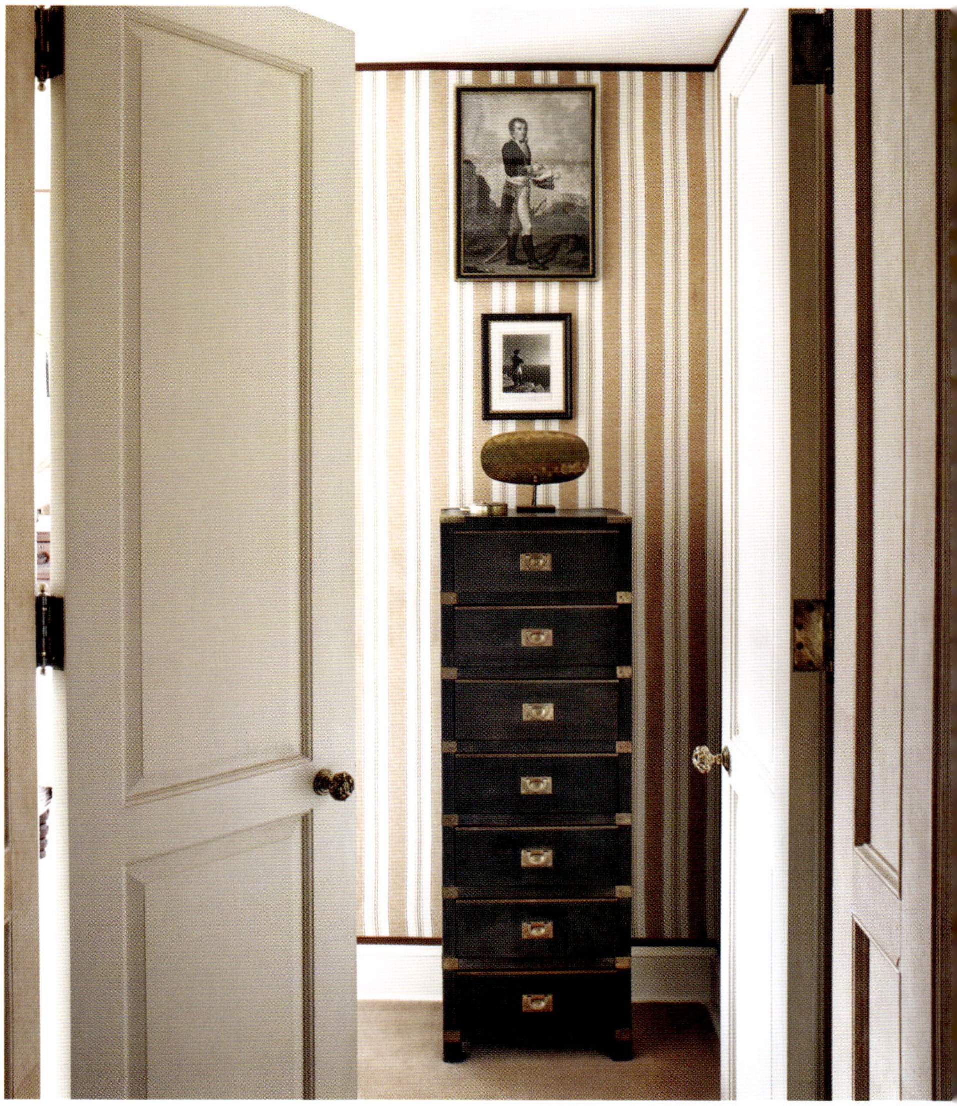

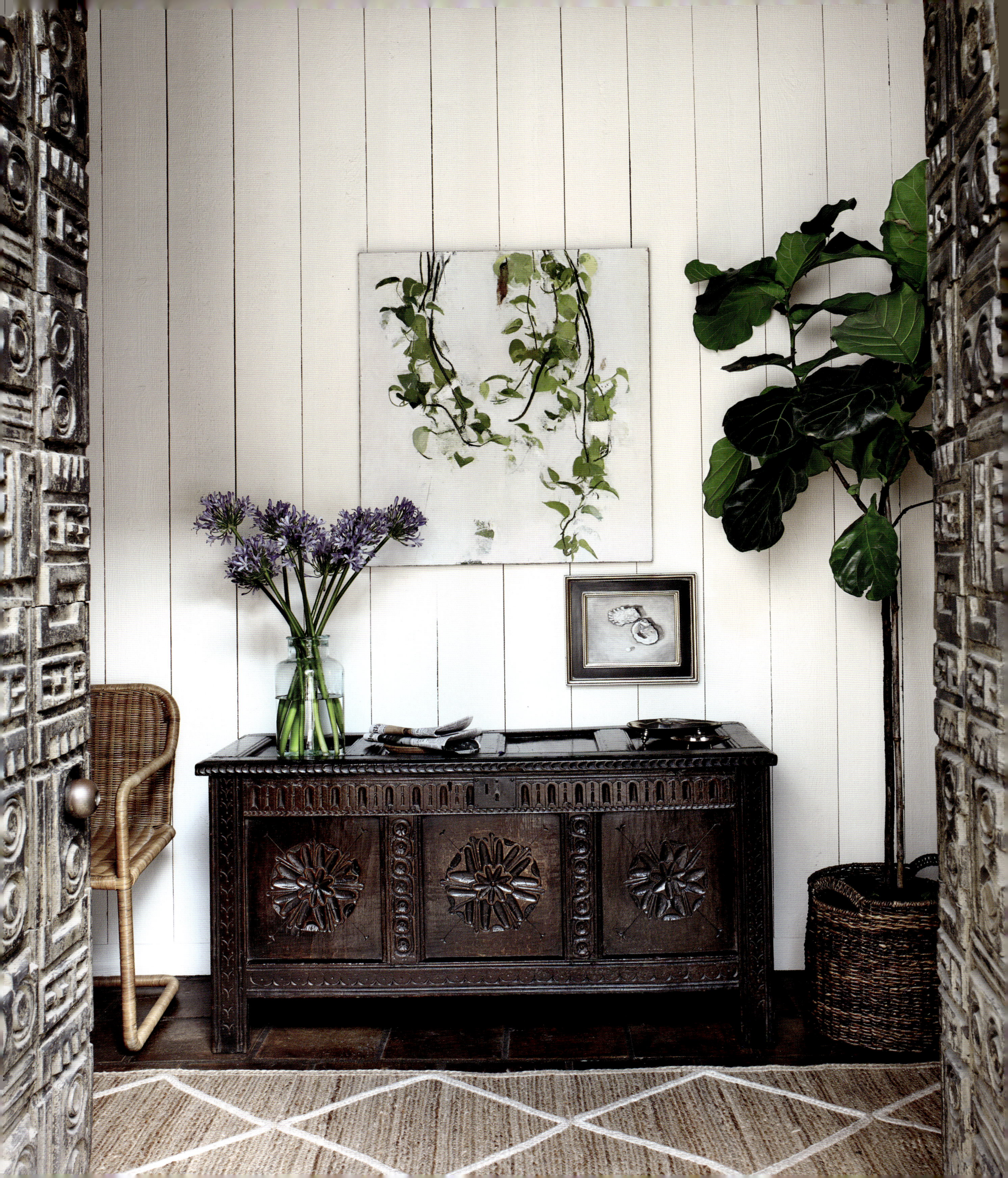

Shock and Awe

The architect of this unusual Houston house, I. W. "Ike" Colburn, is one of my early heroes. I was introduced to his work in 1970 (I remember precisely) by a school friend from Lake Forest, Illinois, where he built several extraordinary houses, which are now iconic among his fans. These houses, many now victims of changing tastes and the wrecking ball, are thankfully documented in old issues of *House & Garden* and have recently been canonized in a dry, almost entirely black-and-white, scholarly monograph.

Colburn's houses are eccentric and extravagant, like those of Paul Rudolph, Philip Johnson, and Wallace K Harrison, his American contemporaries. These were not modernist living machines for the masses but rather resplendent houses for the thinking rich.

Chicago-centric Colburn picked up where David Adler (almost every decorator's favorite architect) left off. His haute haute-bourgeois patrons were looking for a new way to spend lots of money to live well without forgoing the stately comforts provided so liberally by Adler. Modernist houses don't generally come with staff quarters as Ike Colburn's do.

It was a chance encounter and a thrilling rush of school-day memories. While antique crawling through a neighborhood at the edge of River Oaks, we spotted this astonishing house. Its distinctive sculptural chimneys pegged it without question as one of Colburn's. The austere and entirely windowless exterior walls suggested a chic fortress and hinted at a thoroughly private and seductive interior courtyard.

There was no "for sale" sign, but I insisted we dig further. My friend and antiquing companion was, providentially, in the market for a new house and was compliant. Again, providentially, the owner was "absentee" and of the belief that she was holding a white elephant. A deal was quickly struck. My old friend and I often laugh about our "shock and awe" shopping tactic—here it applied to real estate.

The bathrooms and kitchen were the 1977 originals and needed redoing. There was an eccentric and vaguely uneasy entry sequence involving a clattering spiral staircase to one side, an elevator to the other, and a public view from the front door straight through the house. We replaced this layout with a view-shielding, transverse stair sandwiched between wood-clad walls that mirrored the architect's "room divider" at the far end of living room. Thus, a more proper entrance hall was made. Colburn would have approved, we are sure.

The seller of the house left behind a pair of chairs as a gift, with a note saying that they had been left by the original owner and foresighted builder. These Windsor chairs provided our initial decorating cue. Then the stored contents of several houses we had worked on together were edited to fit our "mise-en-scène."

Over the thirty-plus years of our friendship, our decorating language has become entirely coded and succinct. One word evokes a complete room; a phrase takes us directly to the pith of another. "Ike or not Ike" was our mantra for all decisions related to the renovation of the house. As for the decorating, our verbal "shorthand" reached an apogee. Does "Kettles Yard meets Martha Hyder" mean anything to anyone? Maybe not, but it did to us.

OPPOSITE Gutsy ceramic-tile doors, original to the I.W. Colburn house, open into the newly created entrance hall. *Agapanthus* flourishes in Houston's subtropical weather. The jute rug is from West Elm.

ABOVE The painting at the end of the living room is by Sangram Majumdar. A vintage Bielecky coffee table is centered in the room.

ABOVE RIGHT A recently added stairway passes between two new walls: one facing the entry and this one, facing the living room. The blue tape drawing is by Christine Hiebert. RIGHT The Colburn house exterior, unchanged since it was built in 1977.

ABOVE AND OPPOSITE In addition to the living room, there are two sitting rooms on the ground floor. In this one, French doors open to a seating area and fireplace under a shading crepe myrtle. The pillows on the man-sized, slipcovered Restoration Hardware sofa are in fabrics by John Robshaw and Quadrille. The vintage Eames chair and ottoman face the bookcase.

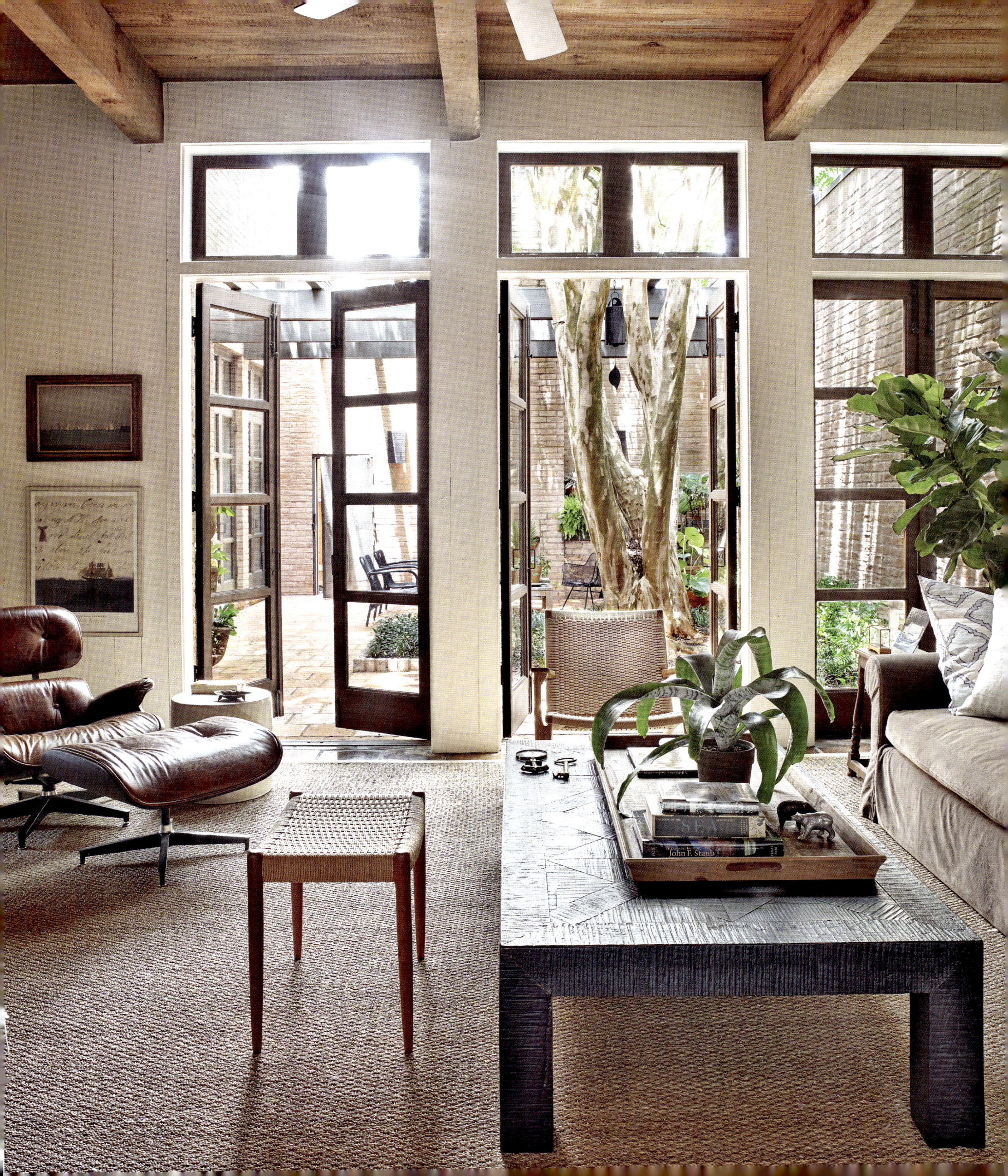
SEA
John F. Staub

ABOVE Wall tiles add color and antique charm to the otherwise white and modern kitchen. The Saltillo floor tiles are original to the house.
OPPOSITE The ceramic light fixtures, also original, were painted white by the decorator. An eclectic mix of vintage and antique furniture, as well as a new peacock chair, contributes to the kitchen's informal, relaxed atmosphere.

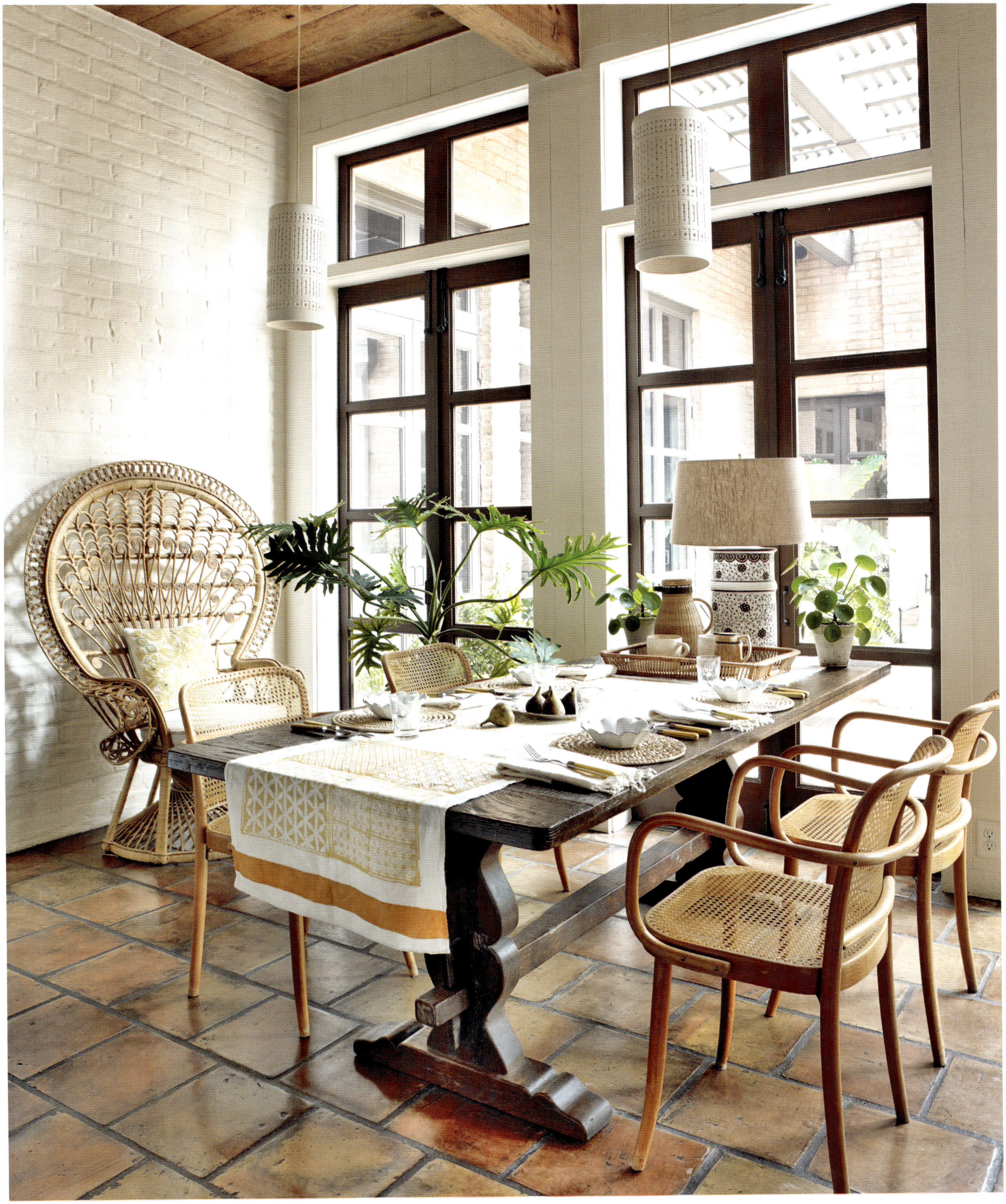

ABOVE A pair of Windsor chairs has been in the house since it was built—a gift from the original owner passed on to the new owner by the previous one. The gilt-tin sconces are from Casas Coloniales in San Miguel de Allende, Mexico.
OPPOSITE The second sitting room has a more feminine air. The object over the sofa once rested atop the mantel in my first New York apartment (see page 15); it is now framed and enclosed in a Plexiglass box. The large camelback sofa was custom made for an apartment in New York and is now slipcovered in white linen with natural jute cording. An early Franco Albini rattan ottoman sits atop one of several carpets from West Elm found throughout the house.

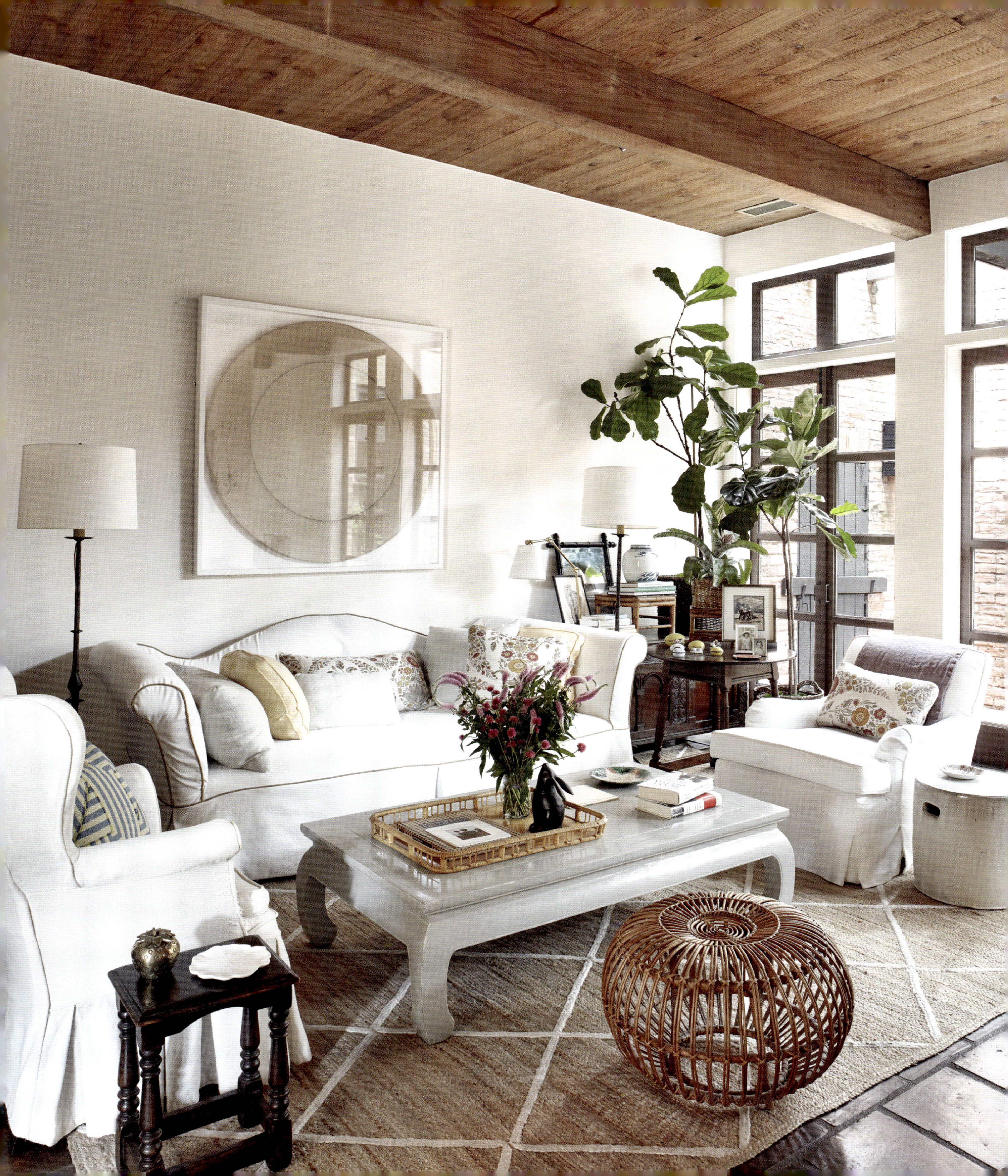

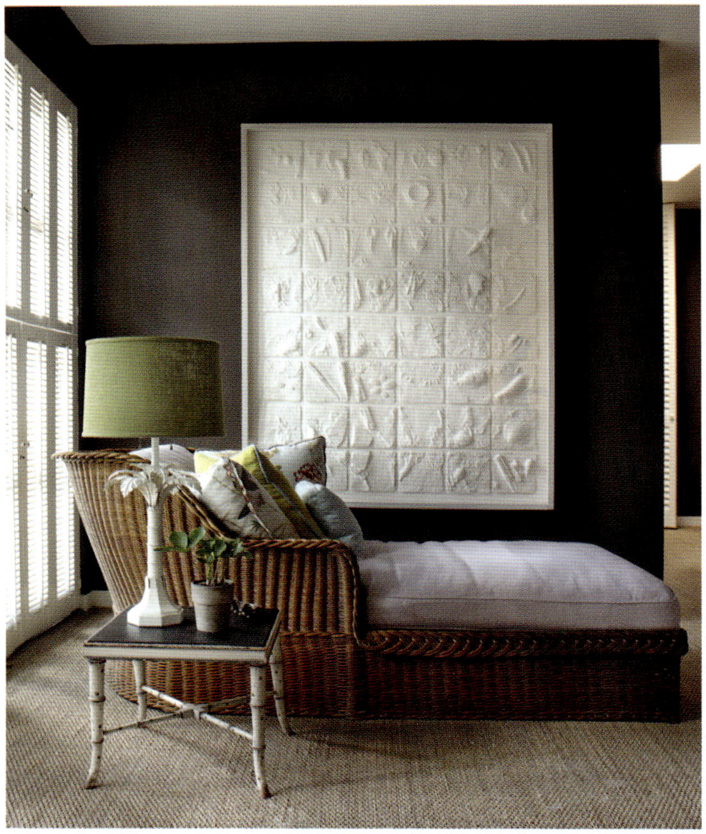
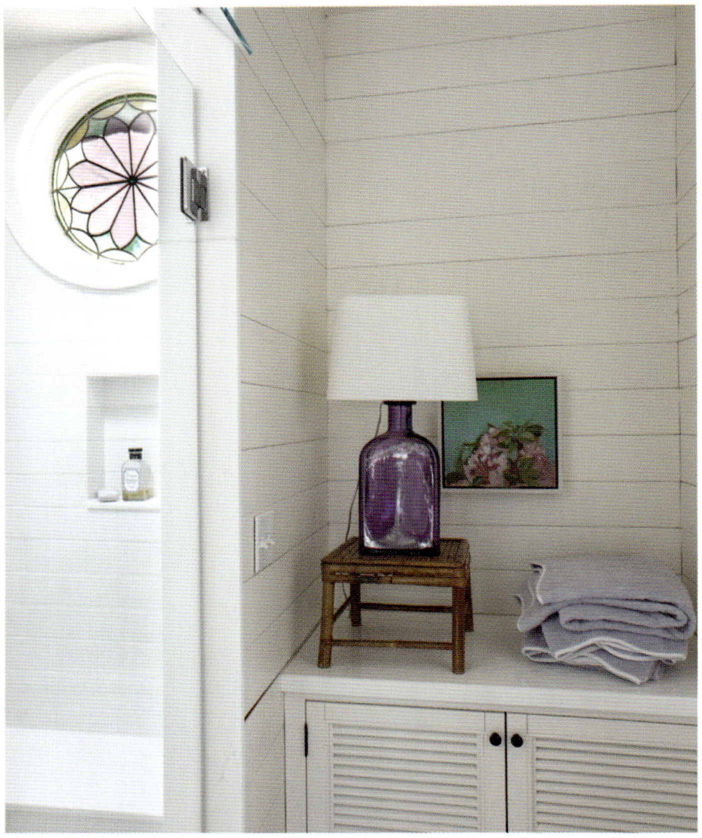
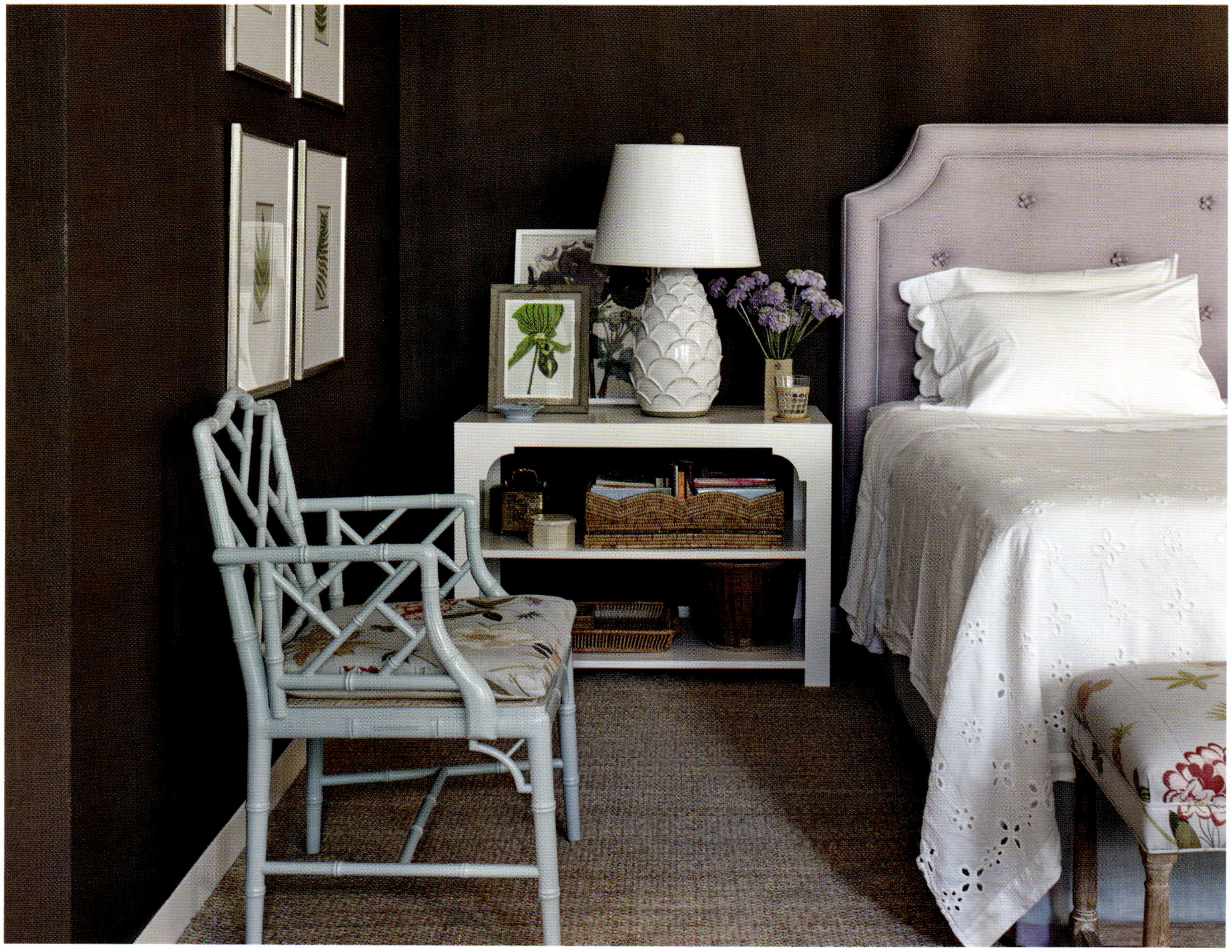

OPPOSITE, CLOCKWISE FROM TOP LEFT In the second-floor master suite, the extra-wide chaise longue from Bielecky has remained with the client through several houses. The master bath was renovated, but the stained-glass roundel window in the shower is original. The entire suite is carpeted with seagrass. **ABOVE** The master bedroom walls were covered in textured burlap before being painted in Benjamin Moore's Clinton Brown. All the doors were cut to the ceiling, reinforcing Ike Coburn's architectural principles. The bench at the foot of the bed is covered in Spring Garden by Raoul Textiles.

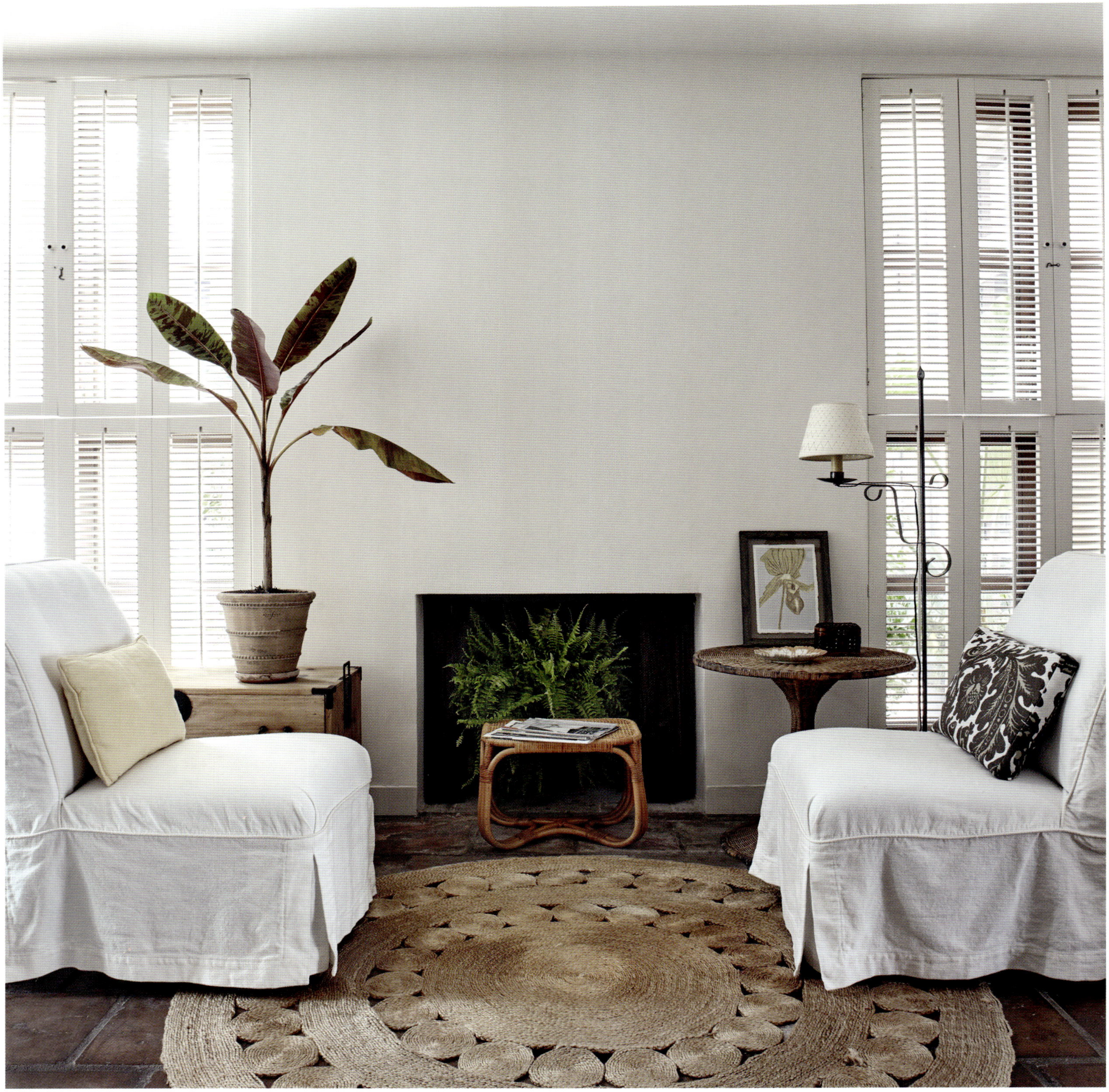

OPPOSITE In the ground-floor guest suite, the round rug, from Serena & Lily, recalls vintage Caribbean straw work. **ABOVE AND RIGHT** The guest suite opens directly to the pool. Its bath doubles as a "cabana." The classic Americana resist print covering the beds' bases and headboards is from Clarence House. Tall doors enhance the height of the rooms optically and reinforce the enfilade. The table lamp serves both beds and resembles those designed by Diego Giacometti for Jean-Michel Frank.

ABOVE AND OPPOSITE Houston weather is hot. The tropics are subtly evoked in the décor, and the pool provides welcome respite. The kitchen, living room, and guest suite all open onto the sunny but shaded L-shaped courtyard, which is overlooked by the second-floor master suite and Colburn's distinctive pierced chimneys.

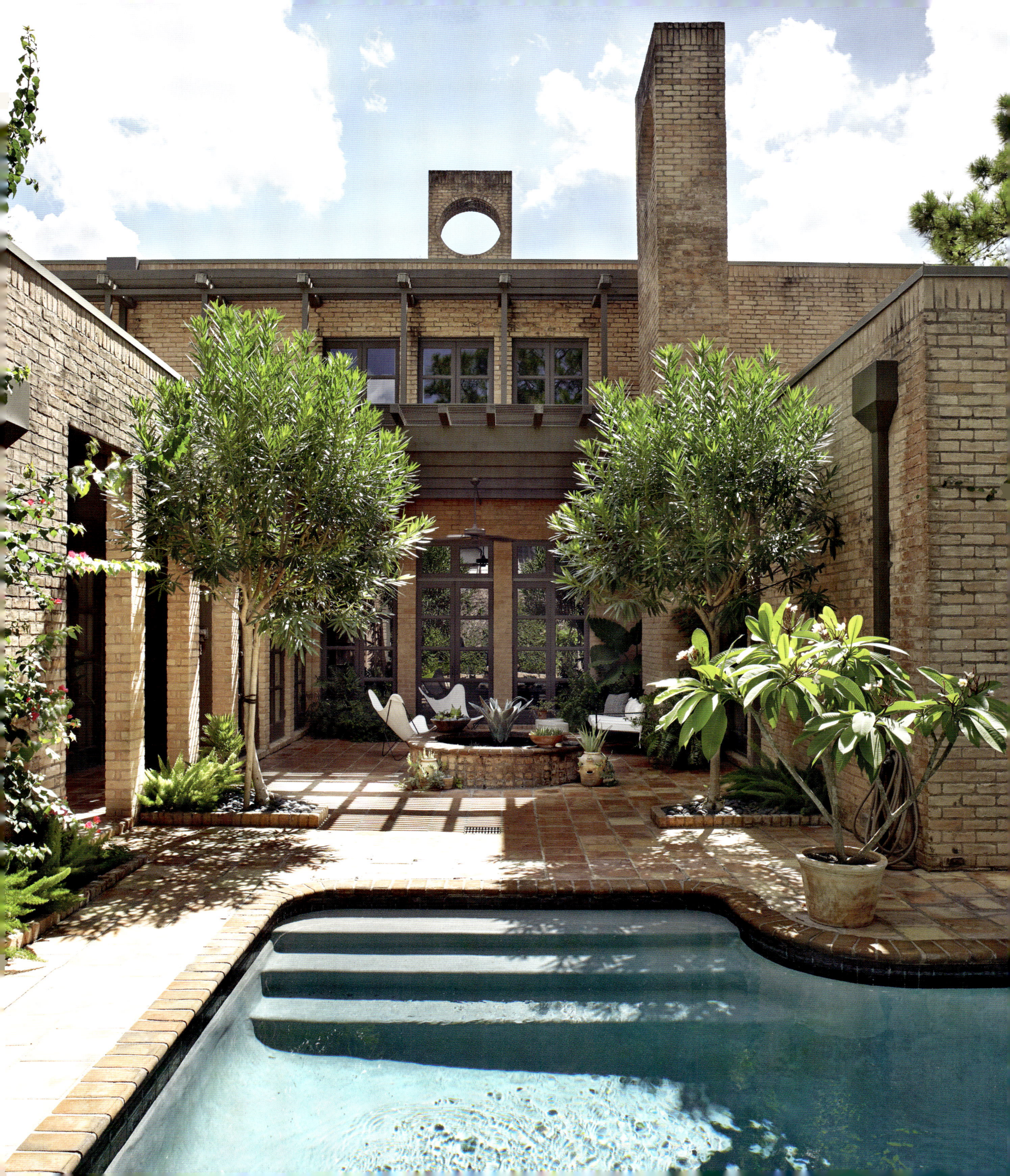

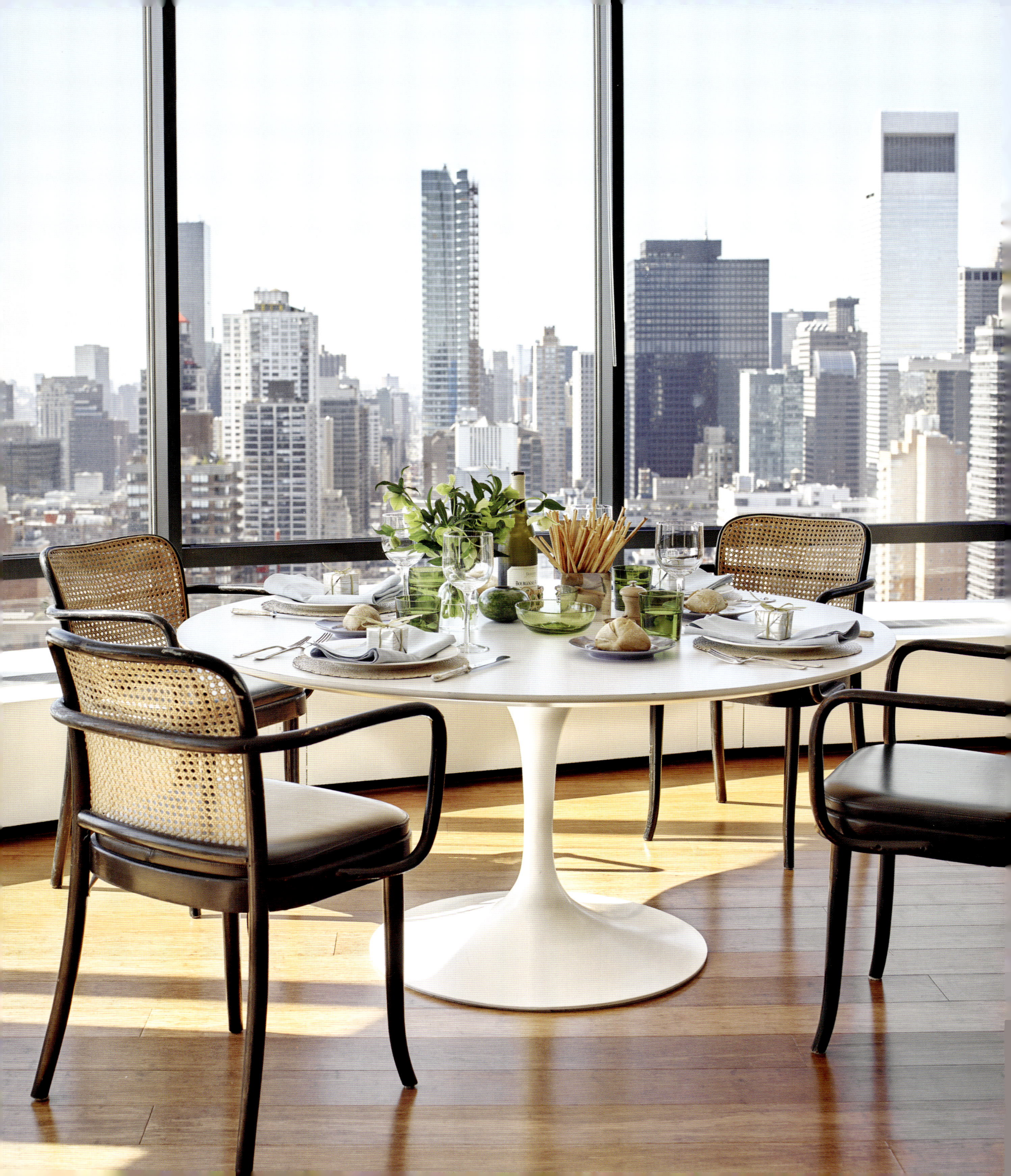

Home Again

A NEW FRIEND, A DINNER PARTY IN HER SUPERB 1980 Ward Bennett–designed apartment, and a propitious offer on my Gramercy Park arrangement inspired a hasty and coincidental homecoming. After twenty years downtown (far closer to the ground in a penthouse!), I decided to move. The fortieth-floor rental apartment I found (I only looked at one) was close to my familial uptown roots and a return to a modernist impulse instilled in me at architecture school.

Built in 1980, late for the genre, this may be the most Miesian of all New York apartment buildings. The ovoid tower stands out among the contemporaneous, jumbled postwar boom of efficient white brick apartment blocks. A smooth cylinder of black glass on a dark granite base rises from street to sky. The apartment interior is not particularly high ceilinged, but the maximally high doors, the omission of a cornice and other fussy detail, the curved interior walls and exposed structural columns epitomize the International Style at its "less is more" best.

The view is not a static tableau of a city but a kinetic Panavision spectacle. During the day the city buzzes forty floors below, the East River bustles. The 180-degree sky is alive with traffic: airports in the distance, fine quicksilver streaks of Long Island Sound to the north, and the Atlantic far off to the south. Inside, the fiddle-leaf fig trees are prodigious in the all-day sun, requiring incessant pruning. Orchids thrive, astoundingly blooming over and over.

The decorations quickly coalesced. The landlord's freshening coat of pure white paint was left as it was. The kitchen and bathrooms had just been updated in the plainest, best way, as if I had done them myself, so no upheaval there. Shaped wool velvet area carpets approximating the color of the bamboo flooring were laid throughout.

Within days, a fantastically long and deep sofa arrived from CB2, pre-upholstered in a perfect tweedy beige. Hello again to my bag of tricks and old standbys: artworks and furniture stored at the office from long-gone houses and apartments. The ever-reoccurring Saarinen dining table (this one "conference height" and rare), a sixteenth-century Flemish kas bought at Christie's in the 1980s, my first purchase of "real" furniture. A Bauhaus-inspired suite of clear-lacquered plywood tables that I made for my first New York apartment is home again after moves to several apartments and to my houses in Charleston and the Bahamas. It's all familiar, and most of it is well-traveled stuff.

At night the apartment is equally thrilling. The swoop of dark glass gives way to the 59th Street Bridge with its swagged pearl necklace of lights and glowing sash of red, pulsating tail lights; the downtown traffic diminishing into the distance and, seemingly, from directly under the dining table. Despite the distracting view, dinner guests never fail to recognize post-mid-century vibrations of louche glamour.

Almost without fail they remark that mine could be the most "New York" apartment they know.

OPPOSITE My fortieth-floor apartment looks south over the Manhattan skyline. The ever-present Saarinen table is a special and rare model. Its twenty-seven-inch "Cipriani" height is especially well suited to convivial dining. It is surrounded by original Josef Hoffman Prague 811 chairs. OVERLEAF The living room's very long (132 inches) and deep sofa came directly from CB2. The large velvet and linen pillows reinforce the green theme throughout the apartment. A pair of gouaches from the 1970s by Italian modernist Luciano Mori hangs directly above. My collection of chrome and stainless-steel modernist furnishings came together compatibly for this new apartment. The Motherwell-reminiscent collage is by American artist Stephen Edlich.

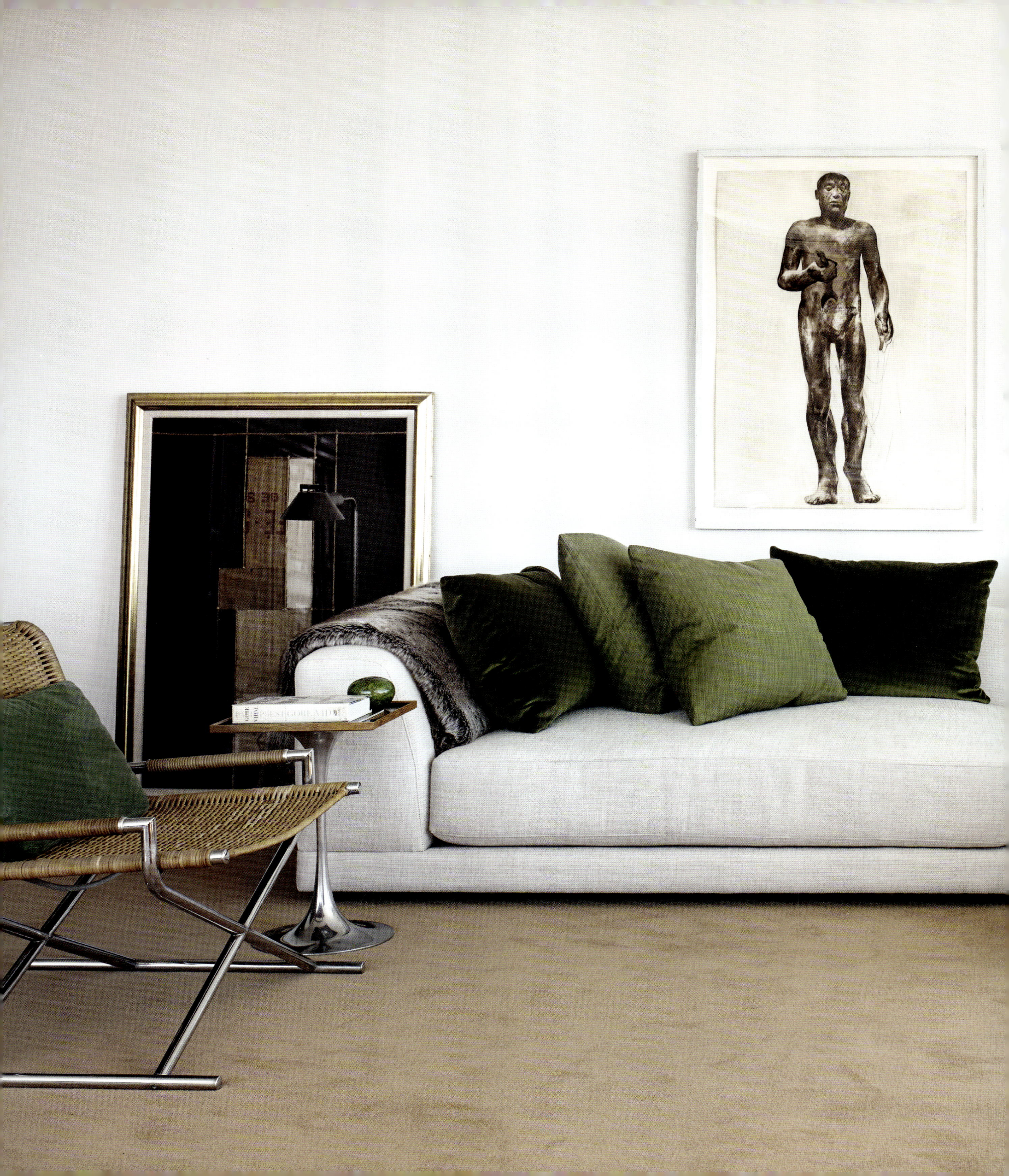
GORE VIDAL

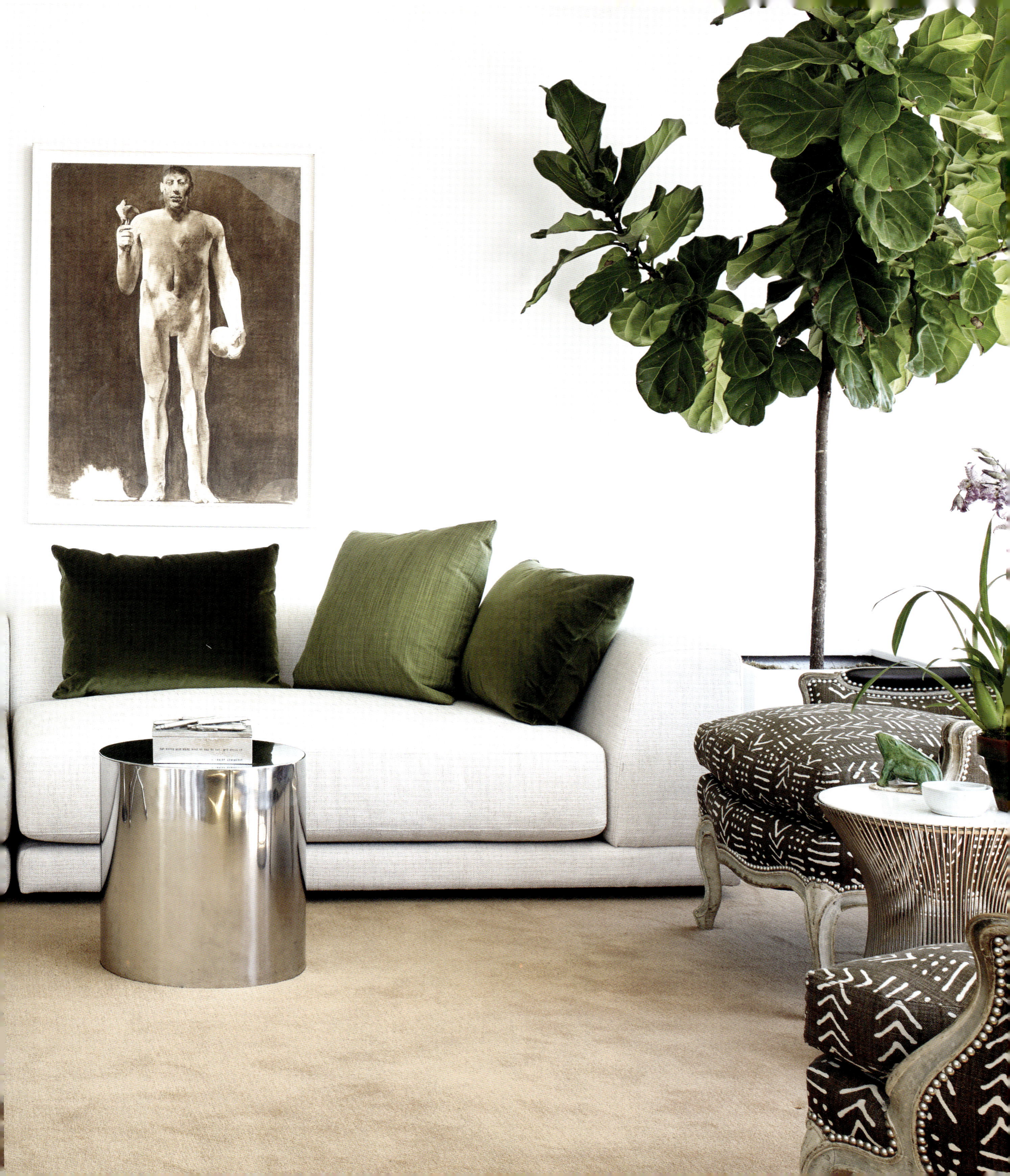

ABOVE The Jansen fauteuils *à la reine* are covered in Penny Morrison's African-inspired Luma print. The bamboo floor is covered with antelope wool velvet carpeting by Studio Four. OPPOSITE The steel-and-rattan sled chair by Ward Bennett is an icon of modernism. It contrasts the seventeenth-century Flemish kas, which houses a television.

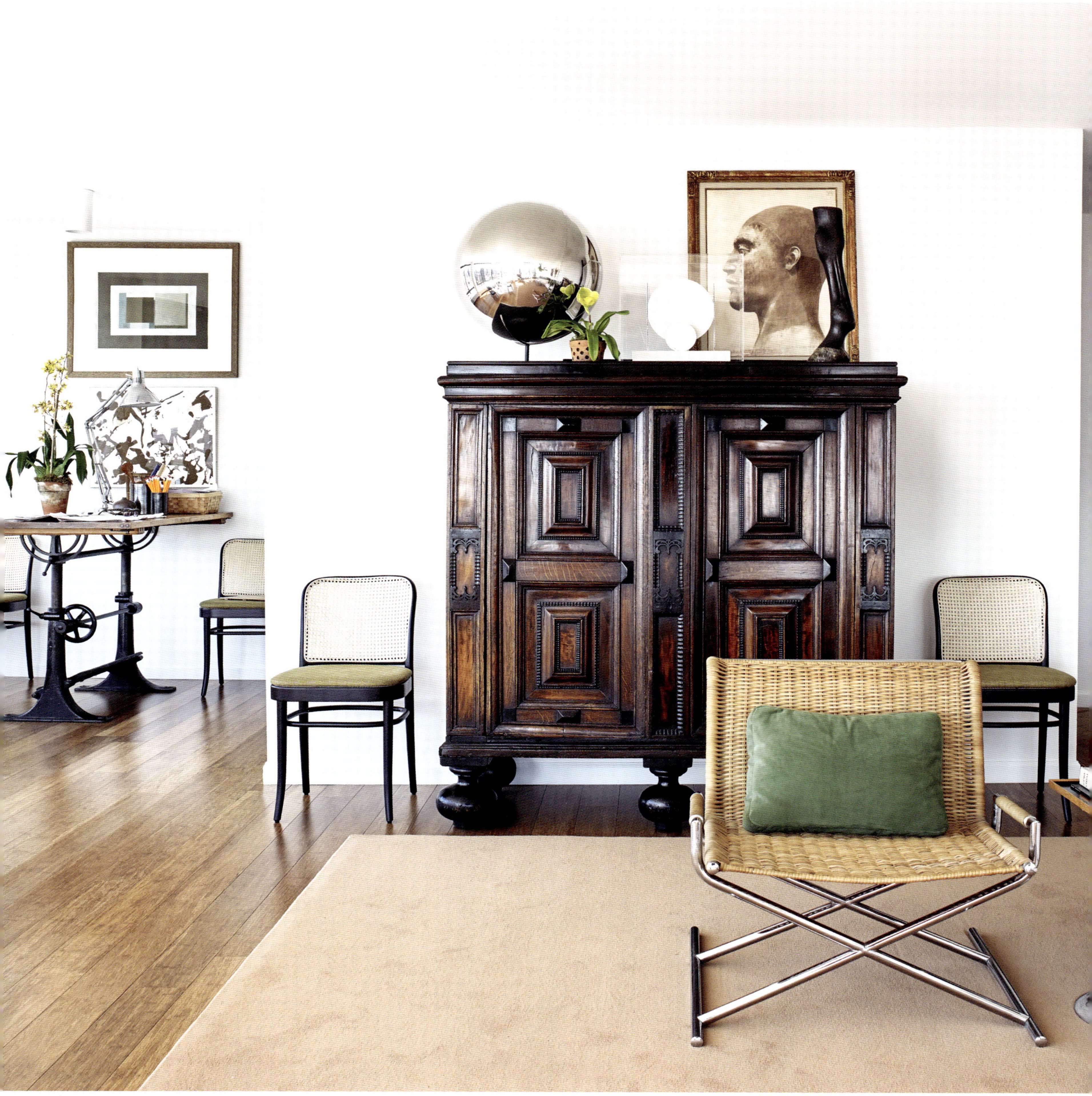

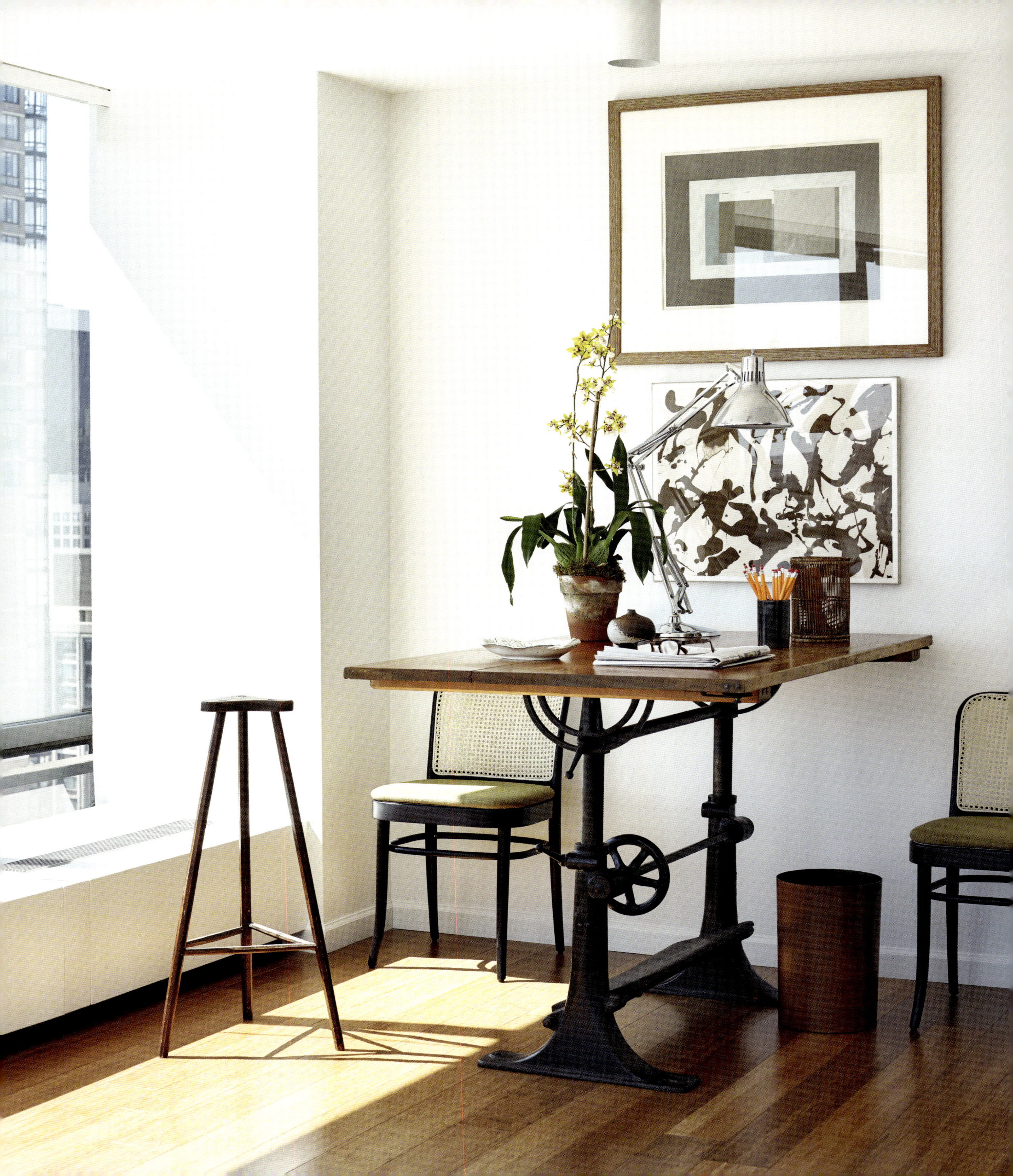

OPPOSITE Above the antique drafting table are works on paper by Ben Nicholson and Lee Krasner. The antique posing stool is lightweight yet superbly sturdy. It came from Angus Wilkie's Cove Landing. **ABOVE** The screen shielding the opening to the kitchen is made from the remaining panels of a larger Chinese screen that I used to make tabletops. The art includes a Joseph Cornell–style shadow box found in a thrift shop and my own painting of a milk jug.

ABOVE The wool velvet carpeting is cut to follow the curving lines of the apartment. OPPOSITE My bedroom contains plywood furniture that I made in 1989 for my 83rd Street apartment. The arrangement of artwork includes pieces by Guy Pène du Bois, Saul Steinberg, and a thrift shop painting recalling my Maine summers. The familiarly swooping Vernon Panton chair is a favorite.

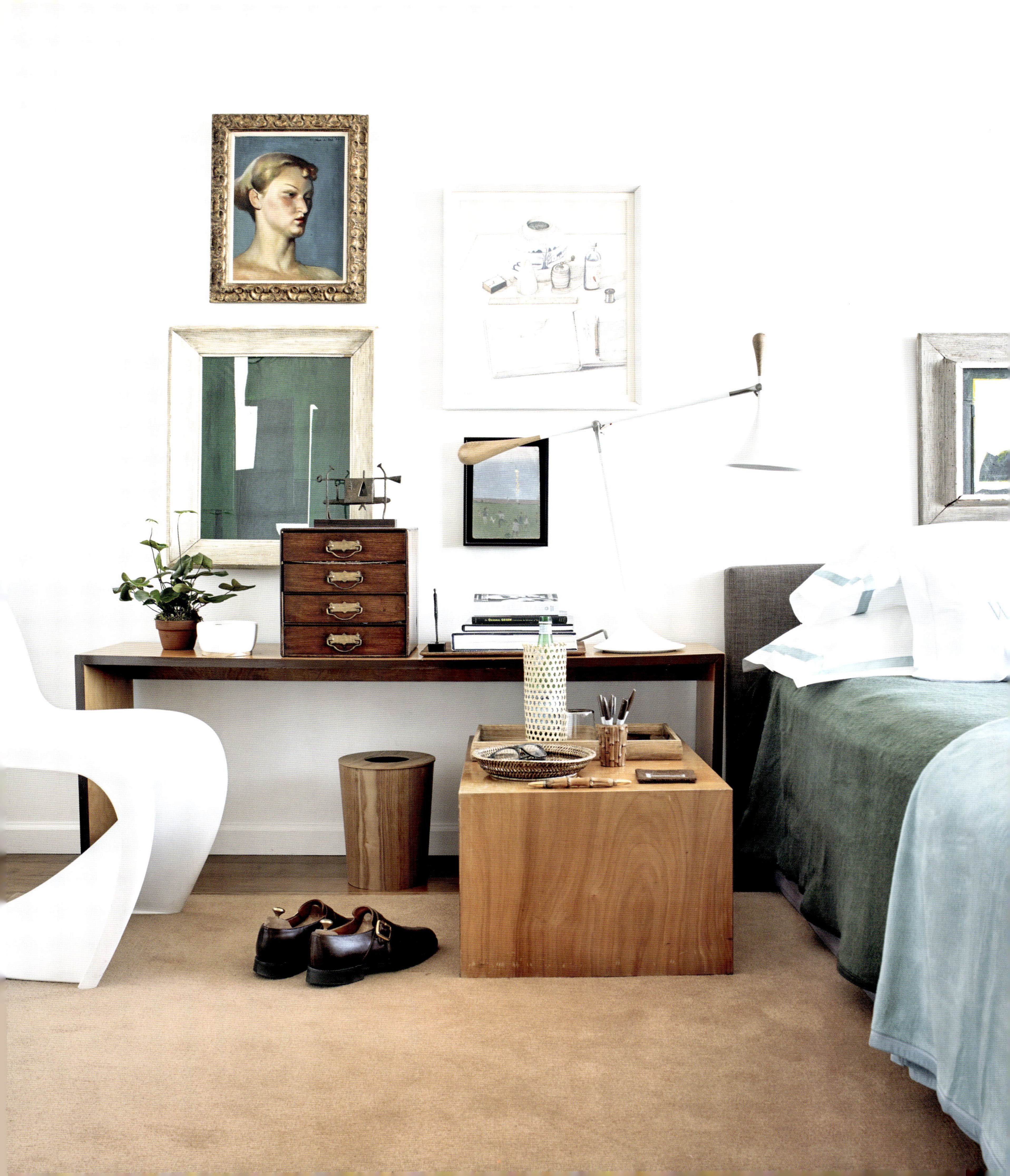

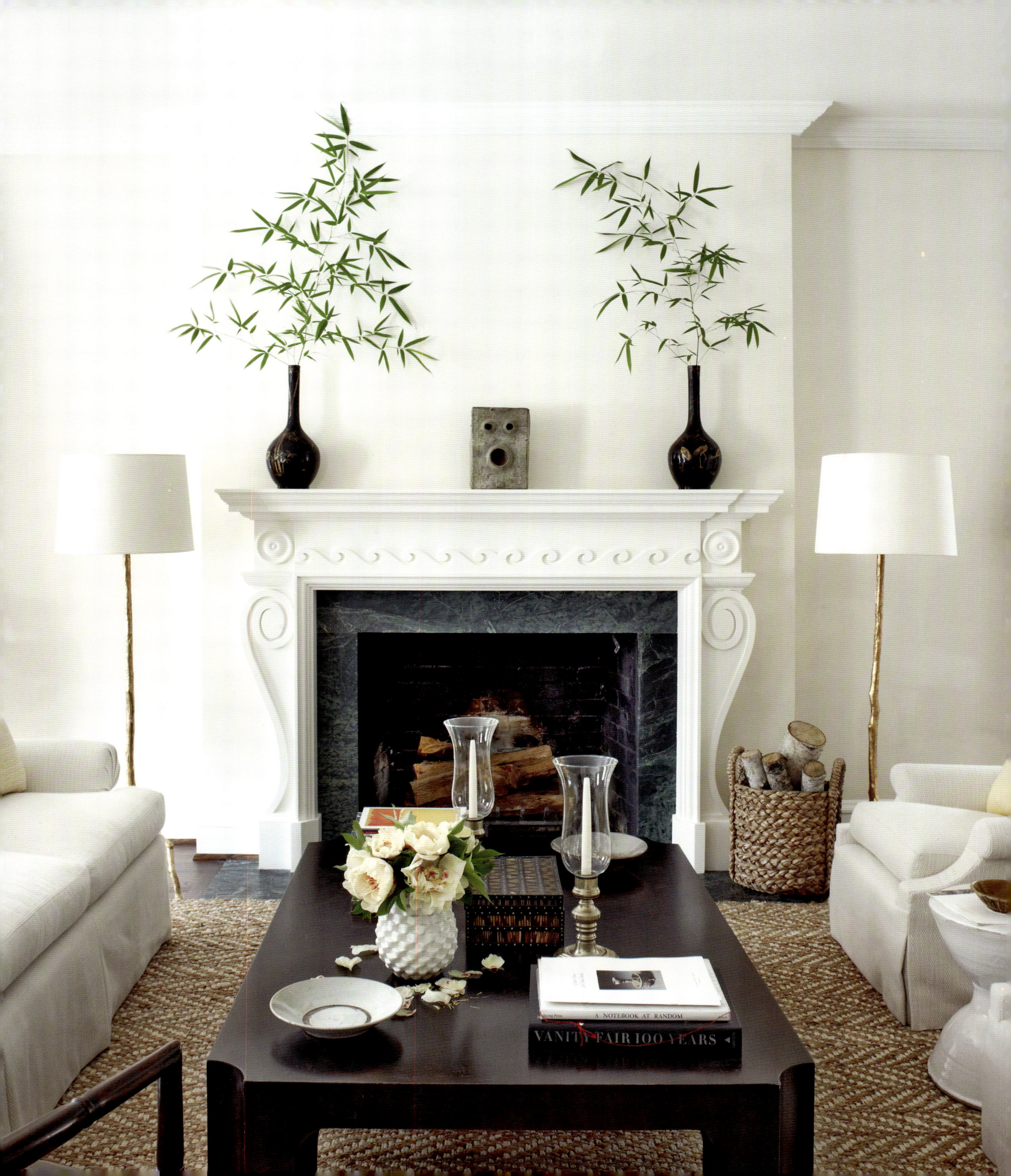
A NOTEBOOK AT RANDOM
VANITY FAIR 100 YEARS

Gentleman's Agreement

This house is a trophy of sorts for the Dallas-born-and-bred New York businessman. With an apartment on Fifth Avenue and a summer house on the West Coast, he wanted something close to home. It's just around the Highland Park corner from where he grew up and his parents still live.

The 1930s "Georgian" has a familiar and old-fashioned grace, now imperiled. So many of its decorous and contemporaneous neighbors are already gone, making way for the notoriously up-sprouting and generally gauche Dallas palaces.

Uncomplicated in its four-square plan, its rooms flow into one another in logical and classic sympathy. And despite the economies of this plan, it is plenty large—it most recently housed a family with eight children!

The owner is traditionalist, well mannered, and as gentlemanly as the house he bought. His primary pursuits outside of his financial career are his thoroughbred horses, the racetrack, and his dog. He is not quite an aesthete, but is keenly interested in furniture and in art contemporary and otherwise. However, he was fully aware of his limitations when it came to doing up a house from scratch.

We had decorated his New York apartment several years earlier with considerable success, and now I was to become the unfettered ghostwriter of his newest and now principal home.

The plot and its outcome came in a single flash—entire rooms fully baked in my mind. With the exception of a few personal objects and books (his other houses were chockablock with borrow-ables), I made every purchase. The owner's character led the way.

The bathrooms were renovated and the systems were modernized, all in keeping with the stature and vintage of this "proper" house. As for the furnishings, nothing obsessively "period," but nothing newfangled or flashy either. English and American brown furniture, handsome and forthright but apparently unfashionable, was languishing in shops and in auction rooms across the map. We had our pick.

Behind the orthodox, unaltered façade we made a vaguely modernizing foray. The traditional 9 over 9 sashed windows were replaced with floor-reaching, single-paned glass doors. They give access to, and picture-framed views of, the pool and gardens flanking the house—all shielded from the street by a high garden wall.

Along the back of the house we made another exception. A bright and crisp kitchen is now open to the white terrazzo-floored dining room and sunroom beyond. Two large, room-defining openings are flanked by hinged folding screens, which can be opened or closed as needed. It makes a flexible and elegant substitution for the ubiquitous, multipurpose but unseemly "family room" or, even worse-named, "great room."

The authorial flash of inspiration came with a bit of full-blown plagiarism. The silver tea-papered corner guest room is a brazen knockoff. The original Frances Elkins room is now famous (to decorators anyway) but had been lurking in my mind since 1971. It was in a 1930s David Adler "Georgian" house belonging to a school friend's Lake Forest family. I first checked the potentially embarrassing appropriation with the gentleman. Thankfully, he agreed there would be no better occasion or a more fitting house for me to free my subconscious.

OPPOSITE The stylized fireplace surround, based on a Georgian prototype, was cast in plaster. On the mantel, a Han dynasty brazier has been stood on end to make a sly but charming reference to Rome's famous Bocca della Verità. The large coffee table is vintage Michael Taylor, repainted.

ABOVE The eagle is an eighteenth-century English architectural fragment. Its enormous weight is supported by a simple, white-painted plywood box. On the sides of the house the traditional, multipaned windows were replaced by single panes of glass that open to the garden and pool, giving the living room an airy, more modern feel. OPPOSITE The potent photographs of thoroughbreds are by Peter Hapak and came from the Trunk Archive. The cane-and-faux-bamboo chairs originally belonged to the Colony Club in New York. The Swedish stone-topped consoles were painted black to echo the racehorse photos above them. OVERLEAF LEFT The sunroom's windows are shaded by retractable black-and-white-striped awnings. I rescaled and recolored my favorite Lyford Trellis wallpaper for both the sunroom and the adjacent dining room. The round coffee table by Robsjohn-Gibbings is surrounded by an artful mix of styles: a Billy Baldwin slipper chair, antique wicker, a Restoration Hardware sofa, and a custom Bridgewater chair from Luther Quintana. The end tables, like the eagle's pedestal, are simple painted plywood boxes. OVERLEAF TOP RIGHT The ironwood Queen Anne–style dining chairs were purchased at Christie's. They are Chinese export for the English market. OVERLEAF BOTTOM RIGHT The Bridgewater chair is upholstered in Clarence House's Dahlia print.

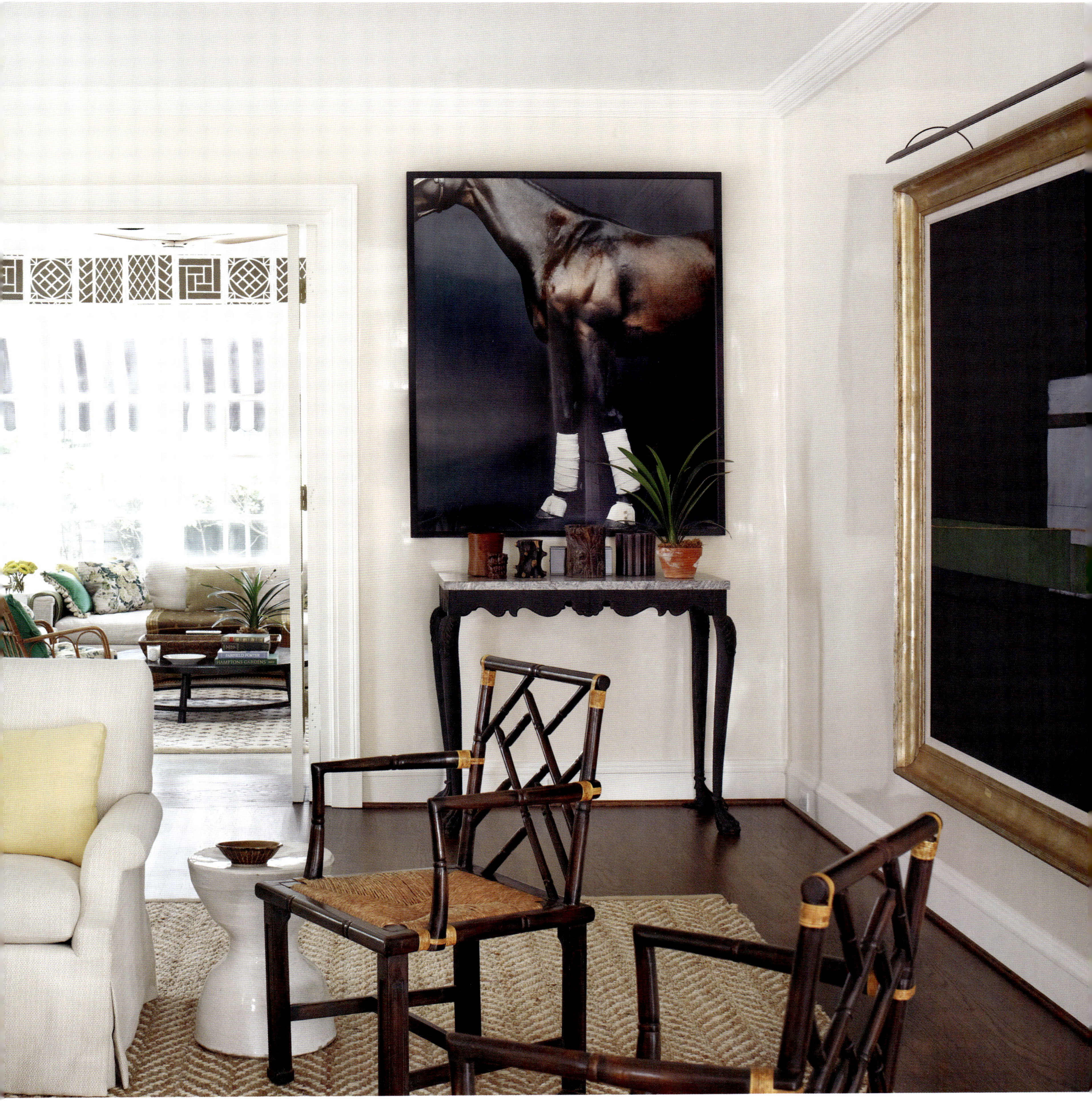

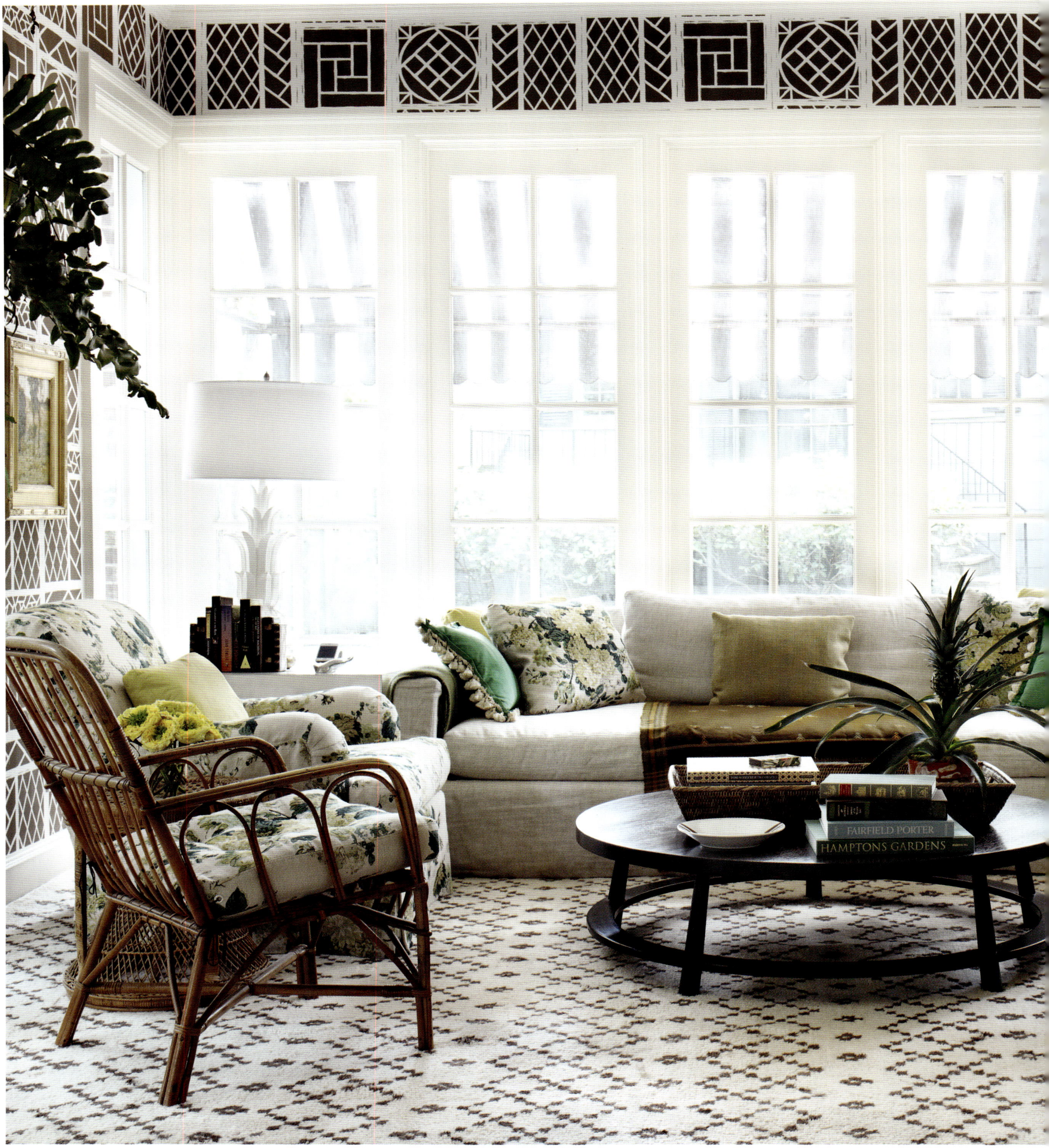
FAIRFIELD PORTER
HAMPTONS GARDENS

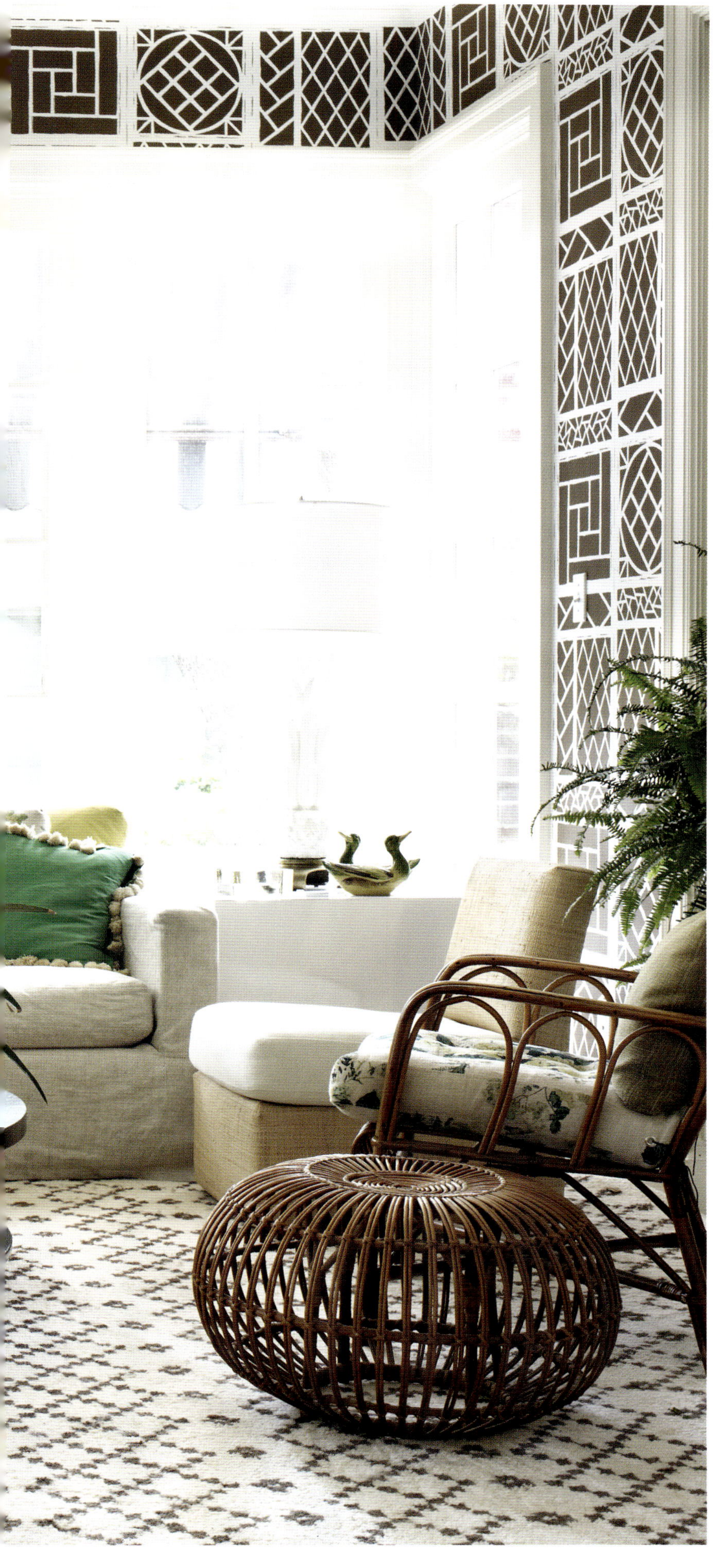
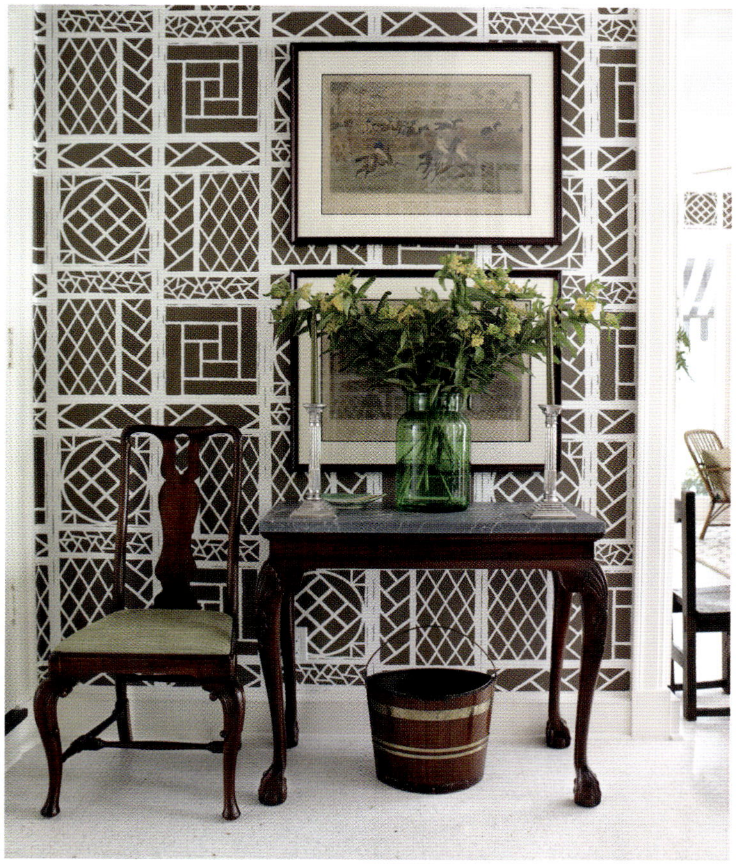
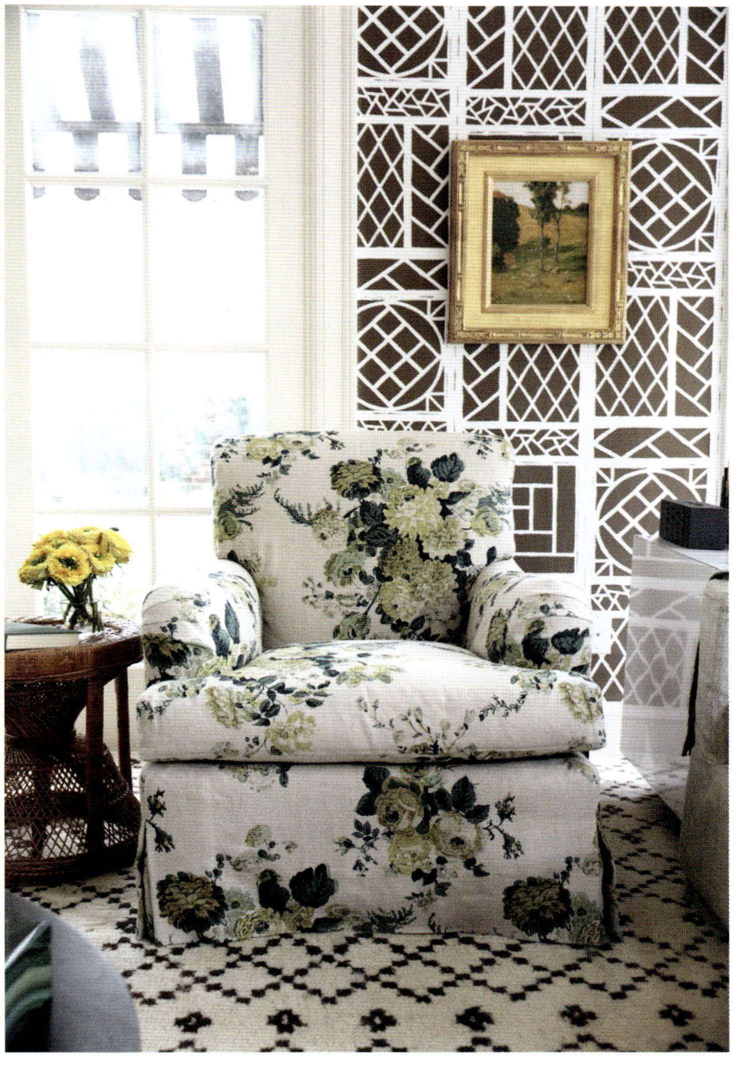

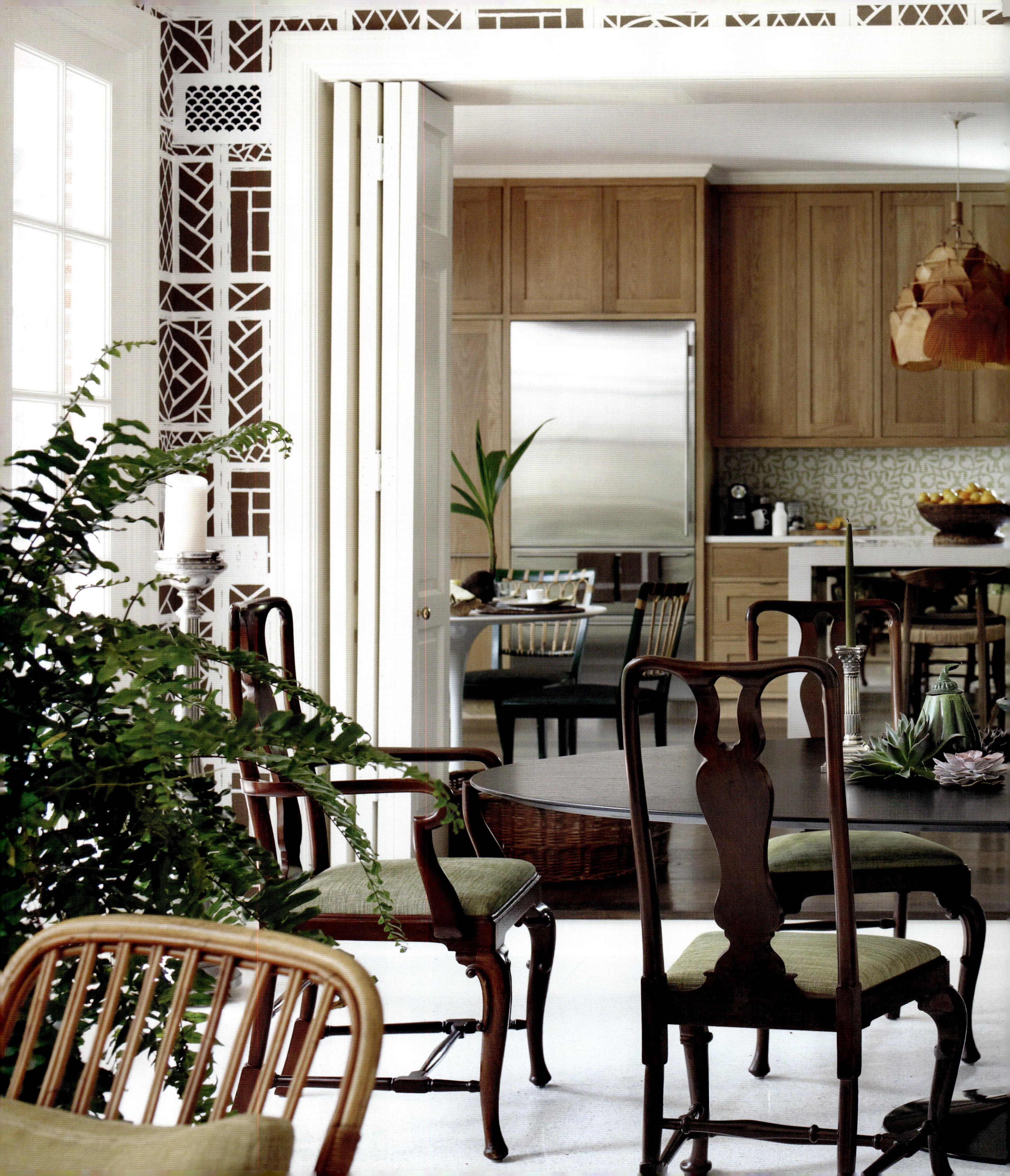

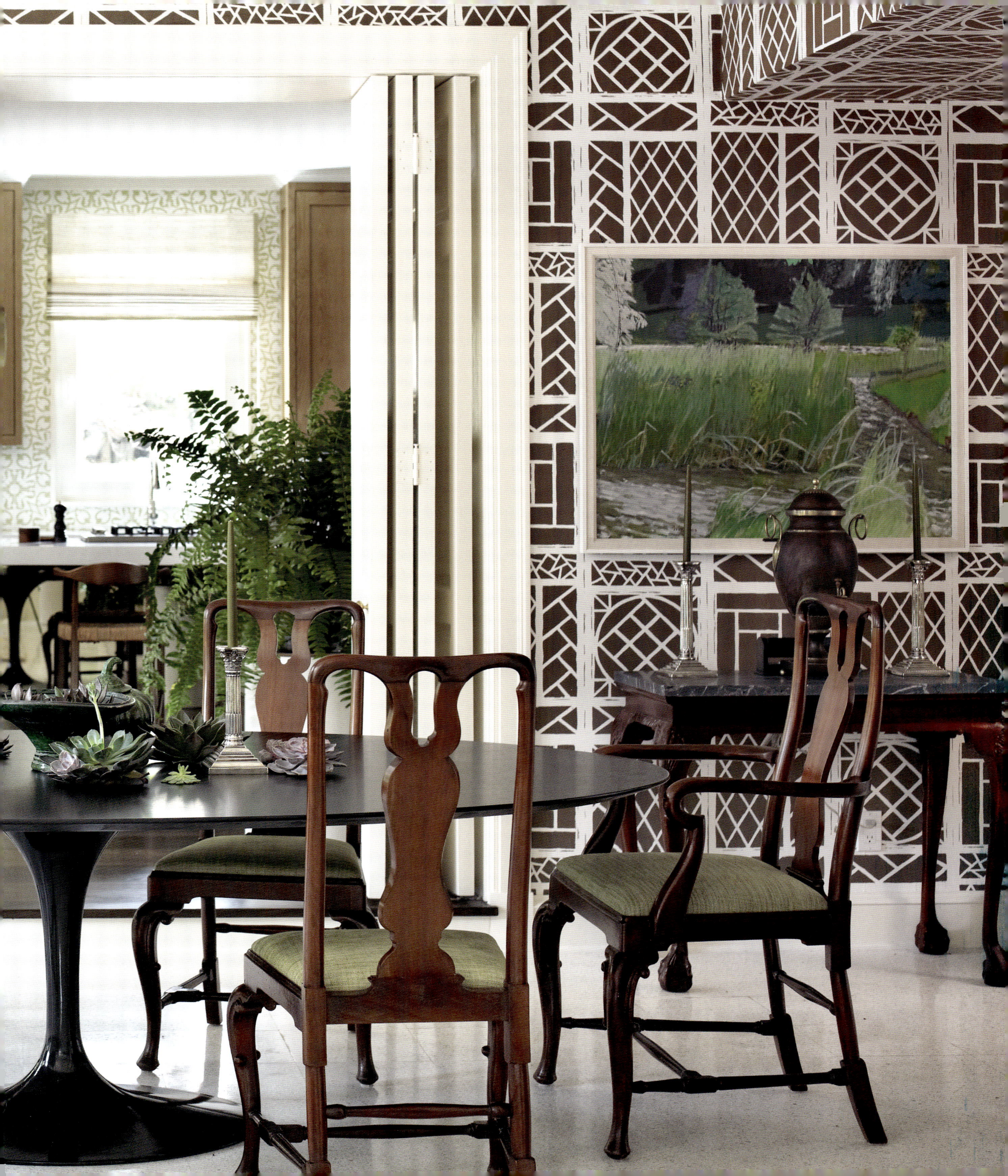

PRECEDING PAGES A Saarinen table with a black base and a dark-stained top is a suitably more traditional iteration for the dining room. We opened the kitchen to the dining room but installed folding screens that can be closed when desired. **ABOVE** The banquette in the breakfast corner was made by Luther Quintana. It's covered in Kravet's "chartreuse" Crypton. The green-lacquered, rattan-backed chairs are by Josef Frank from the 1930s. **OPPOSITE** The recessed mirror beneath the kitchen island shields cabinets and appliances and gives the island the appearance of a light Parsons table rather than a bulky monolith. The vintage Ingo Maurer Uchiwa light fixture is one of a pair. Cuban-style tiles from Villa Lagoon Tile line the backsplash and the walls. The wood flooring was stained in alternating tones to differentiate it from the floors elsewhere in the house.

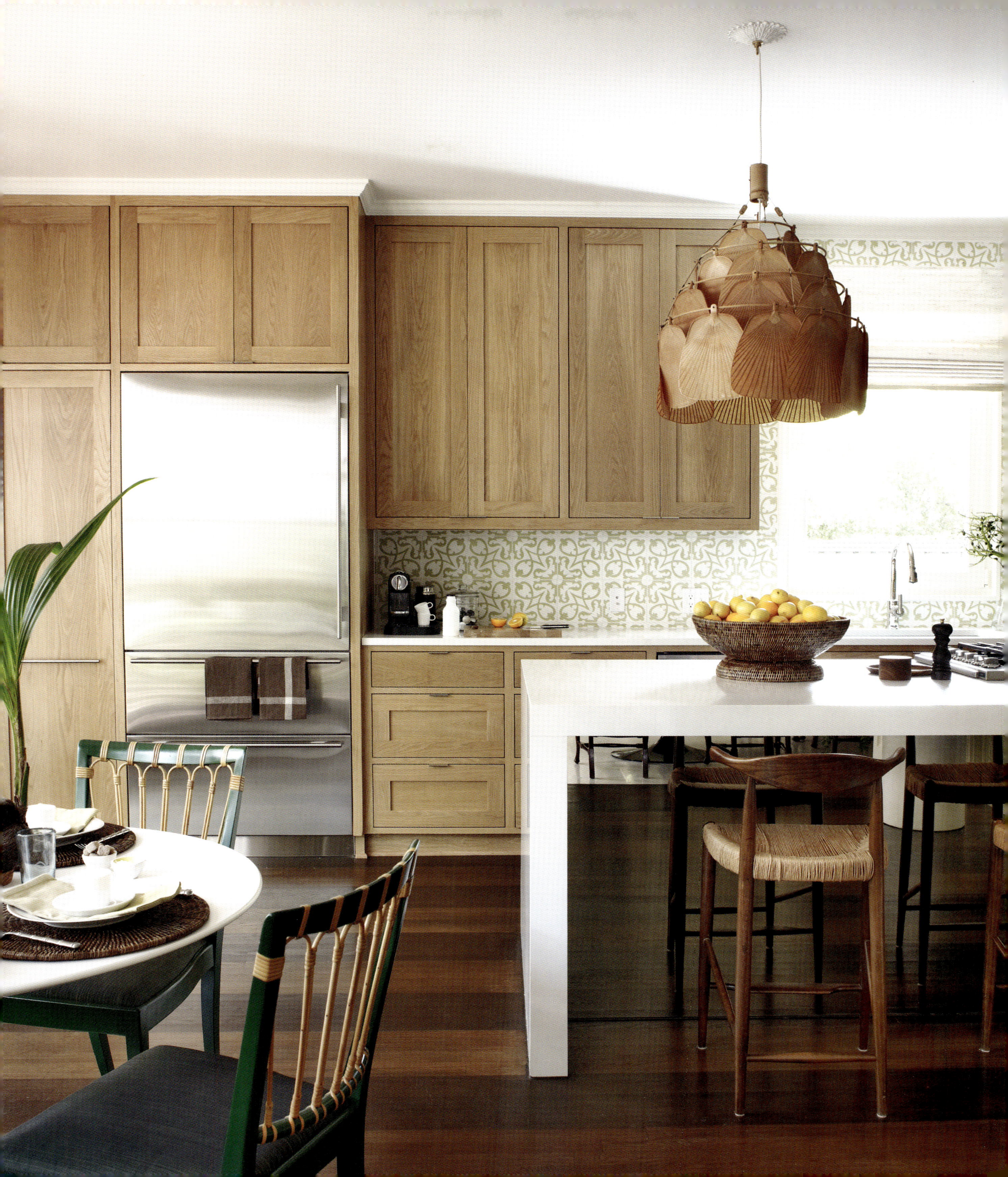

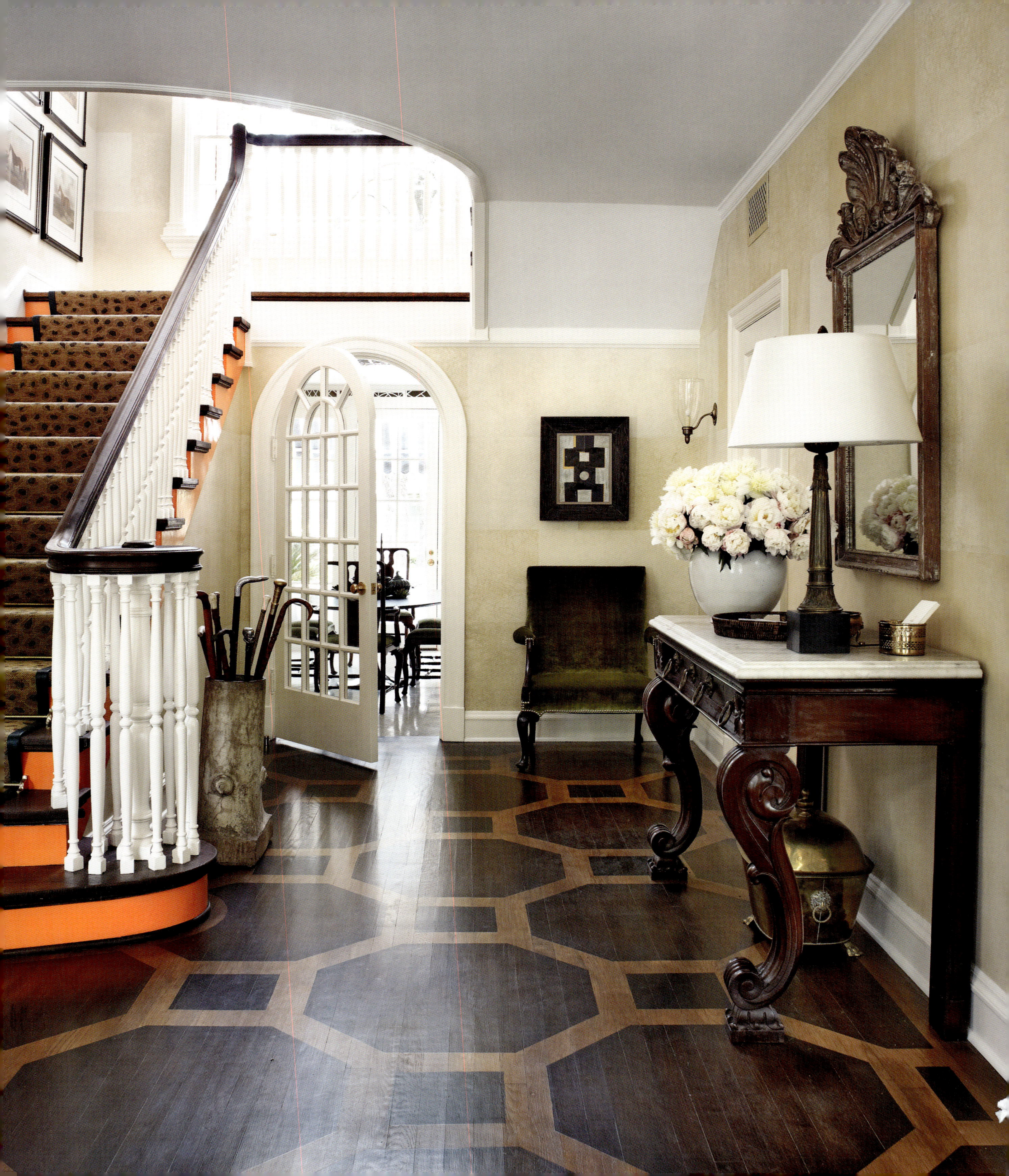

OPPOSITE The entrance hall floor was stained and overglazed in a large-scale pattern recalling the stone floors of English Georgian houses. To take the potential seriousness out of the entry and perpetuate the equestrian theme, the stair risers and stringer were painted Hermès-box orange. **ABOVE, CLOCKWISE FROM TOP LEFT** A series of British steeplechase prints was digitally enlarged to make a scenic wallpaper for the powder room. The actual prints hang in the adjacent dining room. A pair of substantial, well-proportioned eighteenth-century lolling chairs was upholstered in bottle-green silk velvet. A nineteenth-century map of the Hudson River was framed and propped against the wall as a deliberate compositional element. The marvelous English cast-plaster tree trunk–like umbrella stand is from Cove Landing.
OVERLEAF The pair of pickled-teak, pagoda-topped bookcases are freestanding, made in India to match the faux-bois wallpaper by Nobilis. The effect is that of a paneled library. The nineteenth-century horse painting by James Clark, bought in Antwerp, makes a fitting focal point. The fireplace was cast in plaster and is adapted from an English Regency model. The leather-topped, brass-trimmed McGuire campaign-style desk dates to the 1970s.

NEW YORK
VOUET
STALLION REGISTER FOR 2013
CHAMPIONS
FOLK ART IN MAINE
Gone with the Wind
ALBERT BIERSTADT
JO NESBO
Wolf
Richard Diebenkorn The Ocean Park Series

TOO CLOSE TO HOME
AMERICAN IMPRESSIONISM
SARGENT
HAMPTONS GARDENS

ABOVE The walls of the master bedroom are covered in Lisa Fine's Baroda pattern in indigo. The silver-leafed lolling chair came from a Chicago house decorated by Frances Elkins. **OPPOSITE** The upstairs sitting room and adjacent sleeping porch were painted a deep green as a backdrop for the owner's collection of black-and-white photographs by Bill Brandt. Double-wide chaises longues are arranged facing each other, as are the shapely pair of slipcovered Rose Tarlow Edwin armchairs.

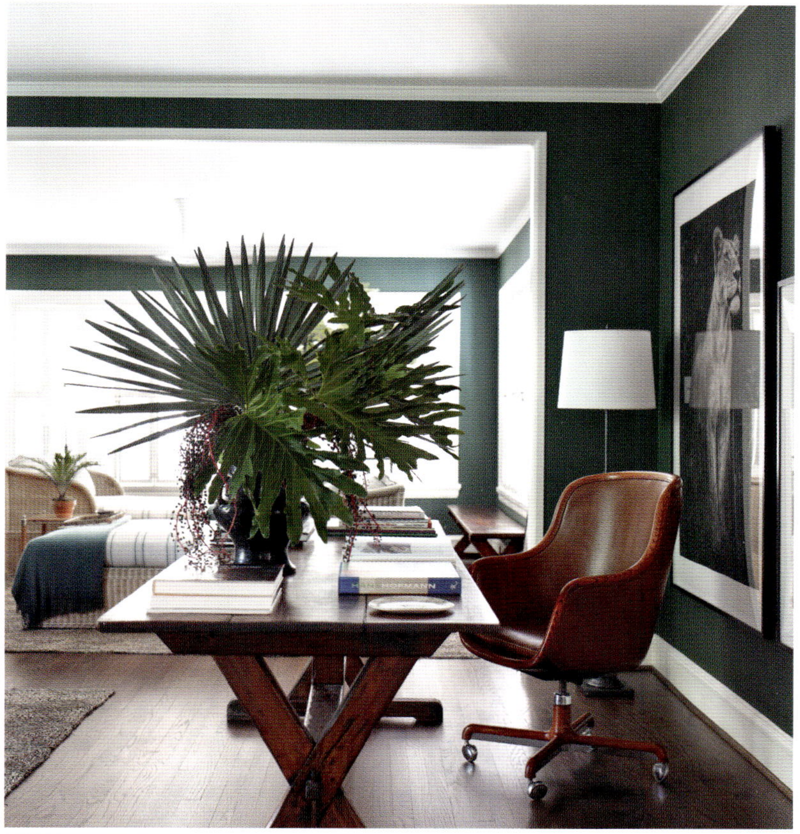

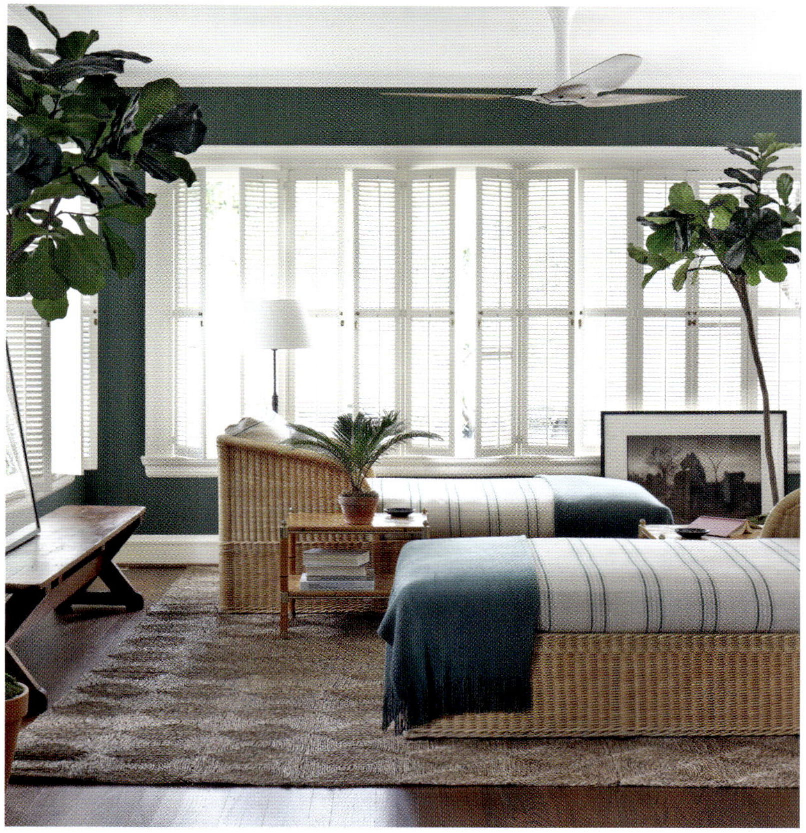

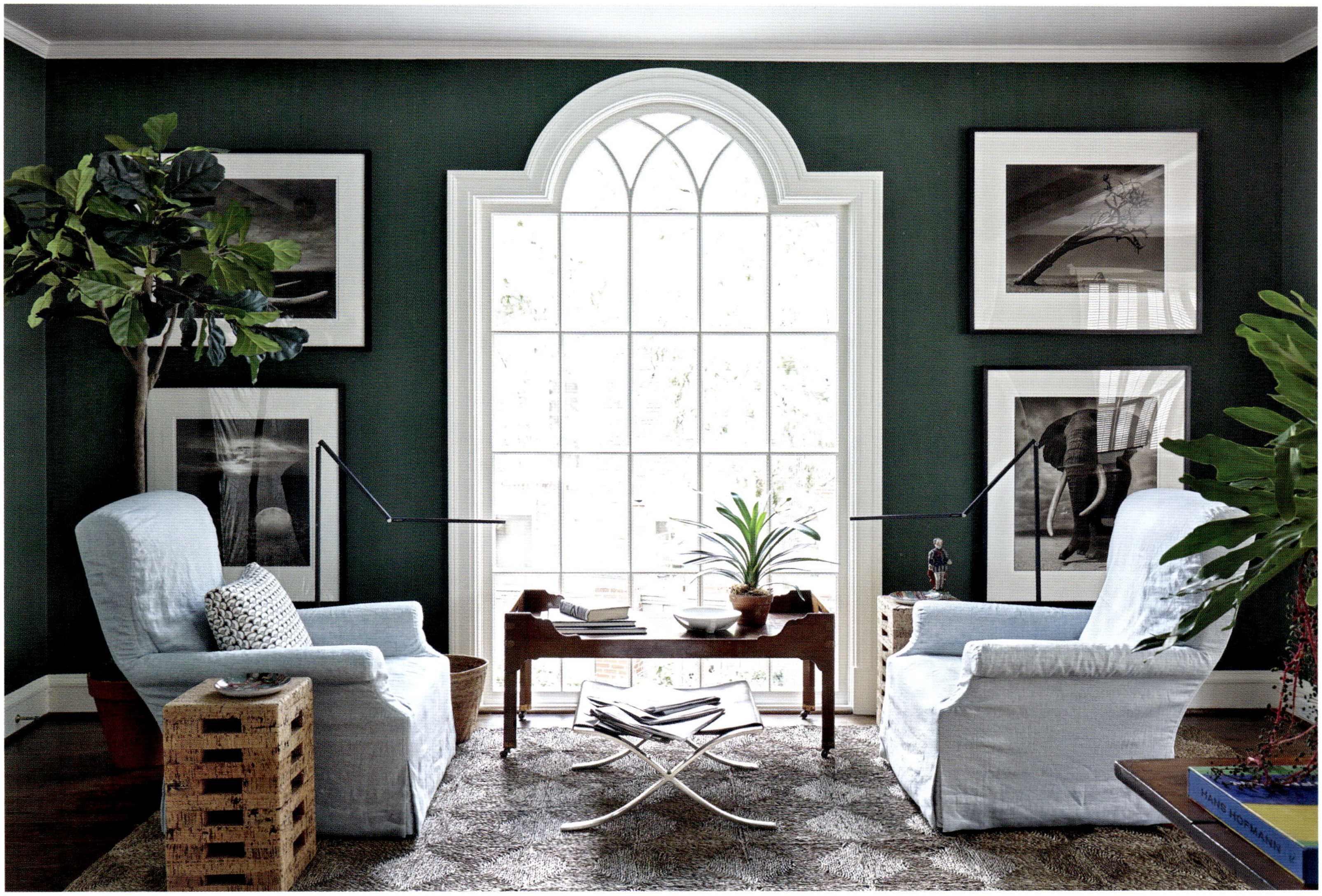

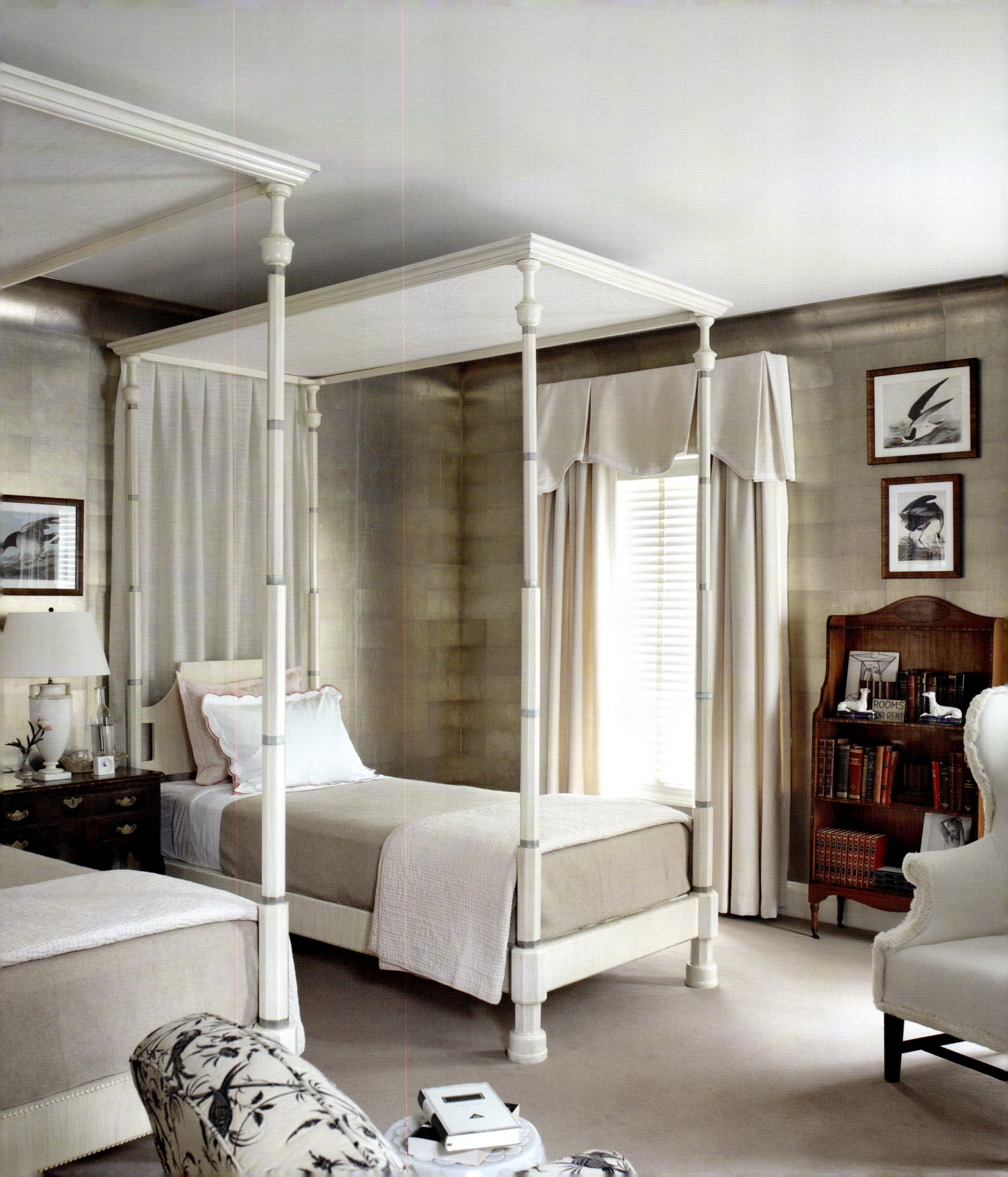
ROOMS
OR RENT

OPPOSITE The guest bedroom's crown moldings were removed to allow the silver tea paper to extend onto the ceiling. The twin beds are faux ivory with silver-gilt accents. They are a simplified version of Frances Elkins originals. The black-and-white fabric covering the armchair is quilted Bird and Thistle from Brunschwig & Fils. Audubon prints further the avian theme. The wall-to-wall carpet is antelope wool velvet from Studio Four. **ABOVE** A fireplace surround was installed for an electric fire. I made the newspaper fan to fill the visual void. The "Venetian" mirror above the mantel is from Restoration Hardware.

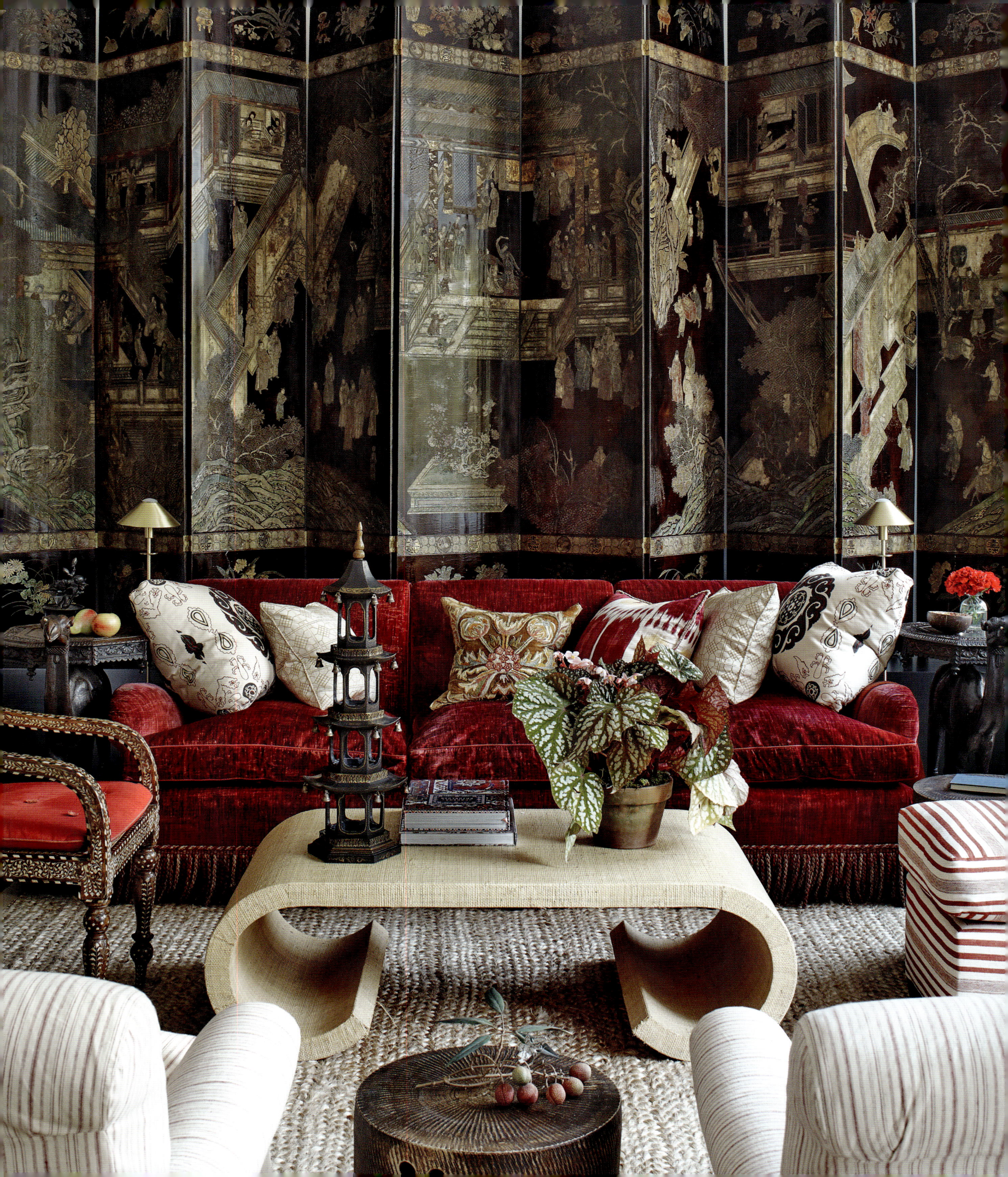

Camping

Their Park Avenue apartment, unspeakably large and wonderfully luxe, had become unwieldy. The rooms and the distances within it were ringing hollow with the children off in their own apartments and at college. The prospect of an entirely new kind of perch was intriguing: perhaps a penthouse, something modern, a view of the park?

Suitable buildings in their own uptown neighborhood were identified and vetted, but no smaller apartments fitting or thrilling were on offer. A scheme was thereby hatched to rent a place, perhaps off their familiar grid, as a practicality and an adventure of sorts, until something might arise to suit a long-term New York plan.

The couple settled on an airy and freshly renovated loft-style apartment, architecturally undistinguished but beautifully situated on Madison Square, with large windows overlooking an imposing obelisk monument and the deep green park beyond. The white walls and lack of detail shocked at first, but assurances were made that their uptown chattel, when cleverly arranged, would quickly dispel the air of a slick yoga studio.

I was familiar with the old apartment and looked forward to mining its contents. The principal rooms had been decorated by a venerable London decorating firm and refreshed twenty years later by another New York one. Several others, however, I myself decorated in 2010.

First, a visit was made to the loft to assess the room sizes and elevational possibilities, then a trip uptown to "shop" the recently sold apartment. This would not be an ideal scenario for a more mercenary decorator, rest assured.

Happily, a few things demanded purchase in order to fill out the new plan: a round dining table, bookcases for the office and bedroom, and a pendant light for the front hall, among others. A few fitting pieces of upholstery were ordered and a few of their own were re-covered. Expeditious choices were made on 1st Dibs and at Ikea, knowing these items were unlikely to make the next decampment.

The furniture and objects were arranged, and the pictures were winnowed and hung to new and optimal effect. The Coromandel screen was placed on a specially made plinth so that it would be in scale with the living room's high ceiling. The stage was set and the couple became downtowners.

But within weeks, the prevalence of "landlord white" began to discomfort. Though they reveled in their chic bivouac, they began to hanker for a bit of the atmospheric and cosseting detail of their former apartment. Posthaste the office was lined in rectangles of handmade papyrus paper, lending a scriptorial air entirely apt for this book-publishing ménage. The powder room walls were covered in a deep coffee-bean glossy vinyl to set off the gilt-framed eighteenth-century Chinese ornithological watercolors. The master bedroom walls were faux-extravagantly "upholstered" in digital wallpaper adapted from a Kashmiri challis shawl, yet another intimation of the East. Not an ounce of paint was used in the decoration of this apartment.

Though hardly cursory or slapdash, a spontaneous, improvisational quality is evident in the result. The downtown-haute-bohemian-meets-the-Park-Avenue-patrician atmosphere is fully realized, if ephemeral. All is comfortably and chicly arranged with loved and husbanded objects. The ceilings are high, the light streams in. The couple does not appear to be in any particular rush to get back uptown.

OPPOSITE The luxe atmosphere of this downtown loft was created with objects brought from the clients' former Park Avenue apartment. The nineteenth-century Coromandel screen was raised on a specially made black-lacquered plinth in order for it to reach the ceiling.

ABOVE In the entrance hall, the angular modernist console by Stéphane Ducatteau contrasts the curvaceous 1930s Italian mirror. The plaster cone light fixture is from Rose Uniacke. **OPPOSITE** The clients' collection of pictures from the Subcontinent covers a wall of the living/dining room to accentuate its high ceiling. Leather-covered Louis XVI-style armchairs surround the Saarinen dining table. The red carnations are an old-fashioned and nostalgically fragrant touch. **OVERLEAF** The console table's stone top is arranged with objects from the clients' life of travel and collecting. Behind this assemblage is a nineteenth-century Indian watercolor of an aloe plant.

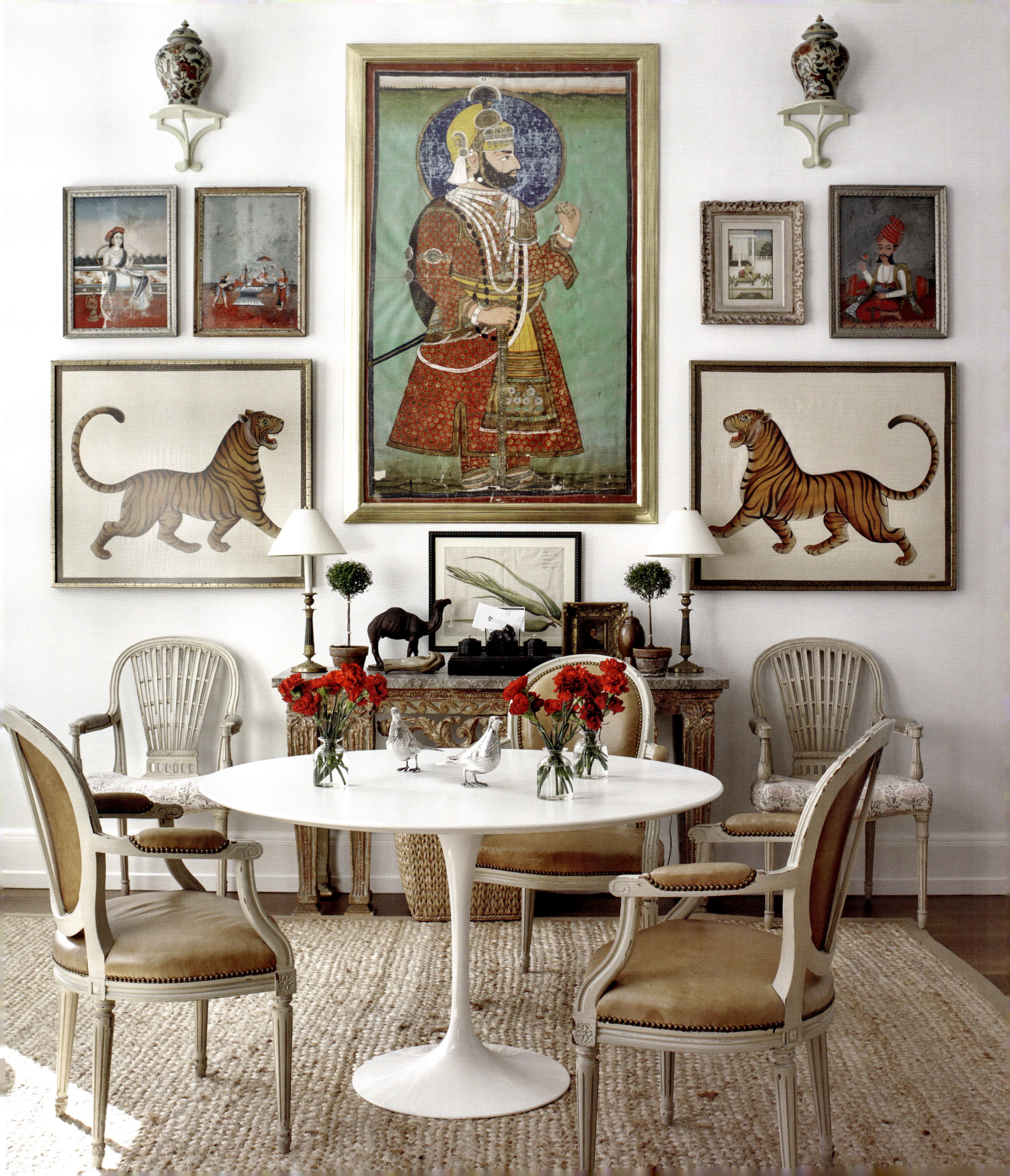

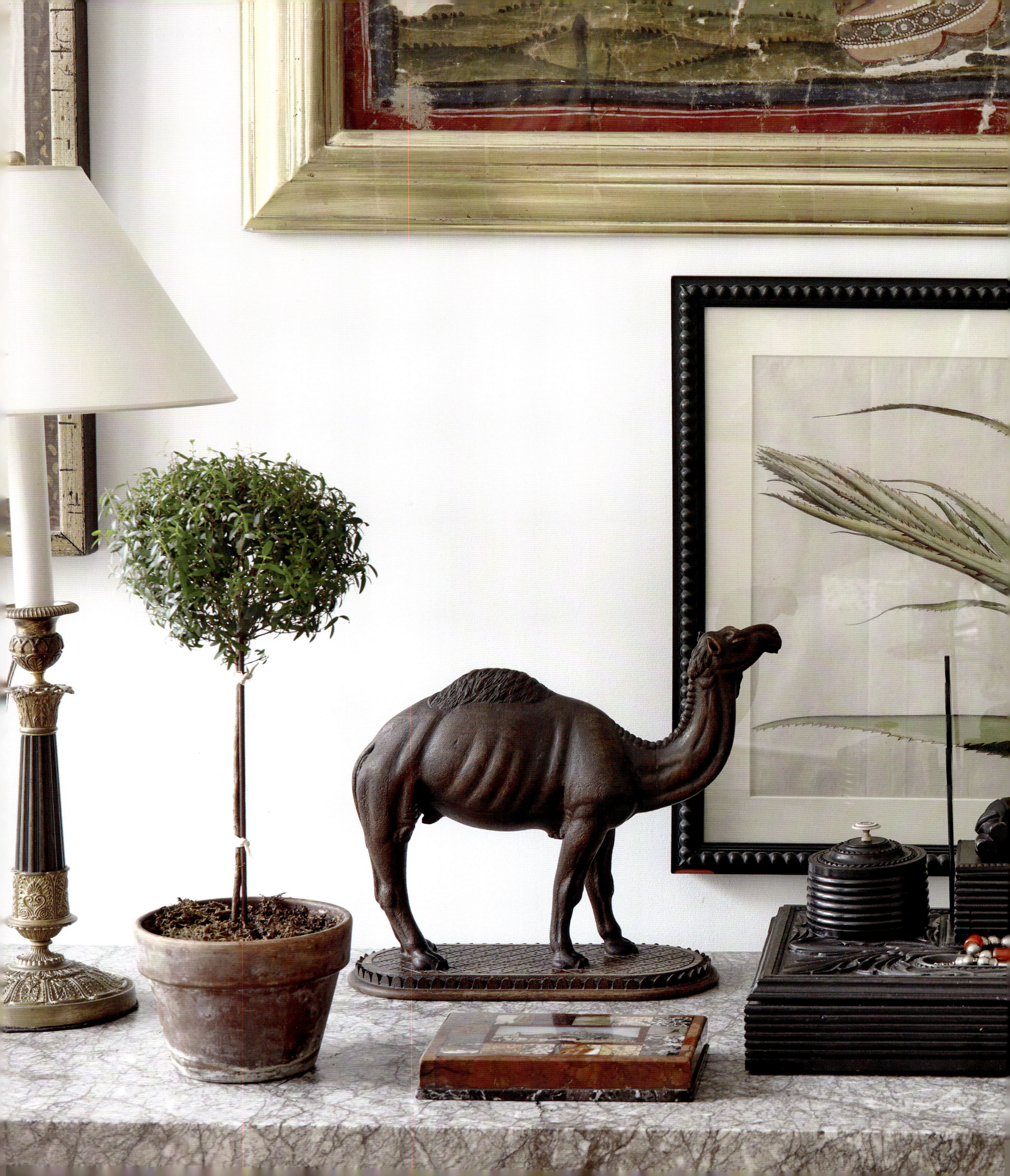

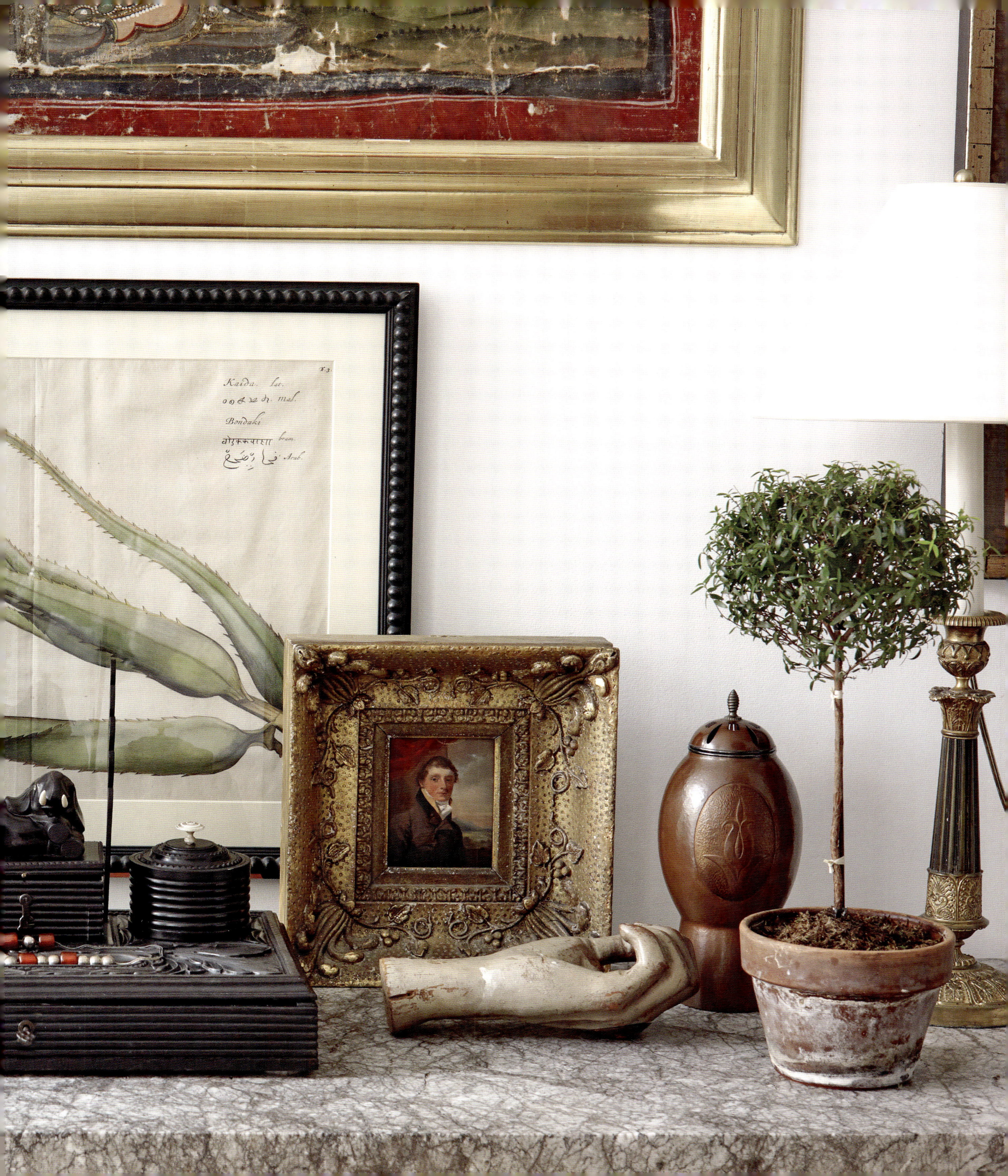
Kaida. lat.
Bondaki

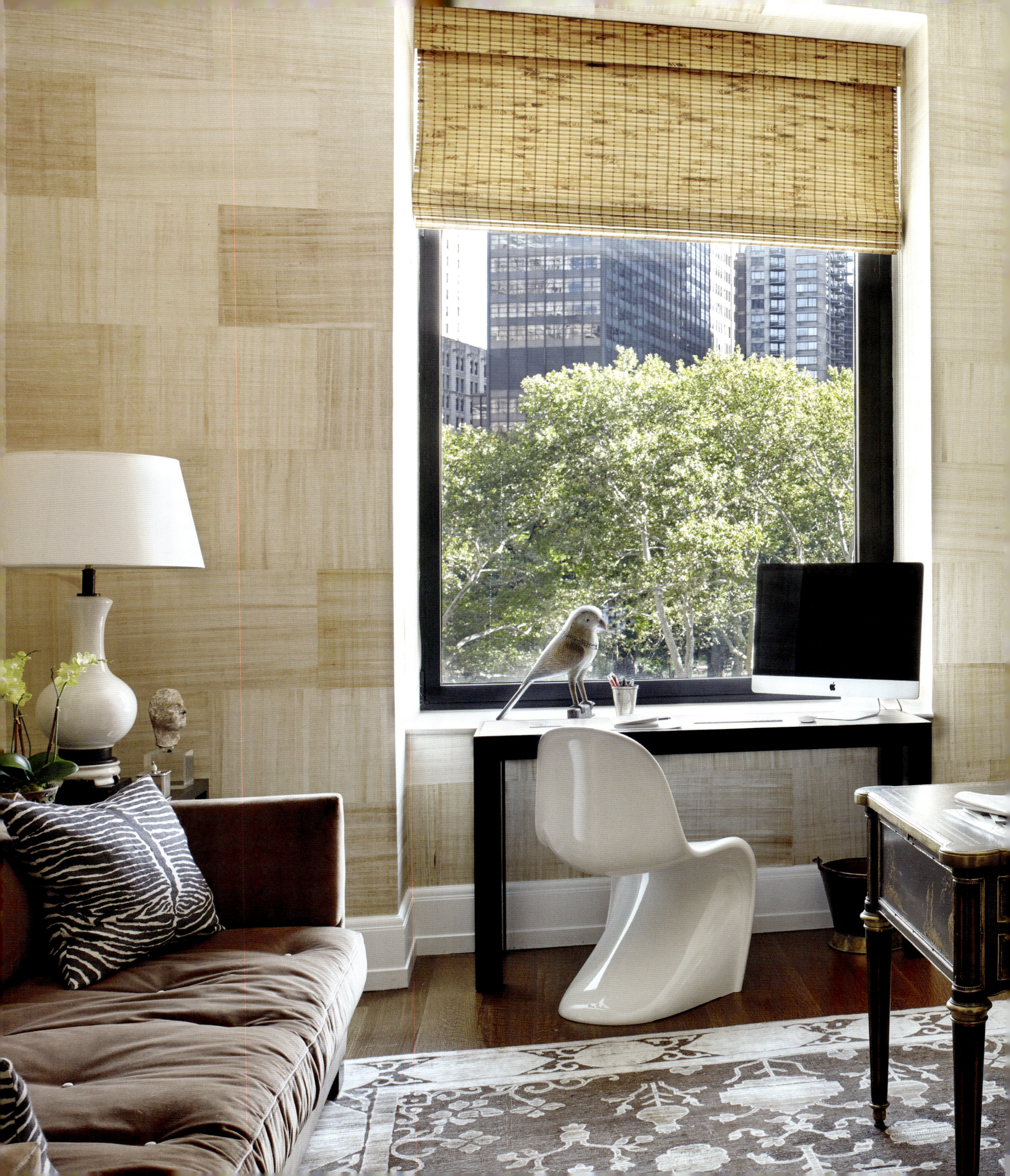

LA CAPPELLA DEGLI SCROVEGNI
LA CAPPELLA BRANCACCI
botero
KARL LAGERFELD THE LITTLE BLACK JACKET CARINE ROITFELD
DICTIONARY
OUTSIDE IN
THE EMERGENT CREATION
AMERICAN WATERCO
The Prado
PIERO DELLA FRANCESCA
THOMAS EAKINS

YESTERDAY'S NEWS
AVEDON
ARCHITECTS OF COMMUNITY
TORTI GALLAS + PARTNERS
SUNNYLANDS

PRECEDING PAGES The publisher's office is aptly lined with sheets of handmade papyrus paper. The Venetian chair and Louis XVI bureau plat add a bit of style and European pomp. A second desk overlooks Madison Square Park. **OPPOSITE** A cotton velvet–covered St. Thomas–style sofa might offer a sumptuous executive catnap. A pair of mid-century lamps emits plenty of light for a working meeting while adding to the domestic charm of the office. **ABOVE** The chic cerused-oak étagères were found in Sag Harbor at Neo Studio. They fit the room perfectly.

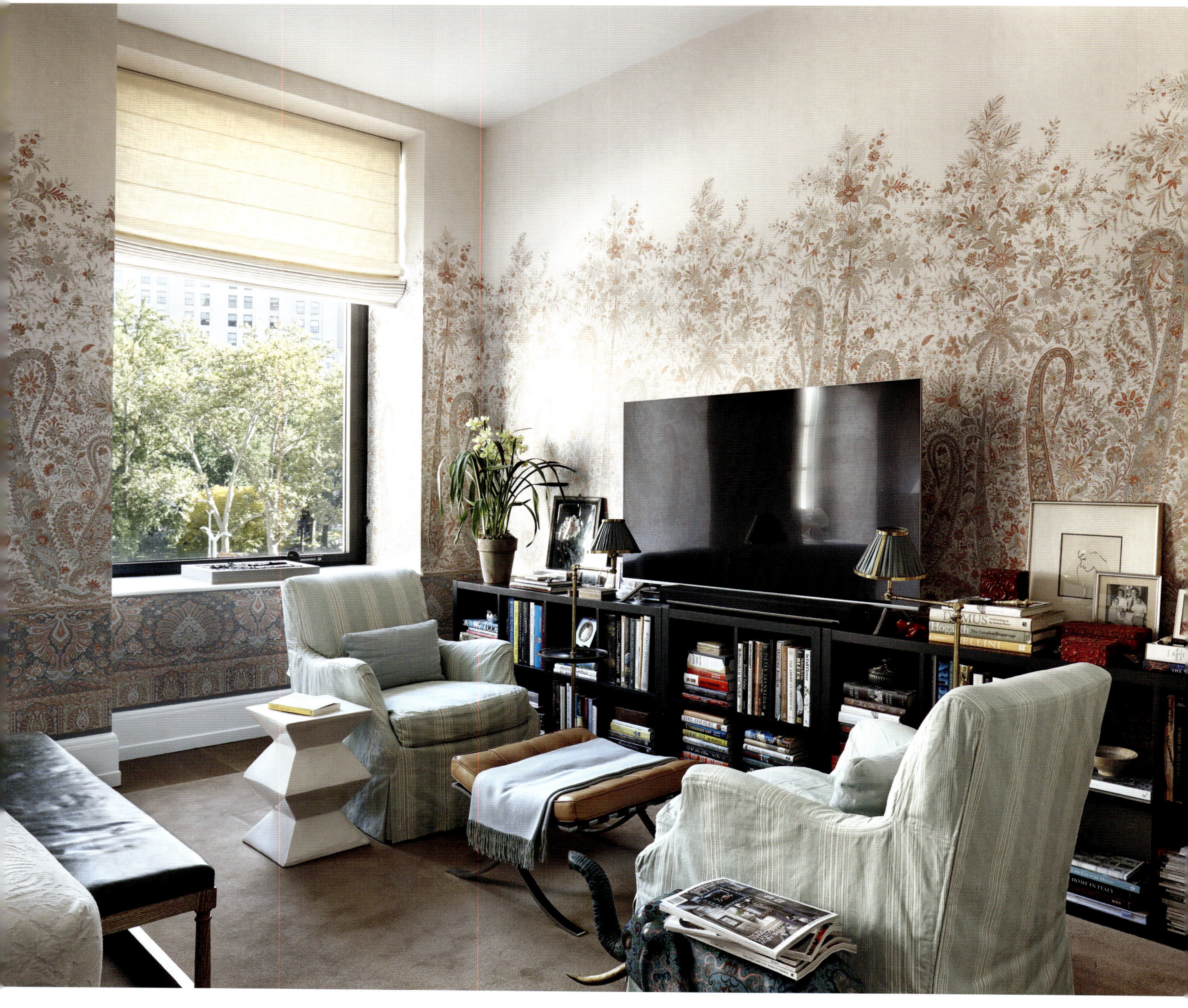

OPPOSITE The facing chairs in the master bedroom are slipcovered in a Peter Fasano striped ticking. The bookcases were delivered from Ikea and were set on their sides, end to end, to span the width of the room. **ABOVE LEFT** Translucent rock crystal lamps on made-to-order white-lacquered nightstands flank the bed. **ABOVE RIGHT** Above the clients' own "transitional" French commode is a Regency mirror from Cove Landing. Looking over the scene is a charming portrait of the publisher as a young boy by Constantin Alajalov. The wallpaper was adapted from a Kashmiri wool challis shawl in a lighter palette suited to this airy bedroom.

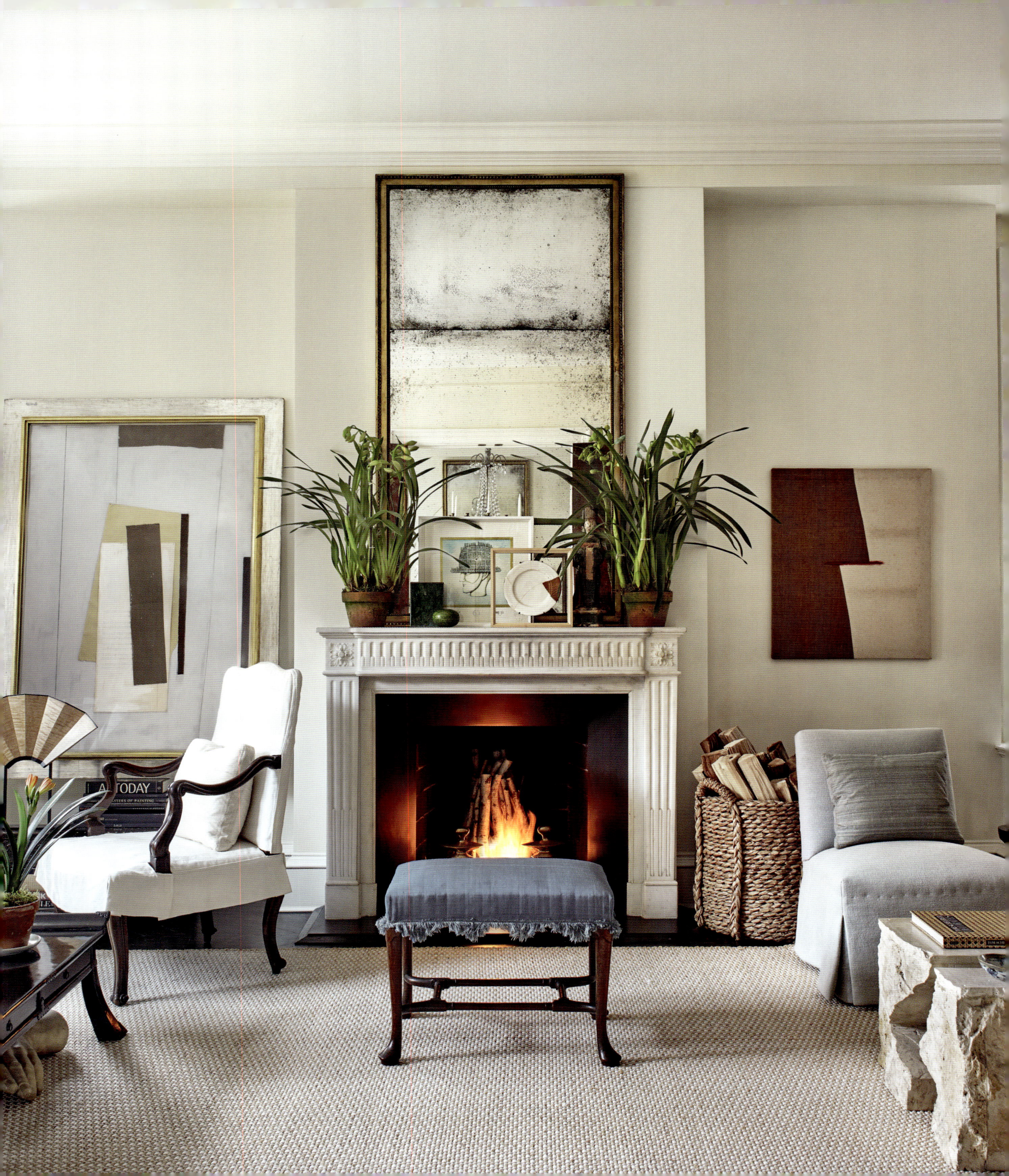
TODAY

Play It Again

WHAT'S A DECORATOR TO DO WHEN A client asks him to redecorate an apartment he had renovated twenty-three years ago that still feels fresh and nearly perfect? He hems and haws and eventually acquiesces, in the hope that the apartment can remain its essential self. God forbid an interloping decorator were to get his hands on it.

This Park Avenue apartment got its "good bones" from our earlier renovation. The original dowdy, closed off, and dark rooms were airily transformed by tall doors that opened up grand axial arrangements. The bathrooms and kitchen were done sensibly, but in keeping with the stature of the apartment, and don't look a bit out of place today.

Handmade bark paper was laid in golden rectangle blocks in the front hall. It still looks as it did then, though a little yellowing may, in fact, have enhanced the effect of rough stone.

The library walls, once richly glazed over a deep brown base, were redone in a fresher, more modern-feeling peacock-ish blue, directly out of its Benjamin Moore can. It's ultra flat like the re-covered wool felt sofa beneath it. The "vanilla ice cream"–lacquered walls in the living room and dining room were laboriously redone to repair the marks from years of picture hanging and some ensuing hairline cracks.

Little of the furniture needed changing. The "Pauline Potter" upholstered settee in the dining room remained, its wide striping merely refreshed with new ribbed cotton. The Georgian chairs' seafoam-blue satin somehow survived—no need of re-covering. The eighteenth-century stone console and facing pair of gilded Louis XVI-style mirrors made for the apartment needed only to be removed during the repainting.

A more modern sofa was ordered and the mix of antique chairs and an English settee were slipcovered in white linen to give the living room a lighter, less formal, more evanescent atmosphere.

The family dog Lefty had died a natural death after a long life. It was now time for the grown-up, if a bit delicate, raffia-and-cotton Cogolin carpet. It had been rejected years back in favor of a more practical sisal one.

A few other elements were deemed to be too old-fashioned. The pleated-silk and fringed lampshades suspended along the bedroom hall were replaced with modern counterparts, and the hall's English-y ivory-striped walls were replaced with reflective and mottled tea paper.

The ca. 1995 silk curtains were only just beginning to show incipient Miss Haversham tatters. We replaced them with more modern layers of shades: in the master bedroom, blackout ones for sleeping, straw scrims for light filtering and privacy, and finally, tailored linen ones to keep the decorator's workroom busy. For the guest room's large window we made a clever bifold screen that obscures neighboring windows while letting in maximum light.

Back in the dining room, the decorator was goaded into replacing his "old saw" of a white Formica Saarinen table for the sake of something new. A glossy top was made of exotic wood (Saarinen's elegant "airplane wing" edge faithfully reproduced). It appears to float on a brass-trimmed, mirrored base that reflects the shiny, dark, zigzag-stained floors. They've held up admirably since 1995, requiring only a fresh topcoat of tinted wax.

Hopefully, this should all last for the next twenty-three years.

OPPOSITE Atop the Cogolin raffia-and-cotton-string carpet sits a varied and wide-ranging collection of furnishings. A 1990 painting by Stephen Edlich in a silver-gilt frame rests to the left of the mantel. **OVERLEAF TOP LEFT** The originally gilded French console in the elevator vestibule was painted a modernizing chalky white and a shaped Perspex slab replaced its marble top. **OVERLEAF BOTTOM LEFT** The lamps in the hall are in the style of Diego Giacometti from the 1930s. The oak columns on which they stand rest firmly on the zigzag-stained floor. **OVERLEAF RIGHT** Through the tall doors of the living room can be seen one of a facing pair of gilded mirrors with antiqued glass made for the apartment by Gill & Lagodich. The painting to the right of the doorway is by Alex Katz.

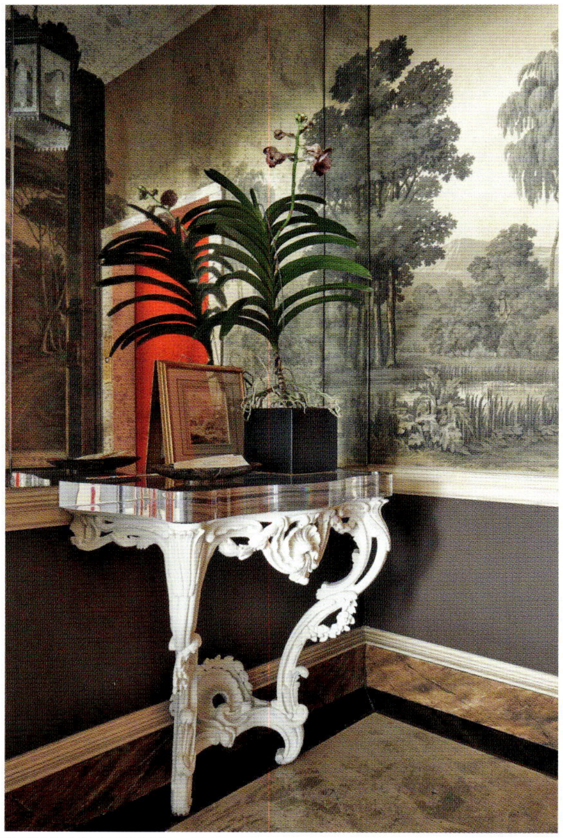
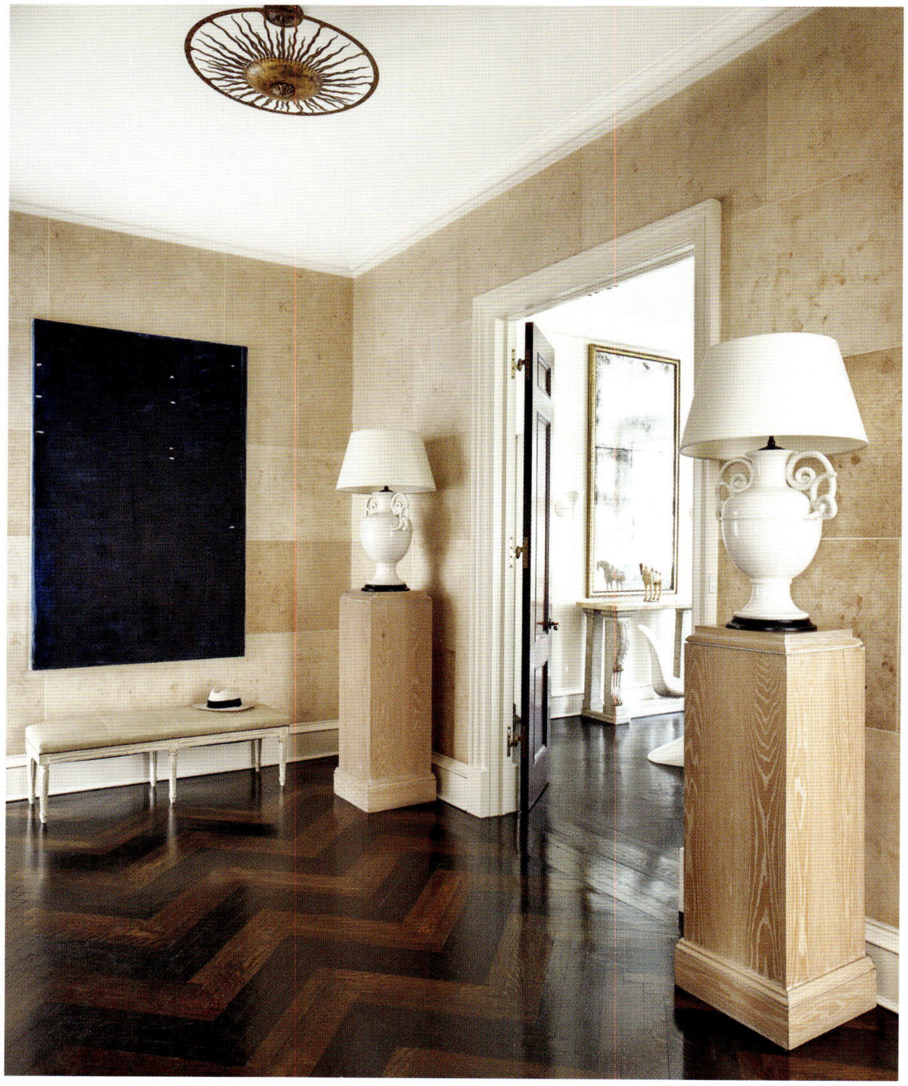
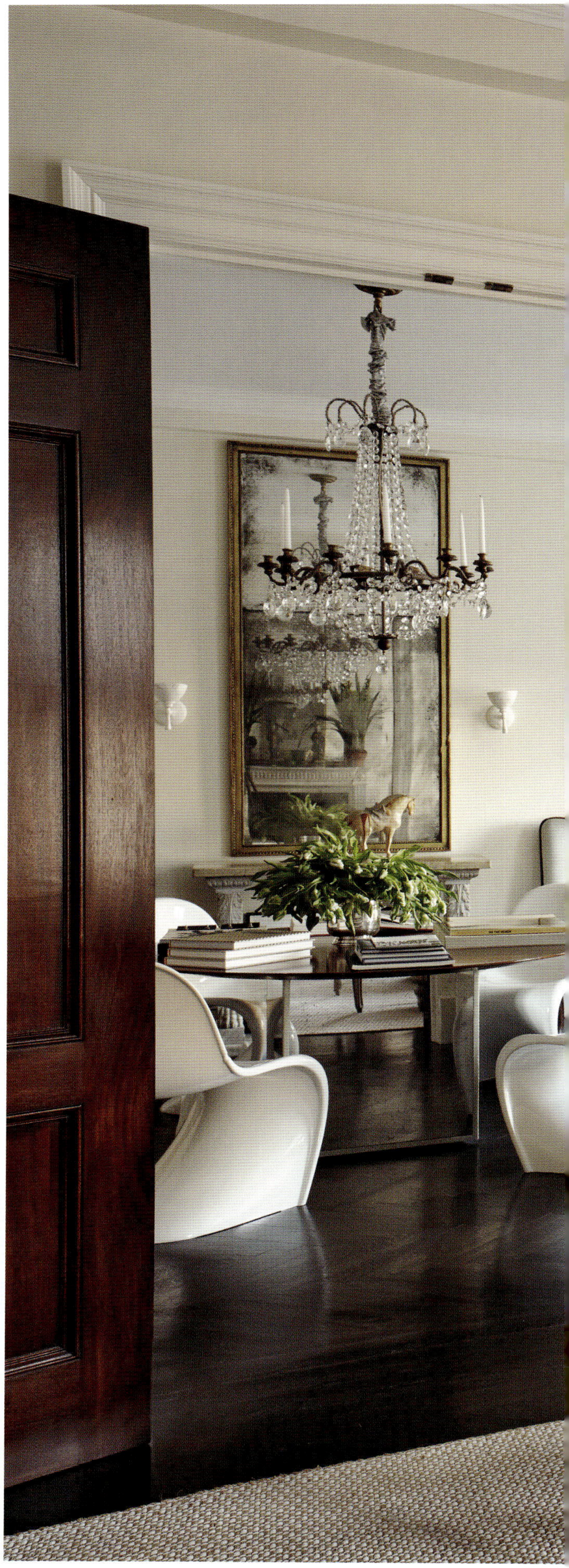

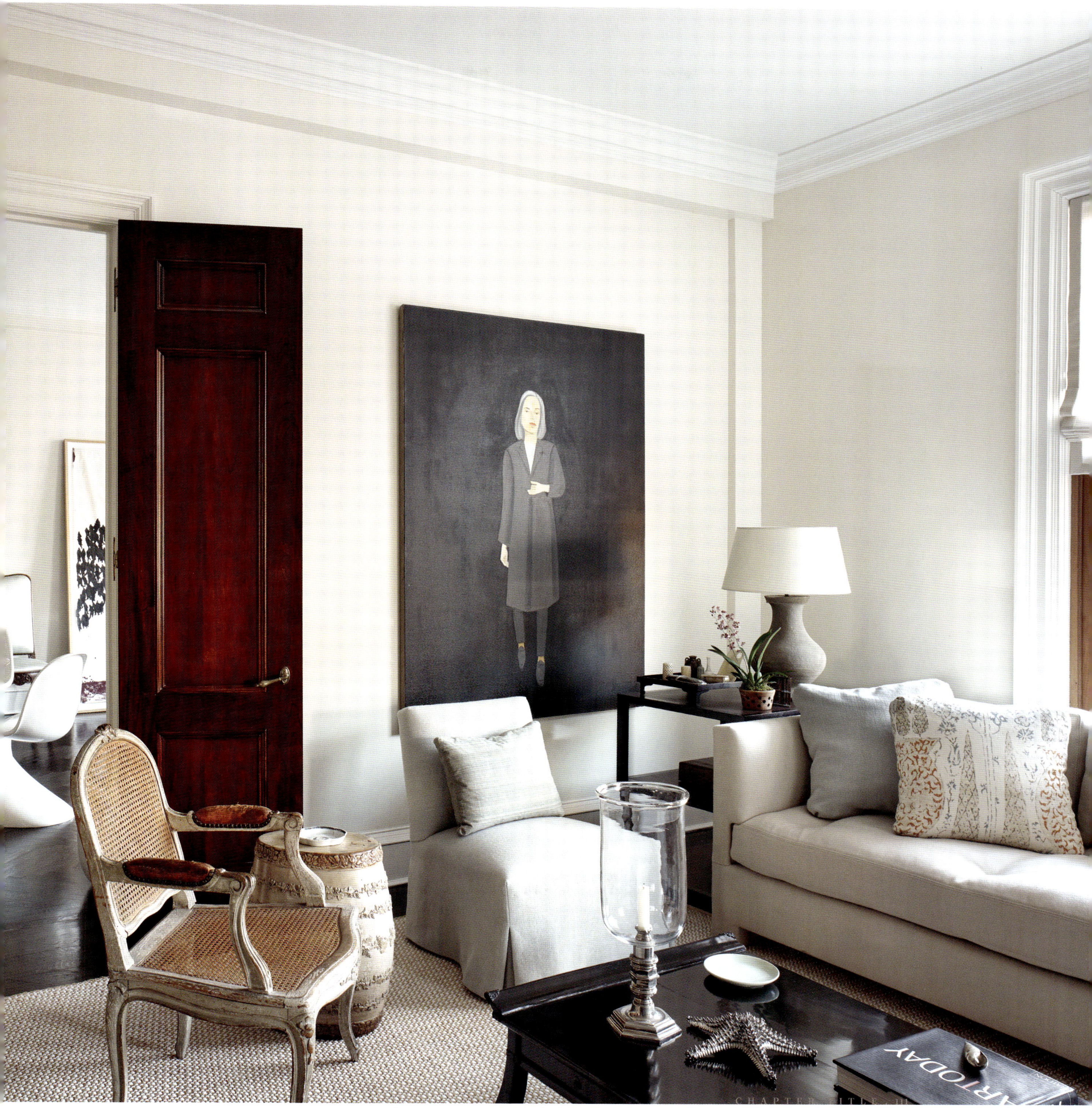

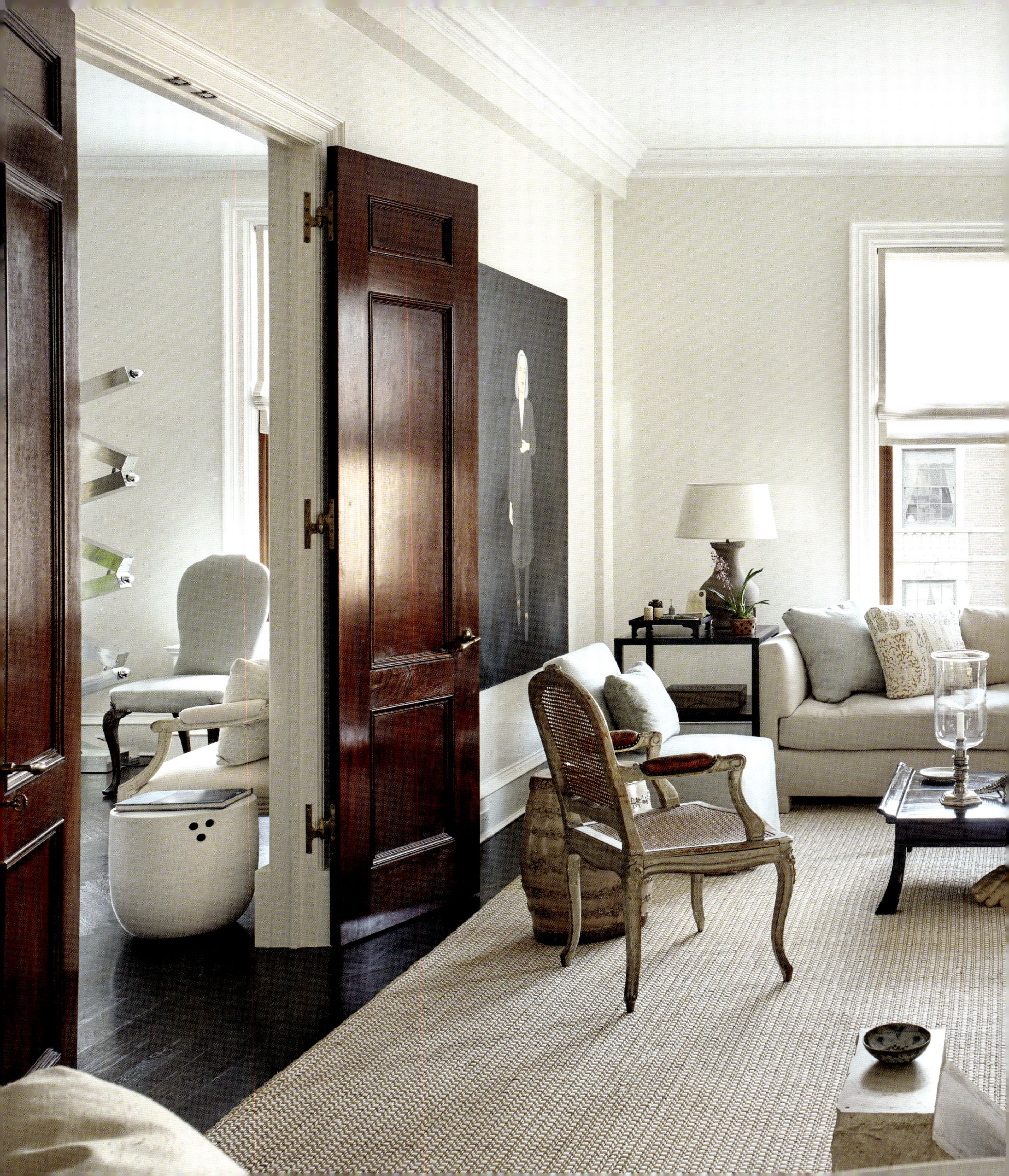

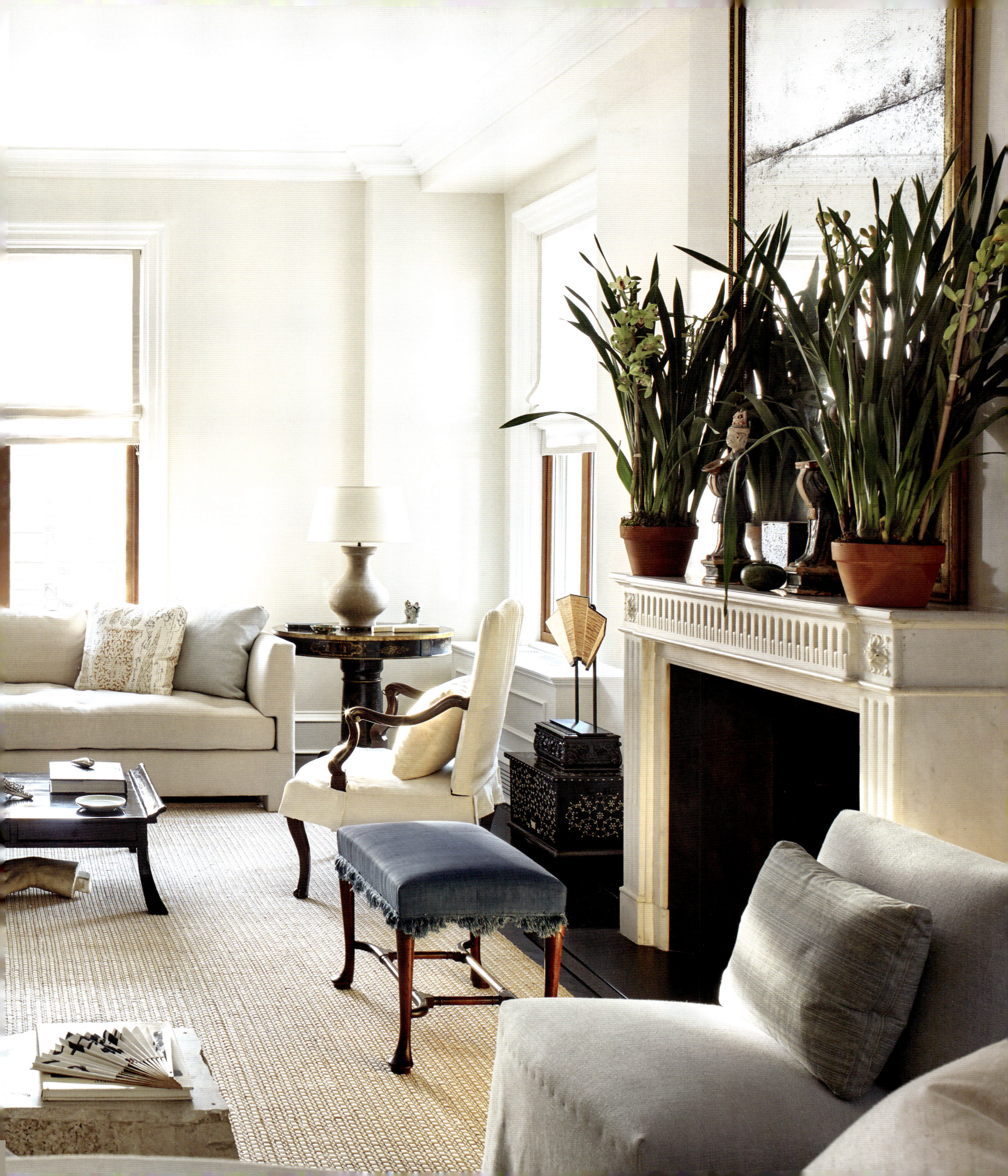

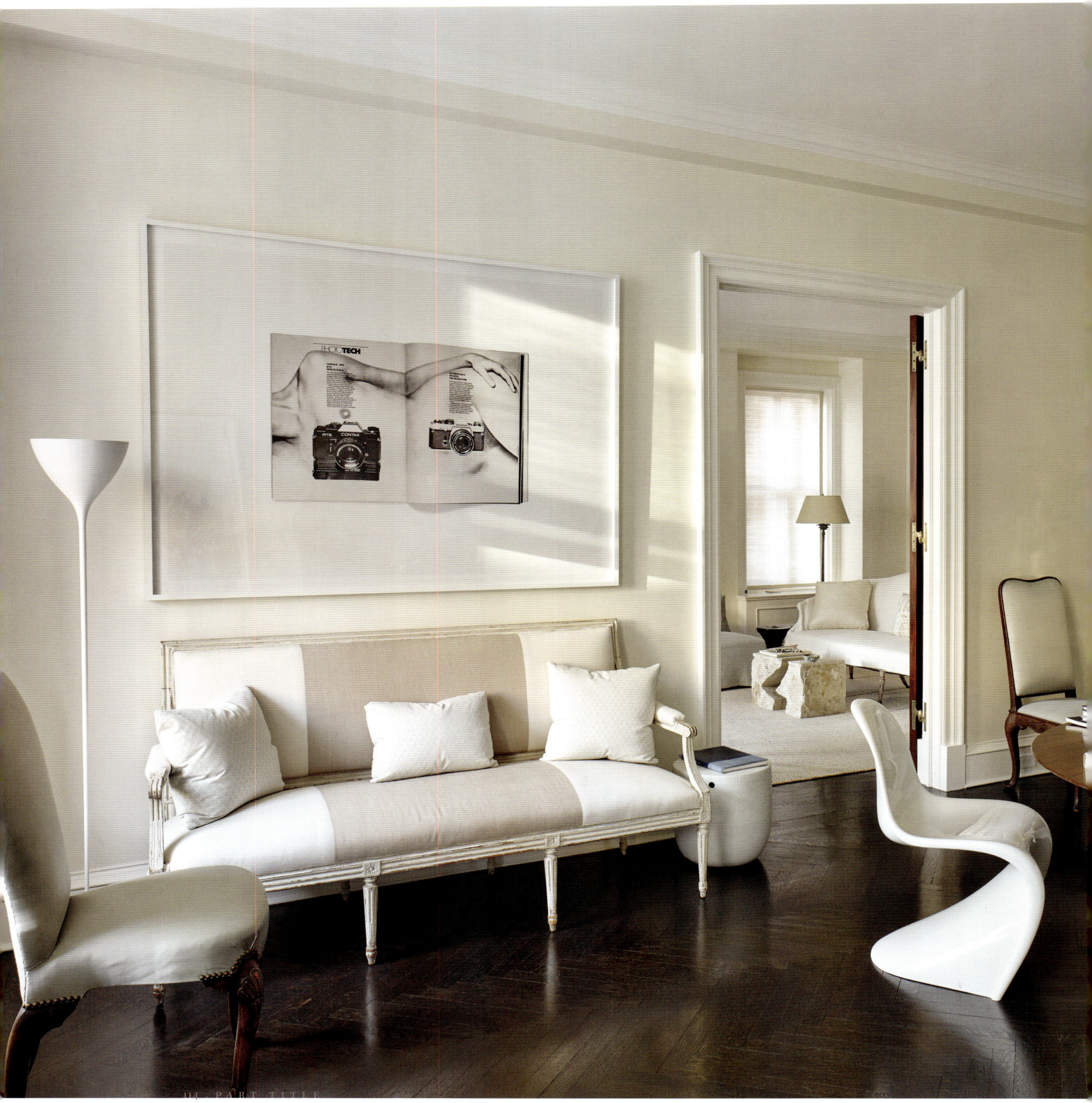
PHOTOTECH
CONTAX

PRECEDING PAGES Han dynasty jars fitted as lamps, a Japanese table from Naga Antiques, an Irish mahogany stool from Cove Landing, a fan-like sculpture by Christopher Hewat, and new but classic custom upholstery span two thousand years of the decorative arts. The living room has a calming sense of balance without resorting to a single "pair." **LEFT** The bold upholstery of the settee was inspired by Pauline Potter, the American wife of Baron Philippe de Rothschild. The dining table base is a mirrored cube that makes the top appear to float. The lacquered Panton chairs remain from the initial 1996 decoration. The Italian chandelier has been electrified to sparkle from within, yet retains a ring of beeswax candles for lighting at night. **ABOVE** The bedroom hall has been re-papered in antiqued but still reflective silver tea paper from Roger Arlington. The light fixtures are by Lumfardo.

ABOVE LEFT In the library, a grouping of Han dynasty jars tops the Chinese cabinet, which has been fitted for a television. **LEFT** A Régence chair, upholstered twenty-three years ago, still presides in the room. The nine-foot bookcases were fashioned from black-lacquered dowels, mahogany shelves, and brass "lamp parts." They are firmly held together by steel tension rods.

ABOVE The library is painted in velvety Blue Muscari from Benjamin Moore's Century collection. The color of the wool felt sofa is a near match to the walls. Above the sofa is a painting by Callum Innes. A superbly comfortable Warren Platner Easy chair, designed in 1966, was added to face the television. **OVERLEAF** The ethereal guest room, formerly a child's room, was redesigned for spa-like comfort. The translucent windows shutters are infilled with Indian cotton cutwork by Schumacher. The shapely John Derian Dromedary loveseat floats like a cloud. It was reupholstered to resemble a perfect and sublimely draped slipcover. The gouaches above the convenient luggage stand are by Robin Cameron.

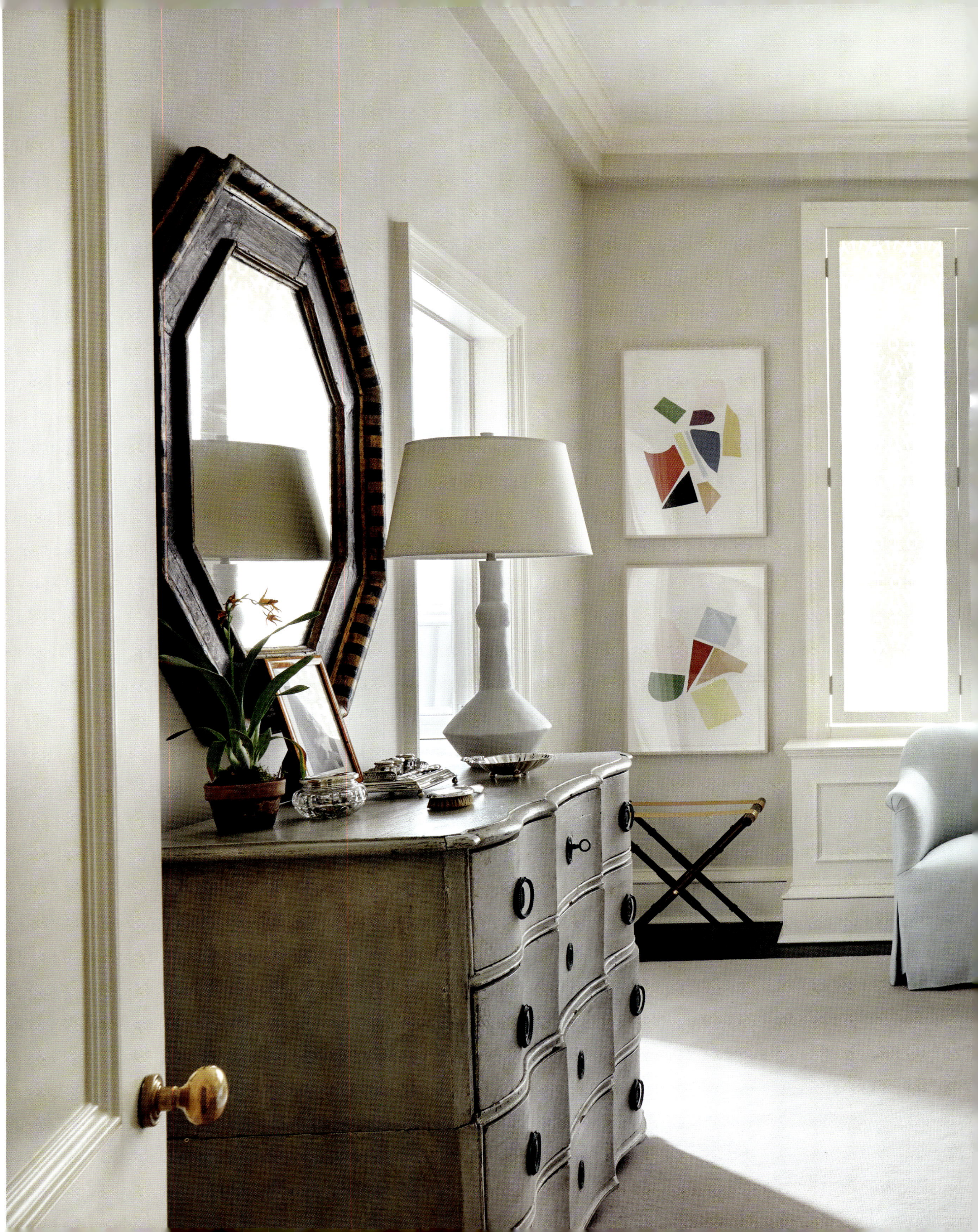

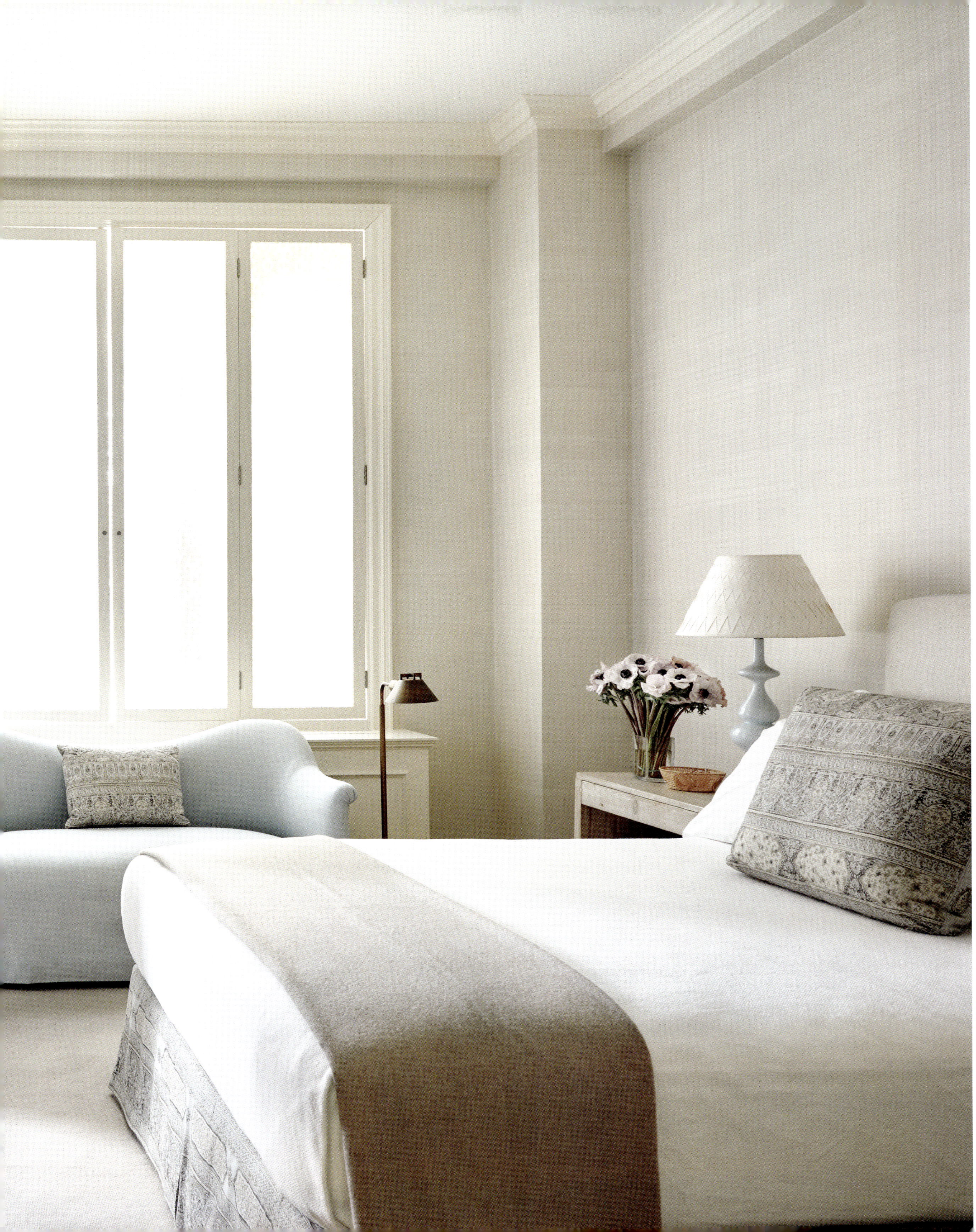

ABOVE The master bedroom is lit with contrasting forms: long-necked Chinese vases fitted as lamps add a splash of color; the industrially designed black Tizio desk lamps flanking the bed are modern classics. The room is softened by Holland & Sherry's whitewashed raffia, which covers the walls. OPPOSITE A serene and ladylike high-back chair by the Swedish designer Frits Henningsen faces the bed. A pair of sinuous oak dressers was painted by Brian Leaver to resemble vellum. They are reminiscent of the iconic variation by Samuel Marx designed for Marshall Field. Coincidentally, they came from a Chicago apartment.

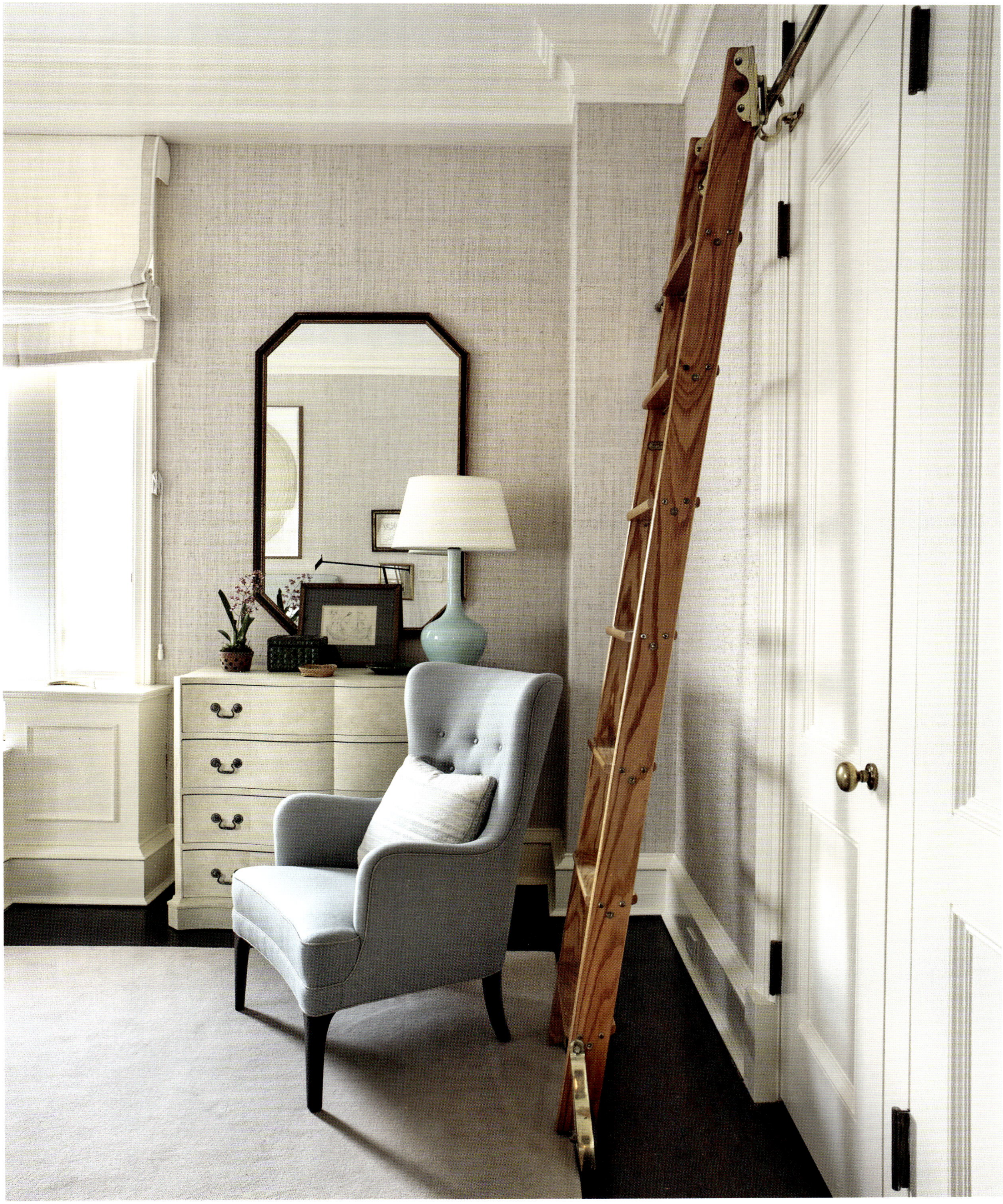

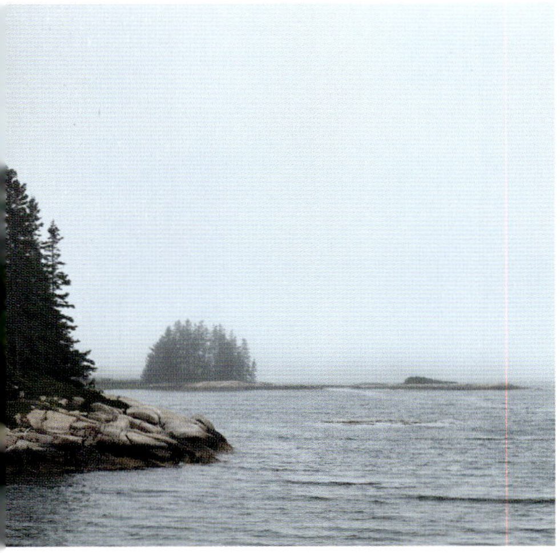
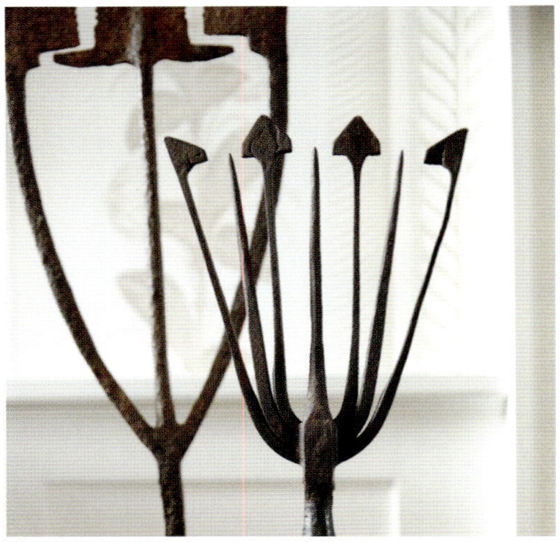
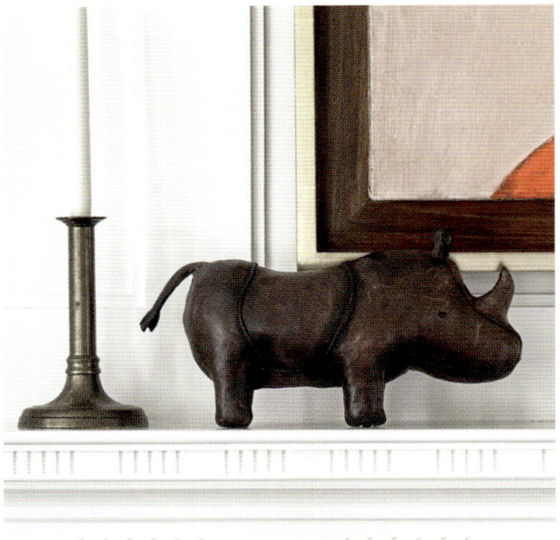

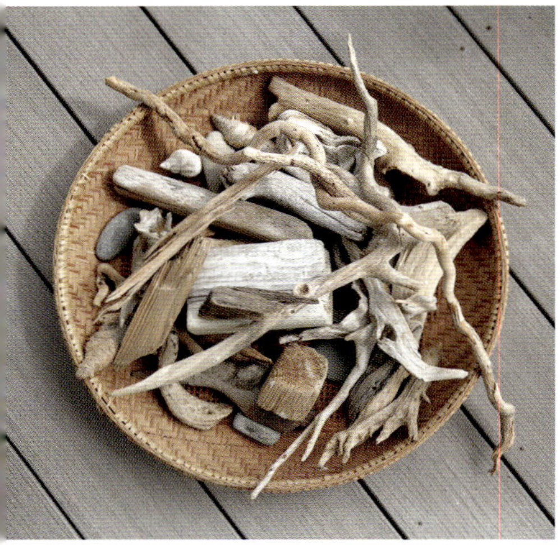
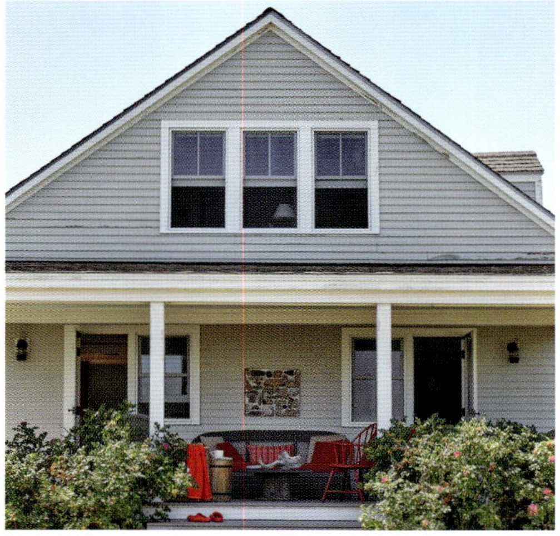
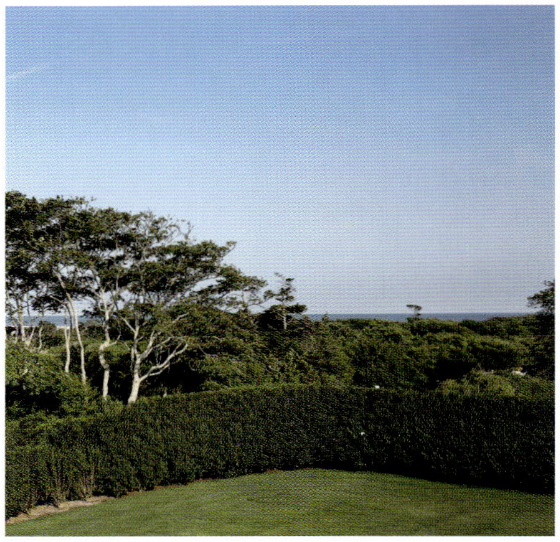
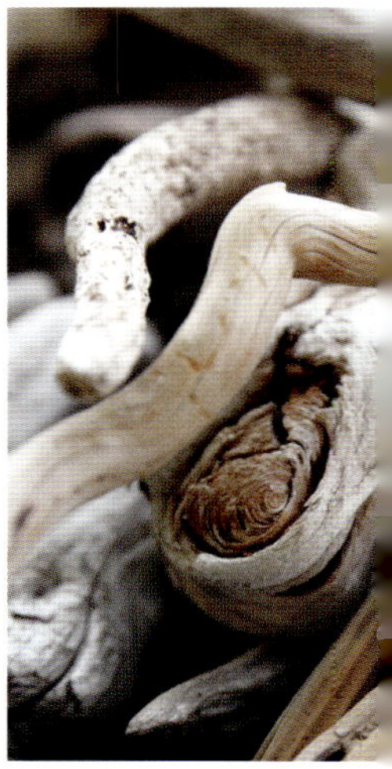
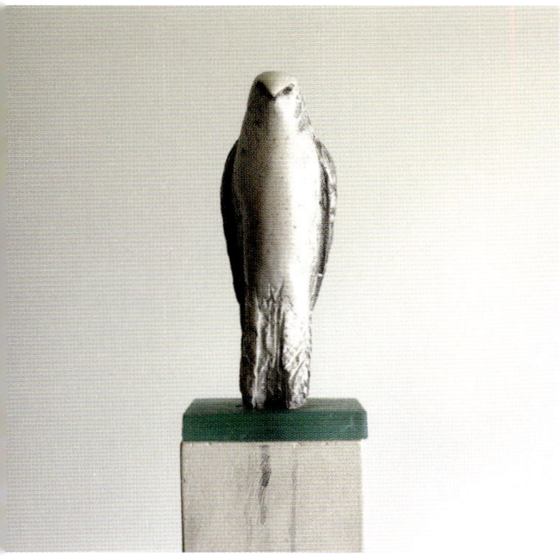
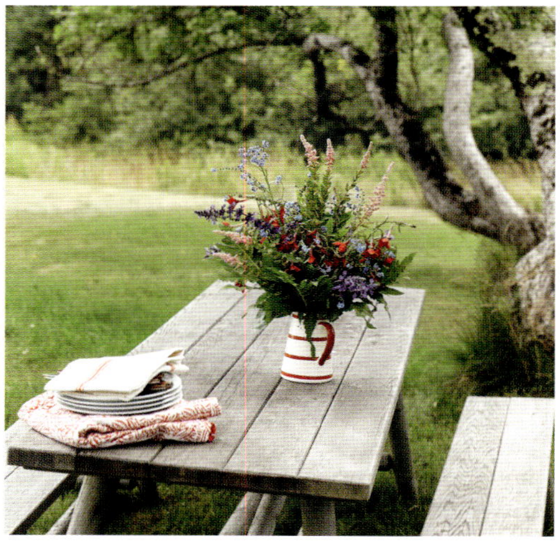
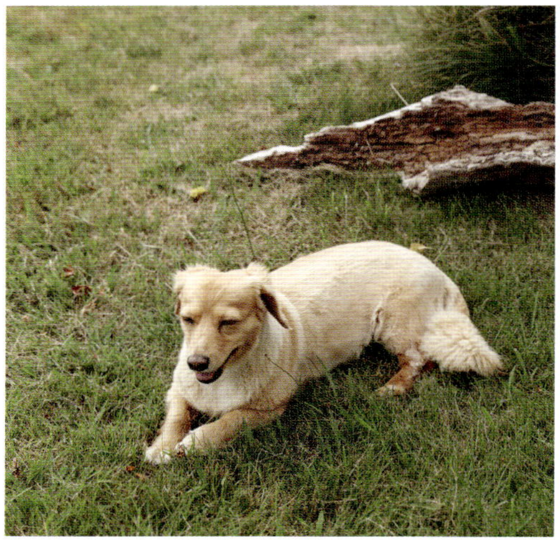
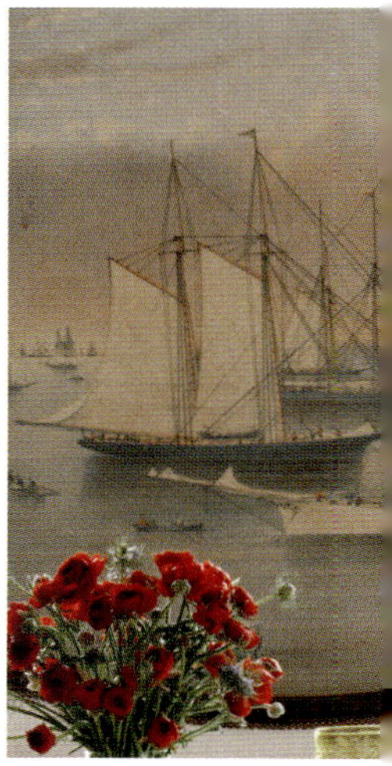
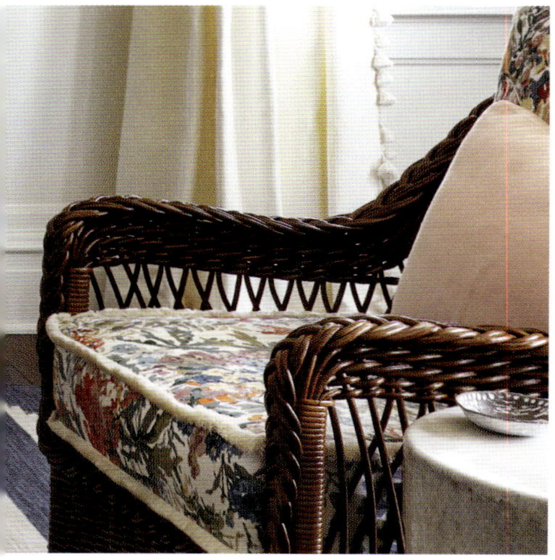
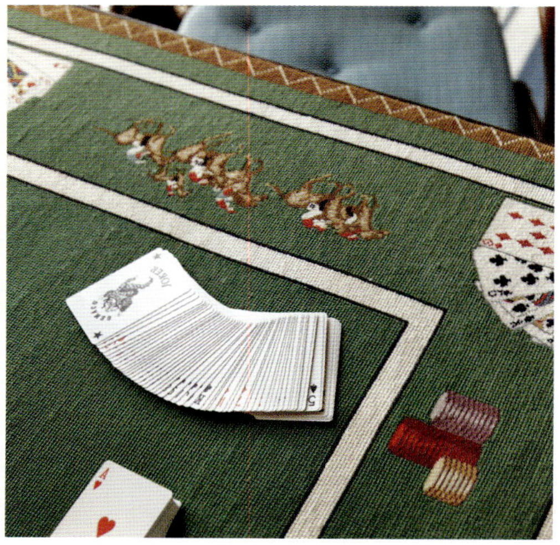
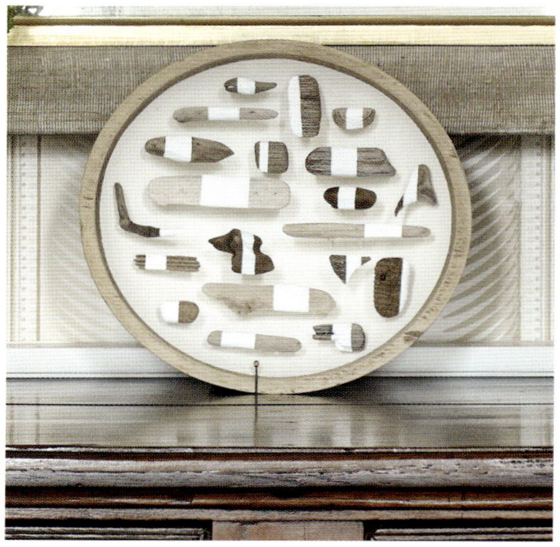
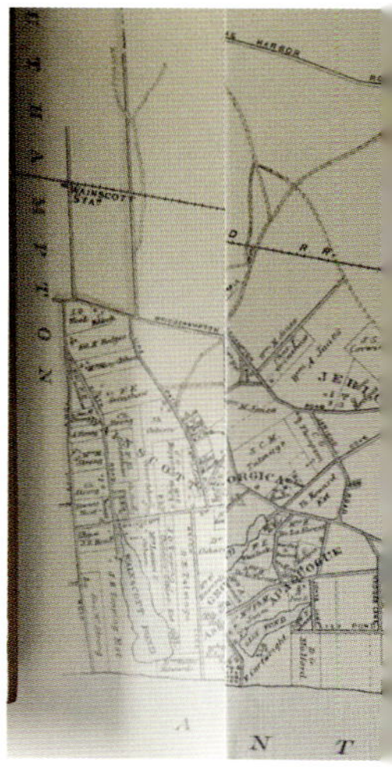

SUMMER

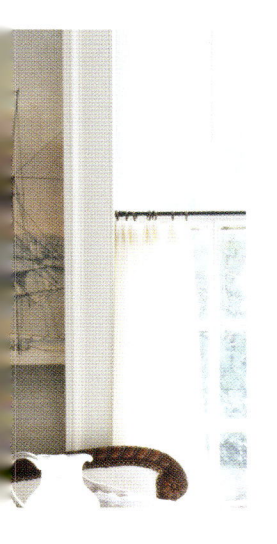

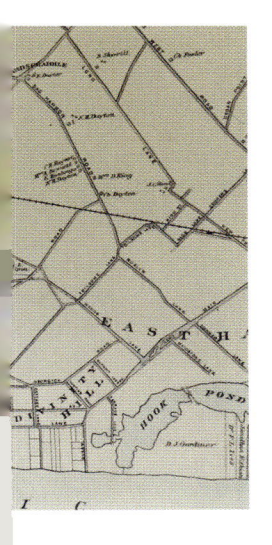

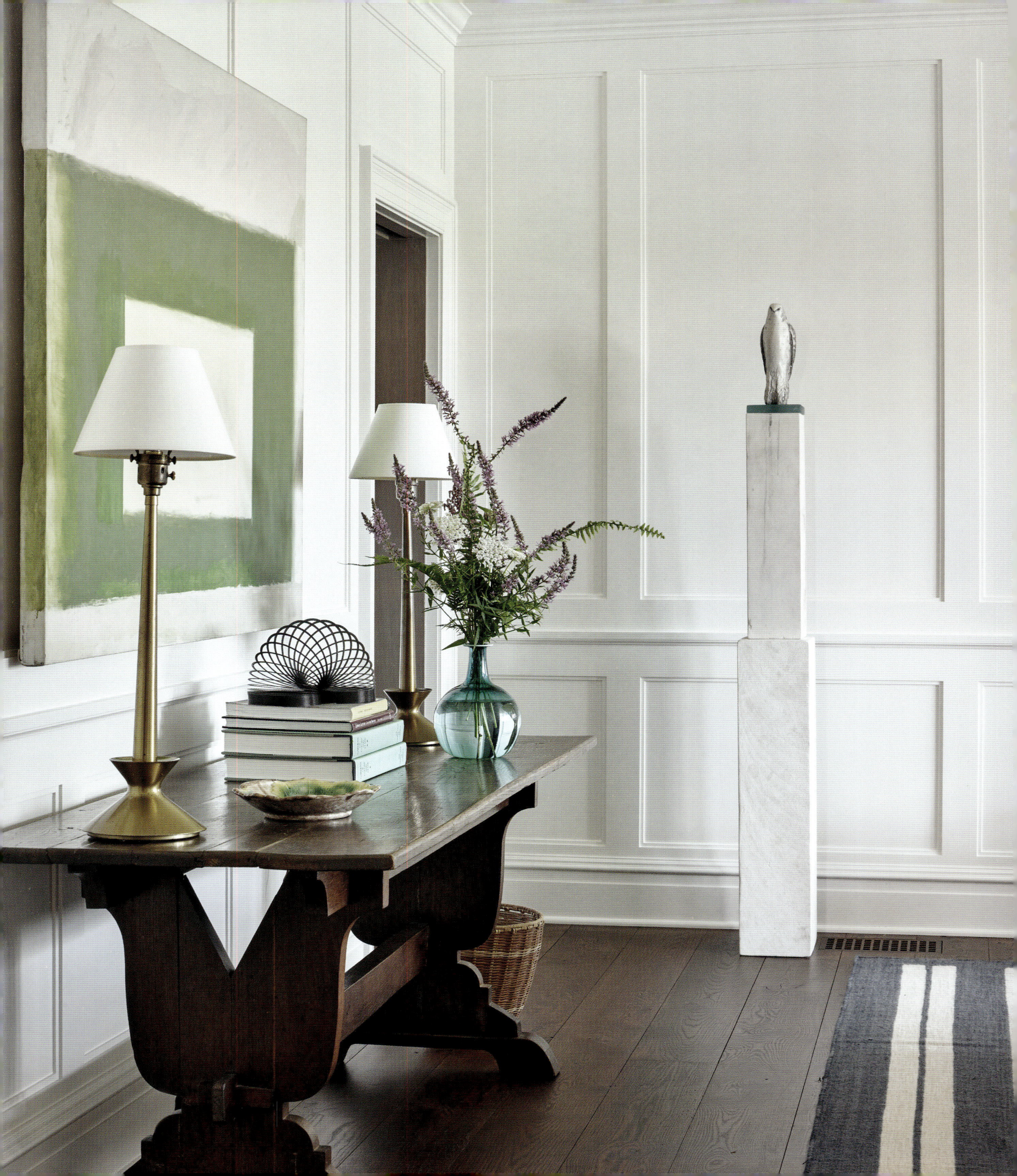

Hedges

THE POTATO FIELDS ON THE SOUTH FORK of Long Island have been under siege for a long time—it's not an entirely new phenomenon. In the mid-nineteenth century the plein-air painters came looking for new fodder. The Hudson River may have been wrung dry by its eponymous school. William Merritt Chase and Thomas Moran were renowned among them and the first to broadcast the unique quality of the South Fork light now touted perennially by the local real estate brokers.

Then, around the turn of the century, came a certain class of summering city folk. They sought an alternative to the fashionable but waning grand hotel and boardwalked resorts within striking distance of New York. My own family made the switch to Long Island's east end in the 1940s from Spring Lake, New Jersey, where the summer traffic had become unbearable and the beach too crowded. Lucky me.

The farmland was parceled up and went cheap, especially near the dunes. Exposure to the salt air was less desirable to the farmers. Lanes were drawn and, little by little, the houses built for generations of summer people transformed it into a privet-hedged patchwork, an intermittently pastoral but still lovely sort of place.

More recently, there's been a disquieting influx. Overly large houses, meant to evoke the enduring Shingle Style cottages, consistently and cluelessly miss their mark. They self-aggrandize behind veritable stockades of privet punctuated by faux-rural yet intimidating electronic gates. The pastiches are awash in familiar materials and details but have so many modern bells, whistles, and general excess that the essence of what makes a good summer house is entirely lost.

This house is not one of those. Its architect was genetically predisposed to the nostalgic and correct, if not precisely historicist. His great-great-grandfather was the principal progenitor of the entire genre: Stanford White.

There are concessions to modern life, yes. The kitchen has an island and exclusive access to a comfortably covered and furnished summer living porch. The bedrooms (every one with two exposures at least) may have baths "en suite," but their closets are closets—not walk-in dressing rooms. There is no upstairs "morning kitchen" and not a wine room, spa, or screening room in sight.

The rooms may be smallish, but there's by no means a stinginess of space. The square footage was used for the things that count. The mistress of this house was unambiguous. She asked for space and air at the expense of large rooms and was well served by her foresight.

So the entrance hall is large—with a soaring stair and airy upper landing. (This extravagance is the essence and wisdom of this house.) But it's not at all imposing. Rather, it is a social and convivial assembly hall and thoroughfare.

Televisions are conspicuously absent in this house (there is but one). Books are taken seriously and provide a principal weekend and summer pastime. The shelves are expectant and will be well filled over time. The upstairs landing was aptly consecrated with the inclusion of a marvelous A. W. N. Pugin oaken library table, the central piece of furniture in the house.

This reading-cum-sitting room opens to the well-used upstairs porch and lookout. The view from there is congenially "borrowed." It looks across a neighbor's low-trimmed border of hedges and lawn toward a tidal pond and the ocean beyond. The blessedly and still uncrowded beach is just a two-minute walk down the lane.

OPPOSITE Several rooms in this Shingle Style house have distinctive forms of paneling. A potent sculpture by Jane Rosen stands guard over the living room. The painting over the oak table is by Perle Fine from the 1970s.

ABOVE Fairfield Porter's daughter appraises the decorating from above the mantel. OPPOSITE With its easy mix of classical and familiar elements, this summer living room could be nowhere but in America. The sofa and the cushions of the Bielecky Brothers wicker chairs are covered in Lee Jofa's Garden Glories chintz. They rest atop a striped cotton dhurrie by Studio Four. The marvelous American Windsor settee, salvaged from the clients' former beach house, is in vibrant, almost music-like, counterpoint to the suite of rectilinear and colorful Agnes Barley gouaches above it.

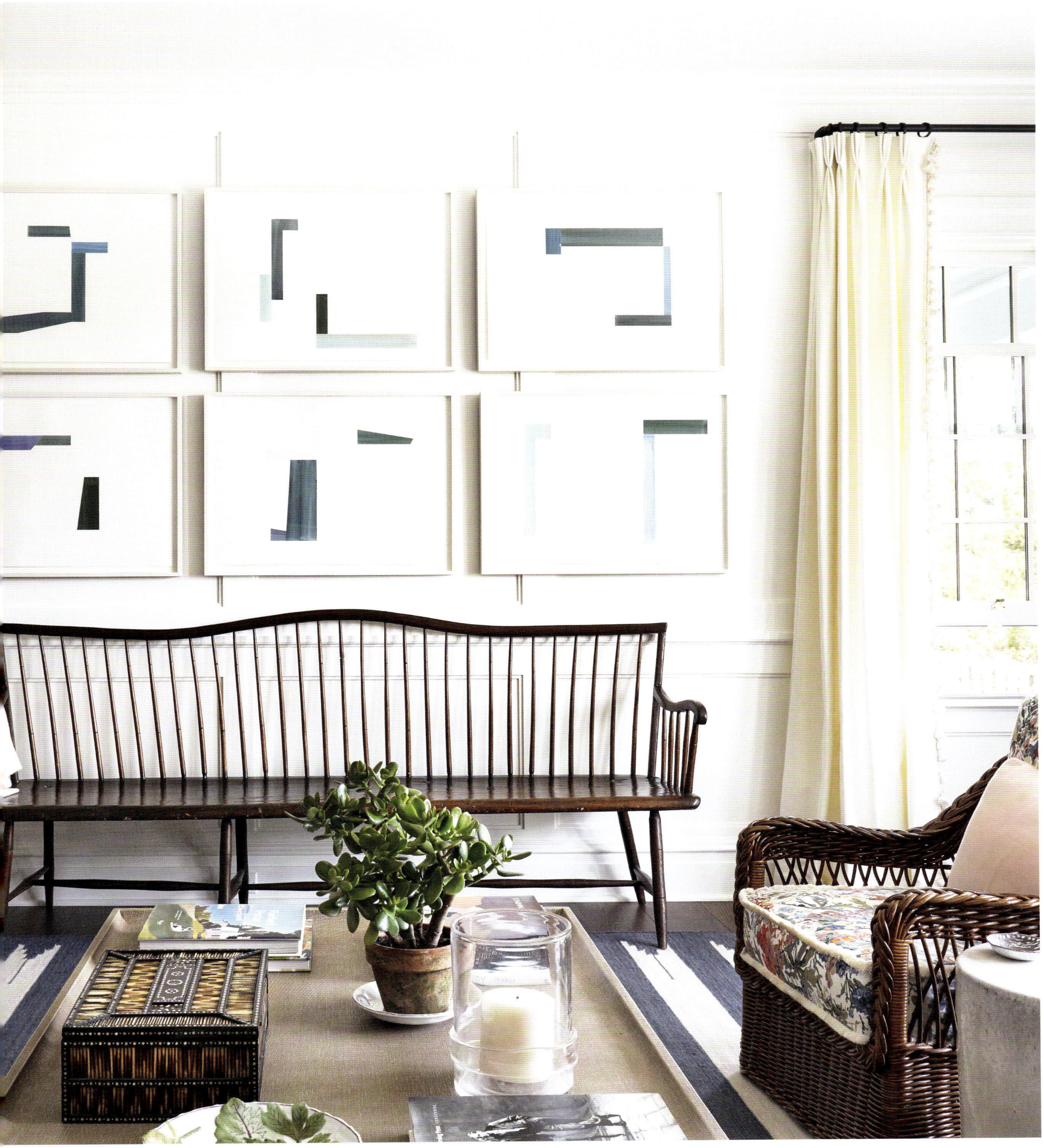

LEFT The entrance hall is papered in Quadrille's Climbing Hydrangea. Hydrangeas are profuse in the garden outside too. A nineteenth-century American painting hangs over the sky-blue settee and is attended by a pair of fishing implements mounted as bold and graphic modernist sculptures. The French wing chair was covered to suggest Americana crewelwork. **ABOVE** An abstract tabletop sculpture by Jane Scheerer Parkes faces the front door. It's made of meticulously painted driftwood floating on pegs in a wooden bowl. **OPPOSITE** The sturdy striped wool-and-jute stair runner was designed to endure many summers of wear and tear. An antique Khotan rug fit the seating area of the entrance hall to a tee, once it was cut down by the decorator.

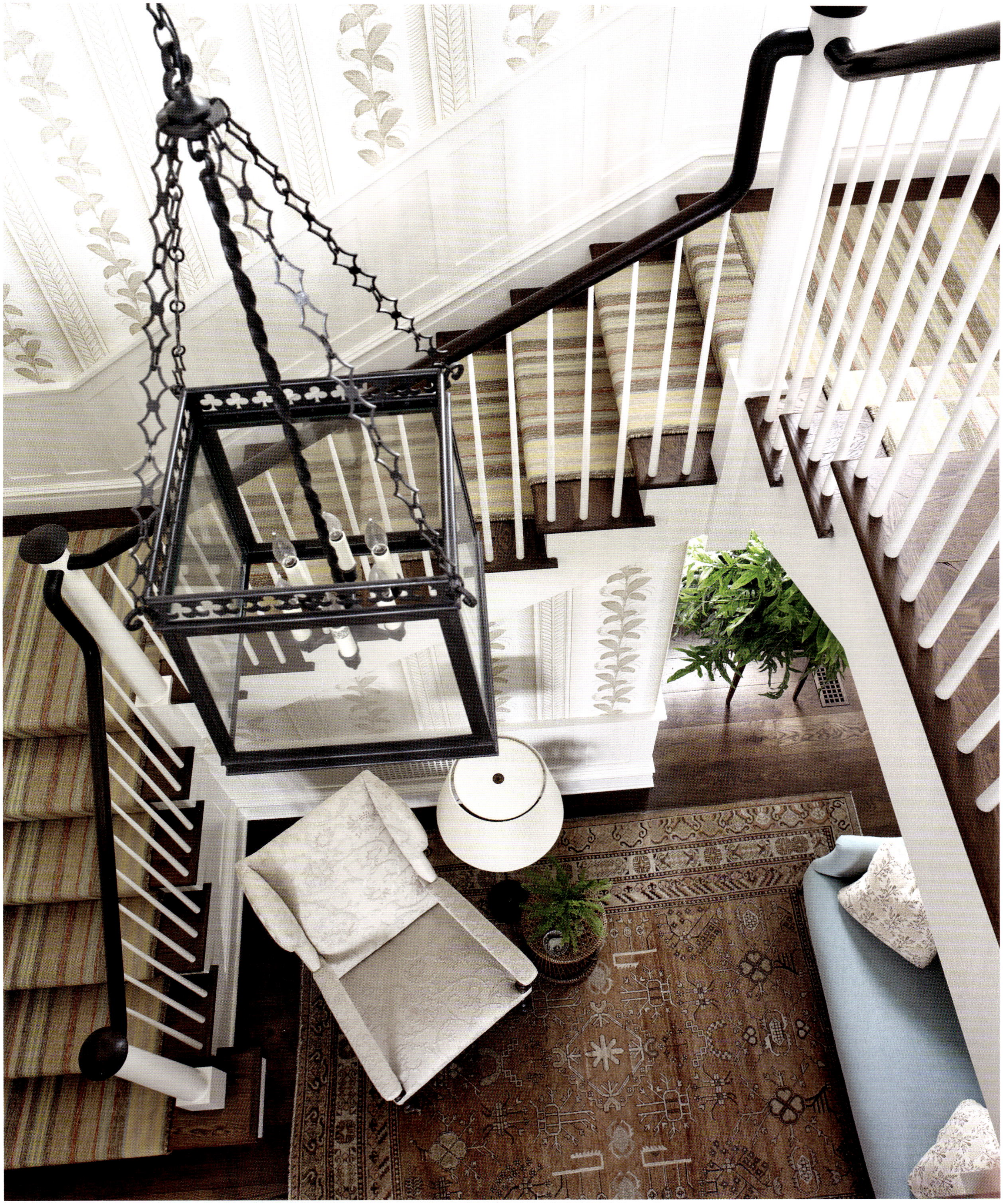

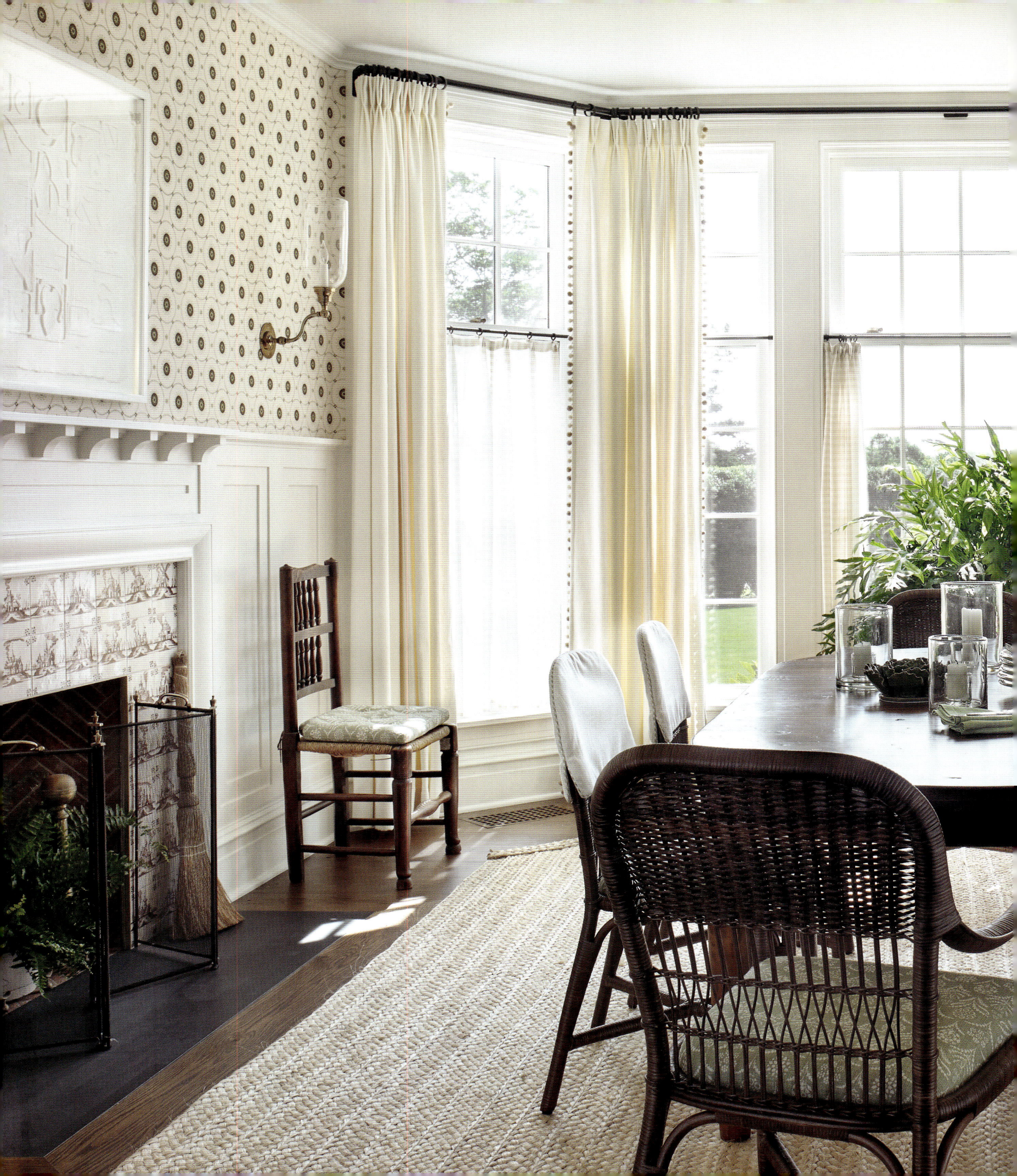

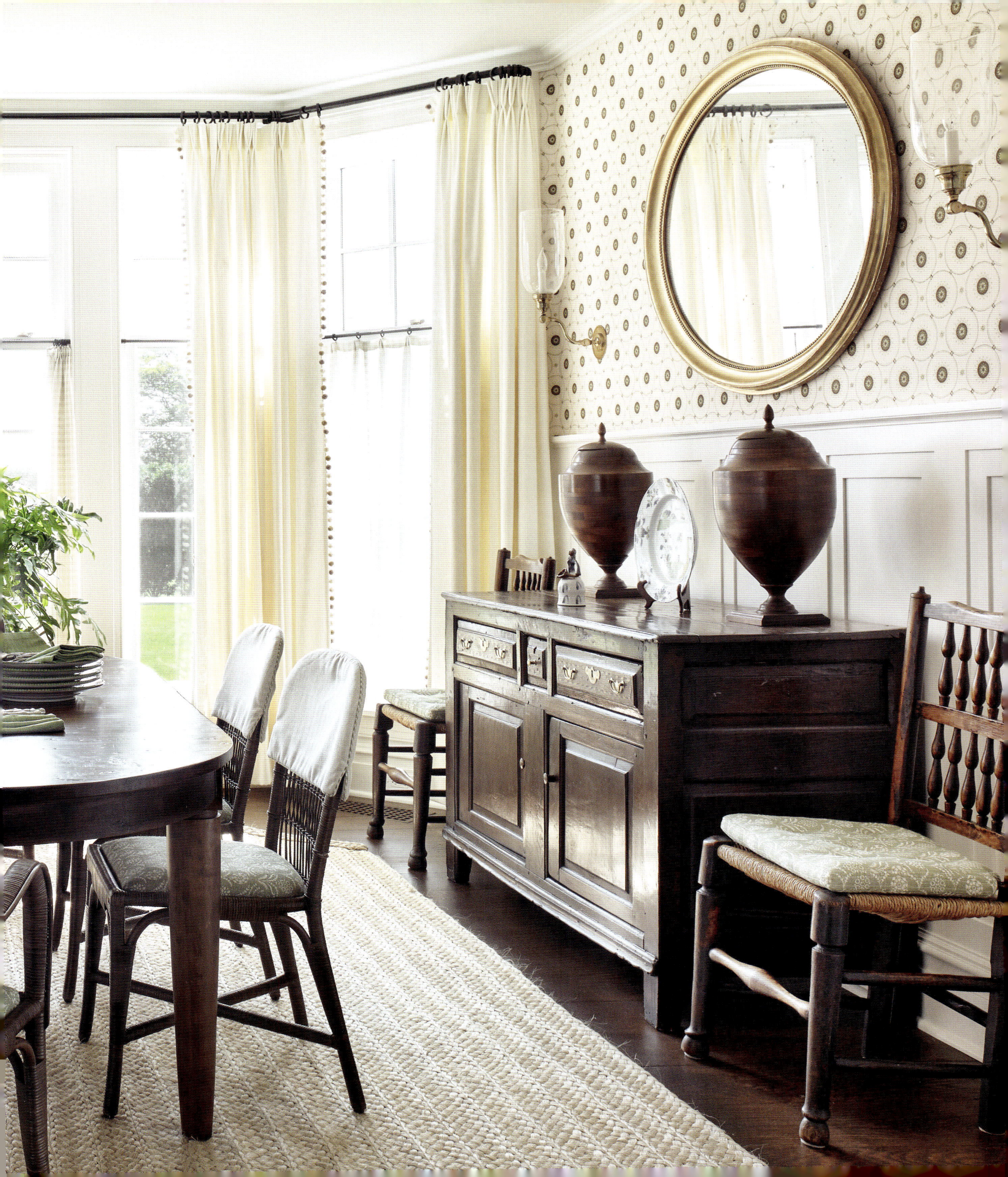

PRECEDING PAGES The antique Delft tiles surrounding the fireplace in the dining room are sepia rather than the more traditional blue. The hand-screened Adena Pin Rings wallpaper was by Adelphi Paper Hangings and is based on an early nineteen-century paper produced by a Philadelphia paperhanging manufacturer. The comfortable and not too serious wicker dining chairs are from Vittorio Bonacina. They surround an extension table by Wolf Hill. The light-admitting curtains are unlined linen edged with linen fringe. The Louise Nevelson three-dimensional "drawing" over the mantel is a welcome modern counterpoint in the room. **ABOVE** The banquette in the breakfast area of the kitchen is covered in Tyler Graphic Paisley. It is set against windows that open onto the deep, covered living porch. A traditional trestle table was designed for the white-painted American Empire chairs. The more modern and practical white Formica top was made from a tracing of a Saarinen table. **OPPOSITE** The client wanted the kitchen sink to have the best view, and it does. The collection of blue-and-white spatterware came from various shops in nearby Sag Harbor. The wide floorboards were stained in alternating shades, giving the floor a bit of snap. The handsome and solid English "tractor seat" stool is from Ann-Morris Antiques.

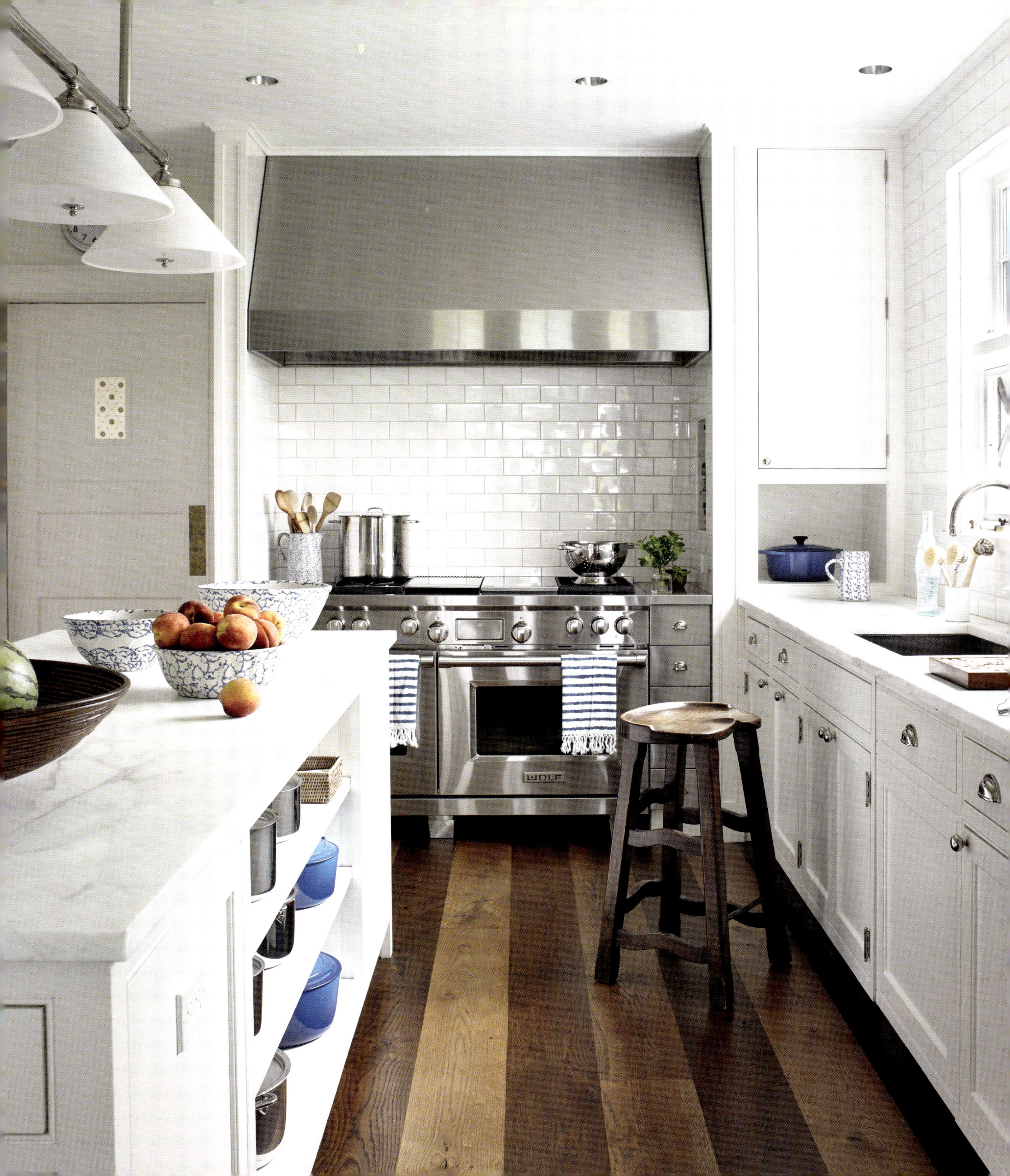
WOLF

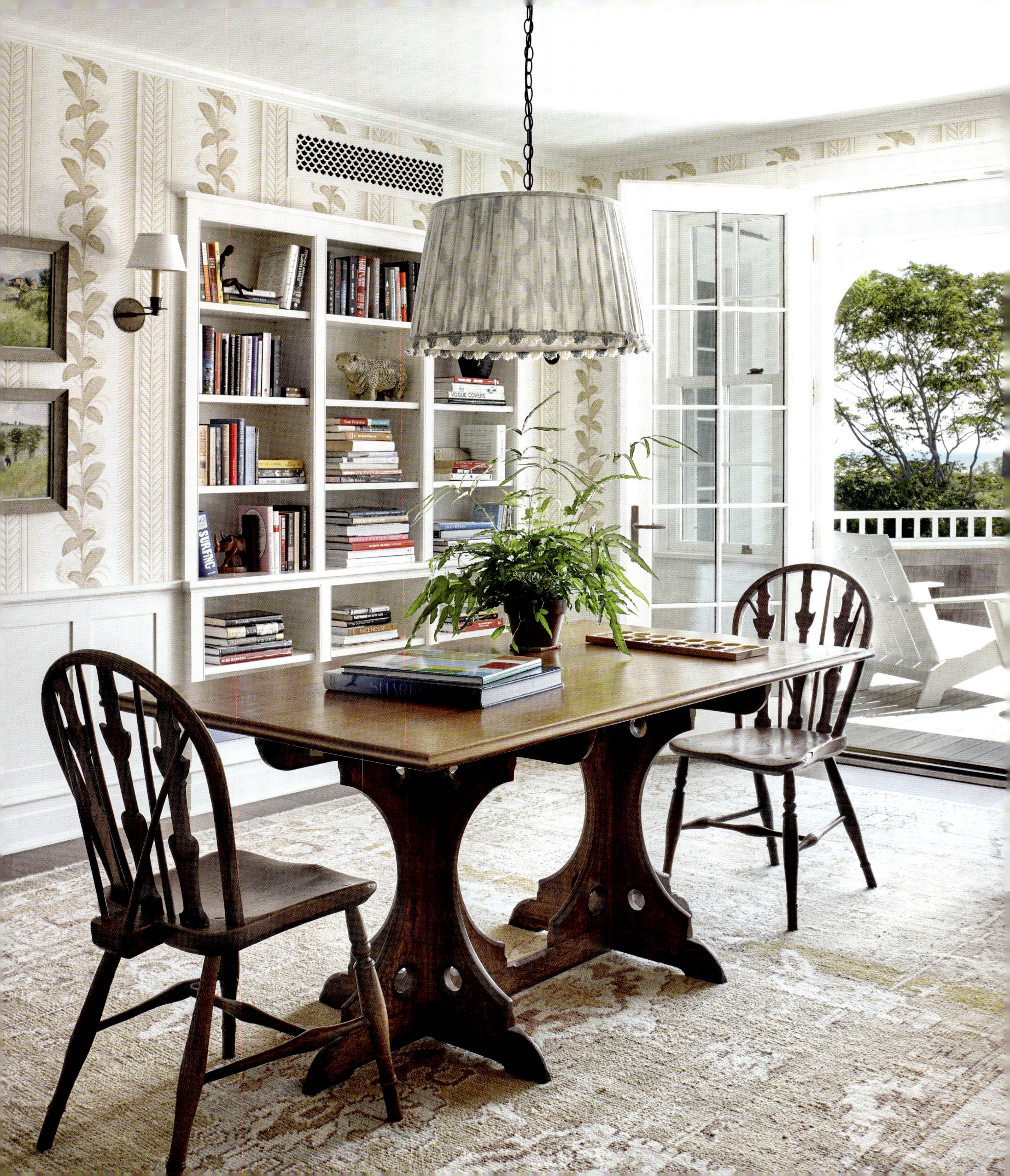

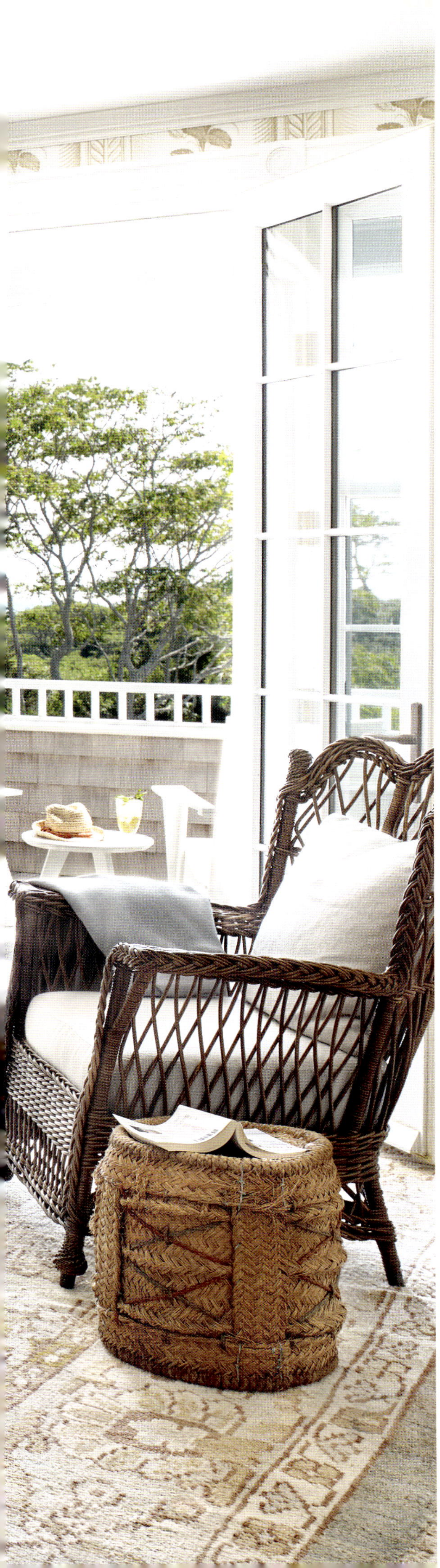
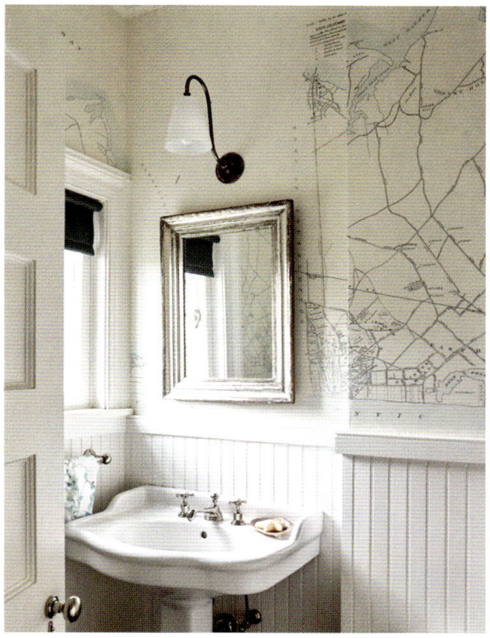
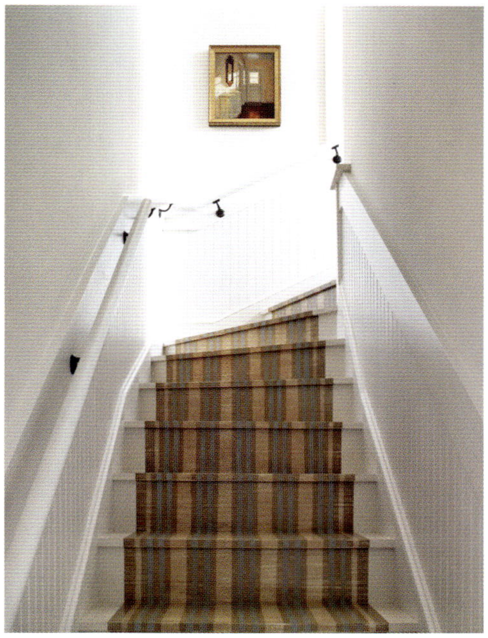
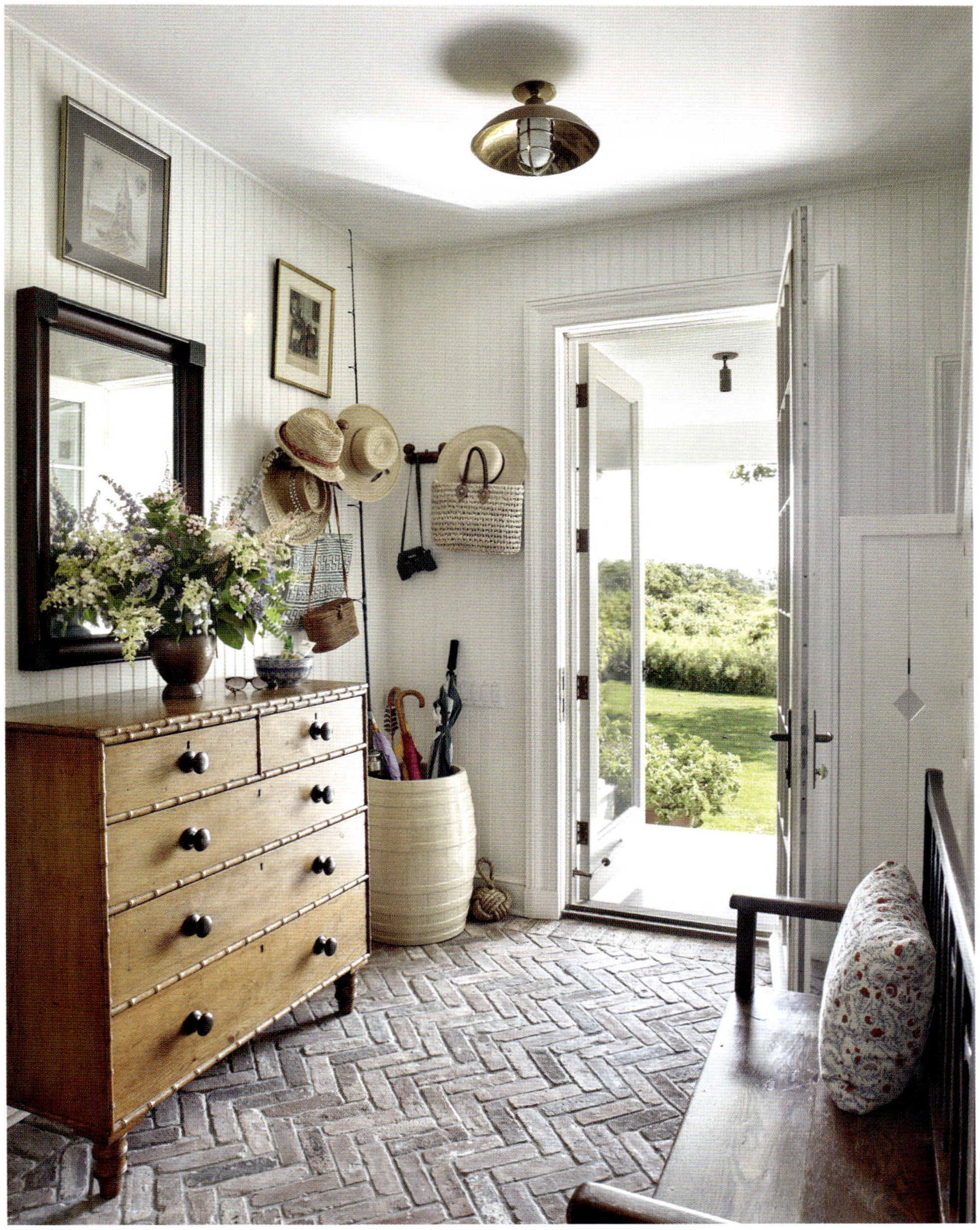

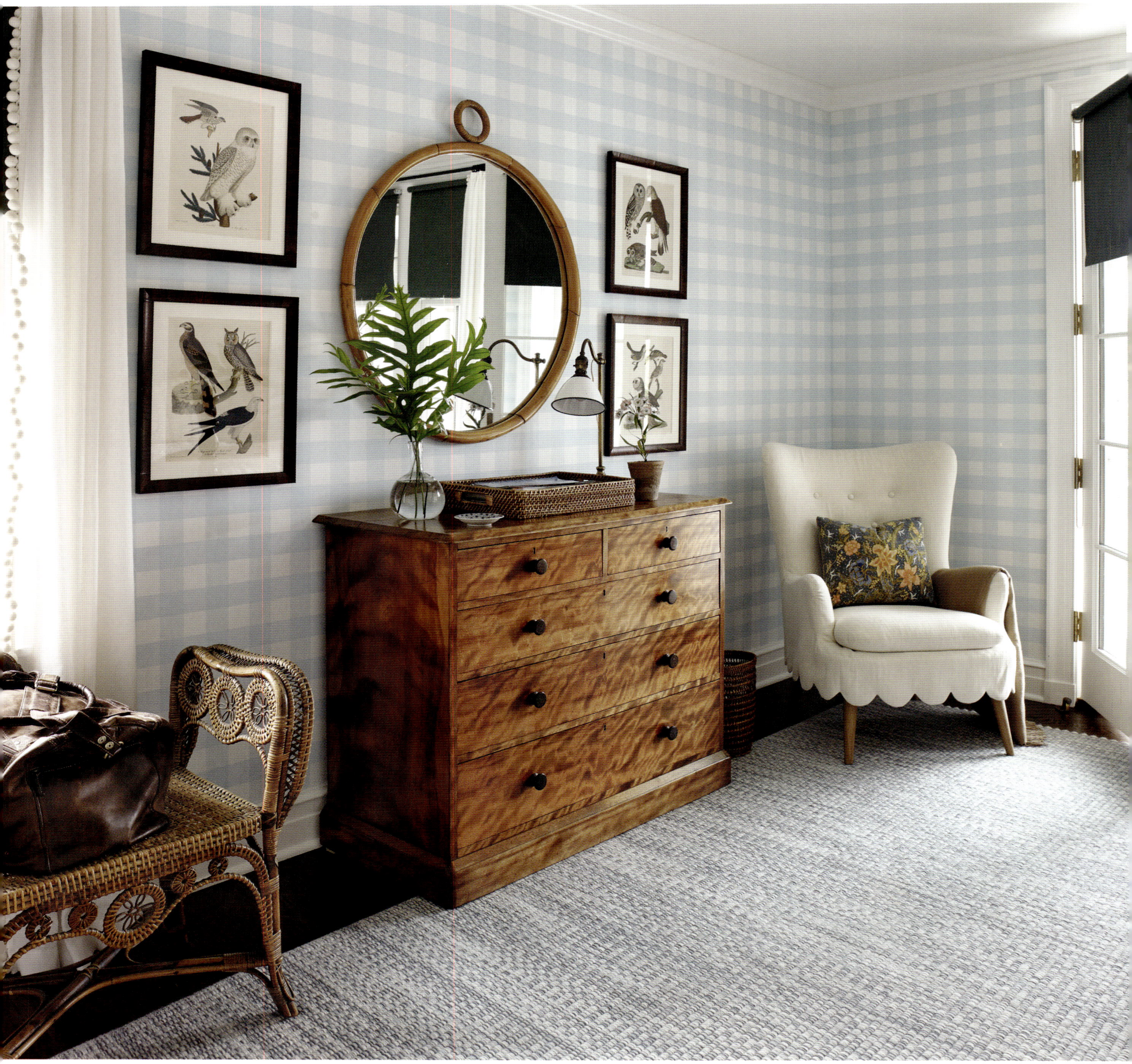

PRECEDING PAGES, CLOCKWISE FROM LEFT The large upstairs landing was transformed into a reading room. It's anchored by an A. W. N. Pugin table, a fine example of English Arts and Crafts furniture. In the downstairs powder room, the wallpaper is adapted from an old map showing the location of the place among potato fields. A lovely interior scene hangs near the top of the back stairs. The faux stair runner was painted by Brian Leaver. The mudroom's herringbone brick floor is not only durable but it camouflages. The porch beyond the mudroom opens to the broad outdoor living area overlooking the lawn. **ABOVE AND OPPOSITE** A downstairs guest room is as old-fashioned as can be. The gingham wallpaper was custom printed by Peter Fasano. Twin beds make a house more flexible for varied combinations of summer guests. Leonards Antiques duplicated the clients' own antique bed to make this pair. The walls are decorated with an eighteenth-century "parliament" of owl prints by the father of American ornithology, Alexander Wilson.

ABOVE The wallpaper for a guest bedroom under the sloping roof is Fuchsia from Twigs Fabrics & Wallpaper. The plain but well-made midcentury dresser was painted to match. Another charming, old-time summery touch is the antique Goofus glass pickle jar fitted as a lamp. The cotton chenille bedspread is a summer house "must-have." **OPPOSITE** A bunk room was devised for future grandchildren but now accommodates overflow guests. The Americana-appearing pattern of the cotton quilts is actually a traditional Hawaiian motif.

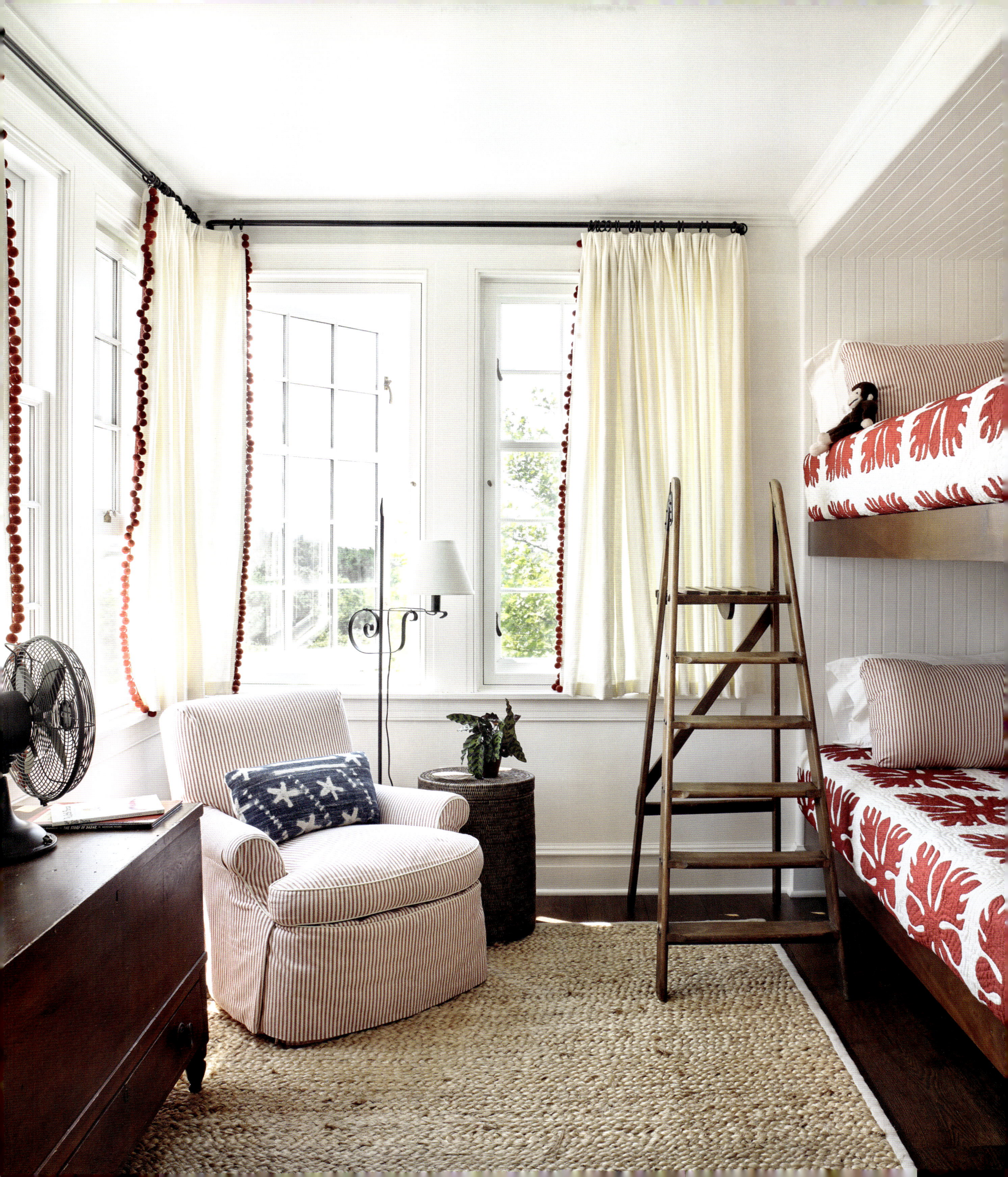

ABOVE The swimming pool is secluded in its own hedge-surrounded precinct and can be seen only from an upstairs bedroom. **RIGHT** The porch off the kitchen is the principal summer living room. It catches the morning and afternoon light, yet remains in deep shade much of the day. The raw teak "paddle-arm" corner sofa has deep cushions covered in a grayish-lavender Perennials fabric. Varied pieces of restored and stained antique "Bar Harbor wicker" encircle the stone-topped table, along with earthy brown garden seats from Tucker Robbins. All the pillows are in outdoor fabrics except for Katie Leede's charming woodpecker print, Isis.

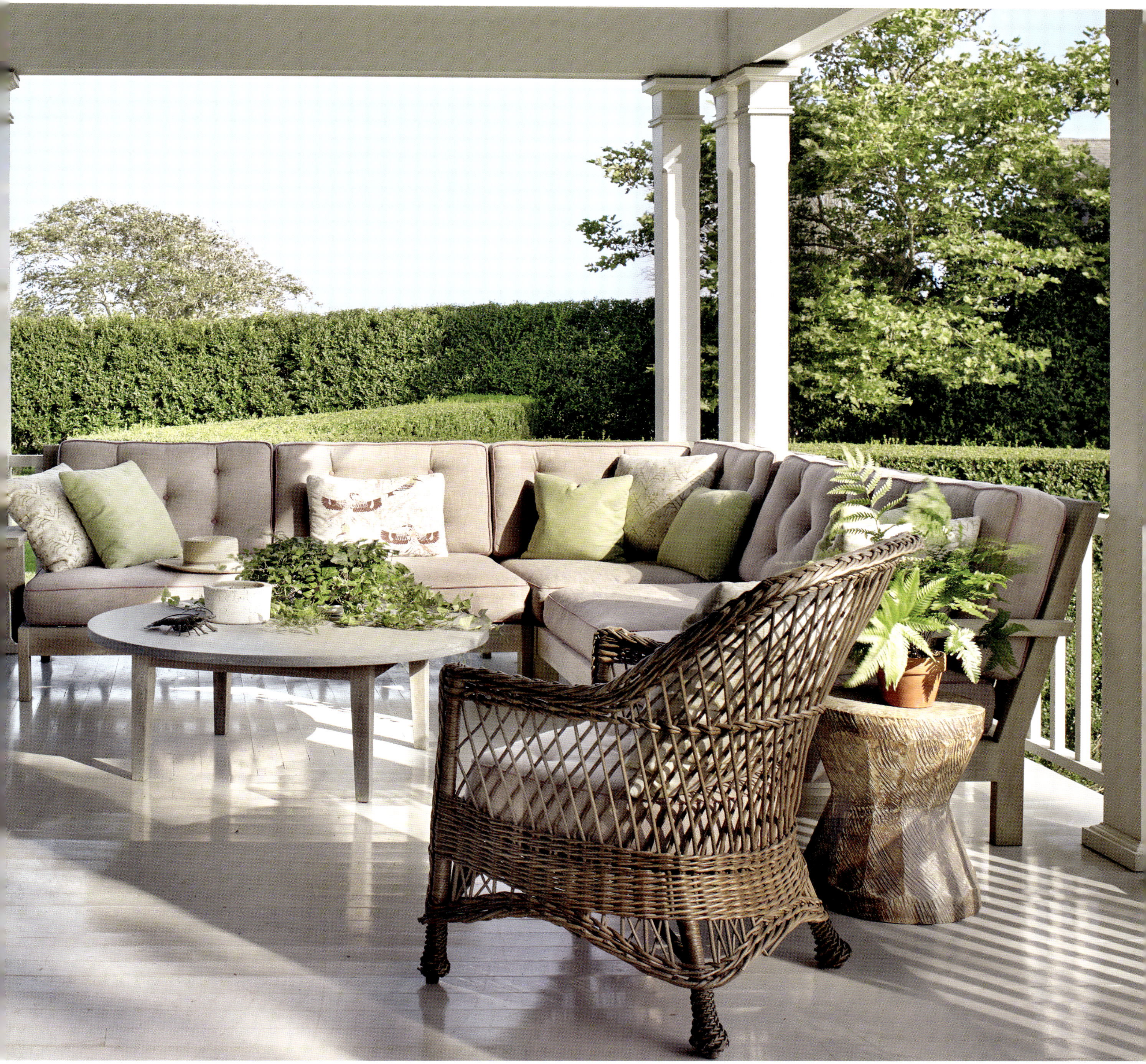

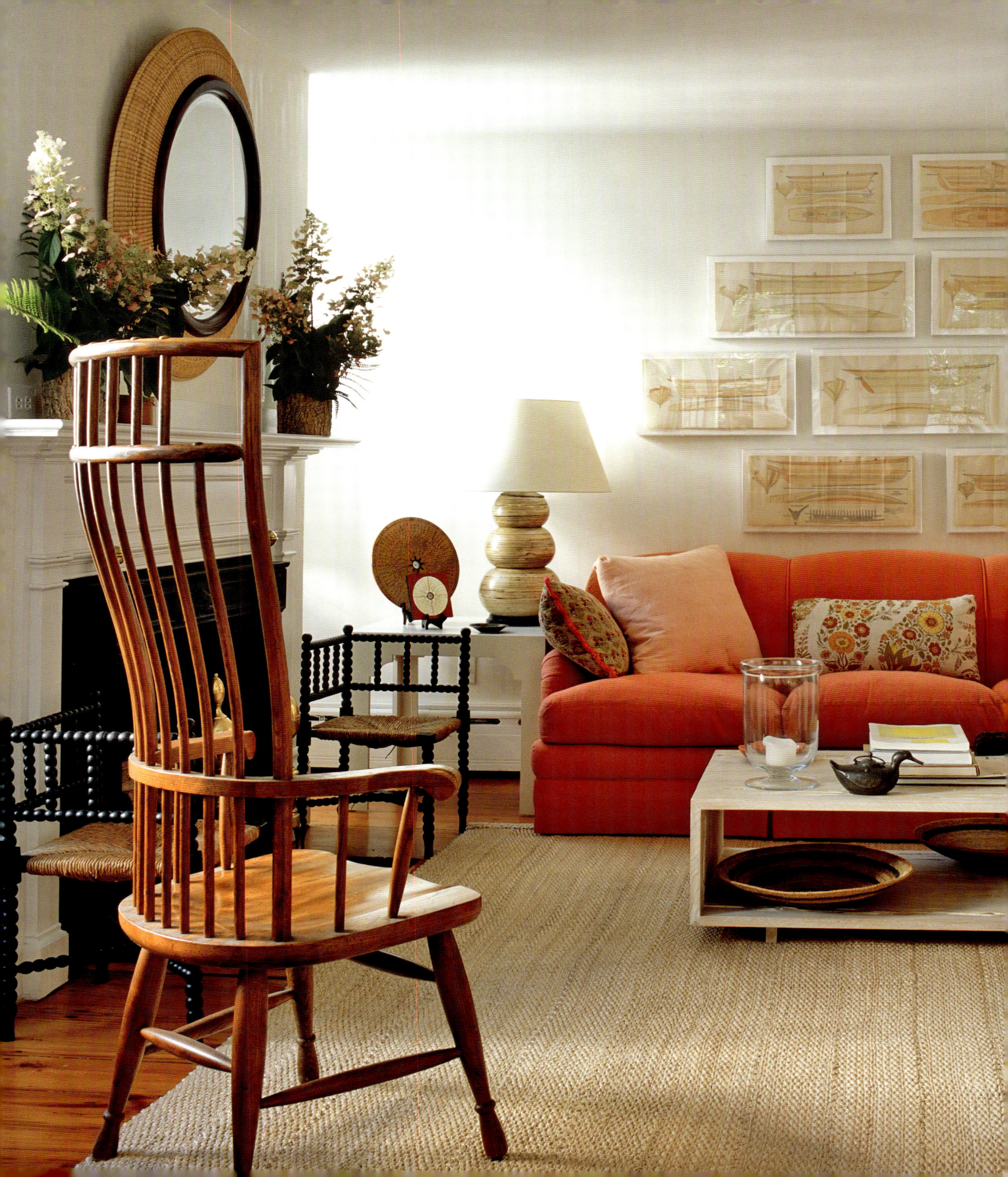

Pink String

Nantucket houses, the old and the fine ones and particularly those in town, do not speak of summer much. They more aptly speak of American history, the romance (and the horrors) of whaling—sea captains' women pacing their widow's walks.

There's a large group of residents, mainly summer people, who revel in this lore—happily trundling the cobbled lanes, eschewing all things modern, clutching the latest *Newtown Bee* along with their scrimshawed lightship baskets.

A parallel group of people espouses a derivative but equally fervent Nantucket style: lots of white and "naturals," contextually shaped houses containing smatterings of Americana and Shaker-like detail. Superior houses in this referential and reverential genre were designed and/or renovated by Hugh Newell Jacobsen. And then there are his less successful adherents.

We would subscribe to neither of these traditions for this fine ca. 1838 Main Street house. This one would be treated with care but without undo reverence. Fortunately, a renovation that had already taken place excused us from that potentially fraught exercise.

Ours would be a buoyant and colorful effort for this all-girl family. It would evoke the mother's own New England childhood, to which I was privy (our parents were great friends). They would now come in July to their own home after years of summer rentals. The three young daughters knew the terroir and would be discerning critics—Nantucket-isms in any pretentious form would be on notice. Cliché would be skirted as much as possible.

We pulled it off quickly and gaily with vivid colors, a host of easy shortcuts, and only a few antiques. Nothing overly wrought or too expensive for the six-weeks-a-year summer house. We did it, as my friend and mentor D. D. Ryan would declaim abstrusely, "with pink string and sealing wax." Her arcane reference, or my interpretation of it anyway, continues to guide me.

We painted white stripes on the catalogue-bought sisal in the dining room as soon as it was unfurled. It begged for something more. In the double parlor, a graphic abstract and modern wall assemblage was made from a sheaf of shipbuilders' drawings found in a dusty thrift shop. Not a thing too serious.

There were bright, pop-y rooms for the girls and an airy but not overly adult bedroom for the lady. Slipcovers were fashioned out of leftover curtains from their bygone house in Philadelphia. The summery chintz evokes the rose-strewn lanes all around. Not too literally though—the printed flowers are camellias.

D. D., coincidently, had once been the chatelaine of the grandest of all Nantucket brick houses. It's just a few doors down. She was a notoriously nimble decorator and though I didn't know her in that era, the house was surely rife with pink string and D. D.'s many other imaginative eccentricities.

She was astounded when I showed her the picture of this double parlor. The pair of modern convex mirrors made by the lightship-basket ladies had not yet been thought up in her Nantucket day. She quickly pronounced them cliché and, more damningly, "chichi." Nevertheless, she then conceded that they were unavoidable and the best possible choice.

OPPOSITE In this half of the double parlor, Nantucket-isms abound, but none is overly cliché. One can almost visualize the sea captain who may have lived here in the distant past seated in the mid-century Windsor-style chair. The mirror is a bold take on the locally made, and much more quaint, "lightship baskets." And a framed assemblage of old shipbuilder's drawings adds a modern touch.

TOP Flags fly up and down Nantucket's main street from the Fourth of July on. **ABOVE** The walls of the entrance hall are painted geranium pink, a far more vibrant color than is commonly used in decorating old Nantucket houses today, but in fact early Americans embraced bold color. **OPPOSITE** Plain board shutters were installed to foil any prying eyes passing by. In this half of the double parlor, the carved "trophy" was installed as a paean to designer Billy Baldwin, who hung a similar one in his erstwhile, tiny cottage around the corner. The club chair is slipcovered in Raoul Textiles' Kashmir.

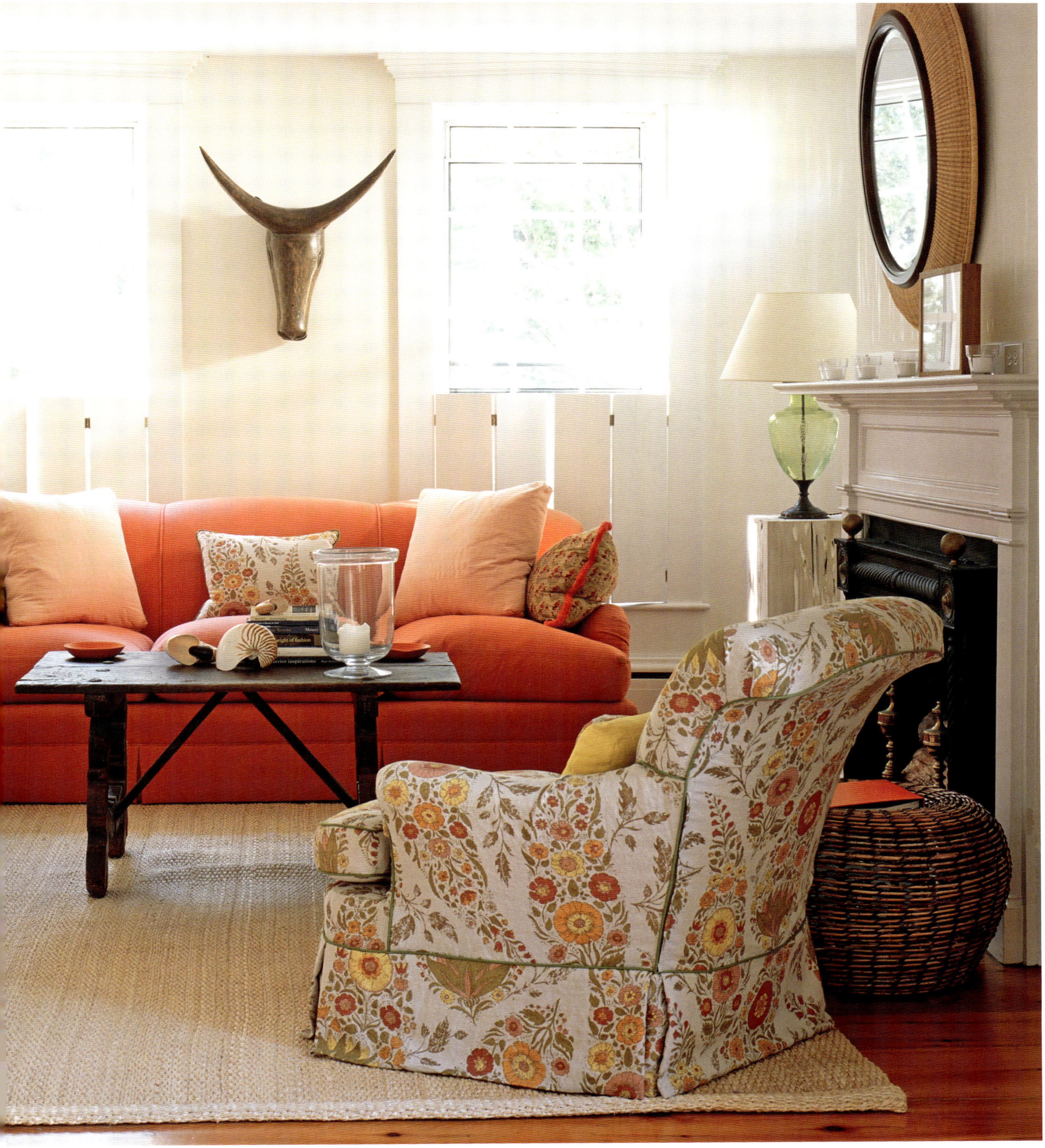

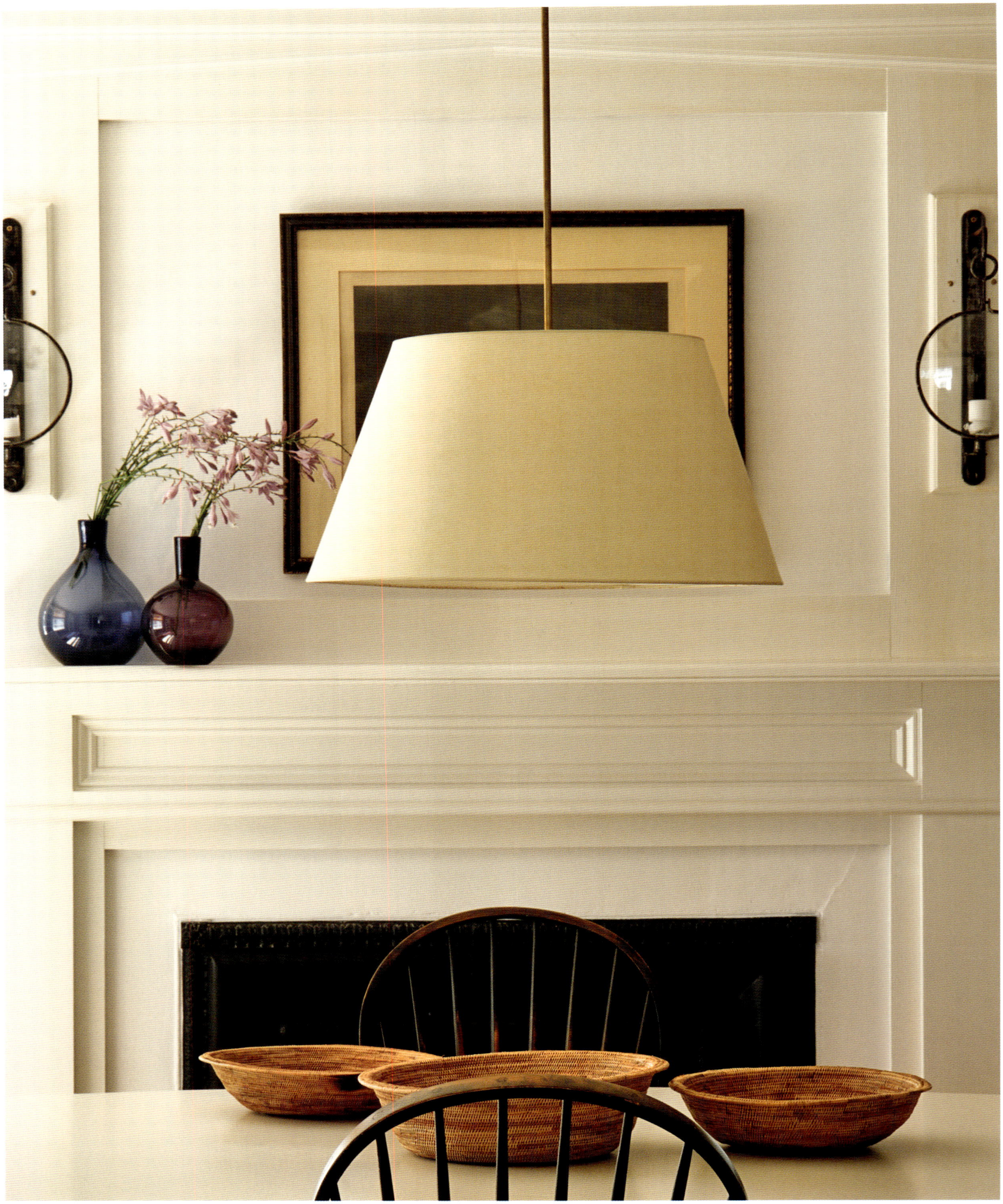

OPPOSITE The sconces that ring the dining room came from a Nantucket shop more than twenty years ago and are now a much-imitated catalogue staple. ABOVE The room is painted a deep seafarer blue with lots of white trim. The white stripes on the sisal rug were painted on—a decorating shortcut. A set of mid-century Windsor-style chairs surrounds an elliptical trestle table made for the room as a compromise between the Saarinen-loving decorator and the more traditional client. OVERLEAF Four bedrooms radiate off the upstairs hall-cum-sitting room. The wallpaper was made famous by Cecil Beaton, who used it as a backdrop for a series of his portraits, Marilyn Monroe most notably. In the absence of a crown molding, the room is delineated like a bandbox with brown paper tape. The wicker is vintage Bielecky.

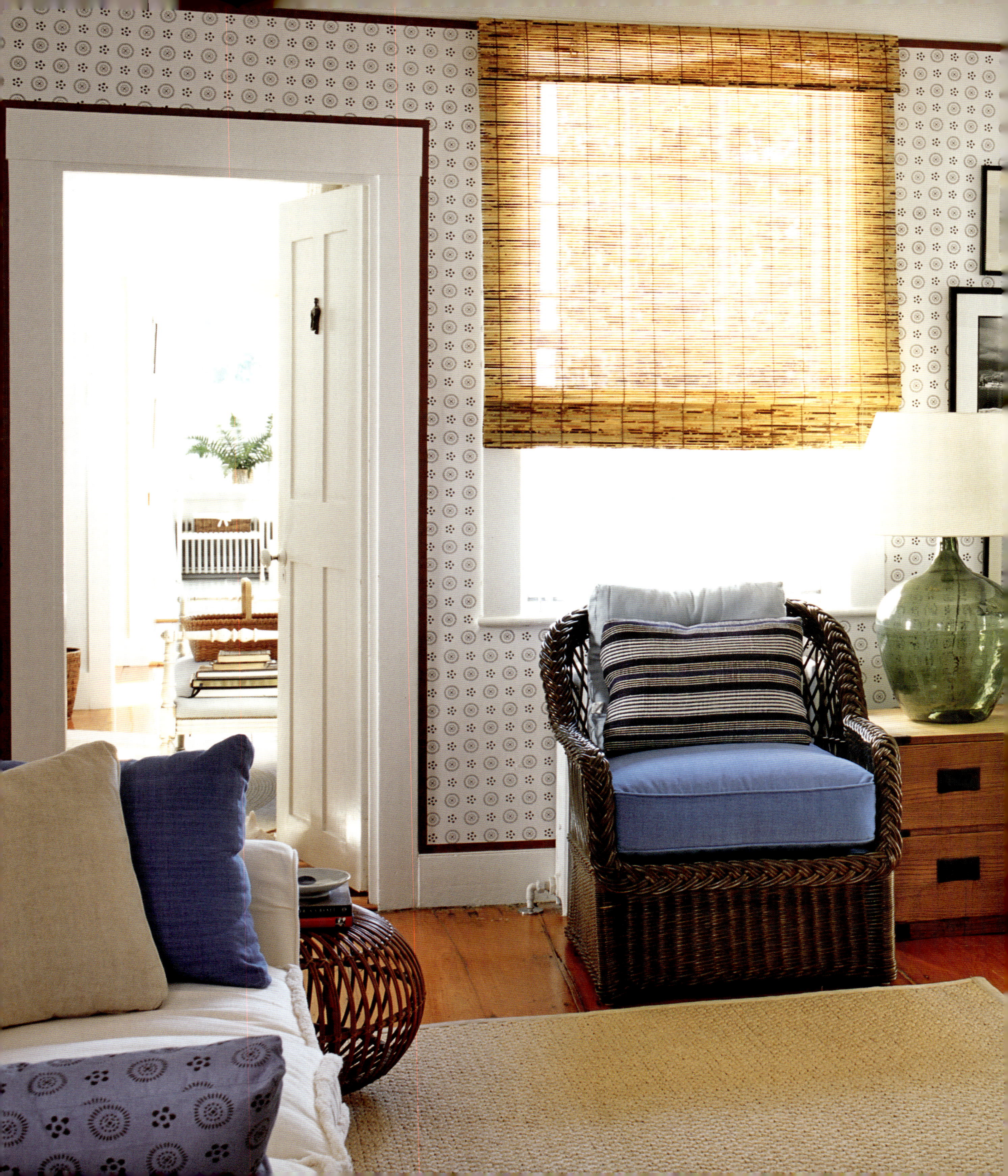

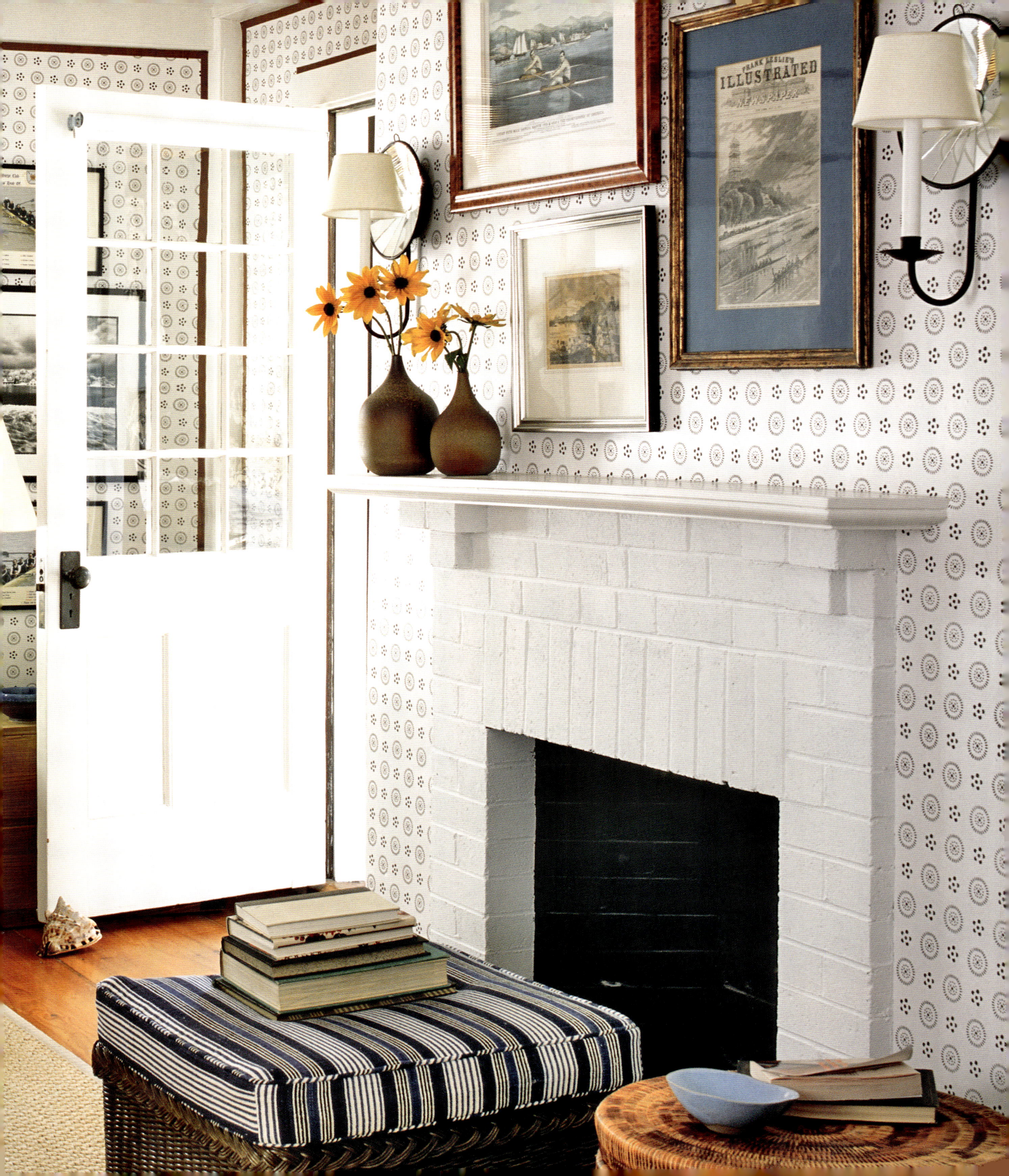
FRANK LESLIE'S
ILLUSTRATED
NEWSPAPER

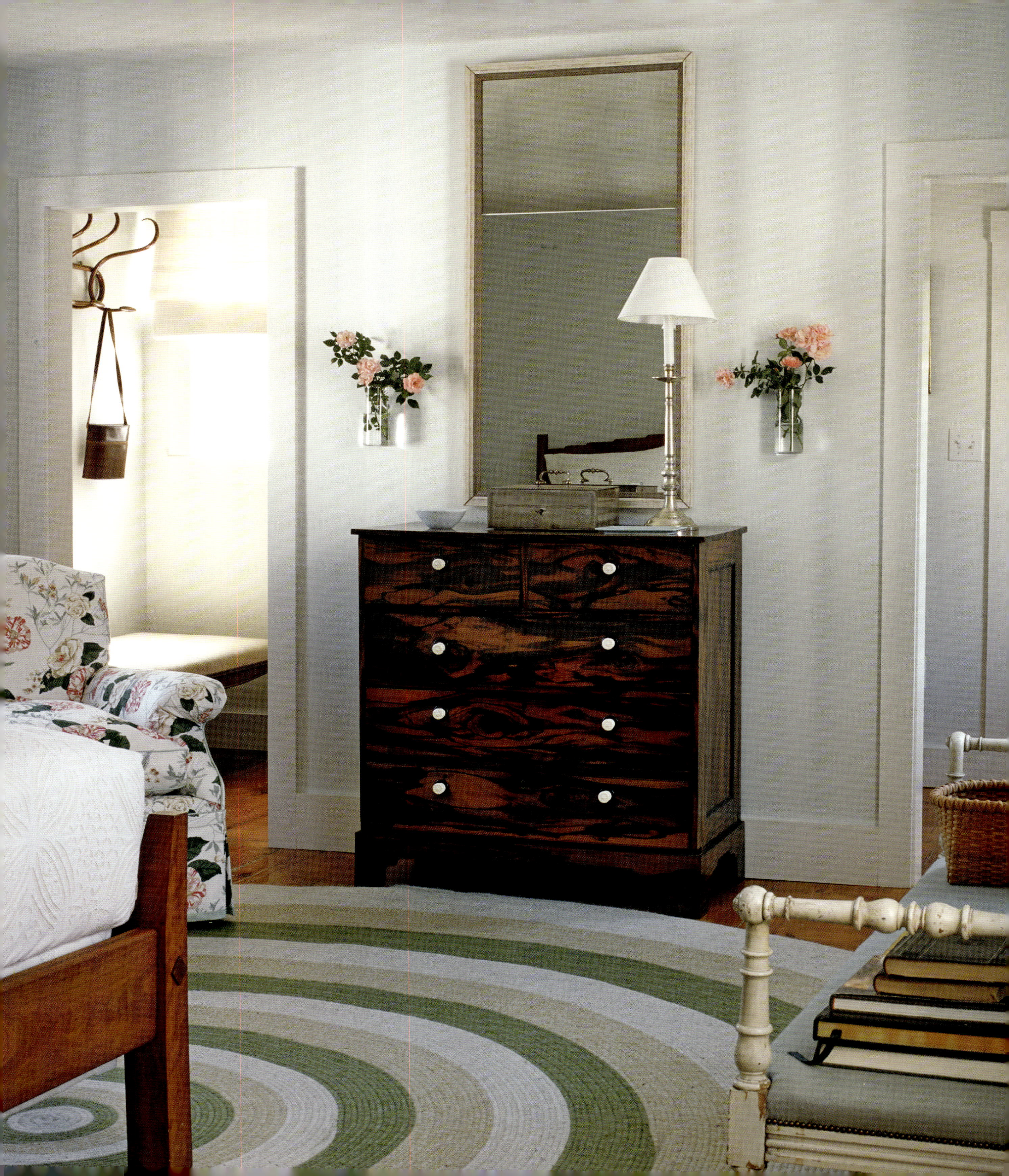

OPPOSITE The braided bull's-eye carpet in the master bedroom is another modern take on Americana decorating. The Indo-Portuguese dresser features exotic materials: figured calamander wood and turned-ivory drawer pulls. The vases hanging on the wall contain Nantucket's profuse New Dawn roses. ABOVE If a chintz could talk, this one—Camellias by Travers—would say "Philadelphia Story." The dressing room continues the flowery theme.

ABOVE AND OPPOSITE A good room has two exposures at least. This guest room has the added benefit of a third. The "shorty" curtains mitigate what would be an overabundance of fabric on the room's six windows.

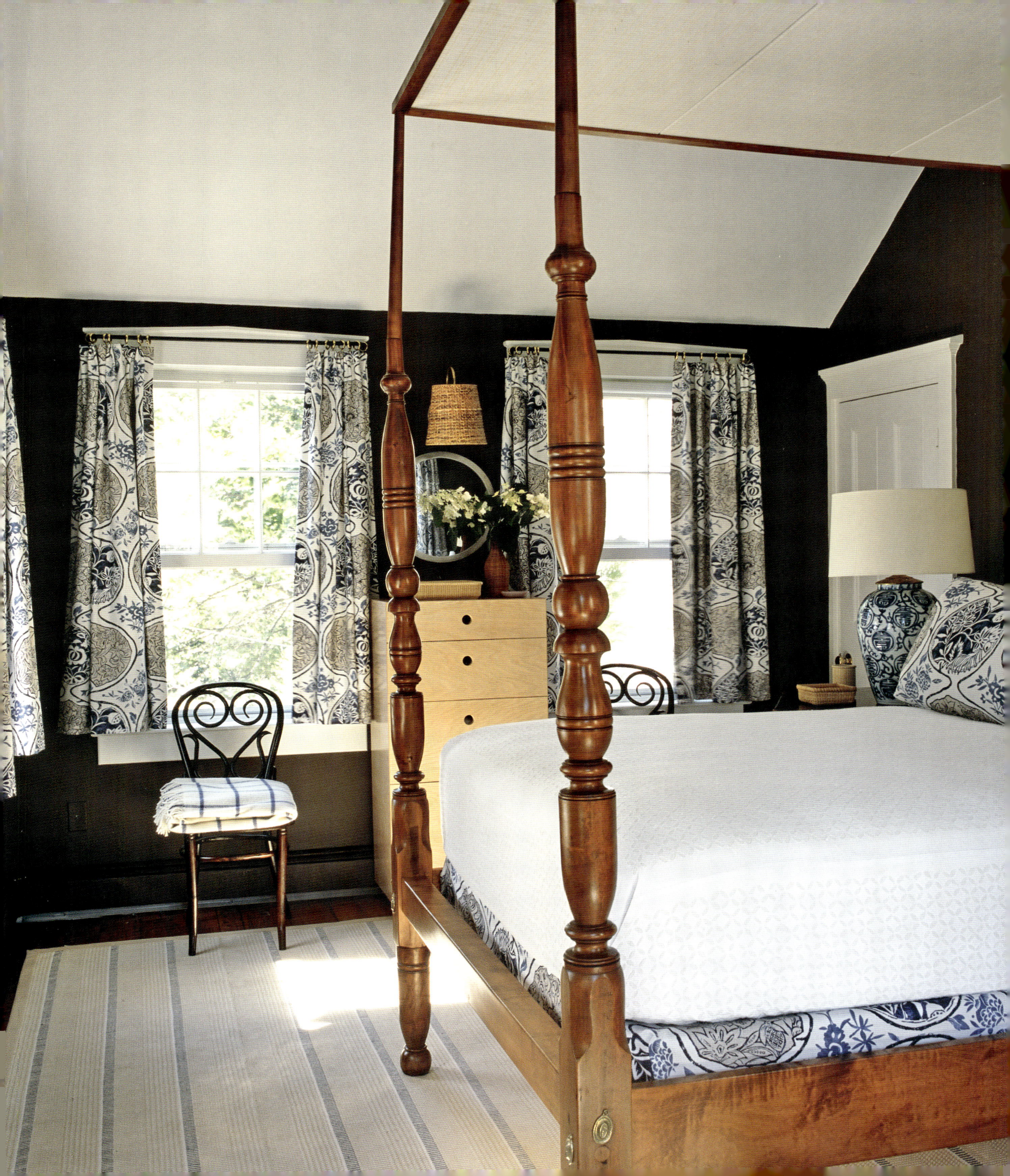

ABOVE AND OPPOSITE The wavy harlequin headboard in this young girl's room is cheerfully buoyant. Floral-print cotton fabrics from Muriel Brandolini, an Indian bedspread, and the winking-eyelash chenille covering the reading chair all contribute to the lighthearted mood. The Pop Art prints are just that; don't call them Warhols.

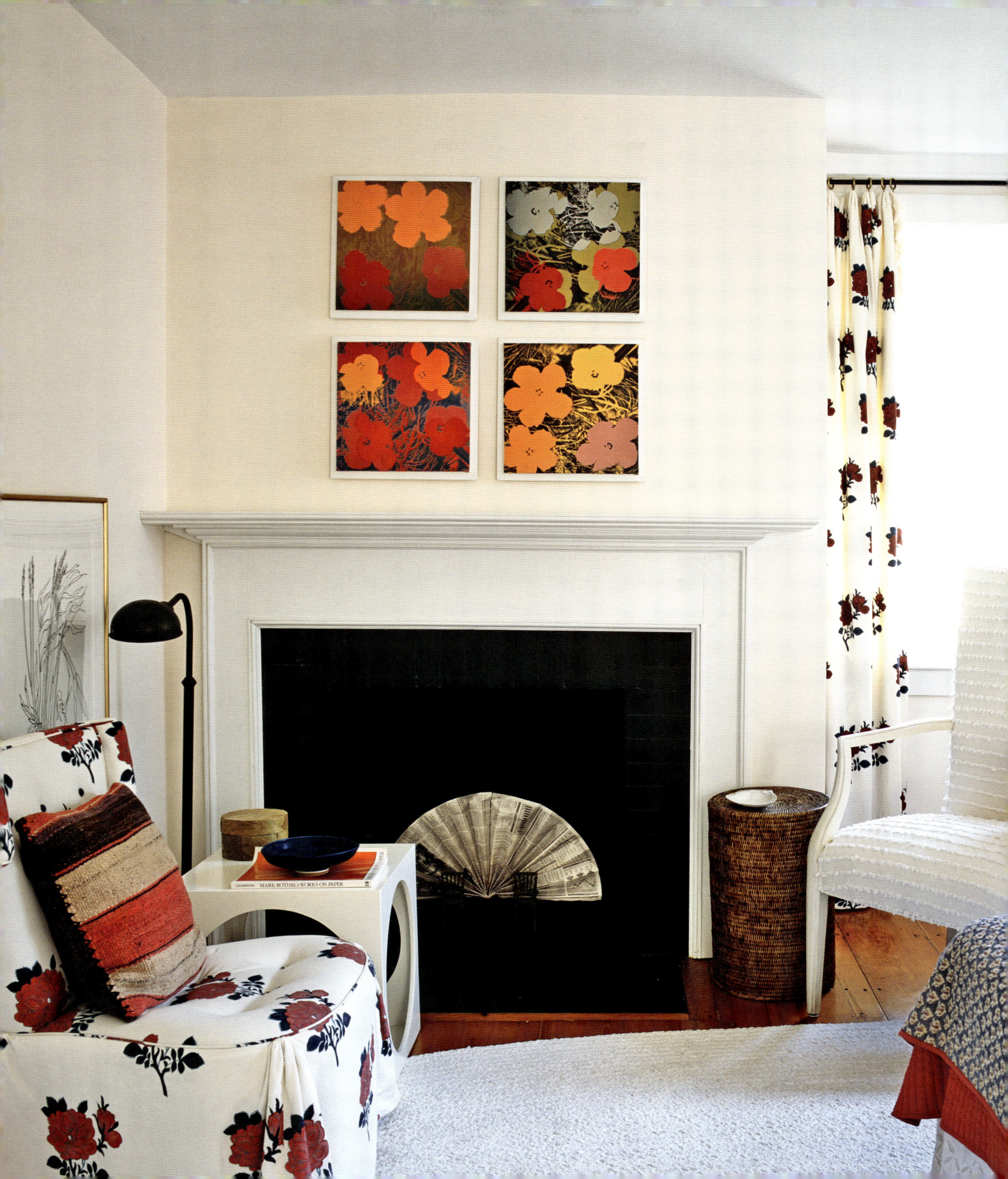
MARK ROTHKO WORKS ON PAPER

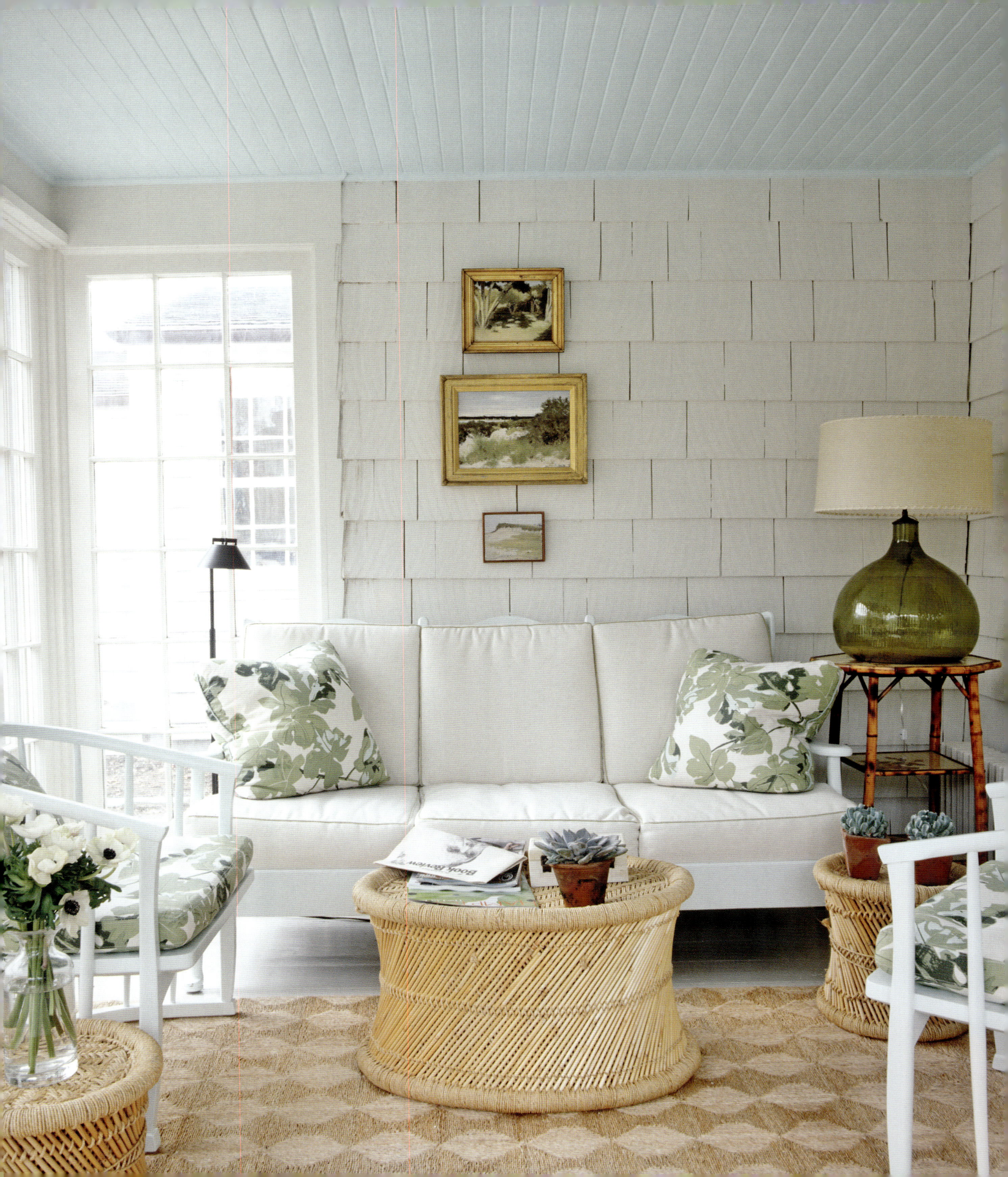

Old East Hampton

THOSE OF A CERTAIN VINTAGE, MYSELF included, remember East Hampton as different from today. We never used the term *the Hamptons*, primarily out of a need to be specific—East Hampton was distinct from its adjacent towns, much more so than it is now.

Southampton was the fancy one. The houses were bigger, and it had a reputation for extravagant, café society behaviors. When invited, we went out of curiosity and to be willfully glamorized by coming-out parties under elaborately decorated tents, by tennis tournaments with dressed-up people viewing from the sidelines, and by shopping at fancy haberdashers on Jobs Lane.

Bridgehampton was just field after field, a place to buy corn and tomatoes. Only a few families from New York could be found summering near the dunes, most in old farmhouses charmingly converted, but some in low-key shingled summer cottages.

East Hampton, however, at the far end, we thought was the happy medium. We considered ourselves more wholesome than those in "South" and more sophisticated and outgoing than those in "Bridge."

Our beach parties came with regularity and often with fireworks. Fairs and sales sponsored by the Ladies Village Improvement Society were a big part of our summer social lives. Tennis and ocean swimming were de rigueur, as was bicycling to town, riding past windmills dormant but lovingly tended by the aforementioned LVIS. In July, flags flew up and down the length of Main Street, as if in a Childe Hassam painting.

East Hampton's architectural styles were more wide ranging; turn-of-the-century summer "cottages" (ours also large but somehow less ostentatious) and seminal (as history later proved) modernist beach houses sprouting here and there. The extant, still inhabited eighteenth-century village and farm houses that were and are part of Colonial America's history were not just the front-porch-plain variety found on the potato fields in other Hamptons.

This house is one of those archetypes. The way we furnished it came easily. Its owner and I were brought up under the auspices of our grandparents, who were neighborly in nearby beach houses. Our affinities and deep knowledge of the milieu were shared and easily parsed for worth as decorating values. It was going to be summer the way we knew it.

The house and its bones were left WASPishly and expediently undisturbed. The waterfowl prints climbing the stair and finding their way into the master bedroom recalled the surrounding cattail-ringed ponds and evoked the days when duck hunting anywhere outside the "village" was allowed almost as soon as summer was over.

The mural encircling the dining room, taken from a Currier and Ives harbor scene, summoned the owner's primary passion for life under sail, while the decorator found it summery and charming. The long pine table, the perfect length and width for the oddly shaped, two-part dining room came with the house. It had been passed from owner to owner since who knows when. In the 1940s, apparently, it was left behind by a family with two daughters, one of whom became the most famous woman in the world—the Bouviers. Or so the story goes.

OPPOSITE Above the sunroom sofa, its pillows covered in Peter Dunham's Fig Leaf, is a stack of three contemporary plein-air paintings. Early twentieth-century artist William Merritt Chase and his circle, who may have painted the very same scenes, are given a run for their money by this artist, Simon Parkes. The rice fiber "china matting" is a longstanding sunroom staple, but it's becoming scarce. The straw hassocks are the common and often exclusive furniture form seen on roadsides, sidewalks, and in doorways throughout India. Here, they serve only as an adjunct to upholstered comfort.

ABOVE The house now faces one of East Hampton's several historic greens. It has been moved twice in its 230-year history. **BELOW** The wistful but charming seaside painting is British from the 1930s and continues the living room's color scheme. Its black frame balances the black hearth opposite it. **RIGHT** The house's main block is intact; there are a few small, more recent additions at the rear. The interior is still relatively undisturbed, with the exception of a few subtly positioned modern conveniences.

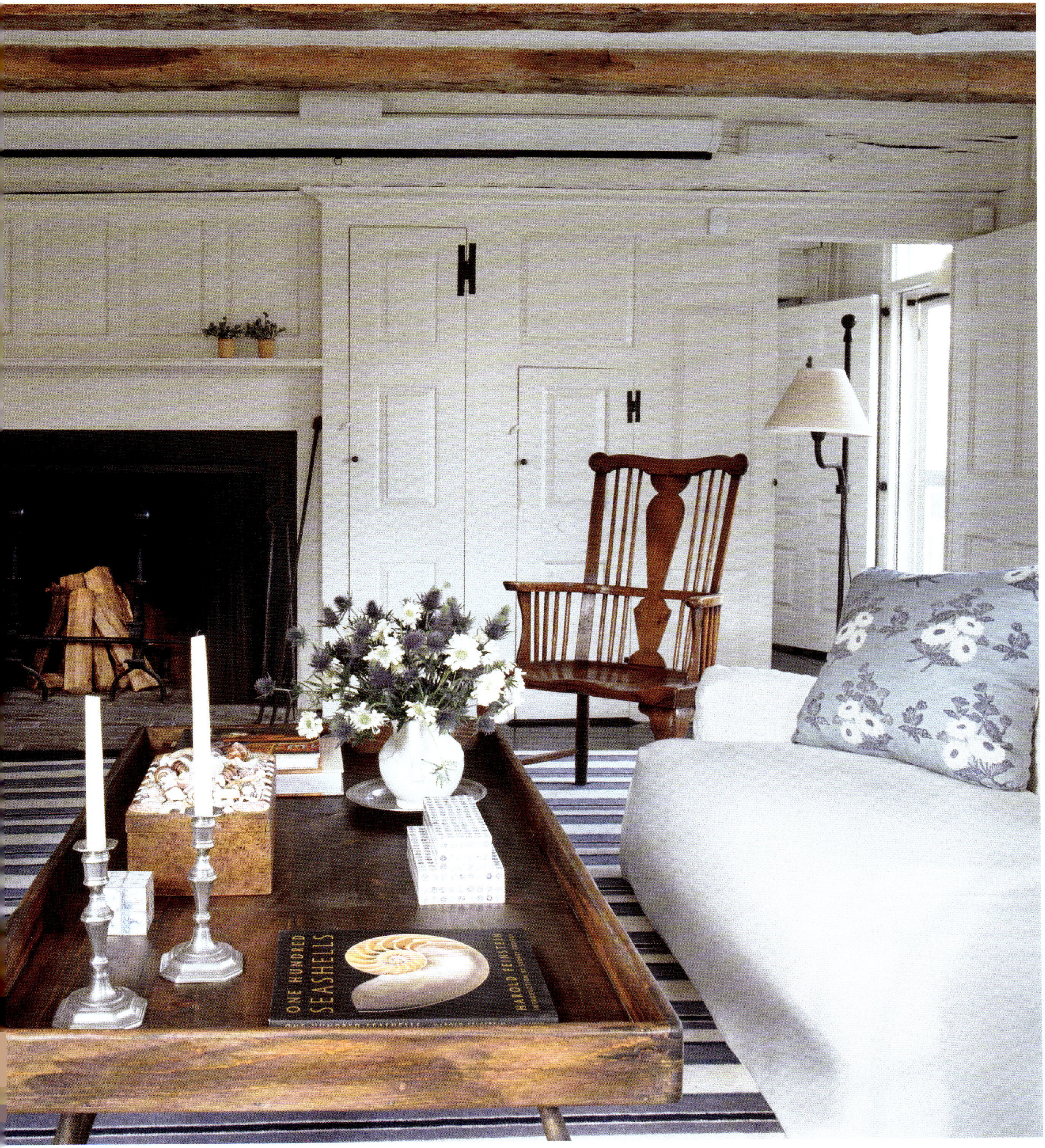
ONE HUNDRED
SEASHELLS
HAROLD FEINSTEIN

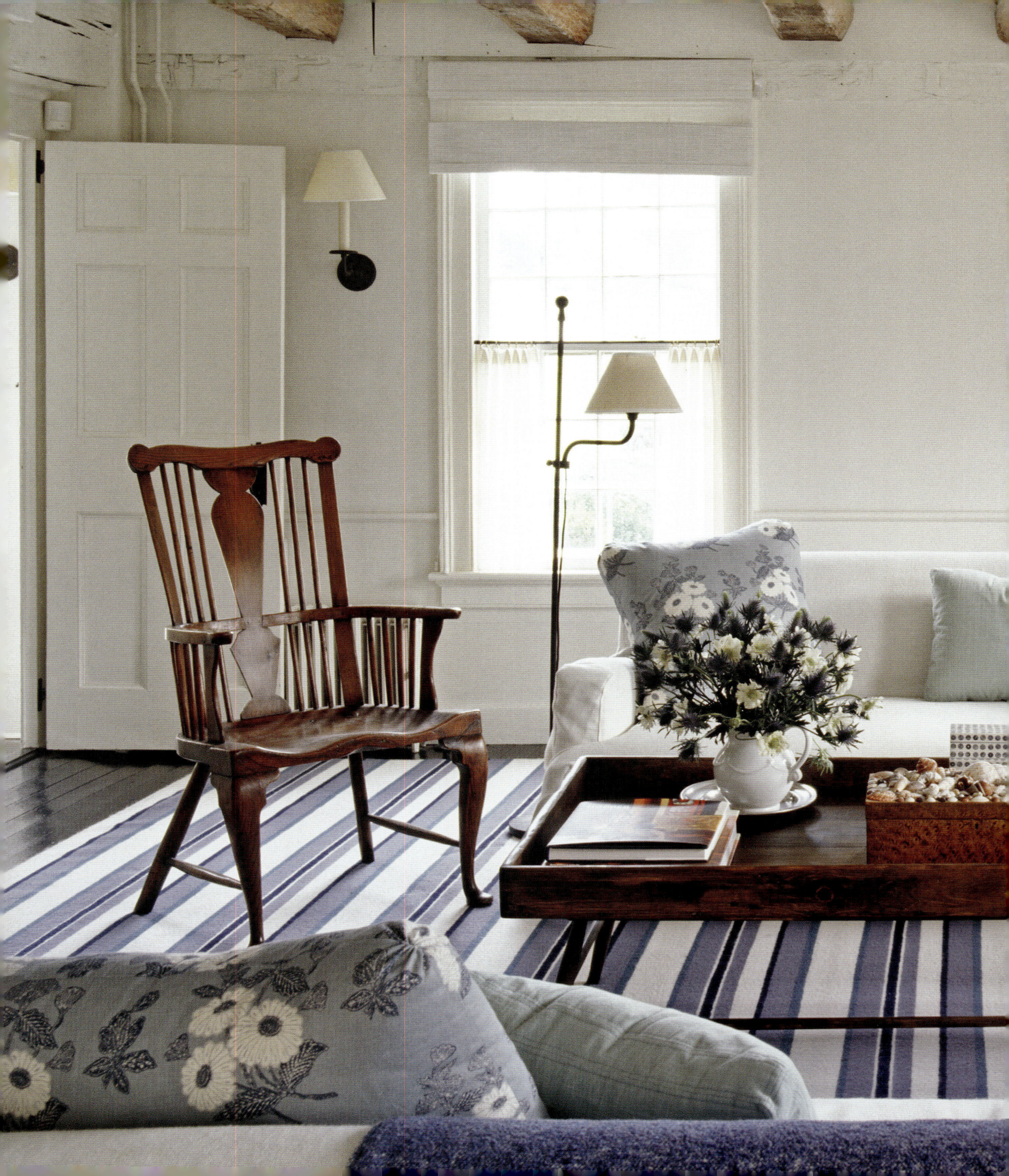

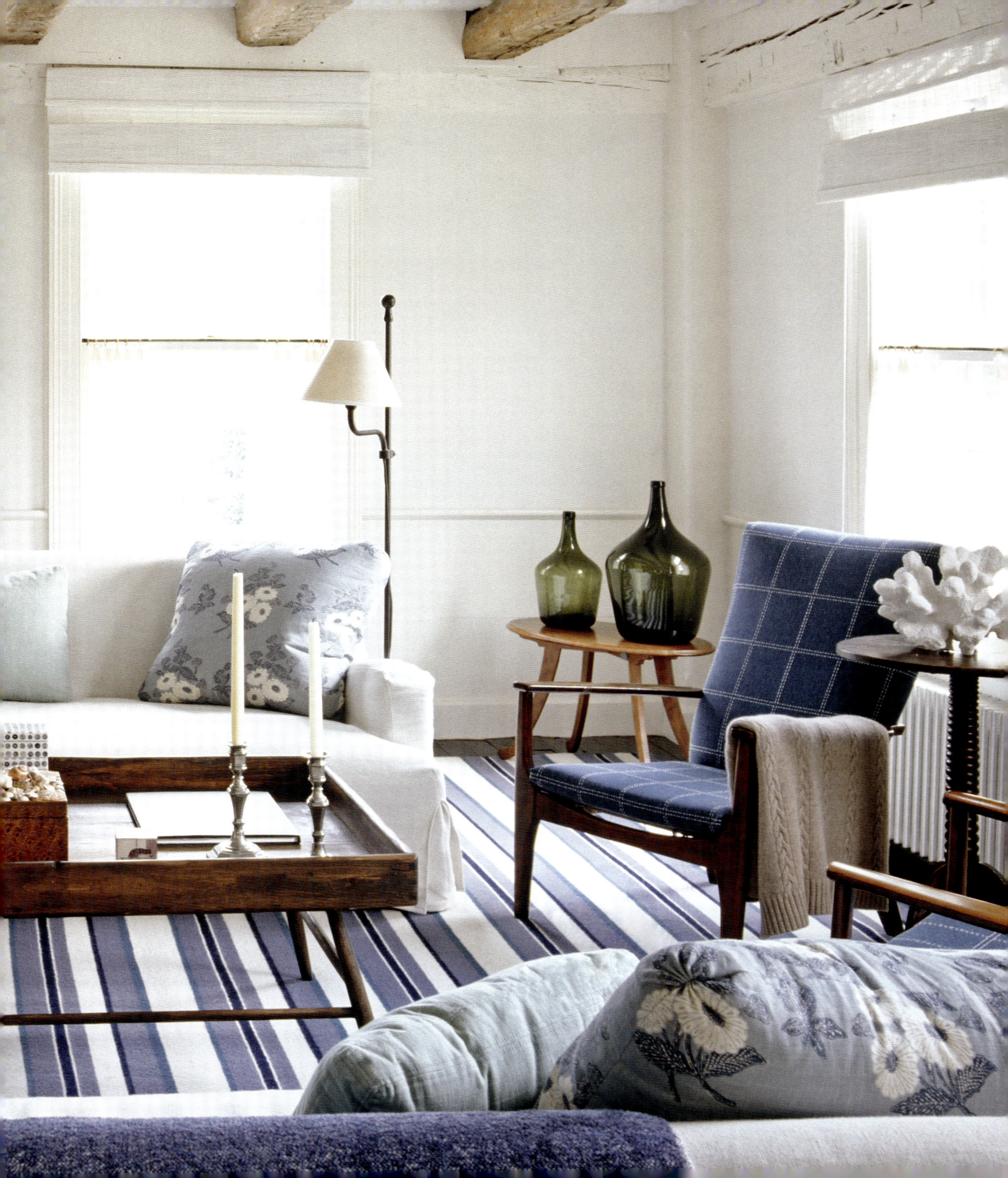

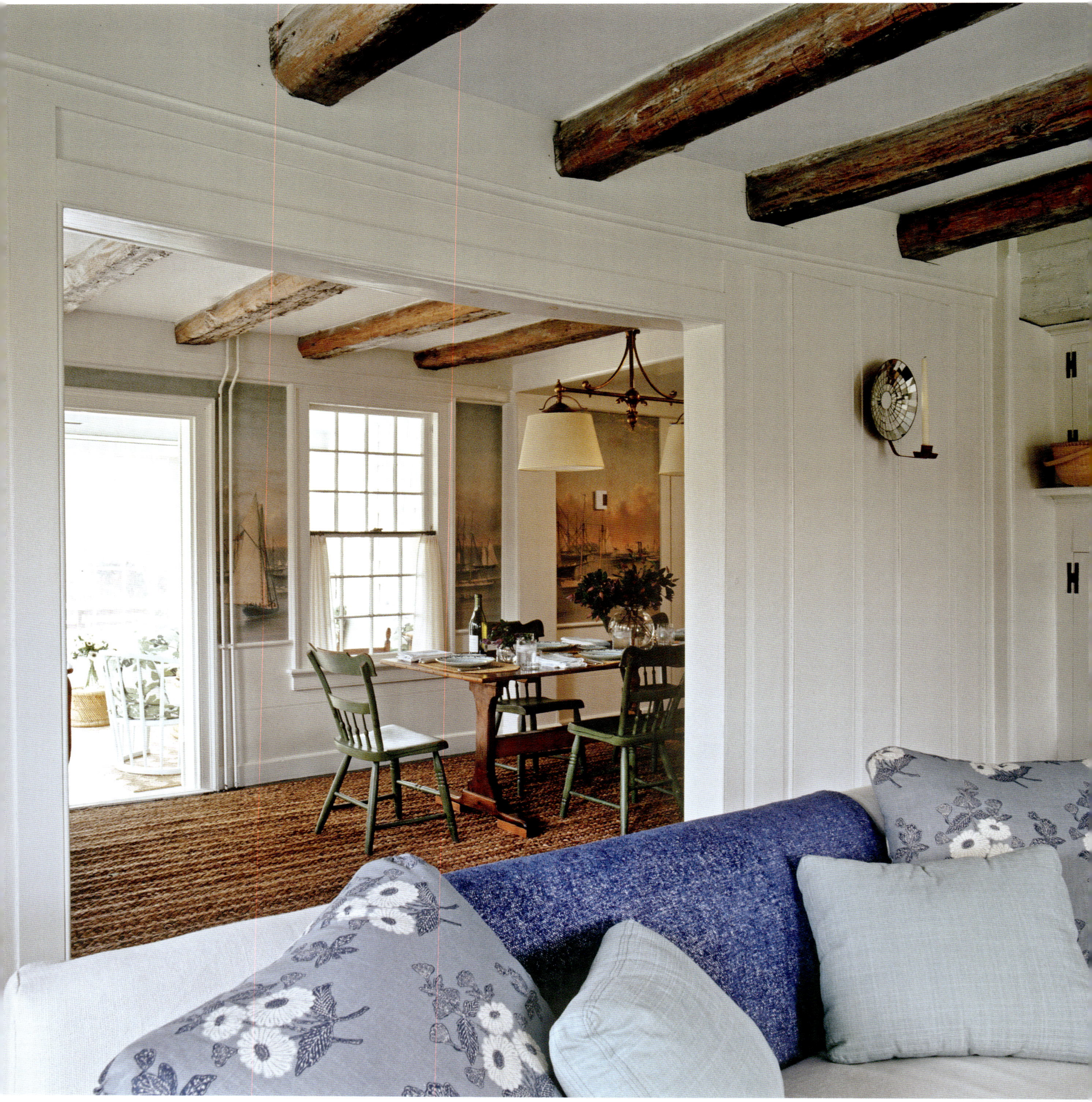

PRECEDING PAGES A new dhurrie carpet lends a fresh and beachy air to the living room. The blue stripes echo the antique beamed ceiling and add to the range of blues, which do anything but match. OPPOSITE A pathway to the sunroom across the dining room's coir castle matting divides the two-table room. ABOVE The smaller dining table sits in front of an Empire settee re-cushioned for dining height. The scenic wallpaper is an enlargement of a Currier and Ives harbor scene. The digital pixilation only enhances the effect. The "antique" iron bridge lamps flanking the sofa are "vintage" Crate & Barrel.

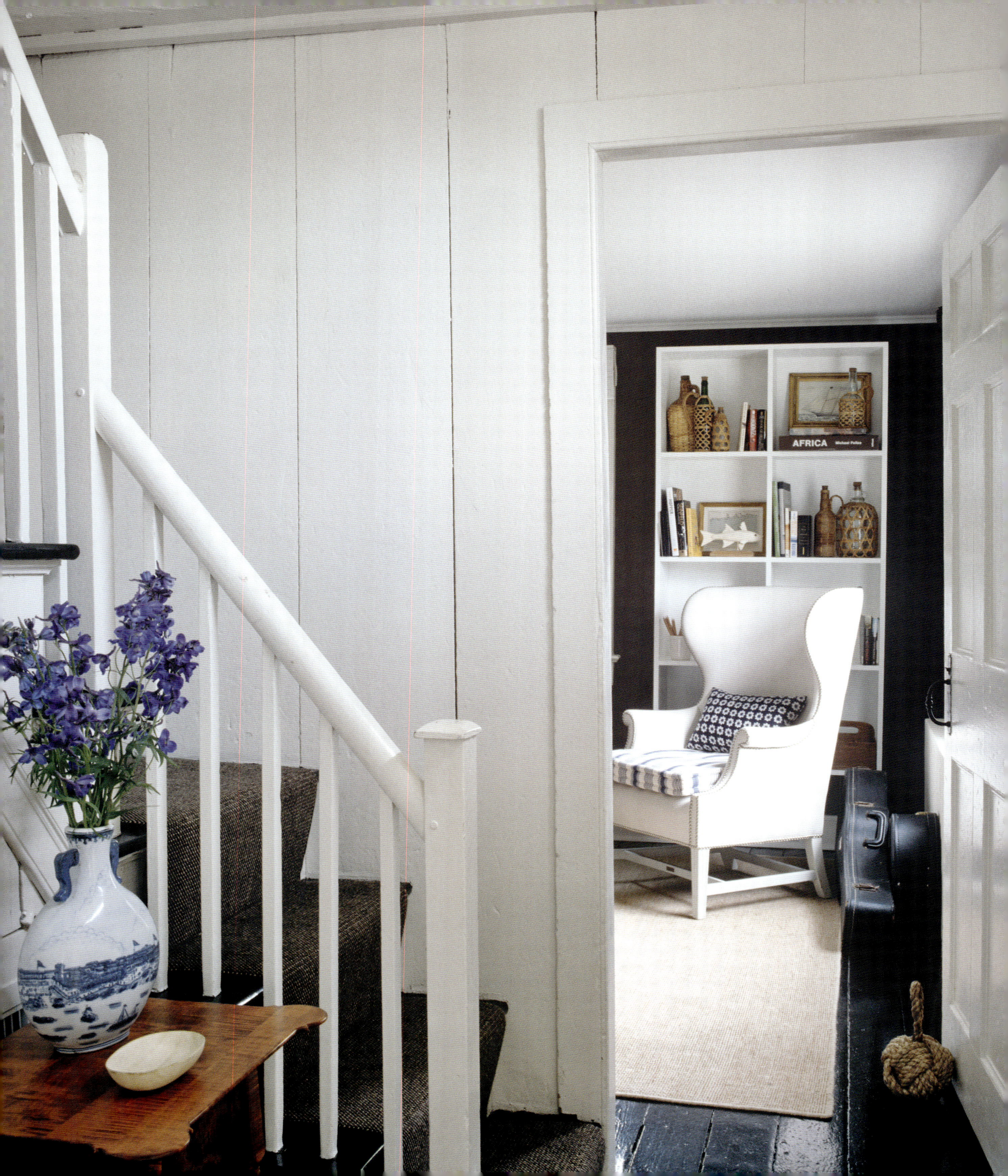
AFRICA

OPPOSITE A newly fashioned study can be glimpsed before ascending the tiny original stair. Floor space is at a premium in the study; the bookcases are mounted on the wall and float above the white-painted skirting. ABOVE An early twentieth-century sprung and swiveling dentist's stool is a conversation starter, evoking comparison with the room's more comfortable seating. Contemporary "folk art" (ship paintings by Mary Maguire) stands out against the deep brown walls.

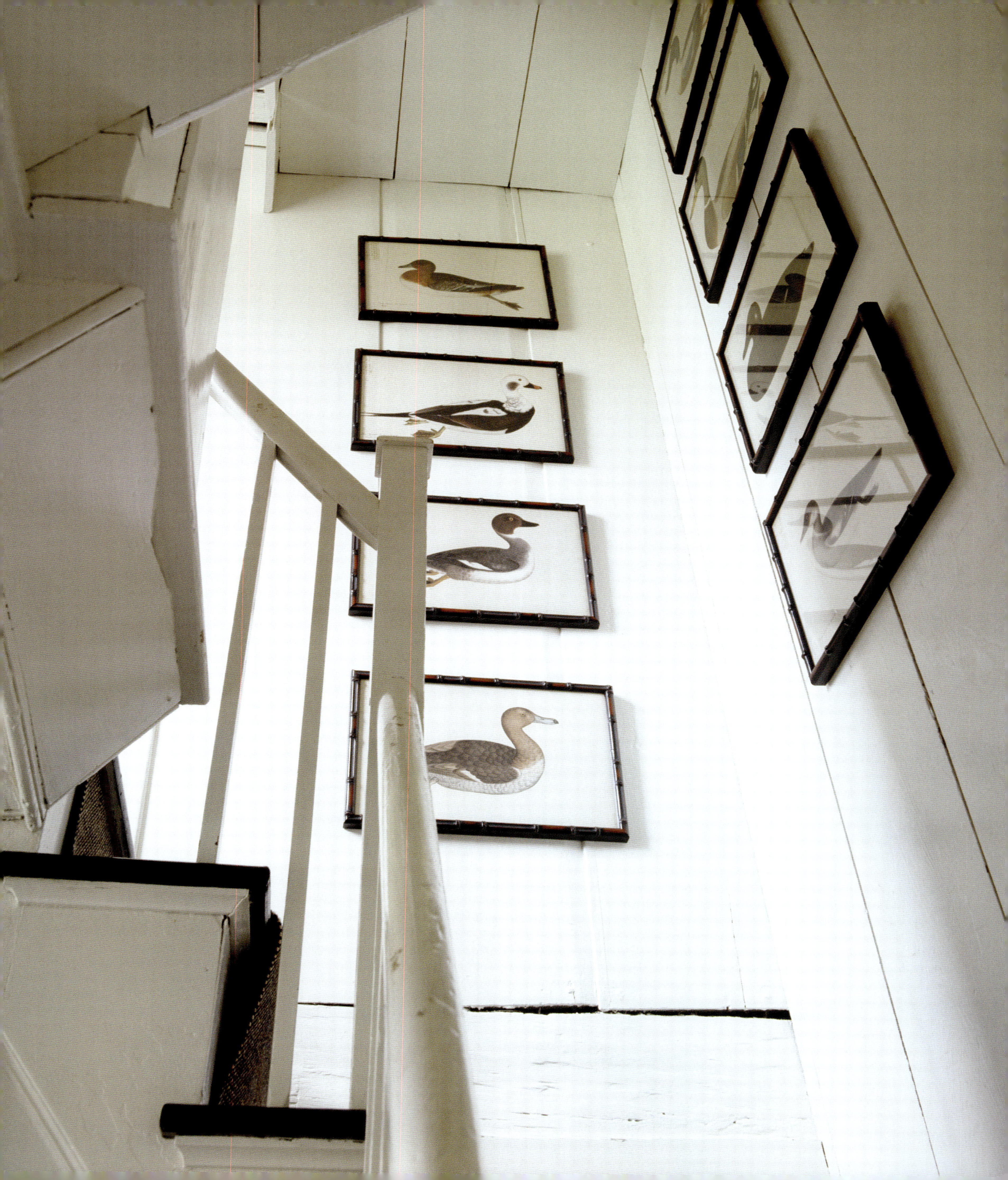

OPPOSITE Reprinted seventeenth-century Swedish waterfowl prints by Olof Rudbeck line the walls of the stair leading to the master bedroom. The original woodwork was barely touched throughout; just a thin veil of paint was applied in order to retain the patina of history. **ABOVE** The tattersall "country" carpeting was laid wall-to-wall over thick padding to mitigate the noise from the irregular and rickety floorboards over the living room. Without dark floorboards at the perimeter, the room seems larger.

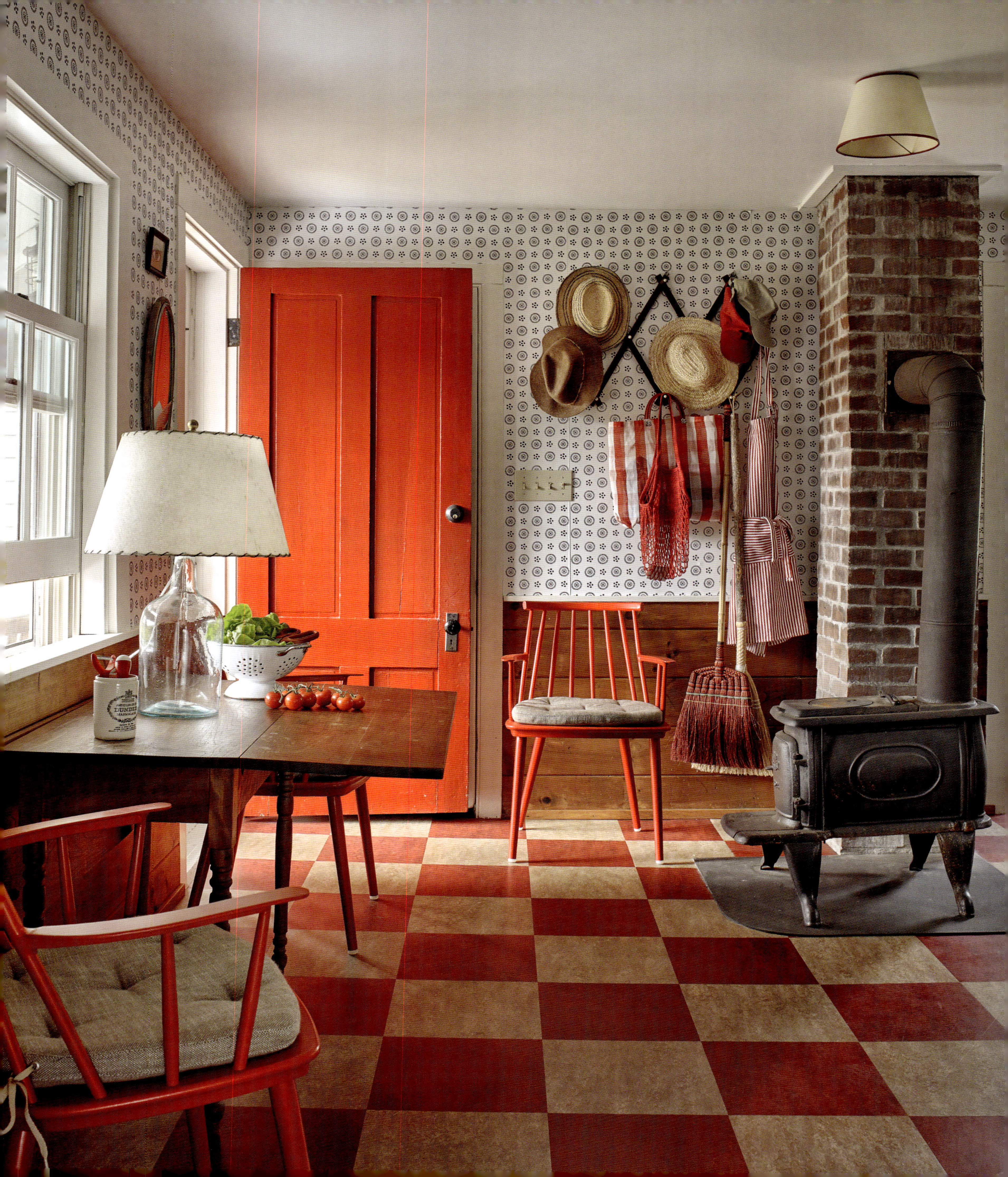

House-keeping

FARAWAYNESS AND RUSTICITY ARE ITS charms. Our island has five ferries a day, one store, five churches, and a clam man. Notoriously, it's one of Maine's "dry" islands; careful provisioning is essential.

The place we found is a farmstead with ancient apple trees, a pasture, and a blueberry field sloping down to a tidal pond and an enormous sickle of a levee formed of loose, smooth rocks. The largest ones, some as large as ostrich eggs, crest this bulwark and then diminish in size down to tiny pebbles at the water's edge.

The water is frigid and clear as glass, but few fish are seen. They are assumed to lurk farther offshore among the lobster pots, whose tutti-frutti buoys carpet the inland sea.

Only in Maine is ours referred to as a "beach." Nevertheless, every rock and stone is a prize. It's a competitive "treasure hunt," the very best are lugged up the path, often cradled in our shirttails, arranged on the decking and then parsed for relative comeliness. This is a principal pastime.

The house was habitable (it had been used as the island's only guesthouse) but had been patched together with DIY plumbing and linoleum, its cornices suggested by contact-paper garlands of apples and other autumn fruits. The first season's work of stripping the walls, the "lobster red" re-making of the kitchen, and the fashioning of two charming upstairs bedrooms out of a single too large one proved to be not enough.

The house cried out for a view-facing porch and a "caboose" of a small twin bedroom, a mudroom, a downstairs bath, and an outdoor shower. These were drawn and ordered up to blend seamlessly with the 1830 house and were laboriously produced over the next several winters by the caretakers. Nothing fancy, but the off-season workdays must have been short.

The barn was unspoiled but required shoring up and some new internal bracing. It should now last a second two hundred years of ten-month winters and two-month summers.

Here in Maine we apply a lifetime of housekeeping lessons, primarily from our mother, who did it all without fuss. We osmosed the seasonal decamping from one house to another to another, brood in tow but making room for dinners and extended house parties, and we do so now with frequency and ease.

We delight in our economies and the rituals of a simple life: sweeping the porch, loading the dishwasher (we are particular experts at this), making soup from last night's lobsters shells. Do we take it too far when, to avoid confusion and excessive laundry, we stitch white football jersey numerals to the dozens of red bath towels?

These observances are pleasures in themselves (I forgot to mention the frisson we get from the opening of a fresh sponge), but they indeed make possible more hours for what we come to Maine for: walks in the shady moss- and fern-profuse woods, dipping in the icy ocean, luxuriant freshwater swims in the relatively warm granite quarry down the road.

We sleep directly under quilts (no fuss with top sheets here), our heads as close as possible to a wide-open window. On a perfect morning, it's cold and it's "pea soup." The only sound is the far off and muffled sputtering of a lobster boat. The fog breaks, and the sun is in our eyes.

OPPOSITE This kitchen was inspired by a lovely woodsy and rustic cottage we once rented on a nearby island. It came with an odd and modern touch—red Formica everywhere. With that memory in mind, as well as Maine's ubiquitous crustaceous leitmotif, "lobster red" seemed a good choice for our own kitchen too.

ABOVE The barn may predate the early nineteenth-century farmhouse. In the distance is the inland sea, sheltered by Mt. Desert and other less-known islands. OPPOSITE The hardy "wicker" is plastic and should last a lifetime of summers without requiring paint. The compromise was welcomed for peace of mind. Beach finds migrate to the heavy granite tabletop, which was quarried and honed on the next island over. It rests on a salvaged and sturdy wooden cable spool.

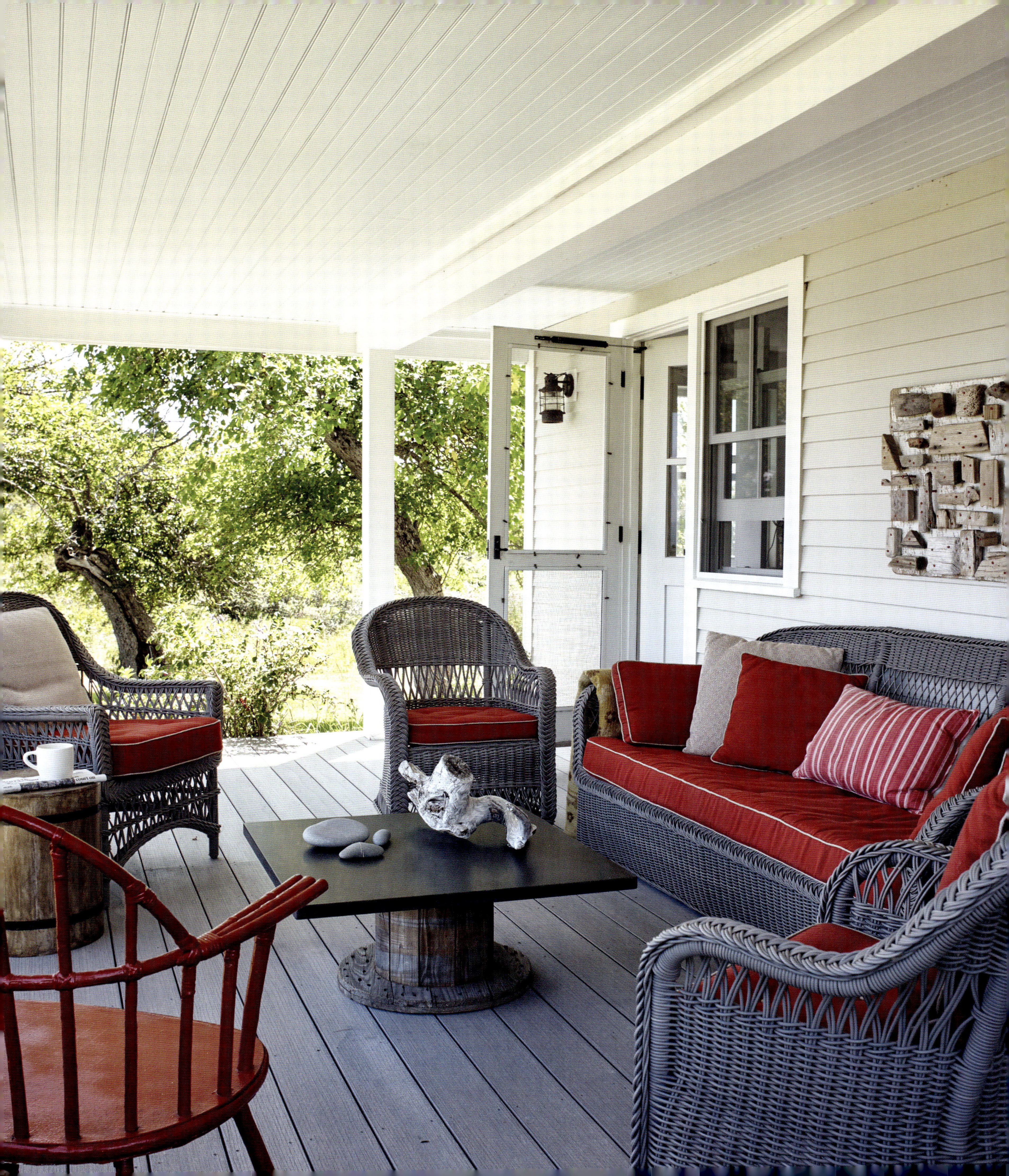

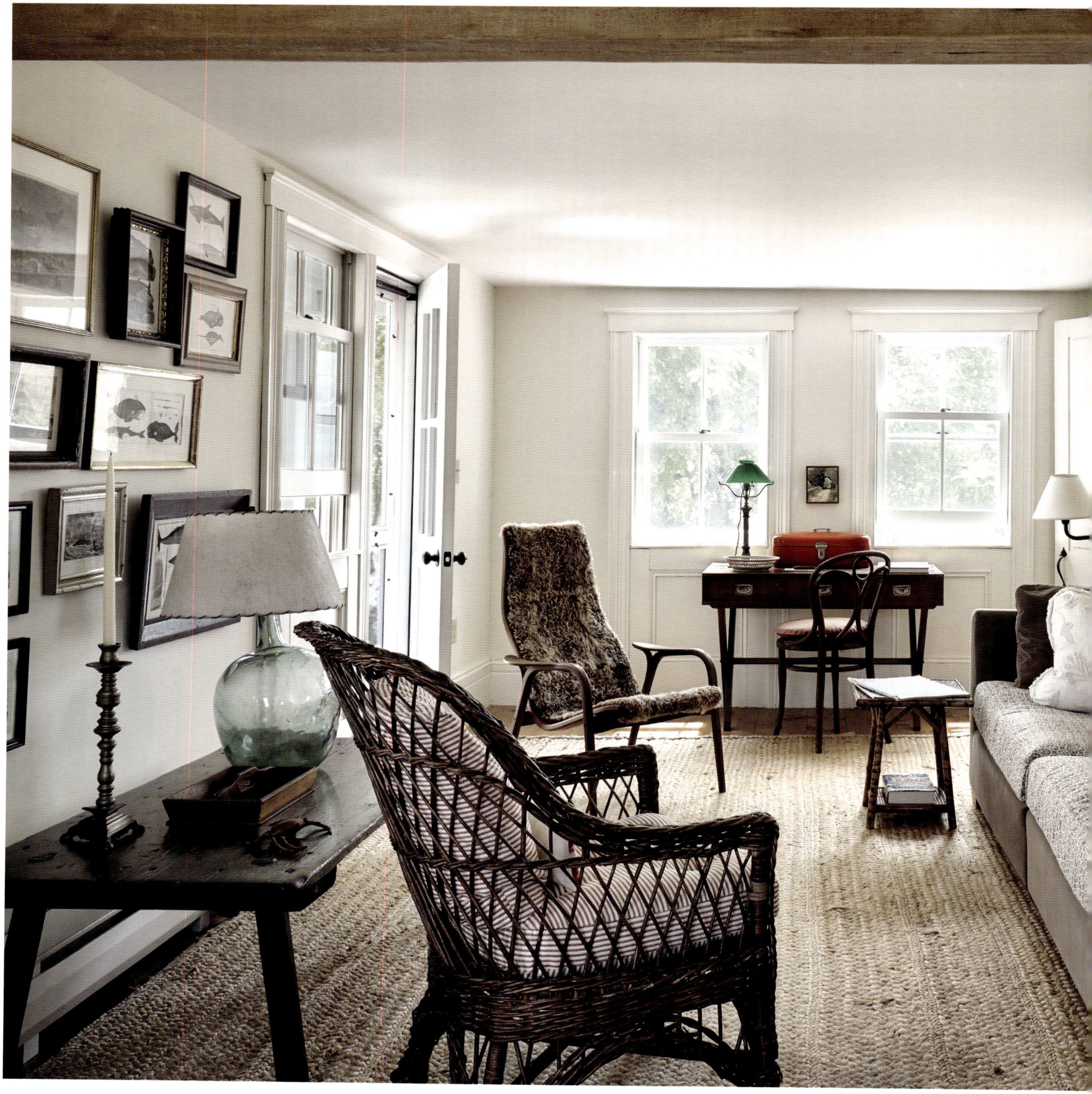

LEFT In one of the two parlors, a collection of whaling prints bought in Sag Harbor, New York, hasn't conjured a whale sighting yet. The ca. 1960 fleece-covered Lamino chair by Yngve Ekström was a precocious and prescient selection by the decorator for his own childhood bedroom. It has been shepherded by family members since then and now is back with its original owner. **ABOVE** These bird print fragments were found in their rustic frames. **OVERLEAF** We transformed the original kitchen into the second parlor. The brick hearth contains ovens on one side. The center table is a marriage between a zoomorphic base found in an antique shop and a top found somewhere else. The pair of sofas with brown wool upholstery came in a box from Ikea. Durable antique wicker is another Maine staple and is used throughout the interior.

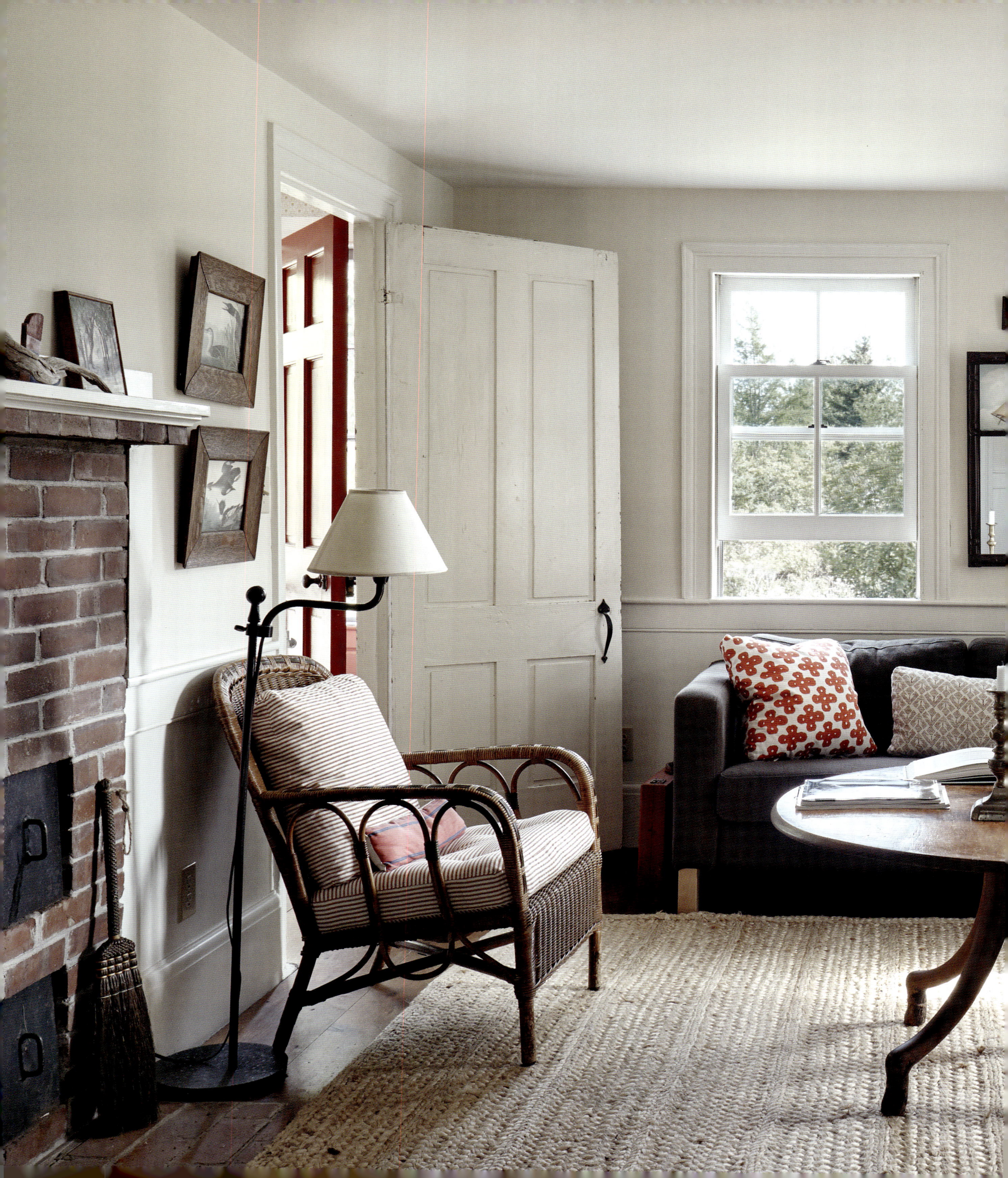

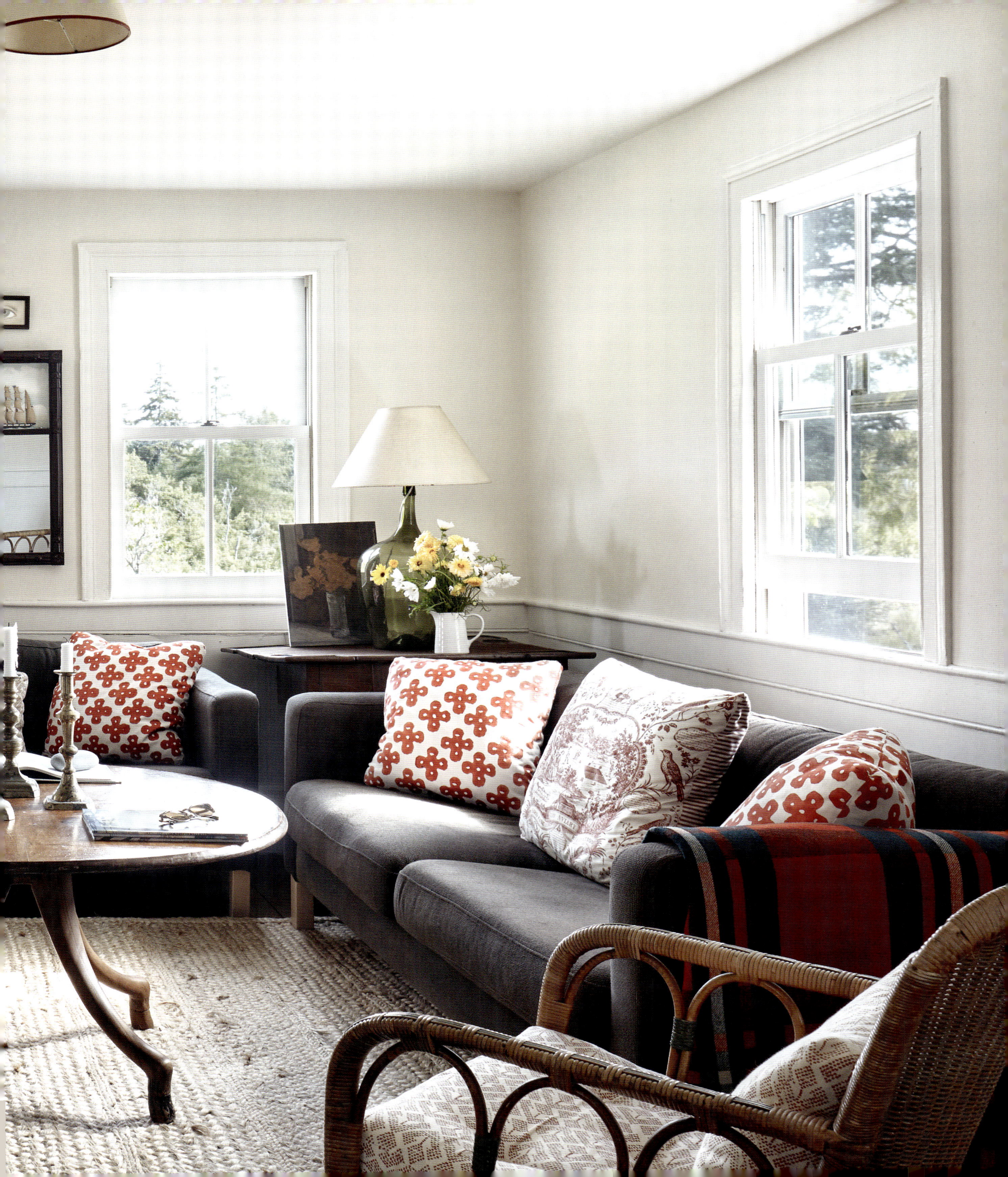

ABOVE The bold checkerboard of the new linoleum kitchen floor set the decorating of the entire house in motion. Seen through the kitchen doorway, resting informally on the mantel shelf, are a 1980s two-part sculpture by Betty Parsons, a small landscape by Simon Parkes, and a piece of driftwood. The "washing up" room, to the left, might be called a butler's pantry in another kind of summer house.
OPPOSITE Houseguests' plein-air painted offerings adorn the shelves of the dining room's Welsh dresser. Days are long in the summer, so the frequent and messy lobster suppers are usually served in twilight. Newsprint makes a readily available and disposable base for the table setting.

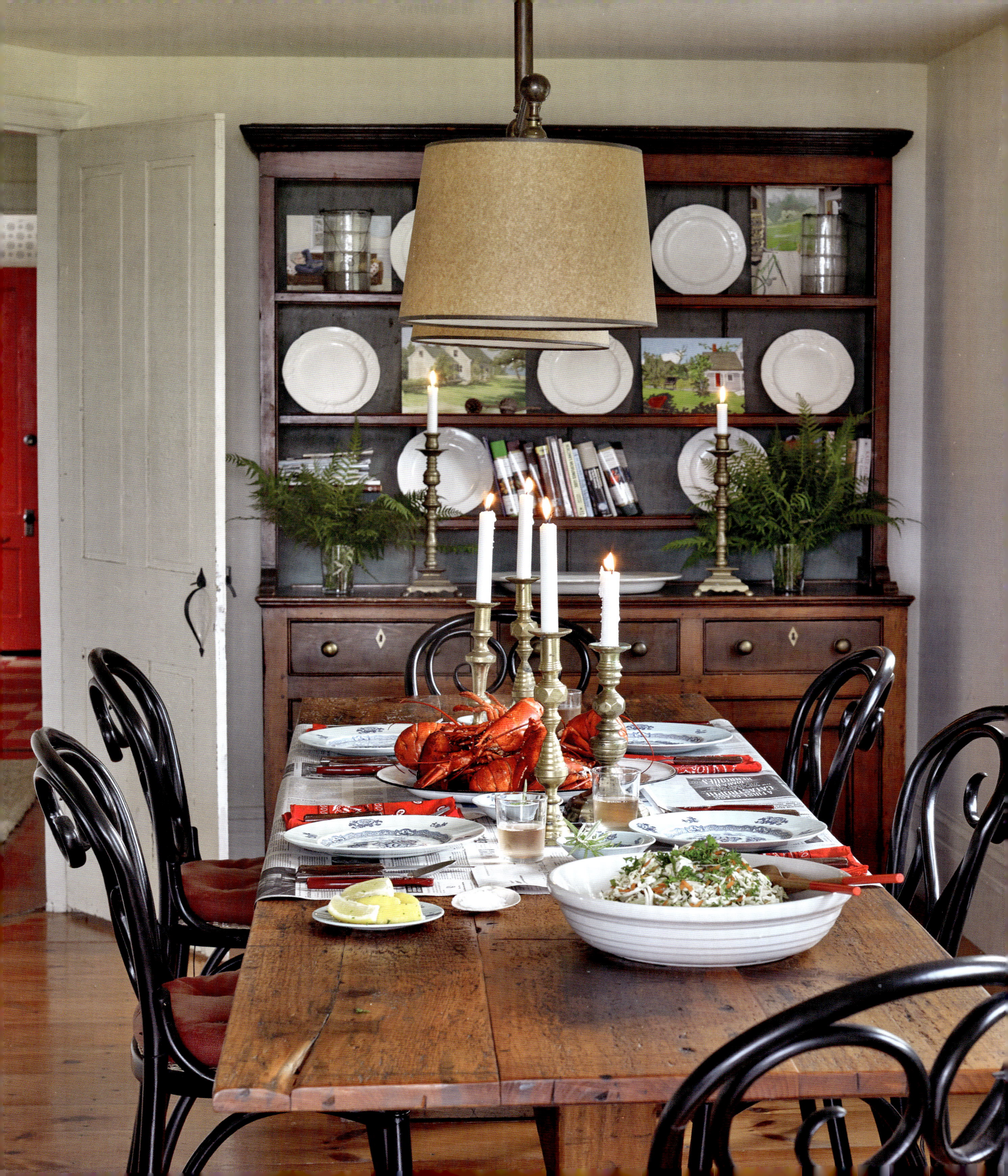

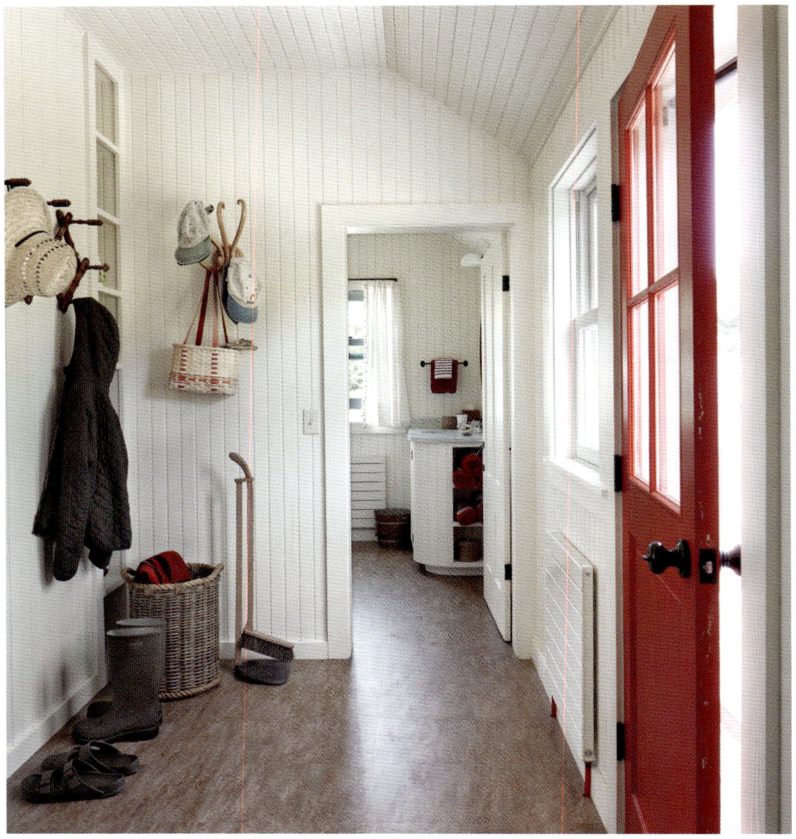

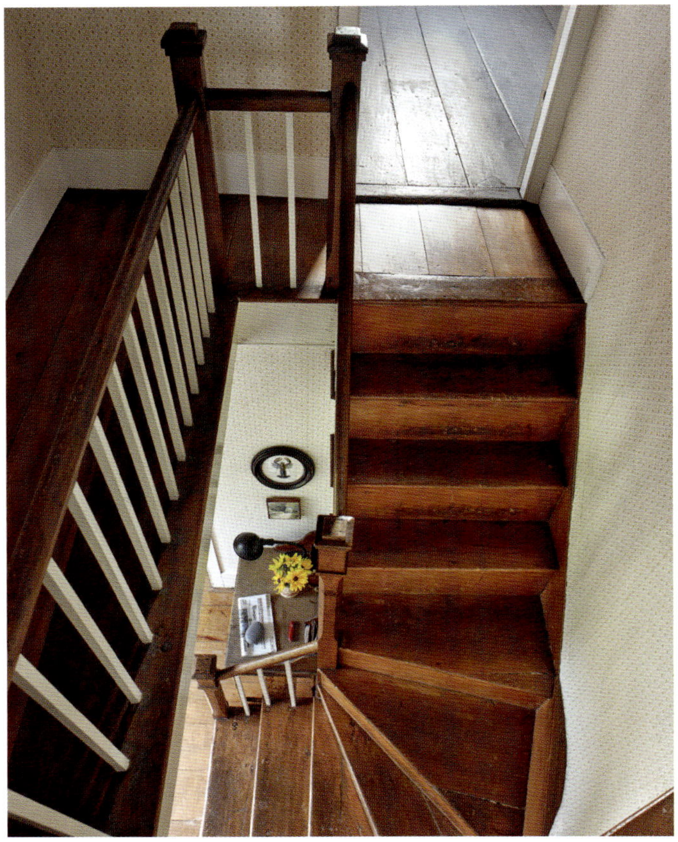

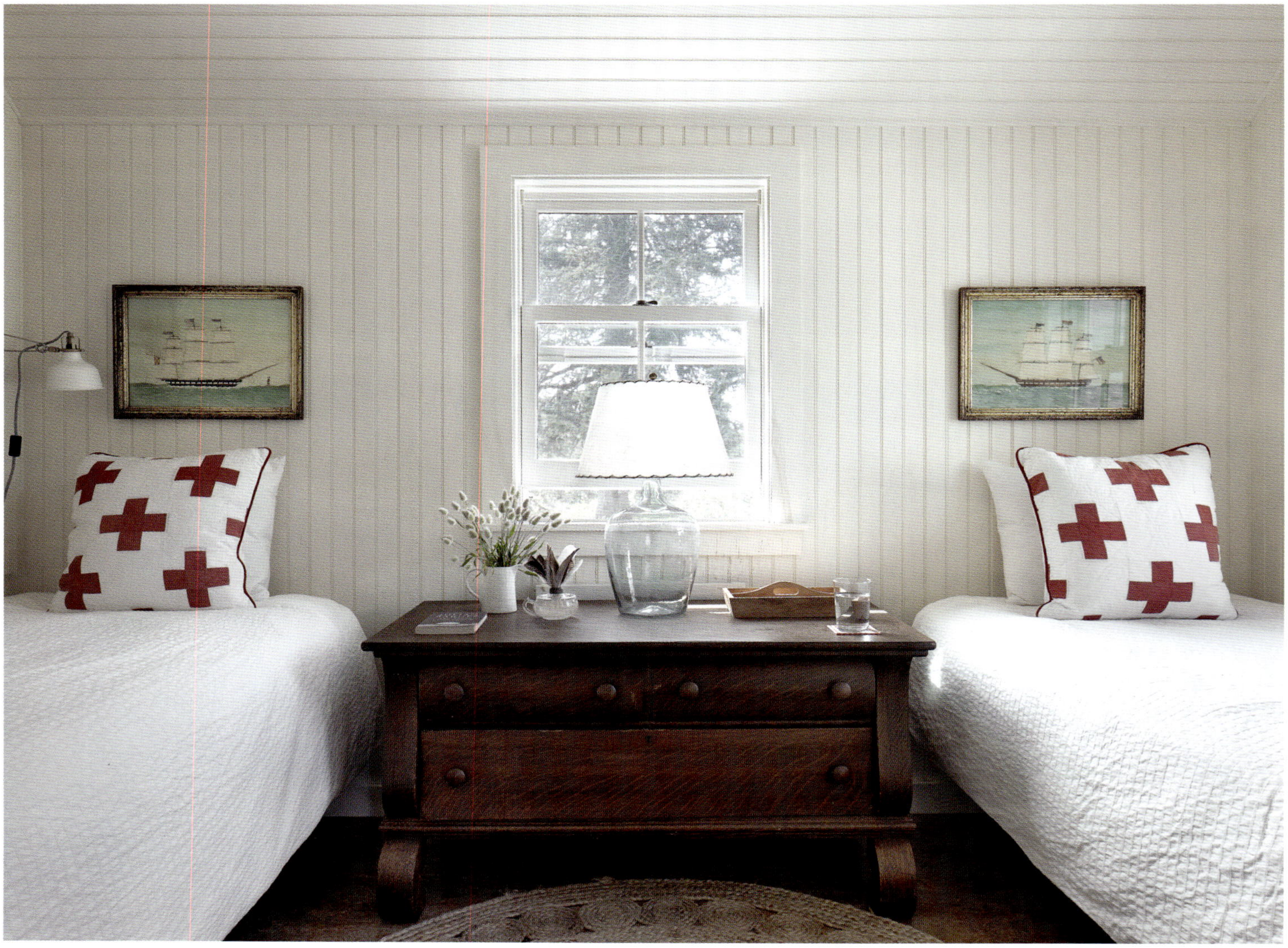

OPPOSITE, CLOCKWISE FROM TOP LEFT At the barn-facing end of the house, we added a linoleum-floored mudroom, a downstairs bath, and a guest room. The corkscrew-like stair and its pine railing were untouched, as were the old floors. The existing yellow patterned wallpaper was nostalgic (we had the same paper in our 1960s childhood home), and so was preserved. The schooner pictures above the beds in the new guest room are faux folk art by contemporary painter Mary Maguire. **ABOVE** The niche in my bedroom was designed with a boat's efficient use of space in mind. A simple wood shelf spans from wall to wall and supports the mattress.

HOUSEKEEPING . 179

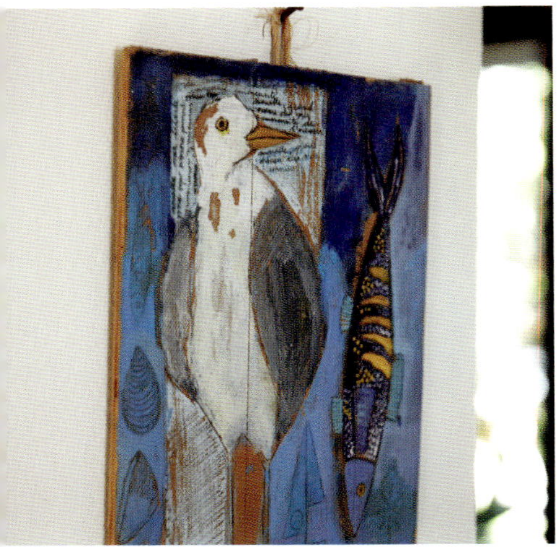
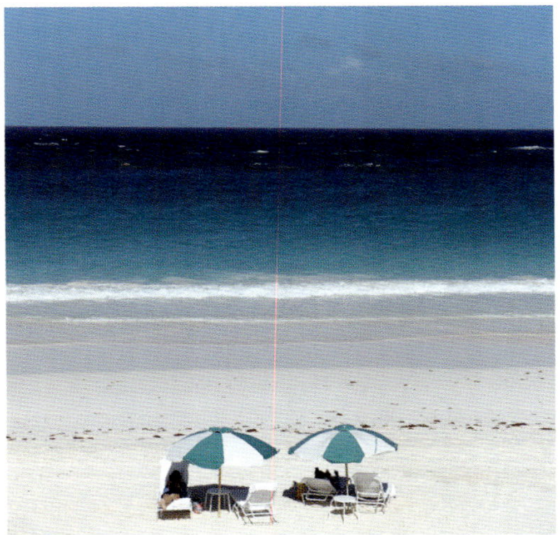
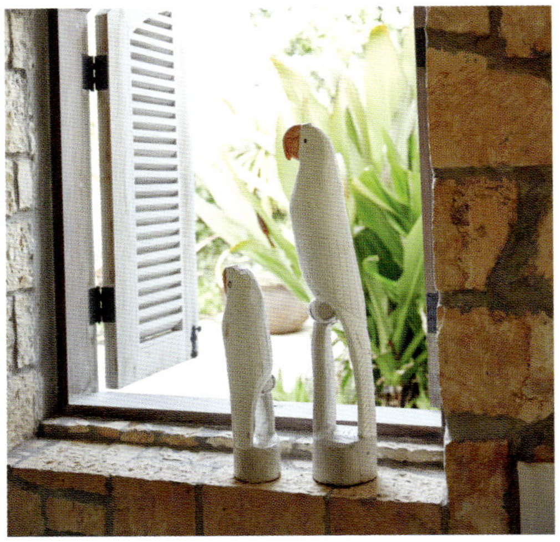
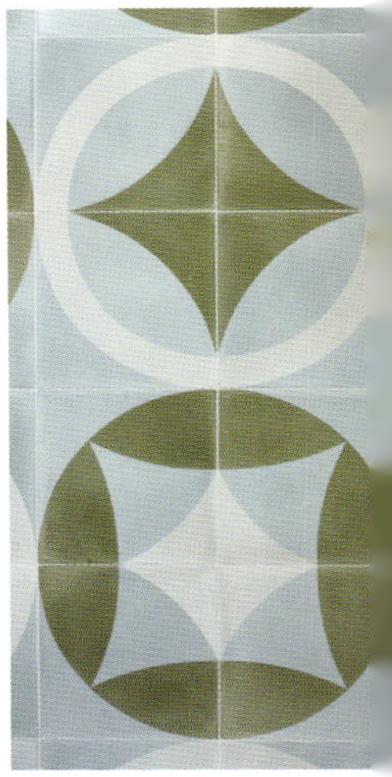
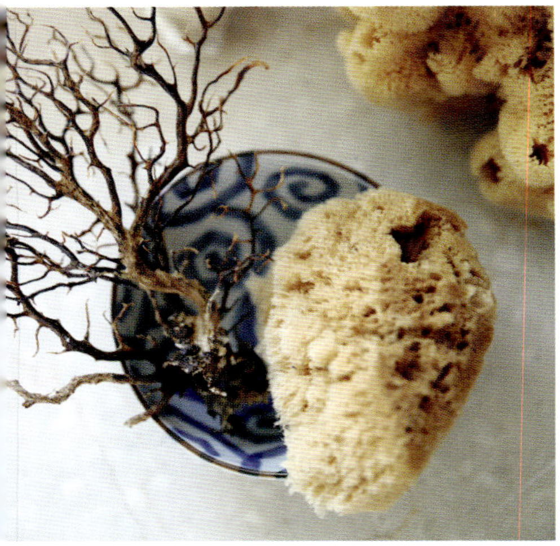
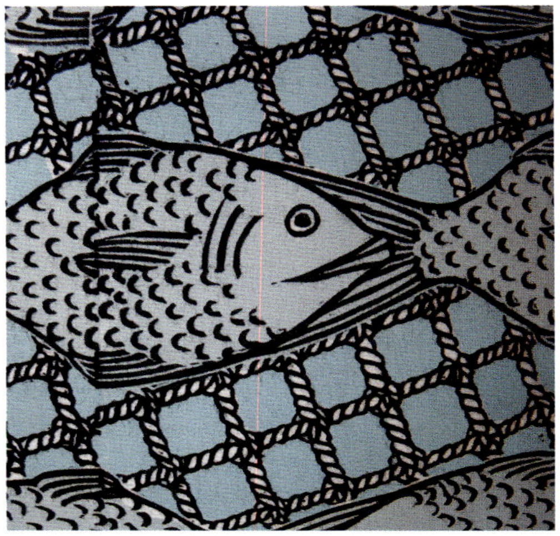
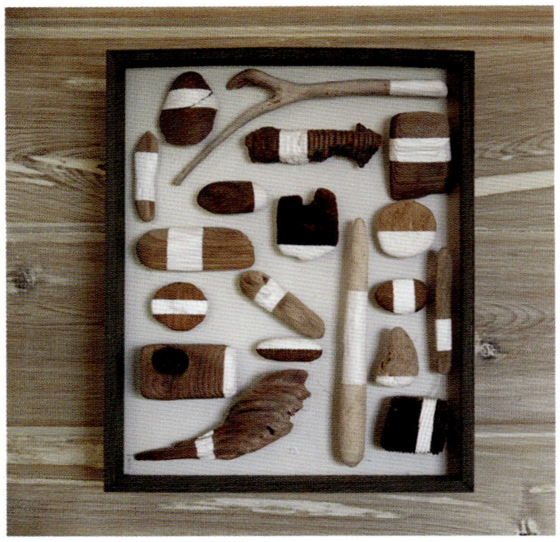
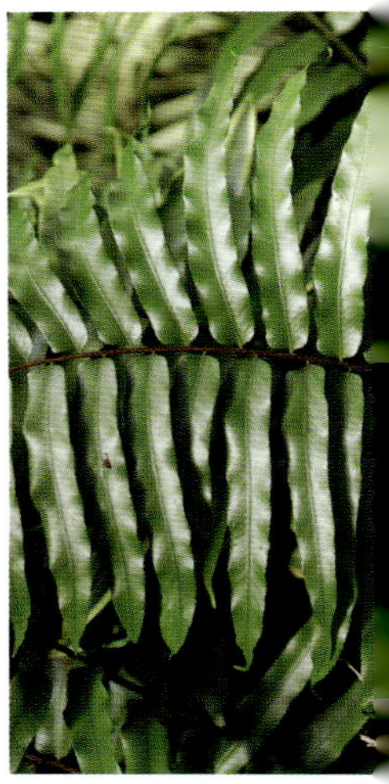
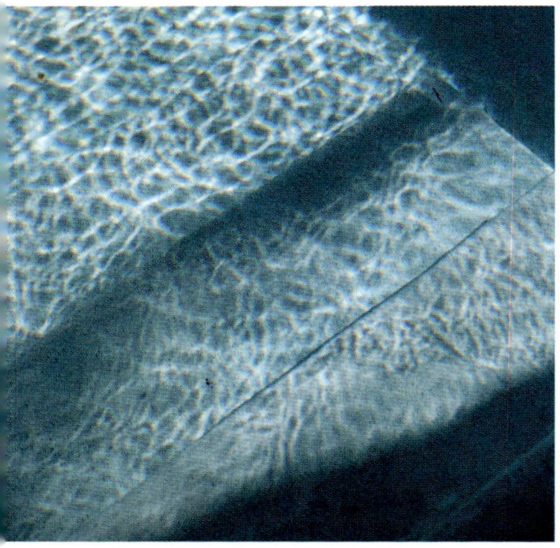
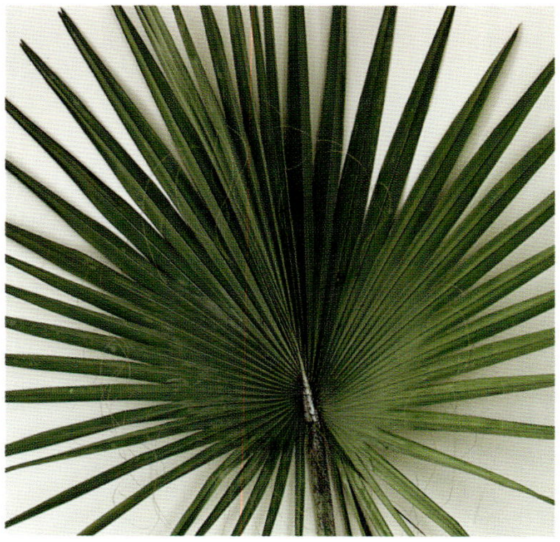
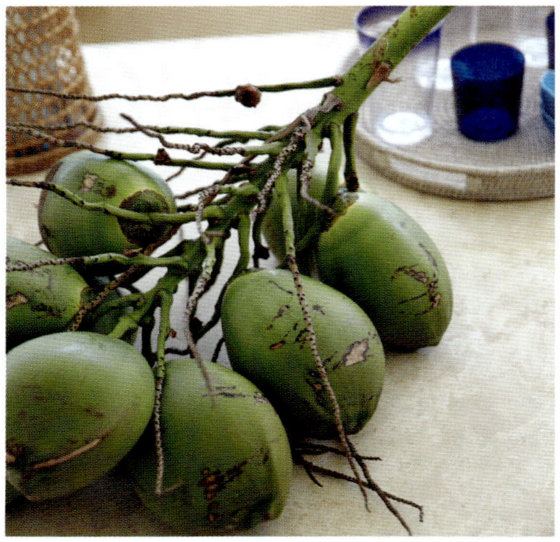
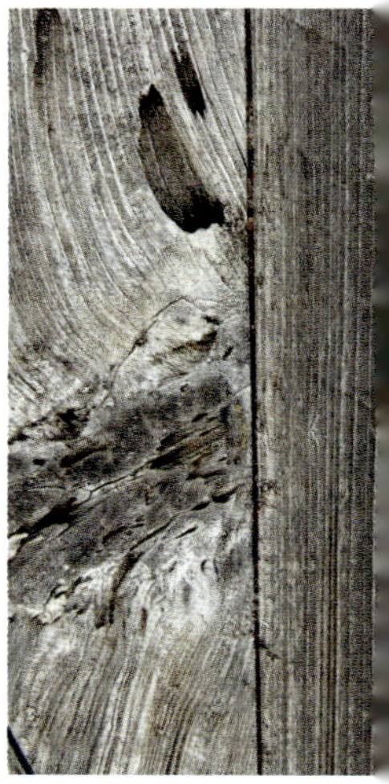
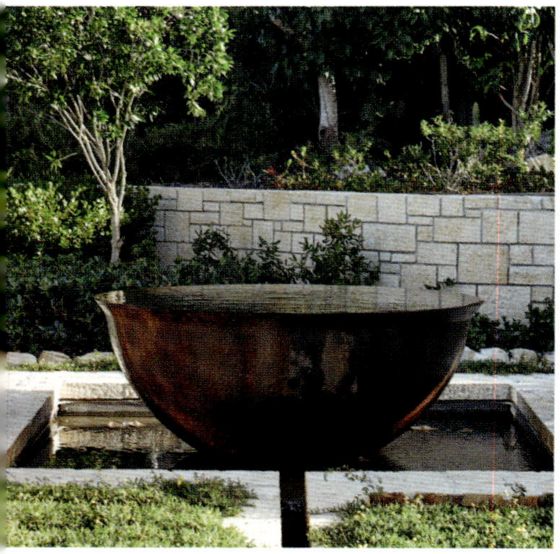
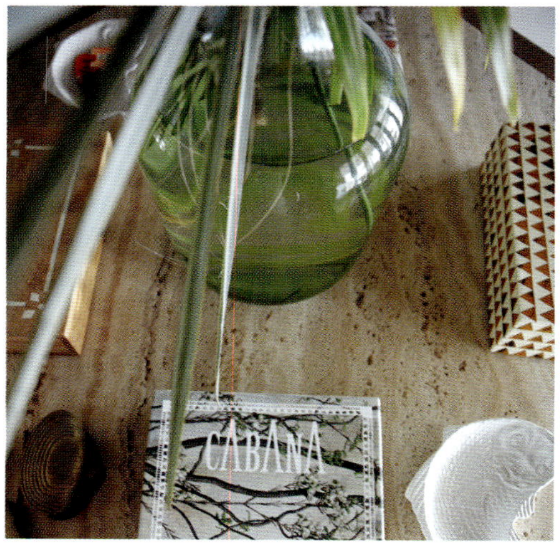
CABANA
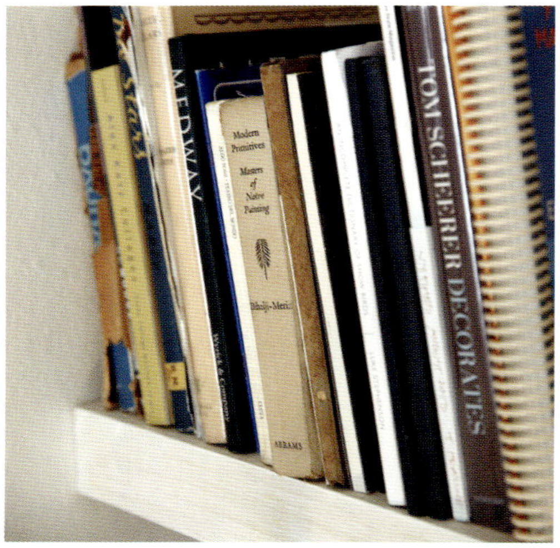
MEDWAY
TOM SCHEERER DECORATES
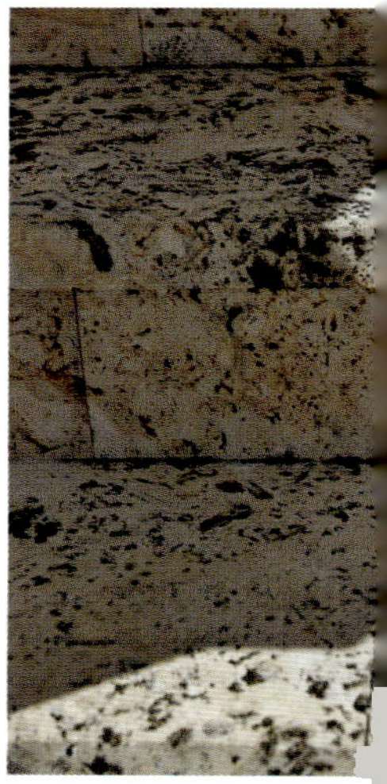

THE TROPICS

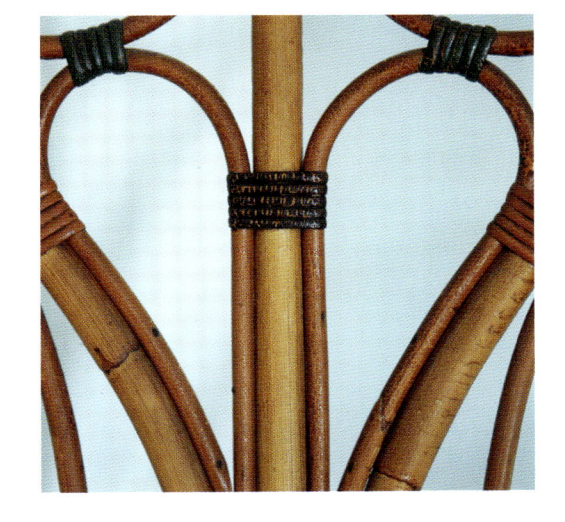

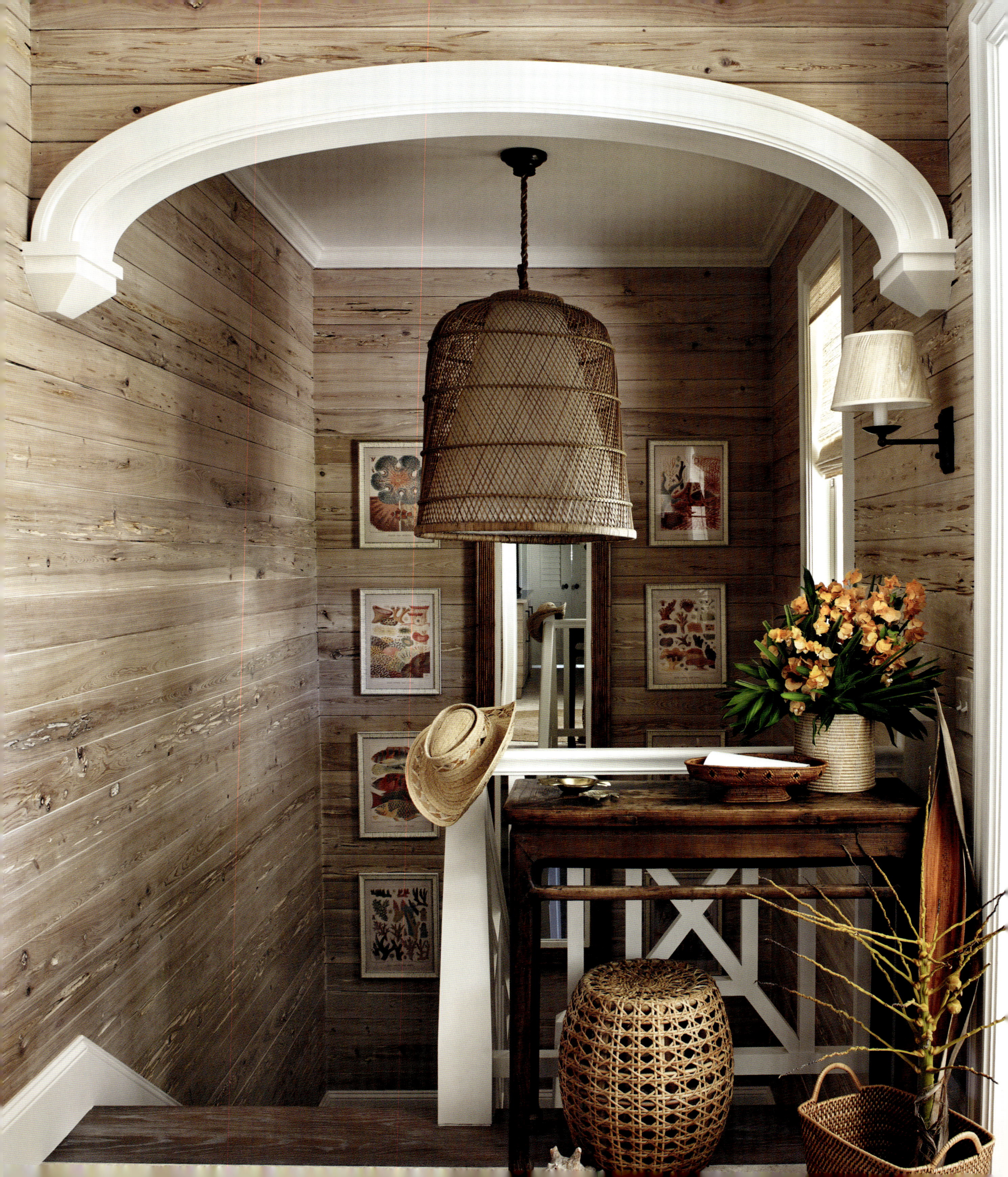

Harbour Island

Dunmore Town on tiny, remote Harbour Island in the Bahamas is a trove of charming houses dating back to the Loyalist era in the late eighteenth century. Vernacular shipwright's cottages made from native pine and a few grander ones made of stuccoed coral stone girded by wooden verandas line the harbor front. Beyond the village, along the two-and-a-half-mile length of the very narrow island, are several generations of straightforward holiday houses for winter residents from all over the world. More recently, Harbour Island has been abuzz with building and has become a hotbed of activity for an international and cosmopolitan group of architects and decorators.

A coconut's throw from the harbor on the windward side, overlooking what is said to be one of the best beaches in the world, is the Dunmore, a beach club and hotel. The rolling, verdant grounds are dotted with guest cottages and a recently constructed series of more elaborate (and staffed) villas built by the hotel's American owner. A single architect provided the common thread for these successively built villas. Stylistically similar, they form a pleasing grouping of syncopated yet compatible volumes in varying materials and subtle colors.

Bahamian building styles were fully embraced but recalibrated for the requirements of today's holiday residents. This house, the fourth in the series, appears to be a modest raftered cottage from the front gate, but is in fact a complex three-bedroom structure equipped with all the latest mod-cons. And down the dune beyond, there's also a guest cottage and pool.

The Dunmore's owner, whose day job is "Texas real estate magnate," took particular interest in the architectural possibilities and the construction process. He was eager to apply the lessons learned about the vagaries of the weather and the arrangement of the rooms from the building of the three earlier villas. Thankfully, he was a laissez-faire decorator. He had left the furnishing of all these successively "flipped" villas to a roster of august decorators. I may have been fourth in the queue but was still happy to oblige.

The materials for the interior are in the vernacular "less-so" category, but none is inappropriate or out of place. Imported pecky cypress and Cuban tile were used liberally. Both are longstanding Harbour Island traditions. Furniture in bug-resistant teak and forgiving rustic finishes was designed and ordered from India. As usual, great emphasis was put on durable fabrics, mostly outdoor ones, used even inside to resist wet bathing suits. The carpets are all close to the color of beach sand.

As usual with projects in these remote places, the decorator arrives prepared. Every single piece of furniture, pillow, sheet, glass, and fork was collected in the States over the construction period, delivered via containers, and installed in one fell swoop. It's a bit like making a birthday cake on a camping trip. Careful planning and strategic preparation are critical.

The cheerful staff of the club was there to greet the new residents when they arrived at their very thoroughly complete house. The veranda seems to hang over the world's best beach. They say this newest house in paradise is "the keeper."

OPPOSITE Pickled pecky cypress takes its first bow in the entrance hall of this Harbour Island house. Though the decorator suggested materials and finishes, Maria de la Guardia of de la Guardia Victoria Architects & Urbanists designed the house and its many charming Caribbean details.

ABOVE AND OPPOSITE Pickled pecky cypress makes a second appearance on the living room ceiling over wide, white-painted plank walls. The rusticated jute-and-wool striped rug is from Studio Four. The decorator designed the octagonal center table and durable inset travertine top. It was finished in a similar driftwood-like "pickling" to echo the ceiling. Above the sofa is a large-scale work on paper by the English artist Christopher Brooks, a frequent Harbour Island visitor. The backgammon table is set with extra Palecek dining chairs. They mimic the vintage Albini "conversation" chairs that are pulled up to the seating areas.

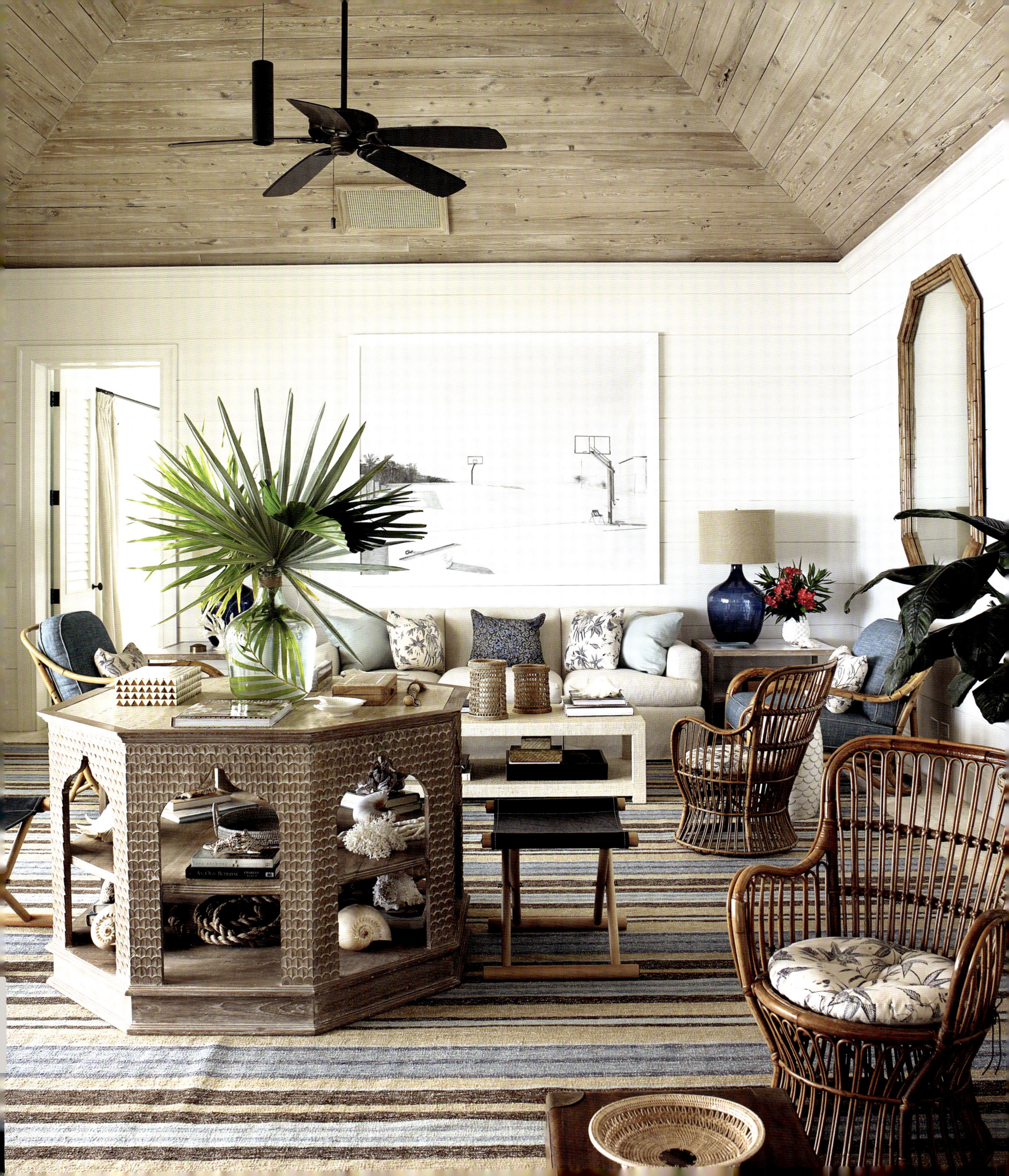

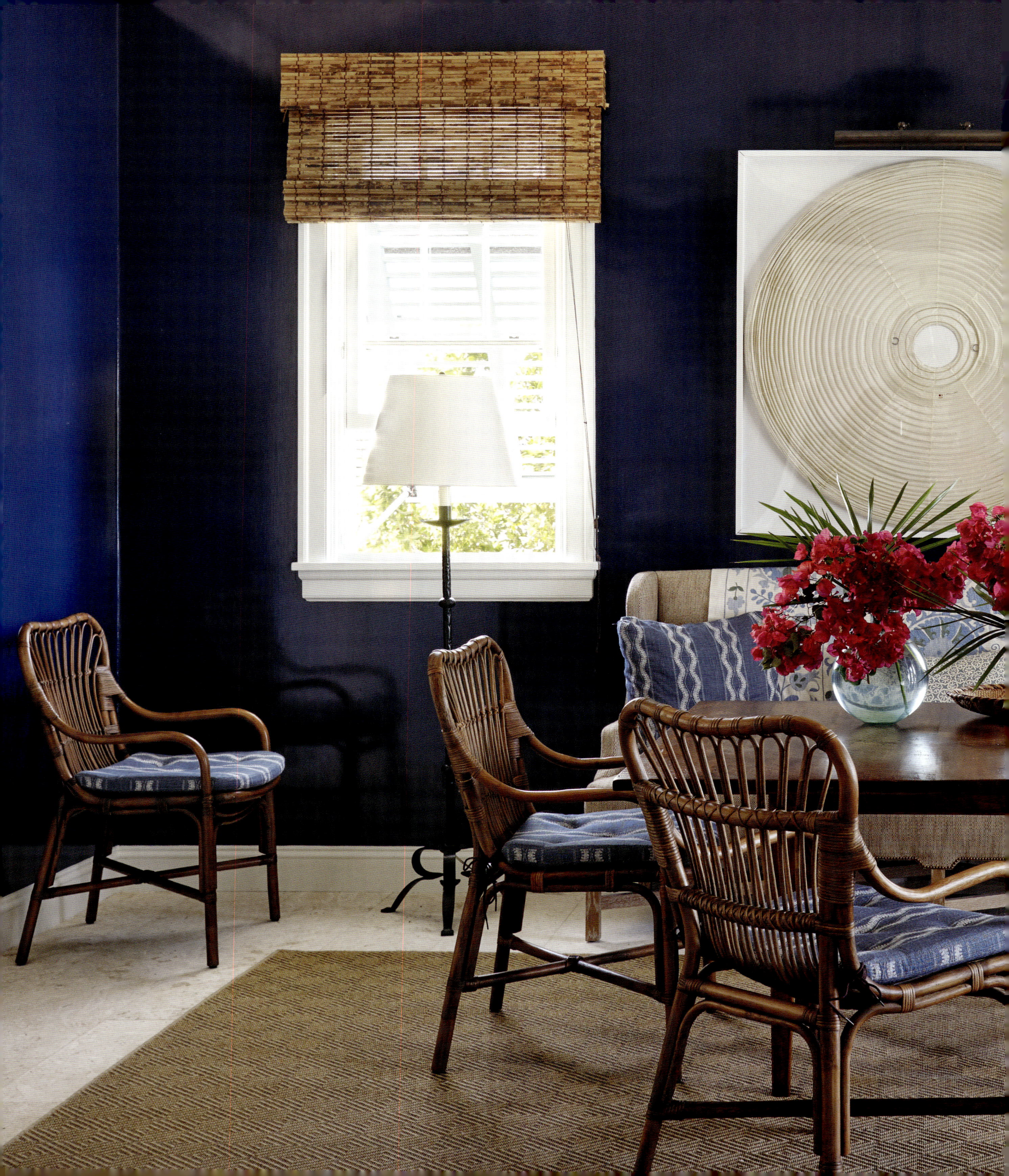

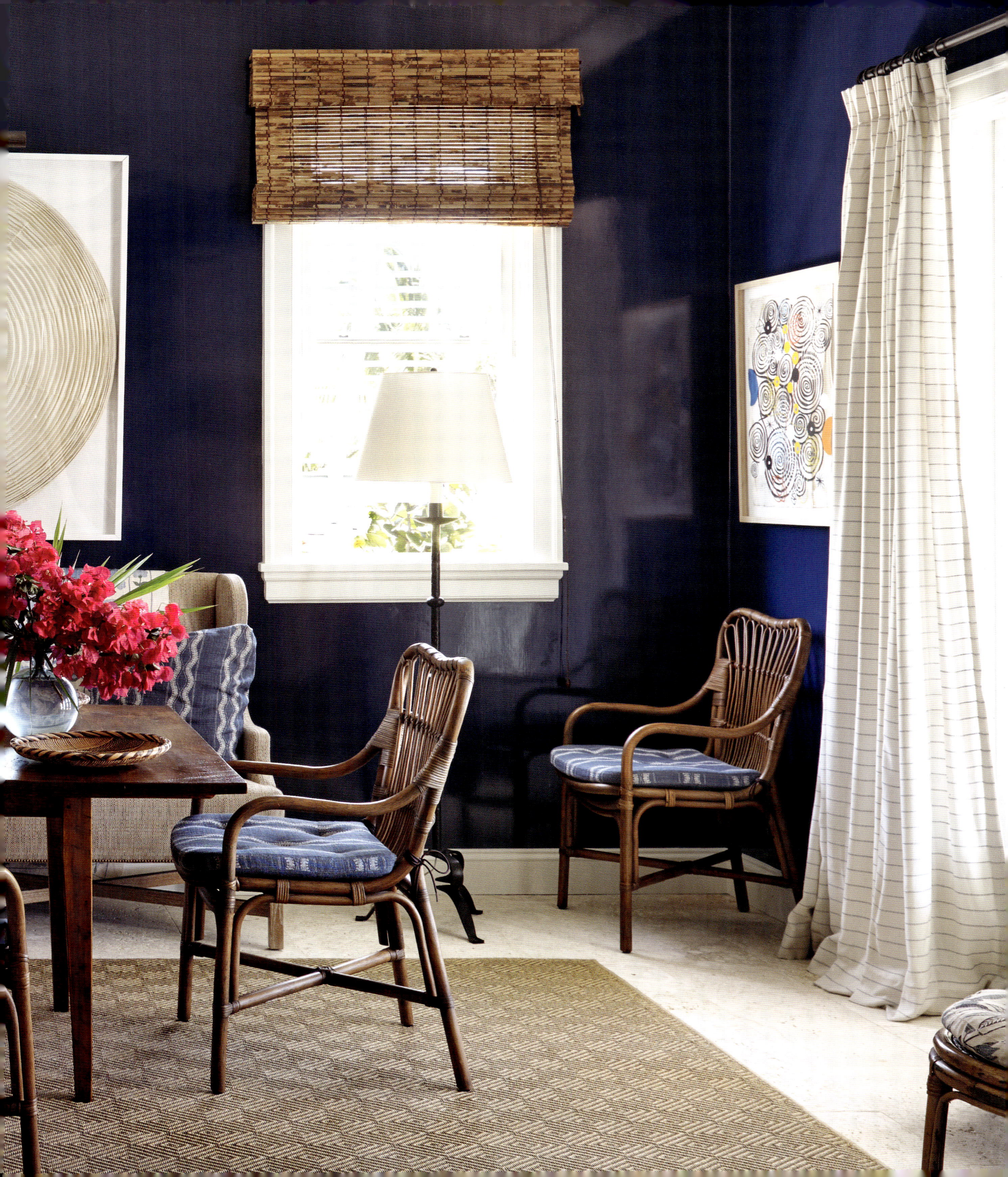

PRECEDING PAGES From the living room, there are two deep blue views: the sea and the dining room. Its walls are painted in Benjamin Moore's high-gloss Champion Cobalt. Most of the time, the square dining table is pulled up to the banquette. When centered in the room, it can be expanded with the semicircle side tables that flank the doorway (out of frame). A framed Noguchi lantern makes a graphic and restorative bull's-eye "painting." The unlined curtains are an indoor/outdoor fabric that withstands the intense Bahamian sun. **ABOVE** Moroccan tile covers the backsplash and the counters of the cozy bar. It is only a few steps from the living room, entrance hall, and front veranda. **OPPOSITE** The decorator eschews upper cabinets whenever possible, allowing patterned kitchen walls to carry the day. The Cuban-style Katie tile is from Villa Lagoon Tile. The Raj Company made the kitchen island, which was fitted with a Caesarstone top after it arrived from Mumbai. The kitchen floor is impervious porcelain, chosen to flow seamlessly into the coral stone–like travertine floors throughout.

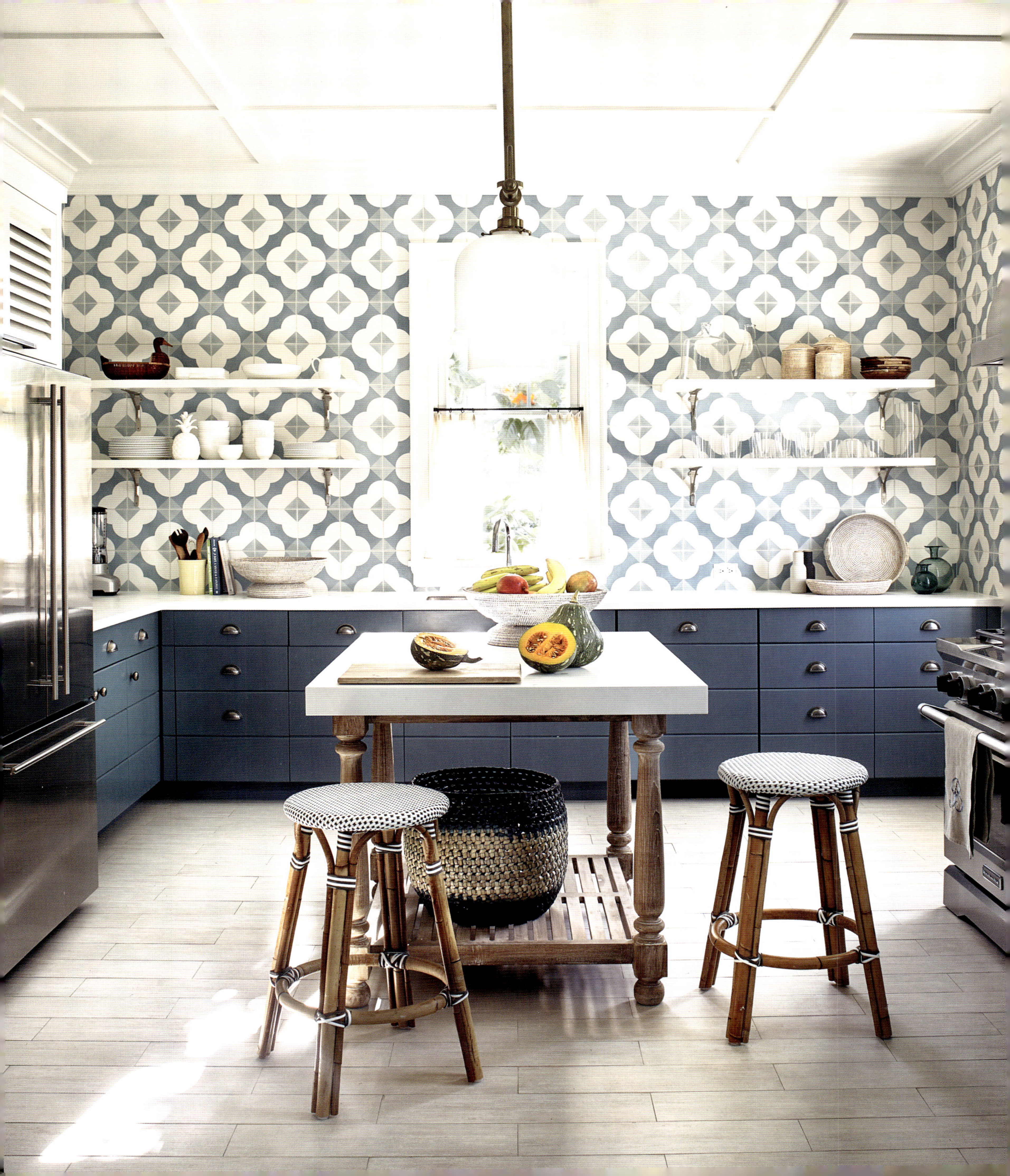

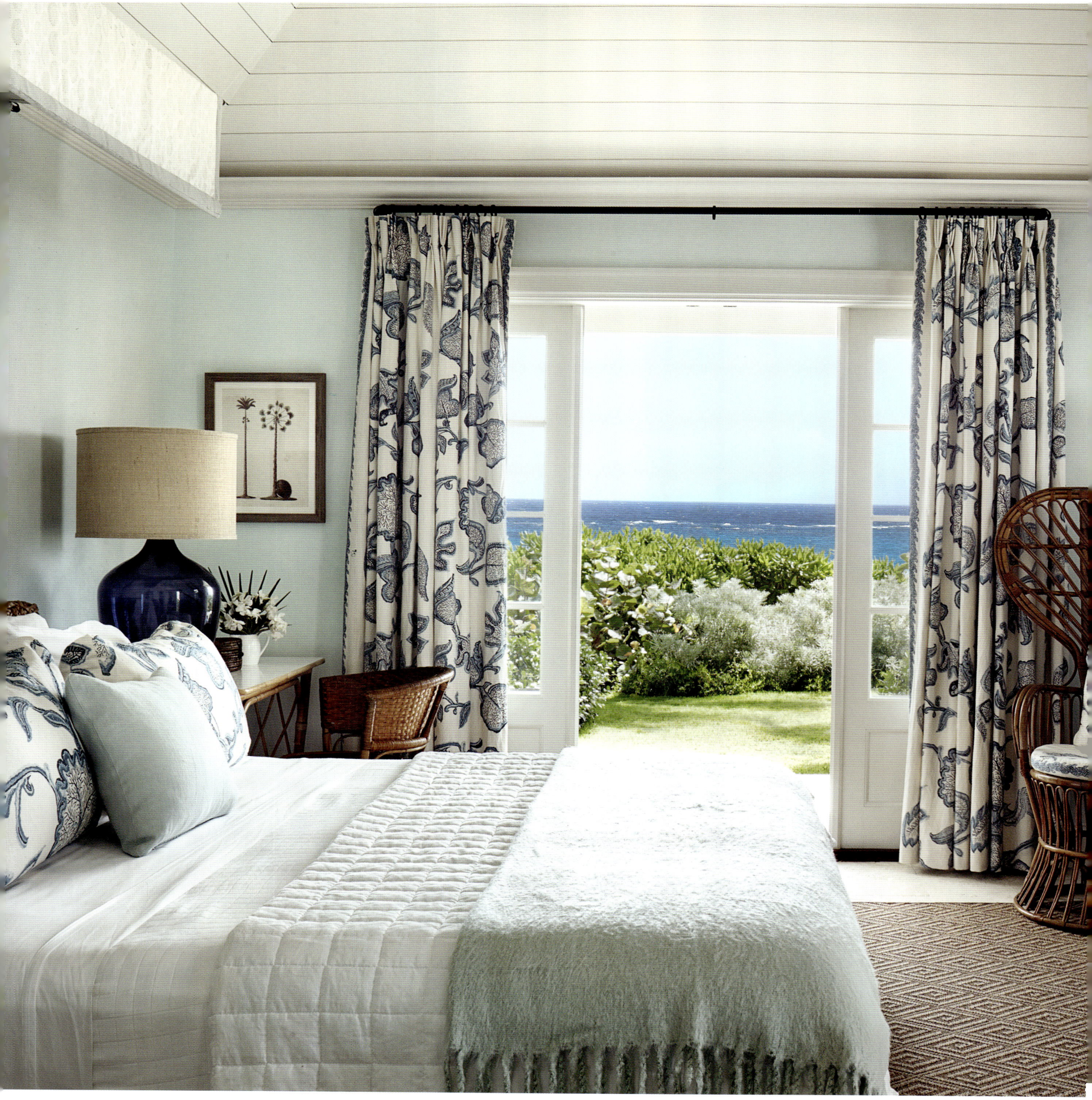

LEFT The guest cottage is approached via the convivial pool terrace but opens to its own private porch and exclusive view. The decorator rarely uses printed fabrics for curtains, but here, Schumacher's relaxed Tree of Life–patterned cotton Palampore seemed apt. The print contains as many blues as can be seen in the ever-changing scene beyond the doors. ABOVE In this guest bathroom, the vanity and its stone top came directly from Restoration Hardware. OVERLEAF LEFT Another bath has a permanent sun-loving guest: an Alex Katz beach towel by the Art Production Fund is framed under glass. OVERLEAF RIGHT A durable Telas de Lenguas woven cotton makes a sensible headboard and upholstered bed platforms for this twin bedroom. The purple colorway is a twist on this traditional, usually blue and white, Majorcan fabric. A one-of-a-kind purple batik sarong had just enough yardage for the two decorative pillows. Palms abound on the property, so the fan-shaped leaves can always be replaced before the arrival of new guests.

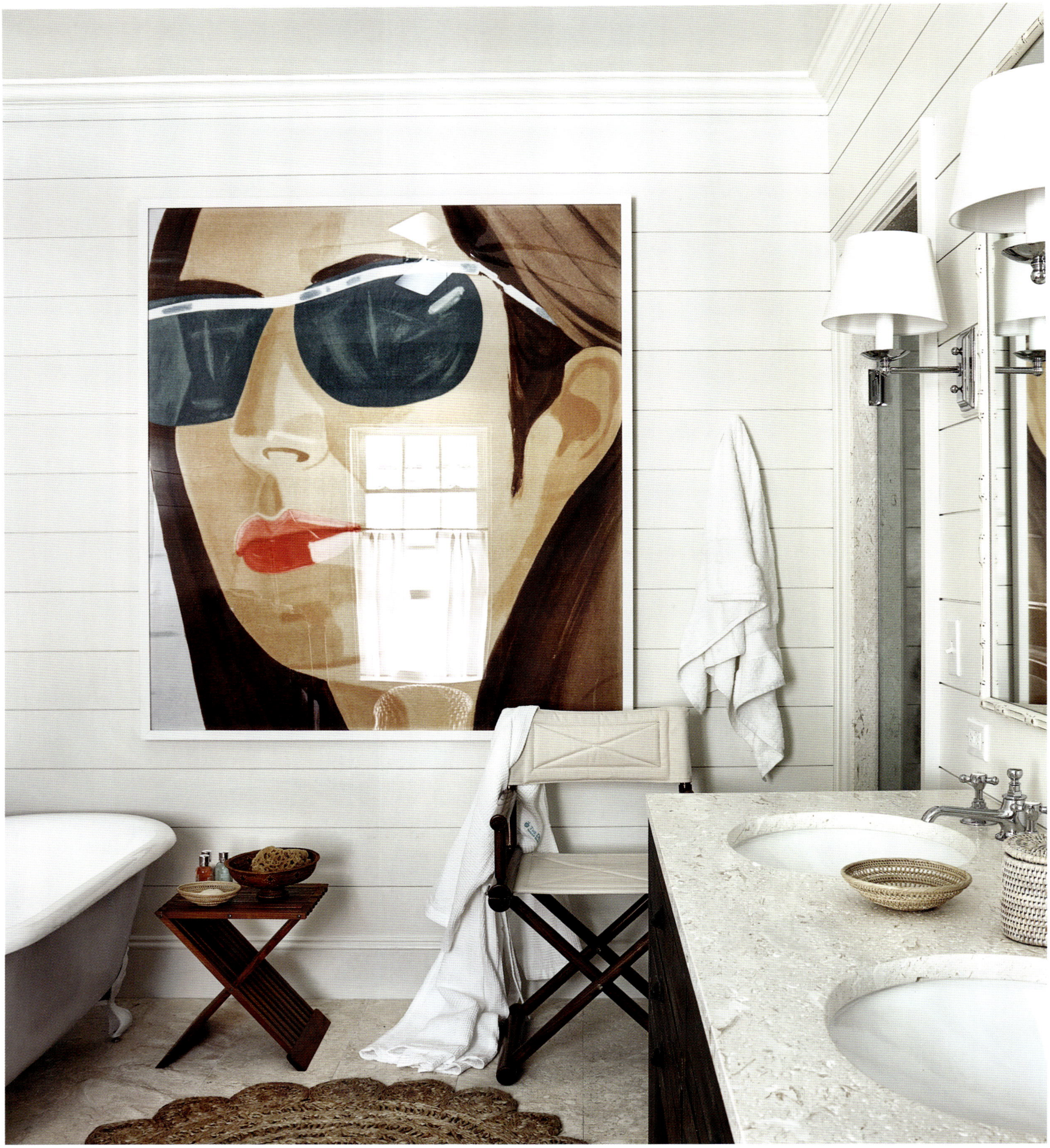

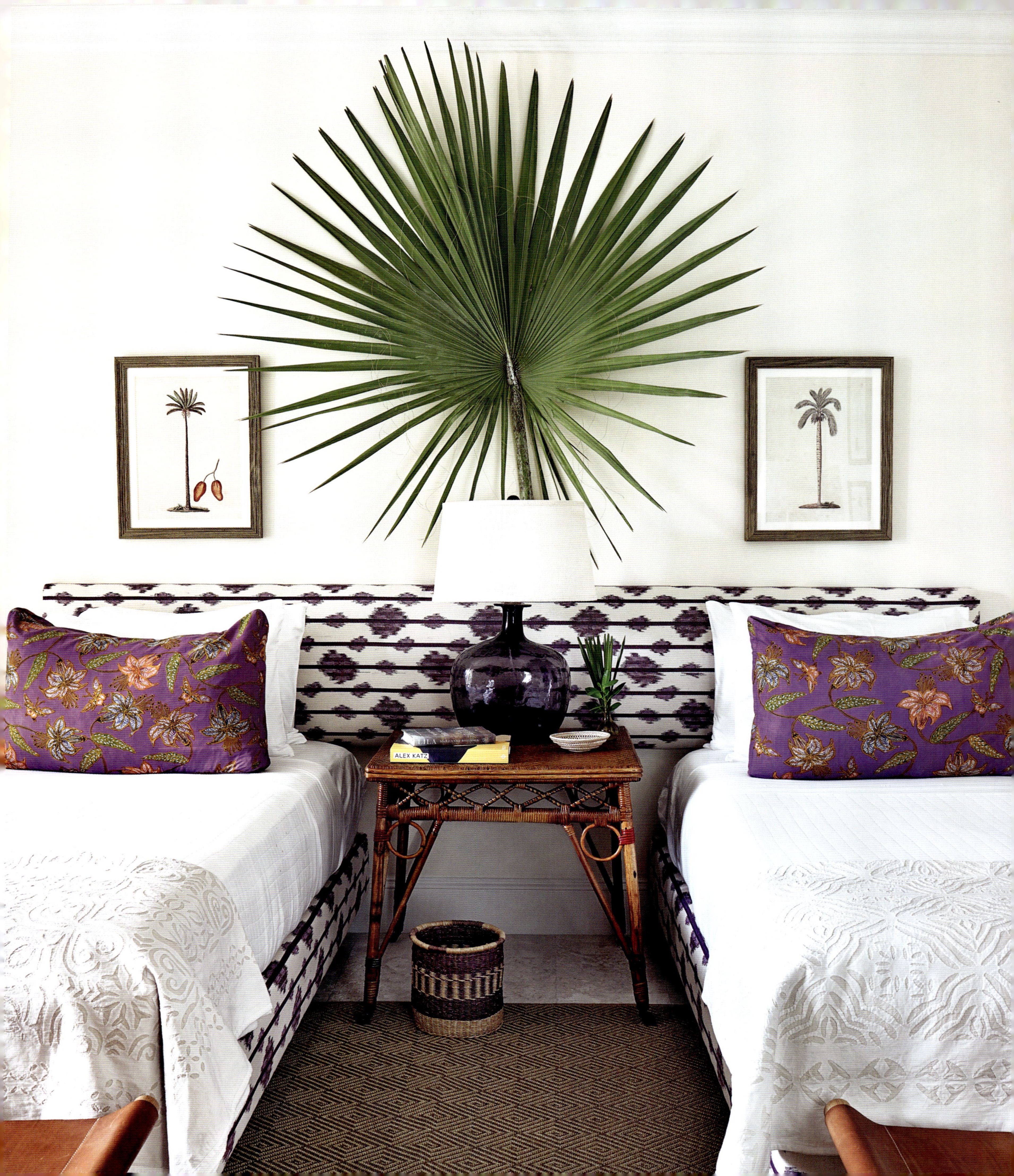

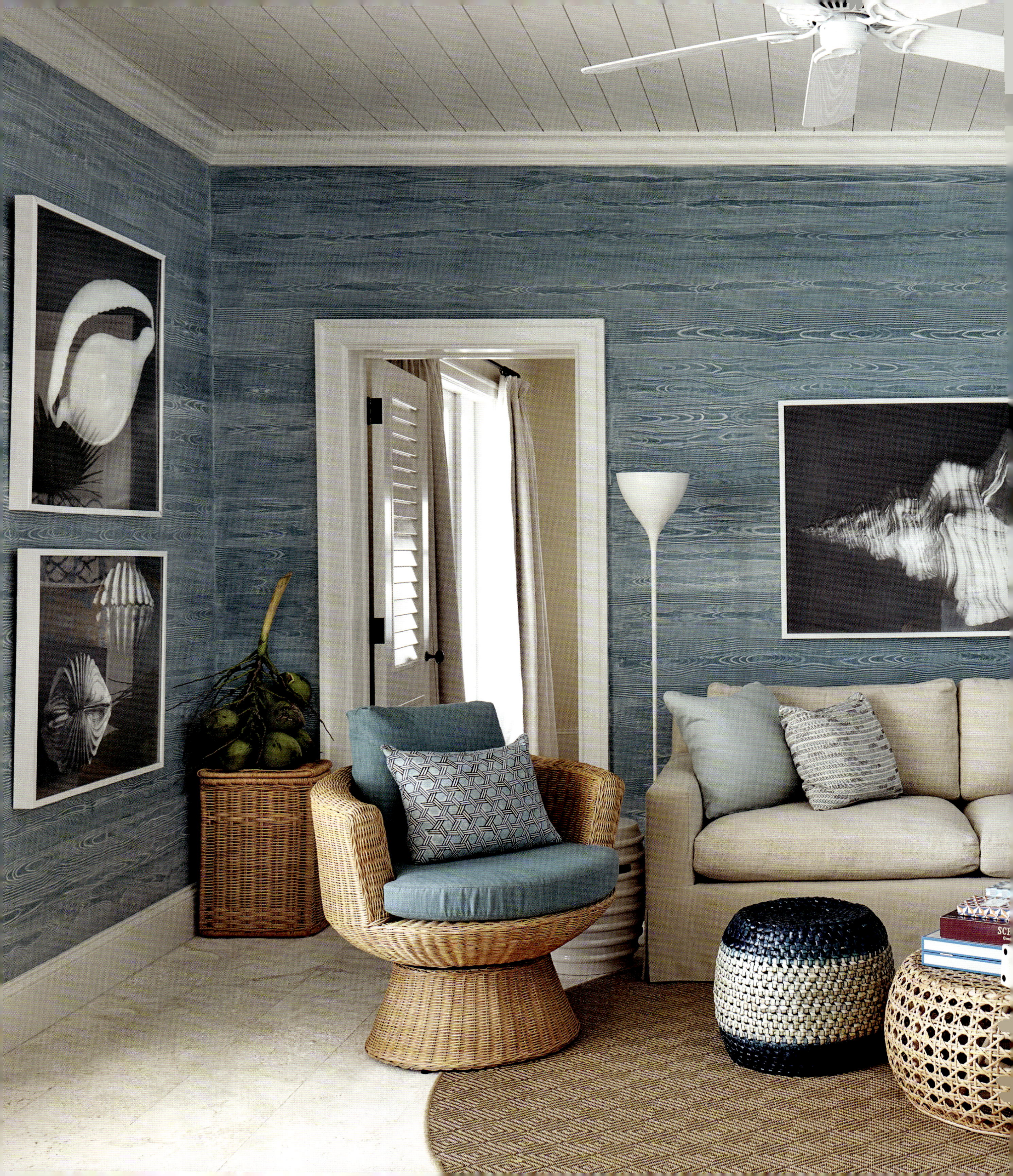

To enliven the playroom, the plaster walls were painted peacock blue in a faux-bois pattern by Frank Reijnen. Black-and-white photos of shells from a vintage conchology book were enlarged and framed for the walls. The wicker chairs swivel toward an unseen and very large television. Vintage "tulip" uplights by Swiss designer Max Bill are classics of modernism. They alleviate any need for ceiling lighting.

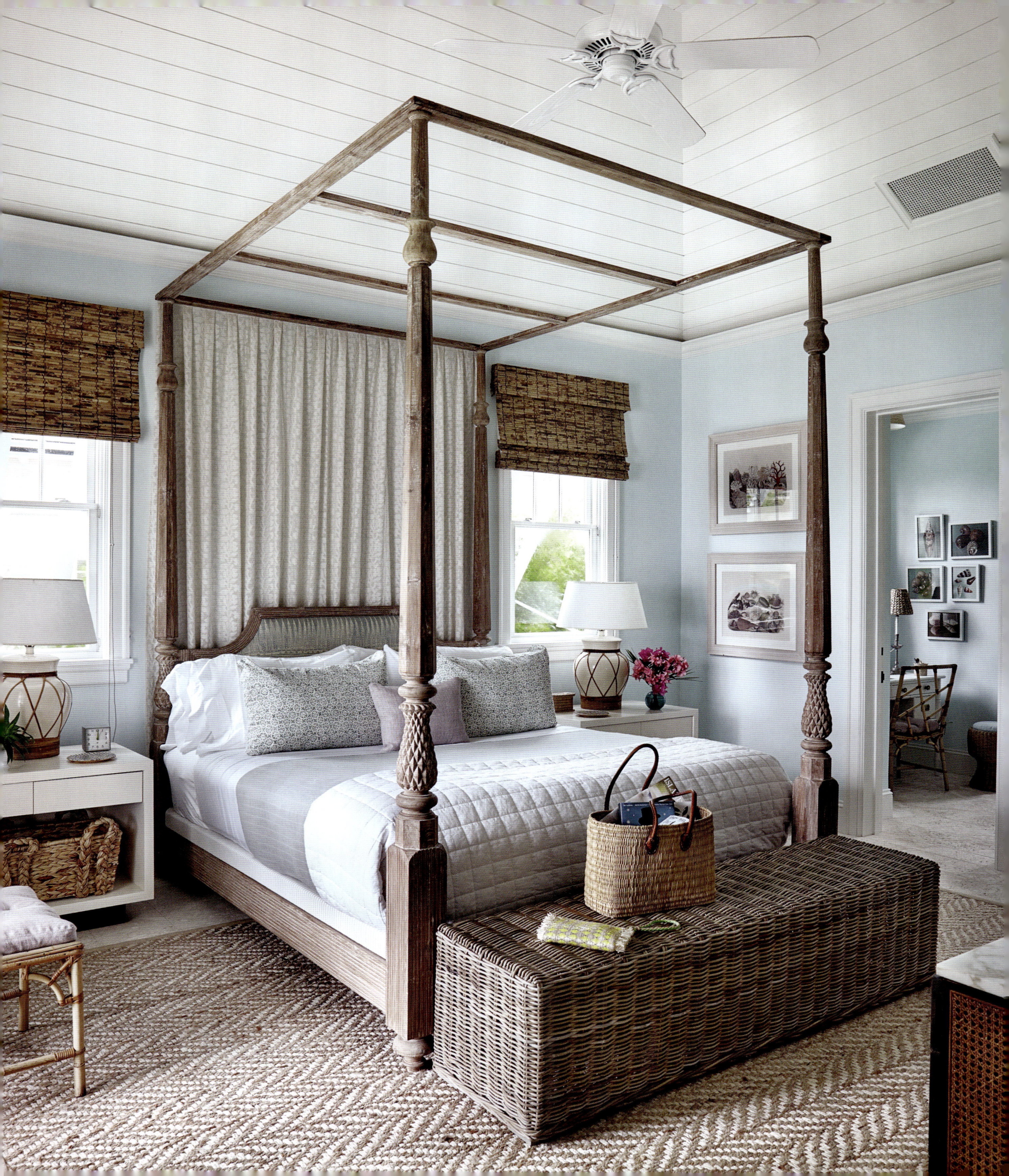

OPPOSITE The tall, pickled-teak tester bed was made in India for the tray-ceilinged master bedroom. Without a canopy and hangings, moving air is unimpeded. Wicker and rattan abound: chairs, dressers, baskets, and accessories. Even the ivory ceramic bedside lamps are lashed in split caning. ABOVE, CLOCKWISE FROM LEFT Another set of shell photographs, these in faded "vintage" color, make a pretty and locally pertinent display. Detail of an exceptionally elegant rattan peacock chair. The single fabric panel behind the bed softens the room in the absence of curtains, which would crowd the windows.

TOP AND ABOVE Hipped roofs, shutters, louvered porches, and intimate scale are several of the Harbour Island traditions skillfully employed by de la Guardia Victoria Architects & Urbanists. **RIGHT** As the pool terrace and the guest cottage are down an incline from the house, the view of the ocean is unobstructed. The comfort of the veranda furniture belies its indoor/outdoor durability. Only a few cotton batik pillows and the two vintage rattan conversation chairs need ever be brought inside.

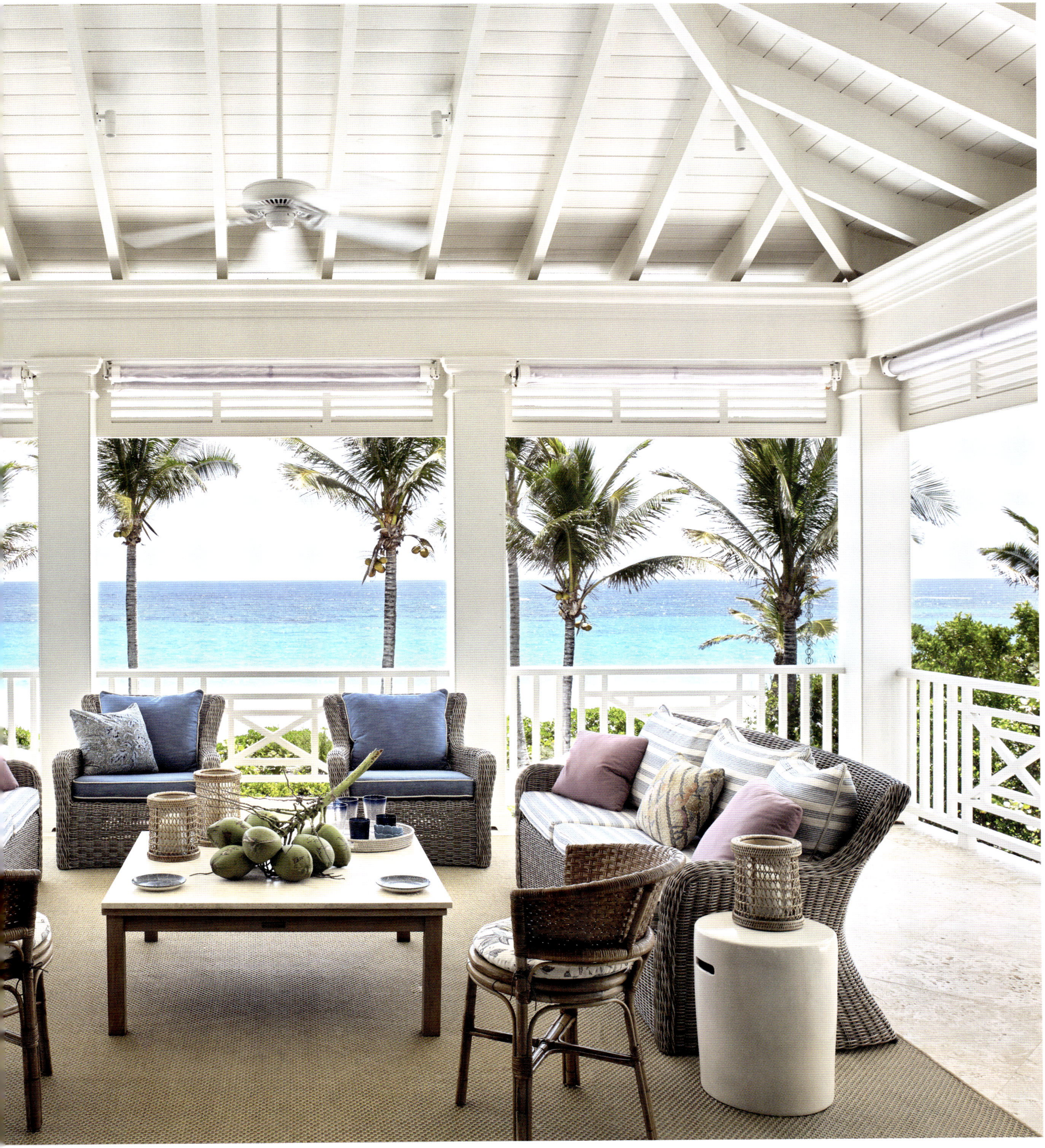

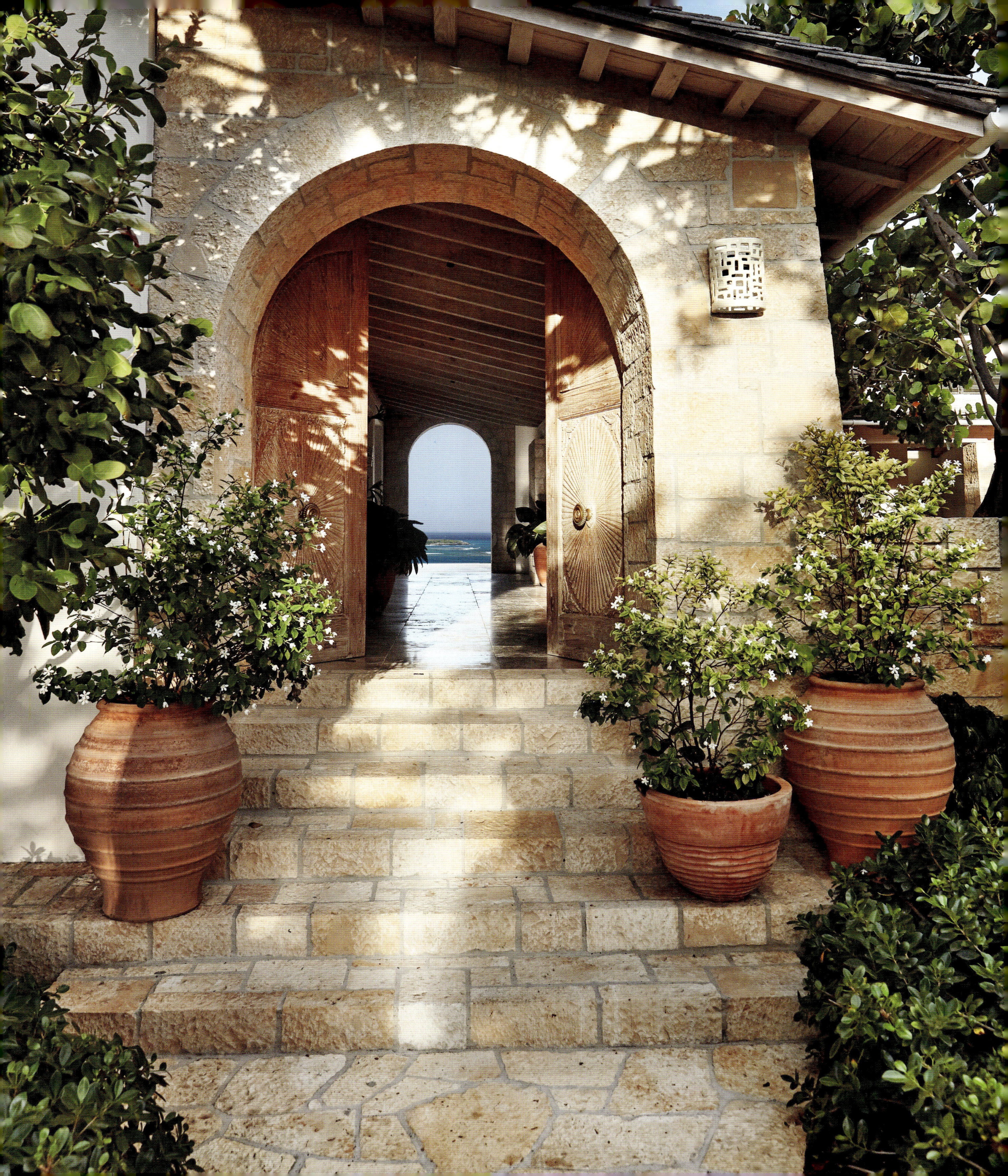

Happy, Alive and Well

ANTIGUA IS MYTHIC TO LOVERS OF THE TROPICS. Topographically it is splendid, with dramatic mountains, a lovely coconut-dotted pastoral heartland, and sugary-white sand beaches. The wild, remote north side of the island remains particularly unspoiled, in large part due to the ongoing custodial efforts of the Mill Reef Club and its forty or so homeowners, who preserve more than 1,500 acres, plus a lushly green and untouched mini-archipelago that forms their view.

The Mill Reef style is known well beyond the club members and their lucky guests. It's been documented in several illustrated books. The principal protagonist of these books is the founder of the club and the father of its style, Robertson "Happy" Ward. His influence as an architect and arbiter of tropical living spread seaward with his work at other much-admired resorts and his many houses on Barbados and in the Bahamas.

At Mill Reef he expressed his inner modernist. Though some of his varied houses were built in charming Colonial style, the best are like the clubhouse itself: bold compositions that interlace architecture and landscape. Echoes of Frank Lloyd Wright's architecture and Roberto Burle Marx's gardens are detectable, but Happy was distinctive and original. Deep and low overhangs, jalousie windows, stone piers that support muscular, arching beams of concrete, and glazed rooms dramatically perched windward and entirely open to the air leeward are his hallmarks.

This new house was conceived some forty years after the last of Happy Ward's, with his dictates still in mind. There are only a few up-to-date touches, and they weren't needed. The house is basic and deliberately short on detail, in the distinctly Ward-ian tropical vernacular, which allows the setting and the elements to take center stage.

Trade winds naturally cool the living spaces, which are mostly outdoors; deep porches and pergolas shade the intense sun. Sheets of glass, which slide into the walls, protect the main living room from the buffeting wind only when required. Yes, the bedrooms have air conditioning, but it's generally frowned upon.

The materials are indigenous wherever possible, as they were by necessity in Ward's day. Full advantage was taken of Antigua's dexterous stonecutters, their precise coral-stone blocks rivaling the Incas'. Ward-worthy mid-century-style breeze-block was cast locally. The encaustic cement wall tile used liberally in baths and kitchen (vaguely retro but in updated colors and patterns) was made in Vietnam—no longer in nearby Cuba, alas.

The sconces, indoors and out, were made in a nearby pottery. They are a rust-proof Mill Reef tradition. The Mondrian-esque pattern gives off twinkling and diffuse "candlelight" at night. An enormous "copper," a potent artifact from Antigua's Colonial rum-producing era, serves as a terminus and focal point in the out-of-the-wind water garden.

The decoration follows suit in its practicality and modernist restraint. The walls are mostly white. The furniture was chosen for durability as well as comfort. The fabrics, with the exception of a few decorative pillows, are all indoor/outdoor and fade-proof against the brilliant sun. The bedrooms were deliberately proportioned for beds to be positioned close to the open jalousies and the view over the precipice.

Wide chaises longues are aligned with the arched breeze-through openings. Daytime lunch tables are set in deep shade, but at dinner they can be placed directly under the sheltering night sky. The spirit of Happy Ward is alive and well.

OPPOSITE The deep stone arches punctuating this house by Merrill, Pastor & Colgan Architects are an homage to the nearby tropical houses of Robertson "Happy" Ward. The entry's massive teak doors were ordered from India. **OVERLEAF** The central view in the living room is through a plate of glass, but the doors flanking it slide into the masonry walls. It's as much about the gentle—and welcome—trade winds as it is about the view.

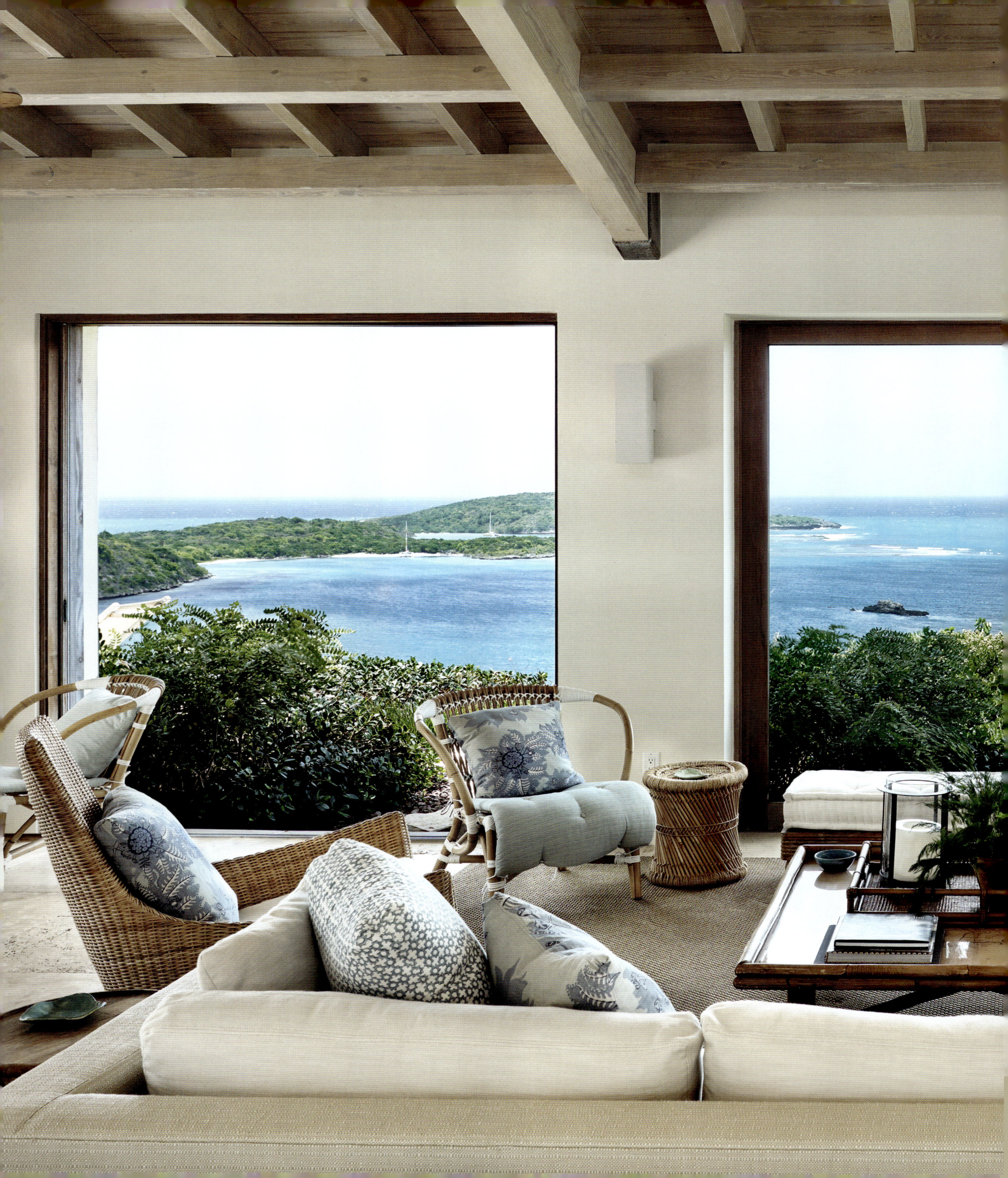

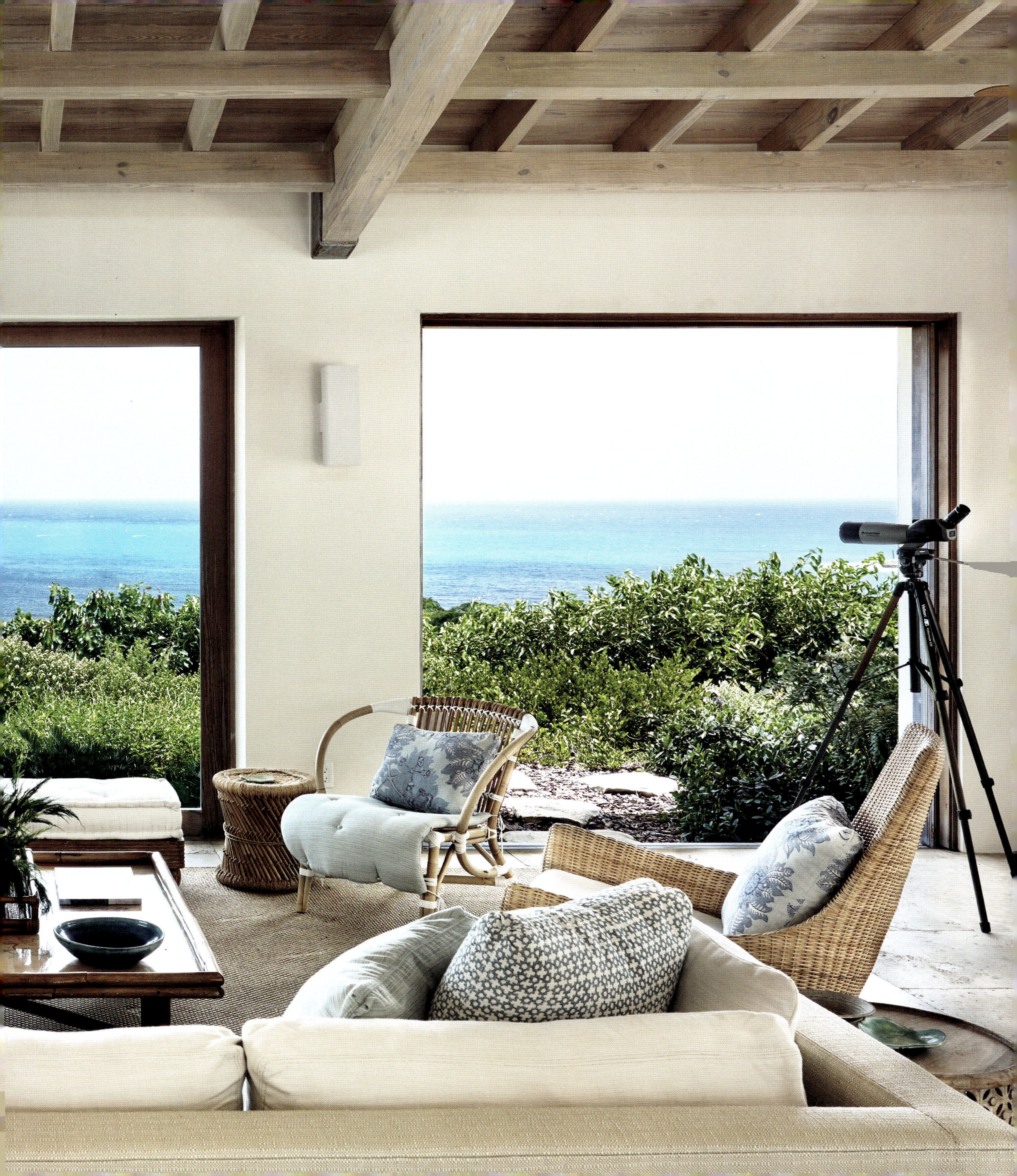

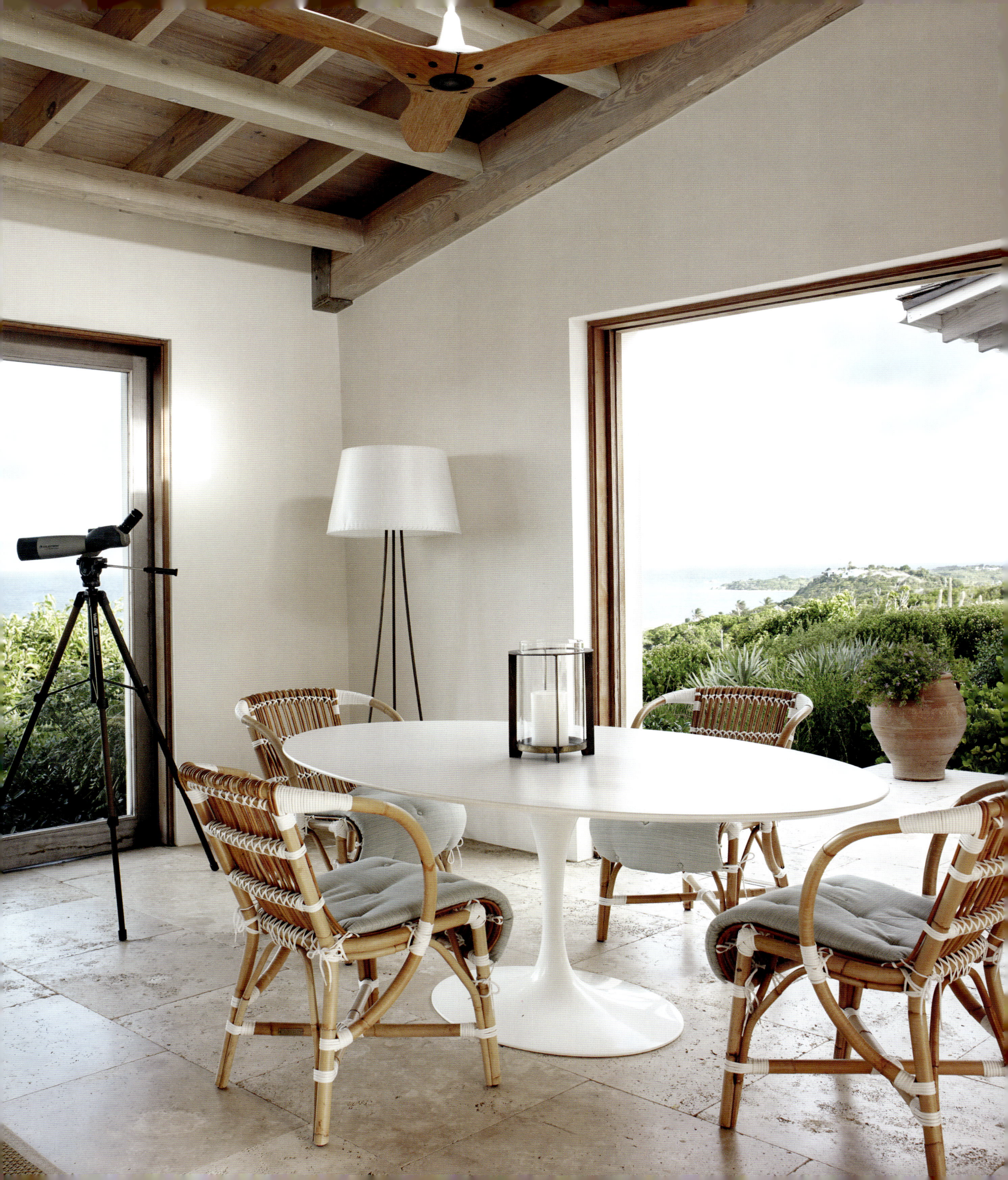

OPPOSITE The familiar Saarinen table is used for games and as an impromptu work surface. The scattered rattan chairs have long-lasting resin bindings and cushions in an outdoor fabric. ABOVE Unlike many Caribbean houses, this one has no need for a central living veranda—the living room serves the purpose. It can be entirely open on all four sides, yet its doors can be modulated as necessary to shield the room from the frequent wind and occasional rain.

ABOVE LEFT A suite of teak-and-resin Isola furniture from Frontgate makes an inviting setting for cocktail hour. **ABOVE RIGHT** An axis running through the house and garden originates at this tile-lined niche and water source. **BELOW** A "walk-up" bar at home is a Mill Reef tradition. At drinks time, the deep green Moroccan tile and mahogany woodwork beckon the thirsty.

ABOVE The dining table is set under a deep overhang on the leeward side of the living room. A sudden heavy rain can make for a dramatic but completely dry dinner party. **OVERLEAF** The water garden was designed by Cecilia de Grelle. At the end of the axis is the extraordinarily large "copper," formerly used to boil down cane juice for distillation into Antiguan rum. Water now spills from it and runs to the square well in the center of the garden. The table is one of five placed around the house for a variety of views at mealtime.

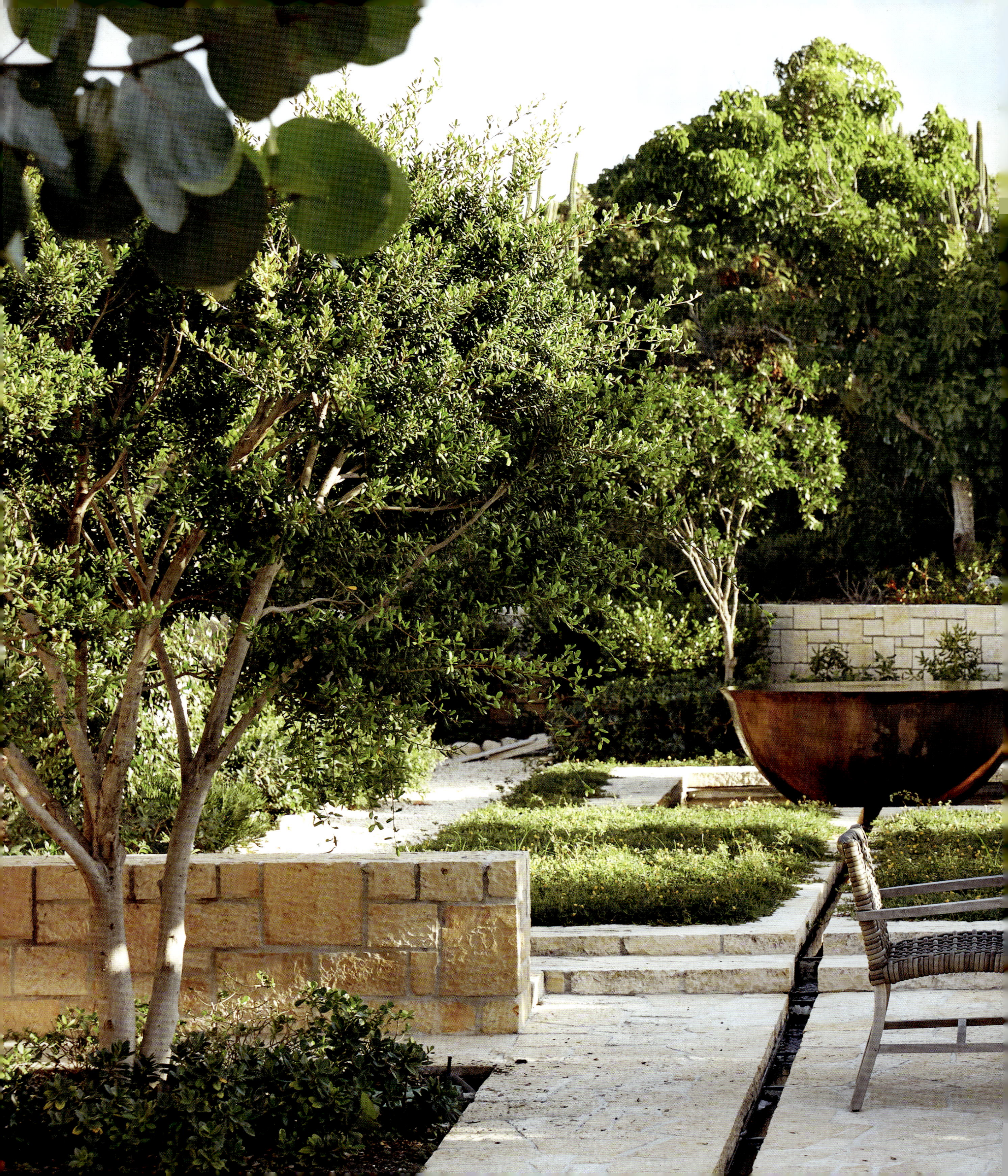

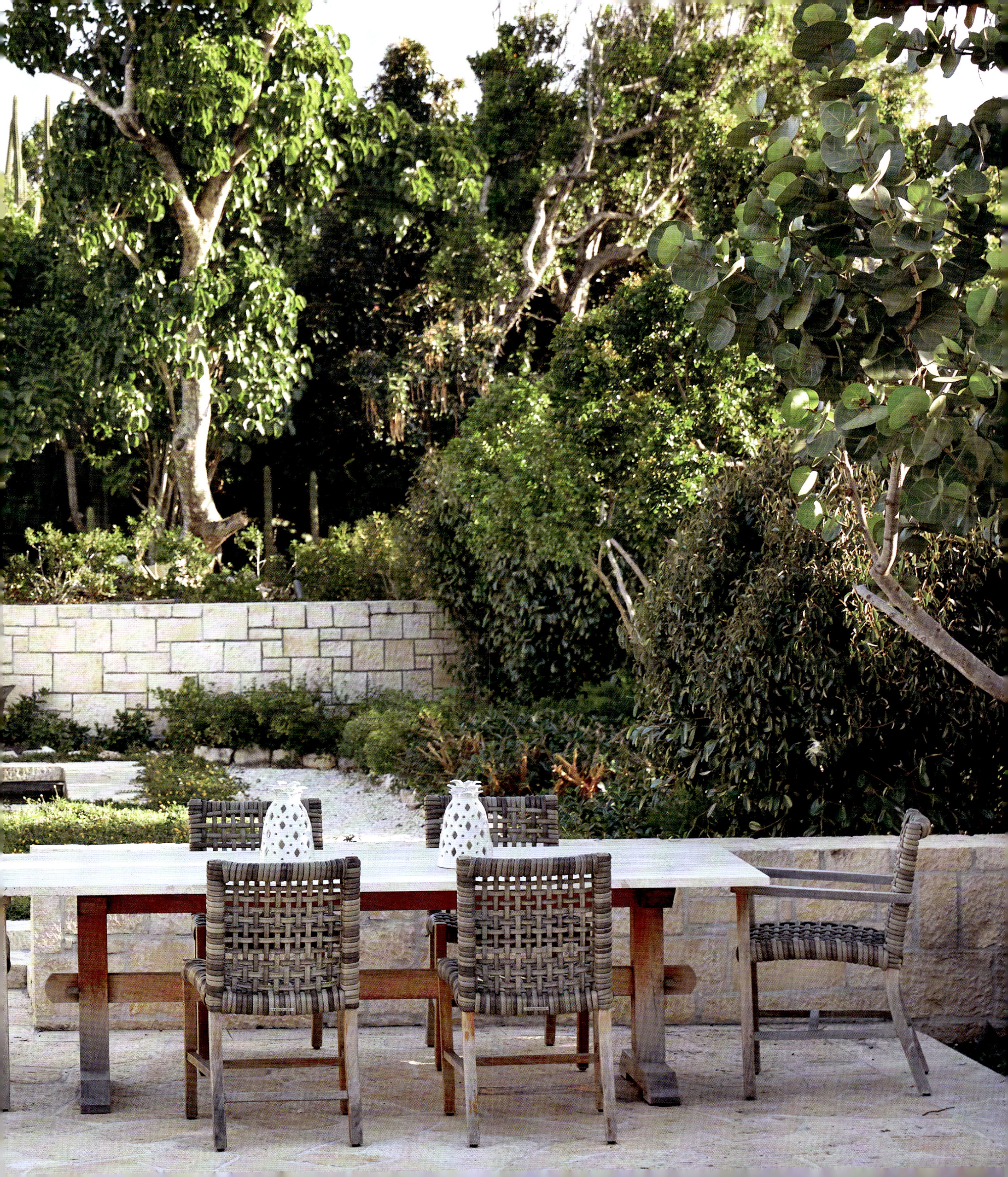

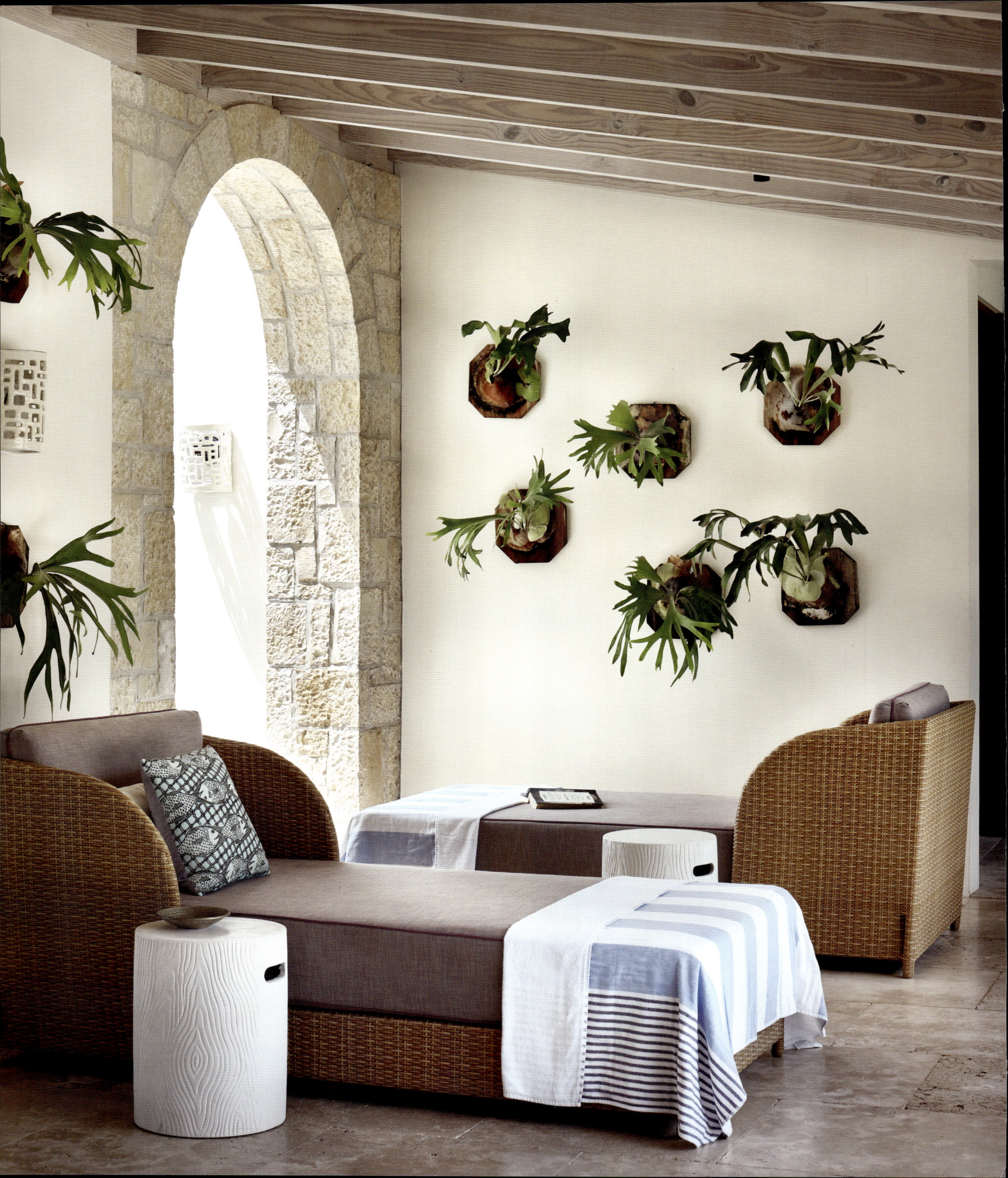

OPPOSITE Wide chaises longues by Walters Wicker are arranged in a spa-like tête-à-tête. Well above the salt spray, staghorn ferns thrive in the shade. The rustproof ceramic sconces, here and throughout the house, are a Mill Reef tradition. **ABOVE** Cuban tile in a large-scale pattern lines the walls and the underside of the Caesarstone kitchen island. The tiles have a retro feel in sync with Happy Ward's precepts.

ABOVE Privacy is not an issue from this bedroom's high perch, but wooden louvers can be slid across the windows to shield the room from the direct morning sun. **OPPOSITE TOP LEFT AND RIGHT** In the master bedroom, the bed frame and headboard are dressed in Bramalta's suitably tropical Palampore print. A cypress-clad dressing unit that doubles as a freestanding wall behind the bed screens the bathroom. Cuban tiles in different patterns and colors line the walls in every bathroom. **OPPOSITE BOTTOM LEFT AND RIGHT** In a tidy twin bedroom, the cross breeze competes with the mirrored view of the blithesome Indian cutwork that hangs behind the beds. The vanity floats off the floor, giving the arrangement an optimally airy and spacious feeling.

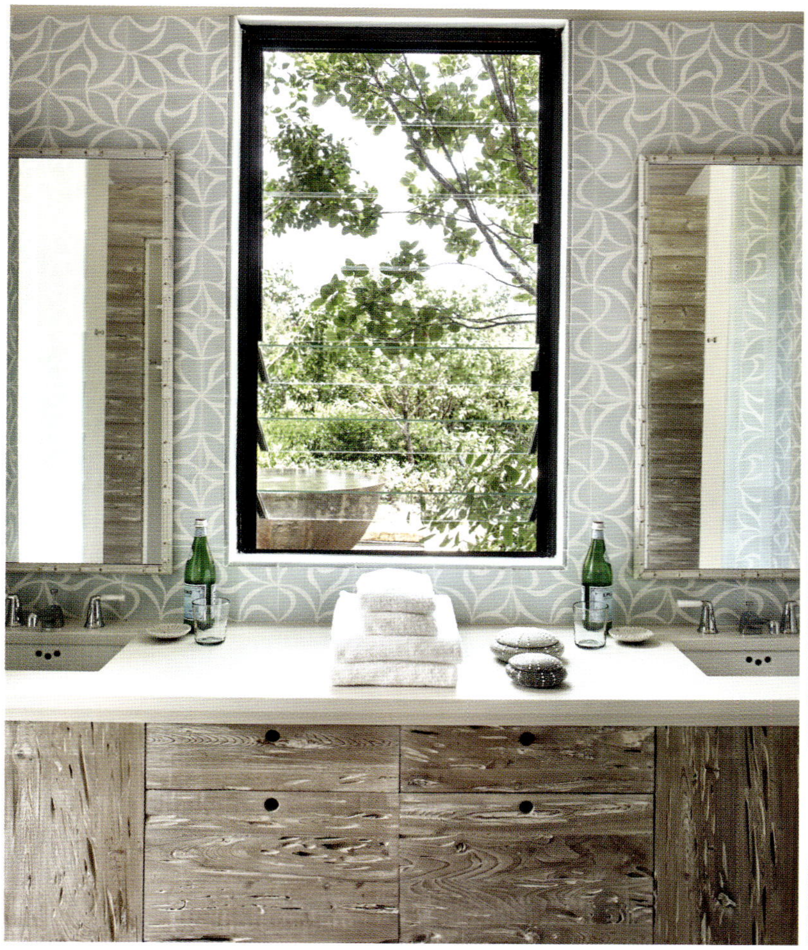
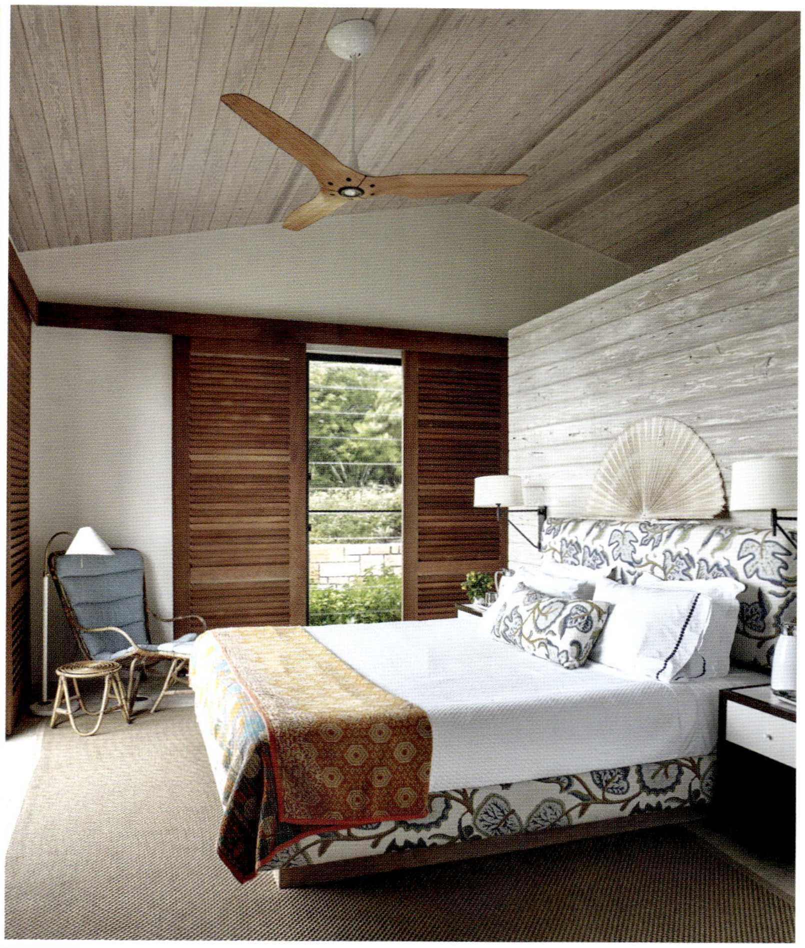
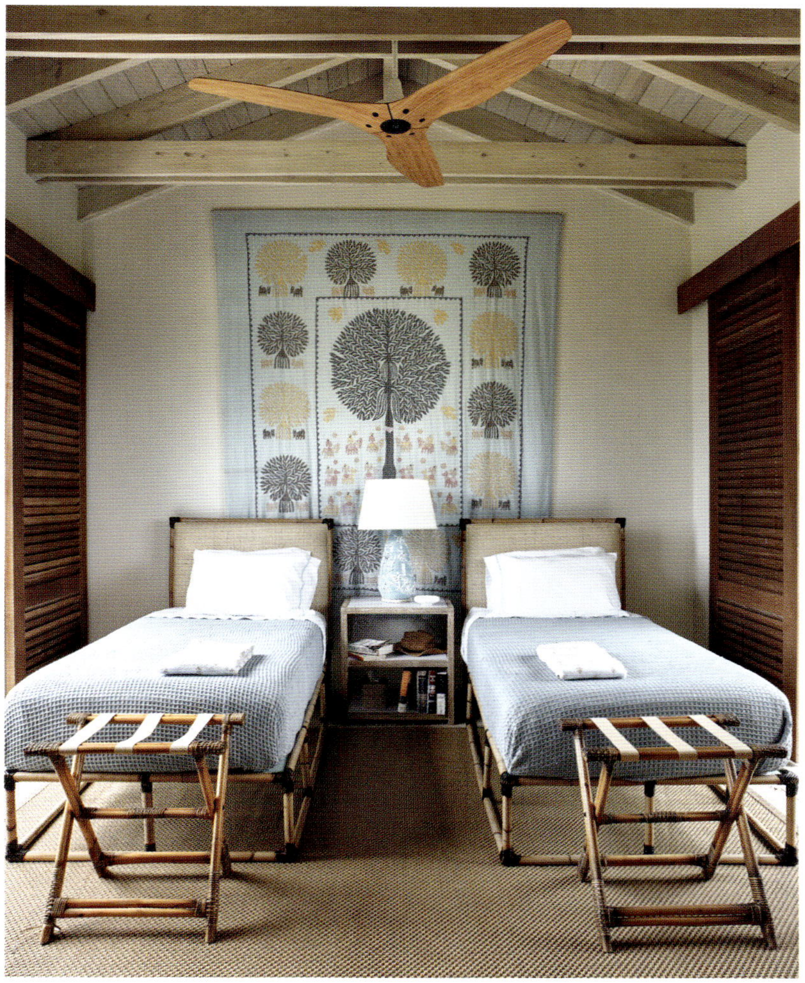
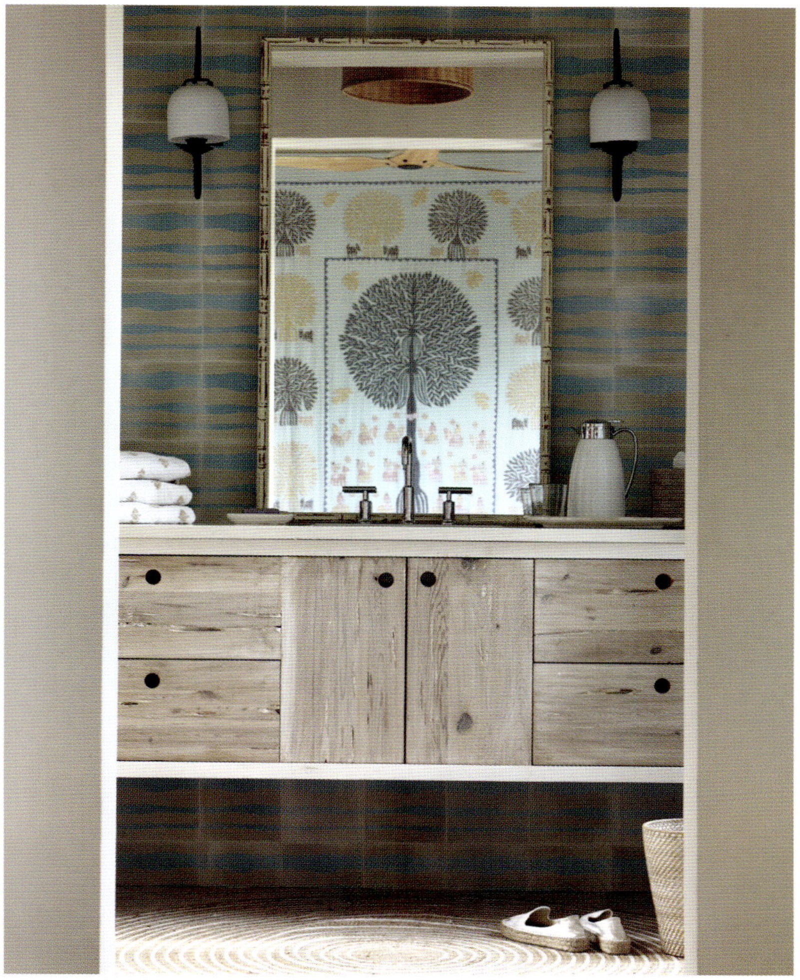

ABOVE Matisse cutouts were appropriated to enliven the walls of two outdoor sitting areas. The artist, Frank Reijnen, hesitated, but ultimately took direction from the decorator. Several loggias and the pergola-shaded terrace above the pool are furnished with teak furniture, which weathers to driftwood gray without any maintenance.

ABOVE It's a steep walk to the beach, so the infinity pool is a frequent and refreshing interlude. Its design is a sensational and sensory feat, reflecting the sky and blending into the sea precisely as intended. **BELOW** A fragment of a 1940s fabric by Folly Cove Designers was used for pillows to complement the vintage batik ones. The chairs are from the Frontgate catalogue, but the corner sofa and outdoor tables were custom made by BenchSmith.

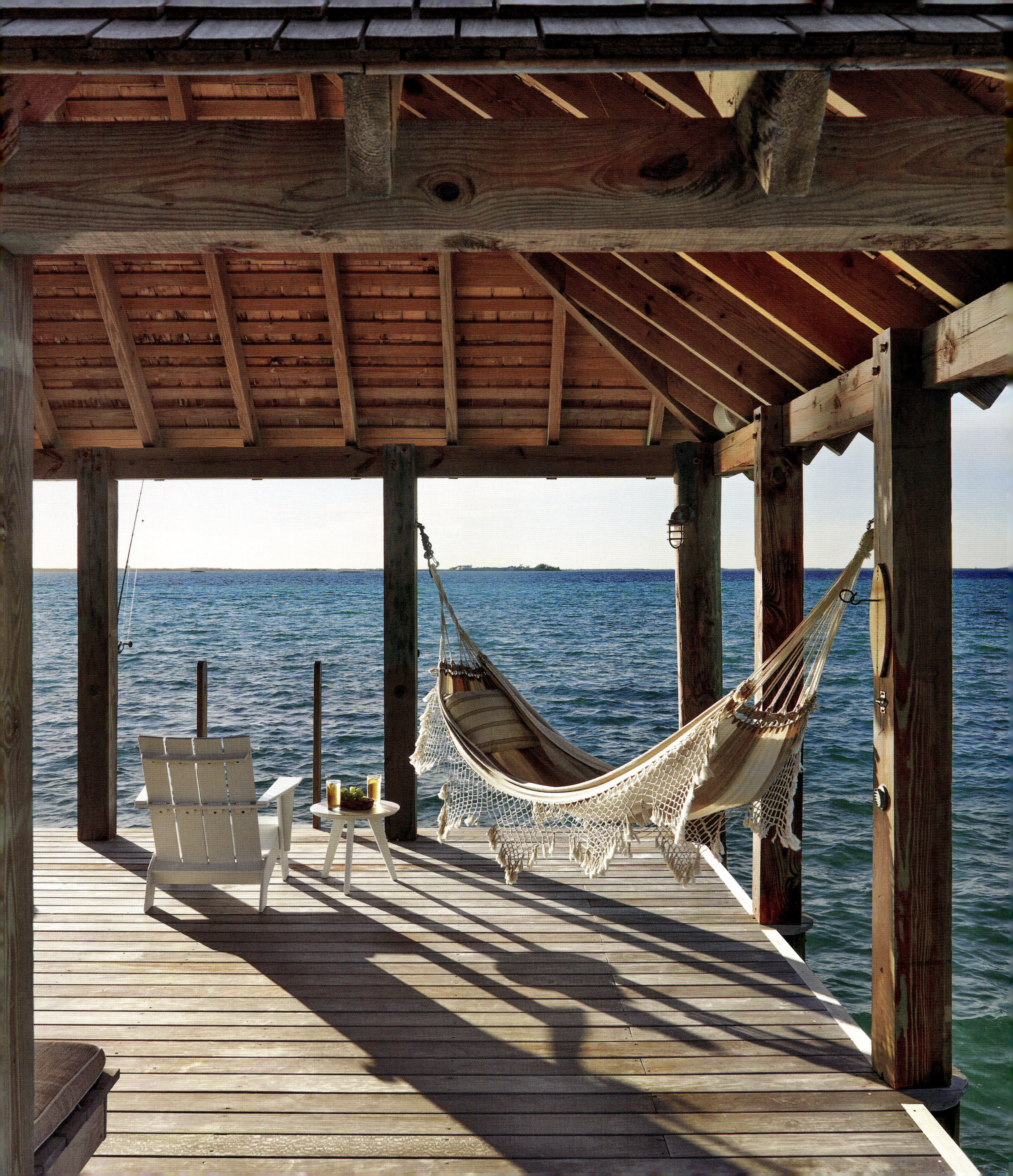

Sunrise and Sunset

At the secluded and narrow end of a tiny barrier island in the tropics is a "compound" imagined and recently built amid an ocean dune, an ancient undulating palm grove, and a rough swath of indigenous "bush" stretching a few hundred yards to a coral-stone escarpment that overlooks a broad, sheltered bay. A large and growing family now comes here for holidays. There are already eight family bedrooms, an additional two for guests, and acreage for more when the time comes.

It was a task of Fitzcarraldo-like complexity. The family, the architect, and the decorator had all worked in this remote and primitive environment before and were well aware of the pitfalls and challenges but managed to keep the faith through a four-year collaboration. And for the decorator, at least, it was a project of a lifetime.

Not one but two complete houses—one facing the ocean and sunrise, the other facing the bay and sunset—are supported by a complex of buildings that are out of sight (and mind). Surrounded by a dense and deliberately planted jungle, this complex includes garages, boat storage, vegetable gardens and fruit trees, staff quarters, and electricity-generating equipment—enough to service a medium-sized village.

Yet there is a gentleness and informality to these houses. They may be large and relatively elaborate, but rather than proclaiming extravagance and luxury, they downplay it. The great size of the ocean-facing house is optically reduced by its H shape and its many individual roofs. It appears to recede into the landscape. The graying cedar shingles, rough stone details, and muted coloring of the shutters were carefully chosen to whisper, not shout.

The approach to the house, a wending drive beneath the canopy of palms, is devoid of pomp and circumstance. One arrives at a winsome portico belying the grandeur within. This self-effacing entrance offers two natural, undisturbed views—the ocean and the palm grove. The Cape Dutch overdoor is decidedly referential and a foretaste of what will be found inside. It's all perfectly appropriate for this family with deep and widespread roots in South Africa.

The bayside house, also H shaped, is approached by another winding road. This one terminates in an informal, coral-paved car park shaded by three irregularly placed, enormous banyan trees. They were barged from Florida, were replanted (a further act of faith), and shot out new branches almost immediately.

The view from here is headlong—the elegant and symmetrical structure makes a casement-windowed picture frame for the brilliantly turquoise bay. The radiating wings, containing several bedrooms and baths, are screened by thick landscaping so that the charming central pleasure pavilion appears to stand alone.

It's as relaxed as can be, perhaps even more than the ocean-side "big house." Here, too, the materials and furnishings were chosen for maximum ease and comfort, and especially for bathing-suited conviviality.

In addition to many seating areas designed to encourage conversation, there are several places allotted for retreat and solitude. One is a spot at the end of the dock, where a hammock is strung between the pilings. In the late afternoon, this is the place to be.

OPPOSITE Day's end in the Bahamas. The dock house makes an intimate spot for reflection and a sundown rum cocktail. The languor-inducing hammock is crocheted. It's a traditional form from far-off Brazil.

ABOVE An artfully planted palm grove shades the lawn while permitting a full view of the ocean from the "big house," the size of which is deceptive from the beach. The small roofs and shaded recesses belie the large mass that looms beyond. Both this house and the bayside house were designed by de la Guardia Architects & Urbanists.

ABOVE RIGHT AND RIGHT The picturesque portico is made from coral stone in Cape Dutch style, a reference to the family's origins and enduring interests in South Africa.

ABOVE The entrance hall's barrel-vaulted ceiling and walls are lined in tropical-appropriate pecky cypress. The rustic, striped jute-and-cotton rug makes a beachy welcome mat. The Anglo-Indian settee is fitted with an antique-style cushion covered in rough, hand-woven jute. The mirror is one of several made for the house by Bamboo & Rattan. OPPOSITE Rare antique maps of Africa and the family's accruing collection of artifacts are arranged above and on a pair of rattan-trimmed console tables made for the entrance hall. OVERLEAF The veranda is comfortably furnished with resin wicker from Casa Mobel, as well as various pieces from Janus et Cie's Lazy Lucy collection.

CARTE REDUITE
D'UNE PARTIE DES COSTES
OCCIDENTALES ET MERIDIONALES
DE L'AFRIQUE

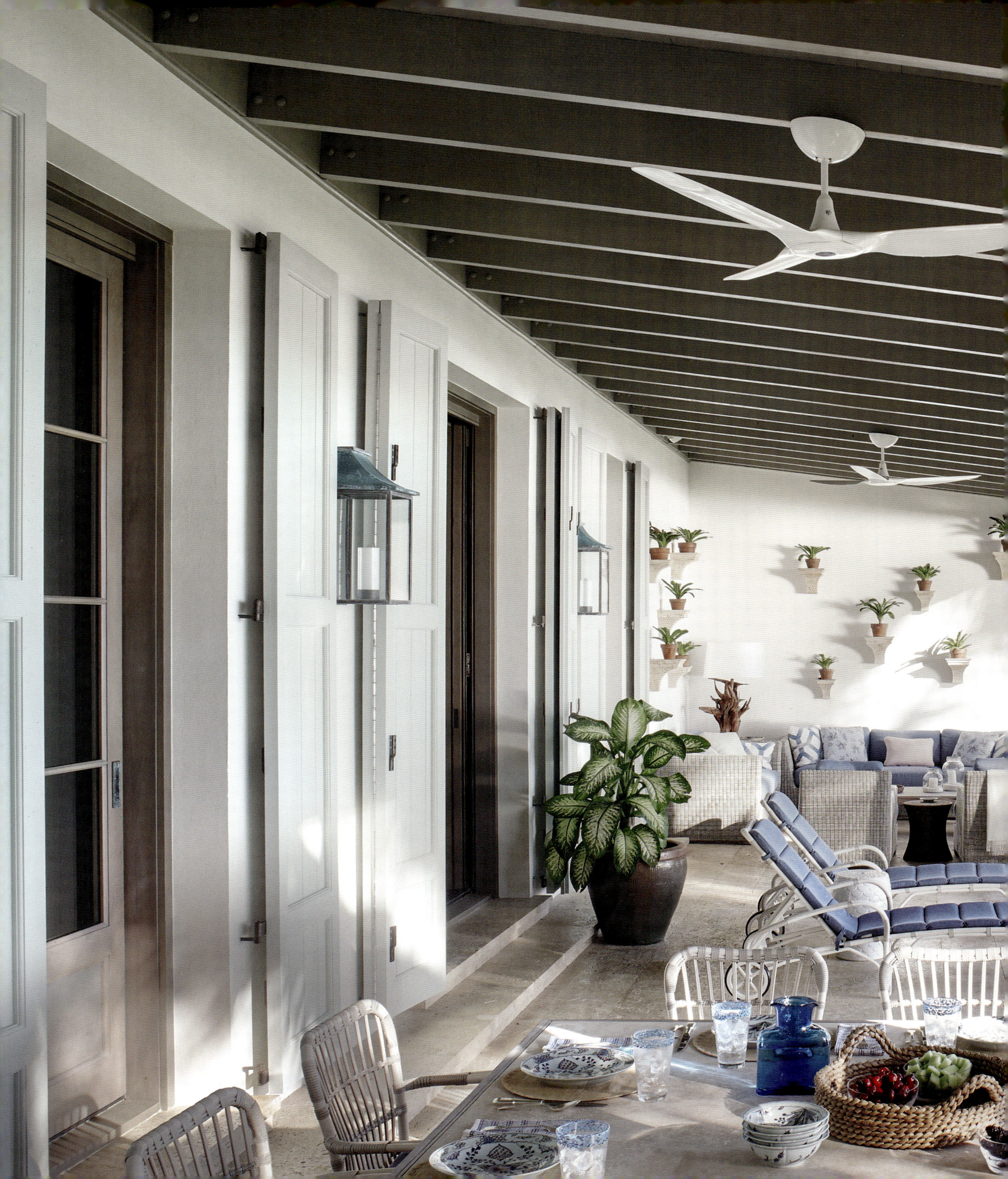

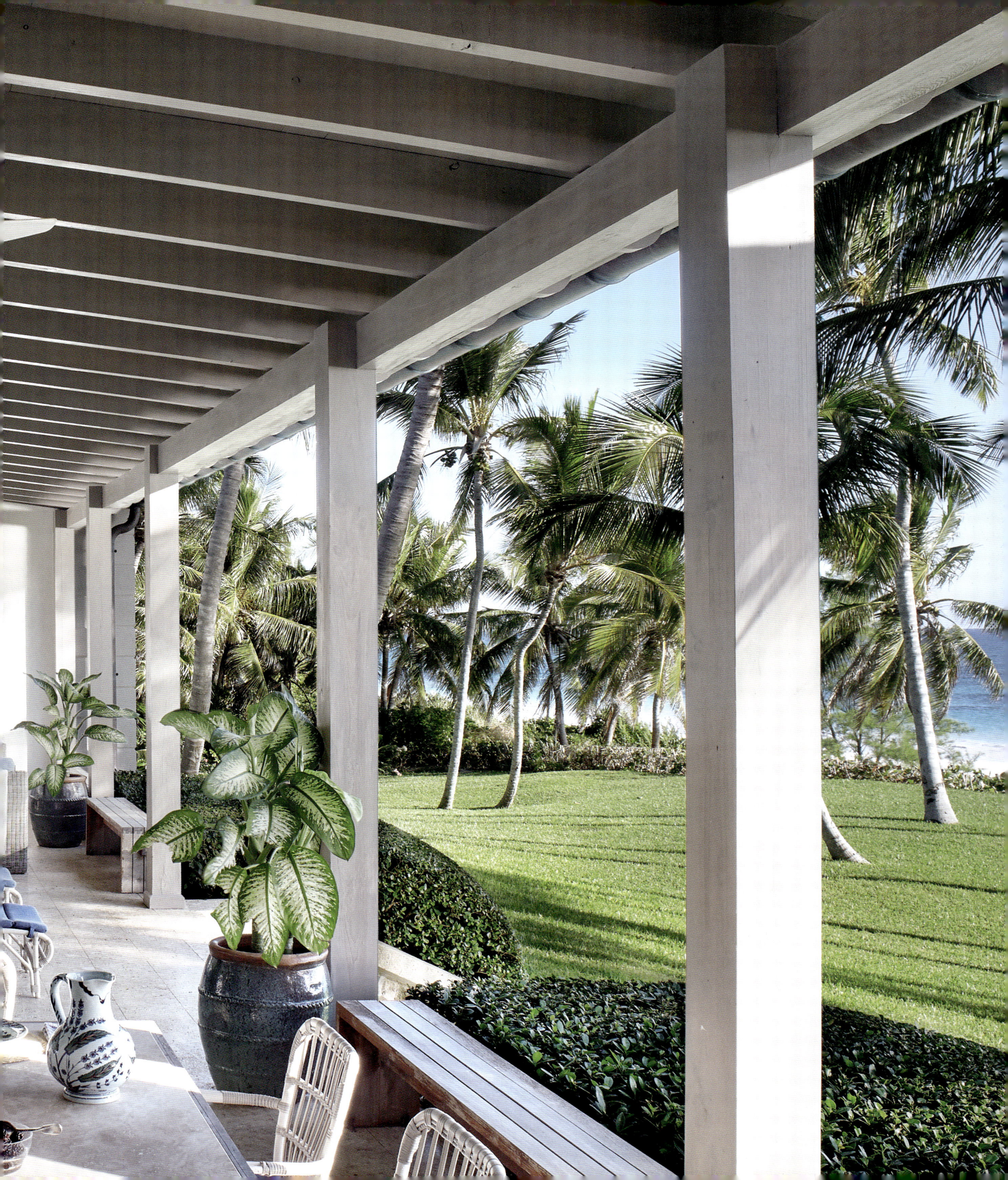

ABOVE The Indian-made mahogany "cabinet of curiosities" is lined with pages torn from the decorator's reproduction copy of Albertus Seba's *Cabinet of Natural Curiosities*. Referential scientific, anthropological, and decorative objects were arranged and now suggest ongoing additions by the family. OPPOSITE The principal room opens to the veranda, to a large courtyard, and to corridors and rooms at all four corners. It's the busy and accommodating social nexus of the house. OVERLEAF Deep back-to-back sofas face the fireplace and the dining area, respectively. They are slipcovered in Perennials' Linen. There's also a relaxed mix of modern rattan, cane-backed antiques, and exotic accessories. A familiar and "easy-for-the-beach" blue-and-white color scheme is accented by bits of orangy-pink coral.

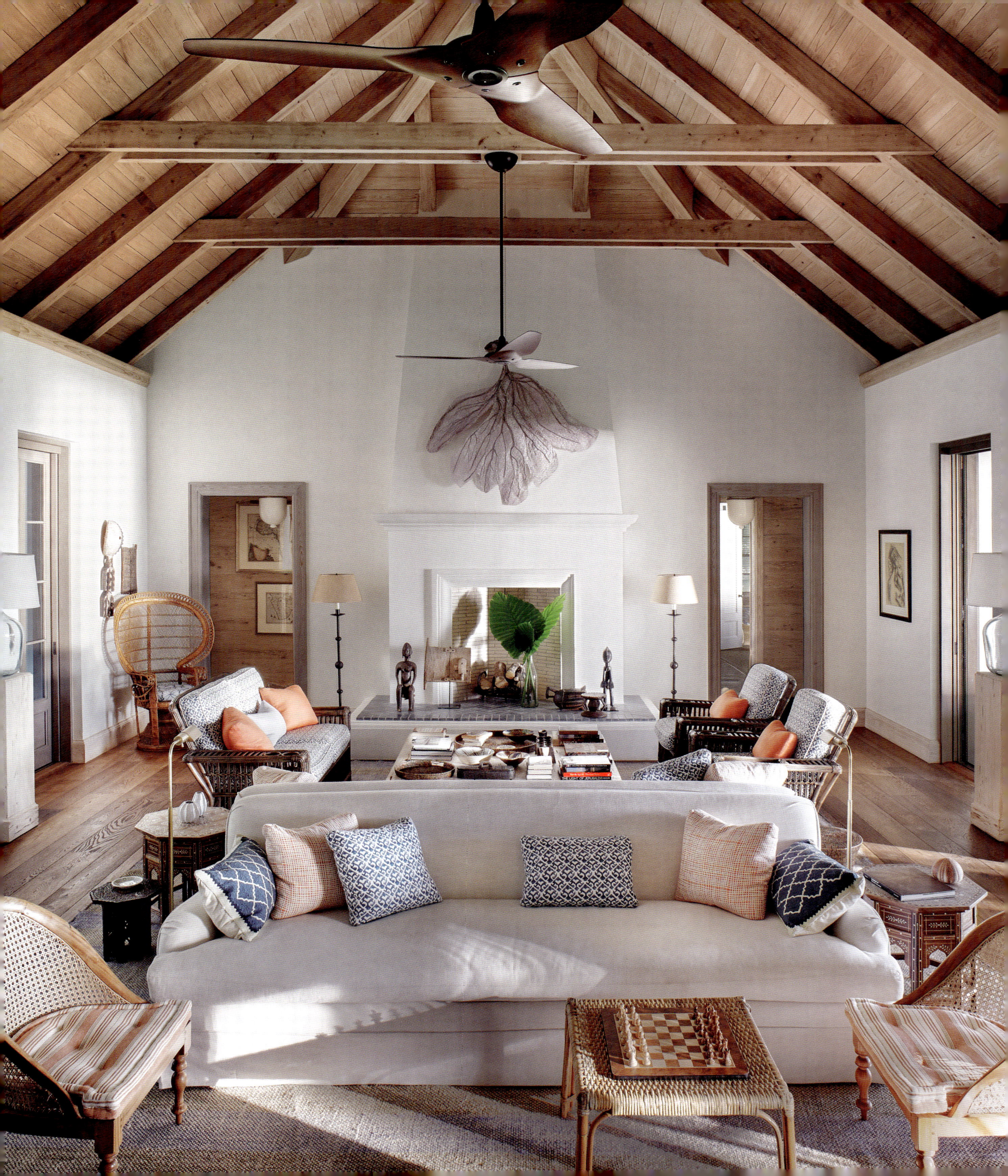

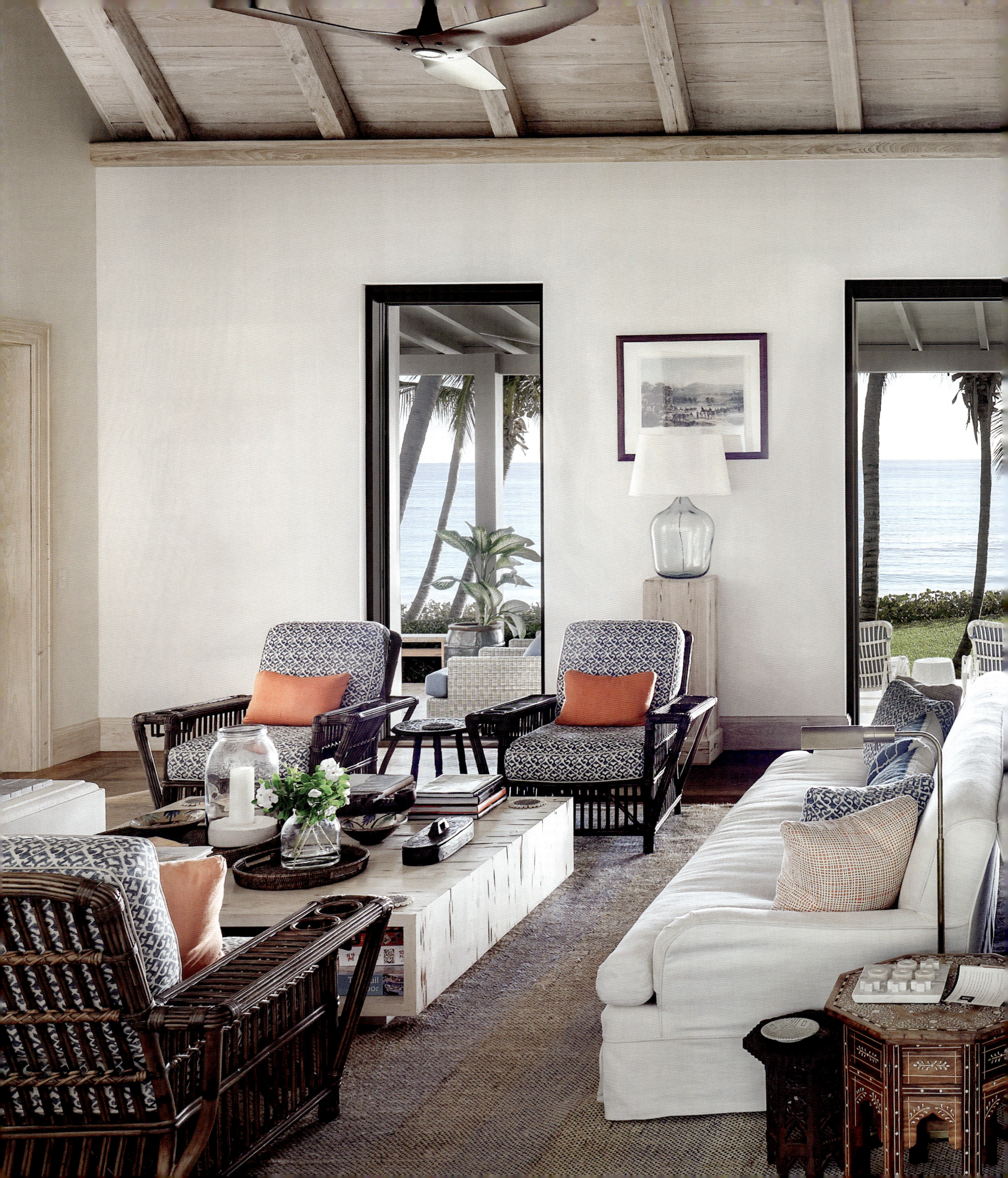

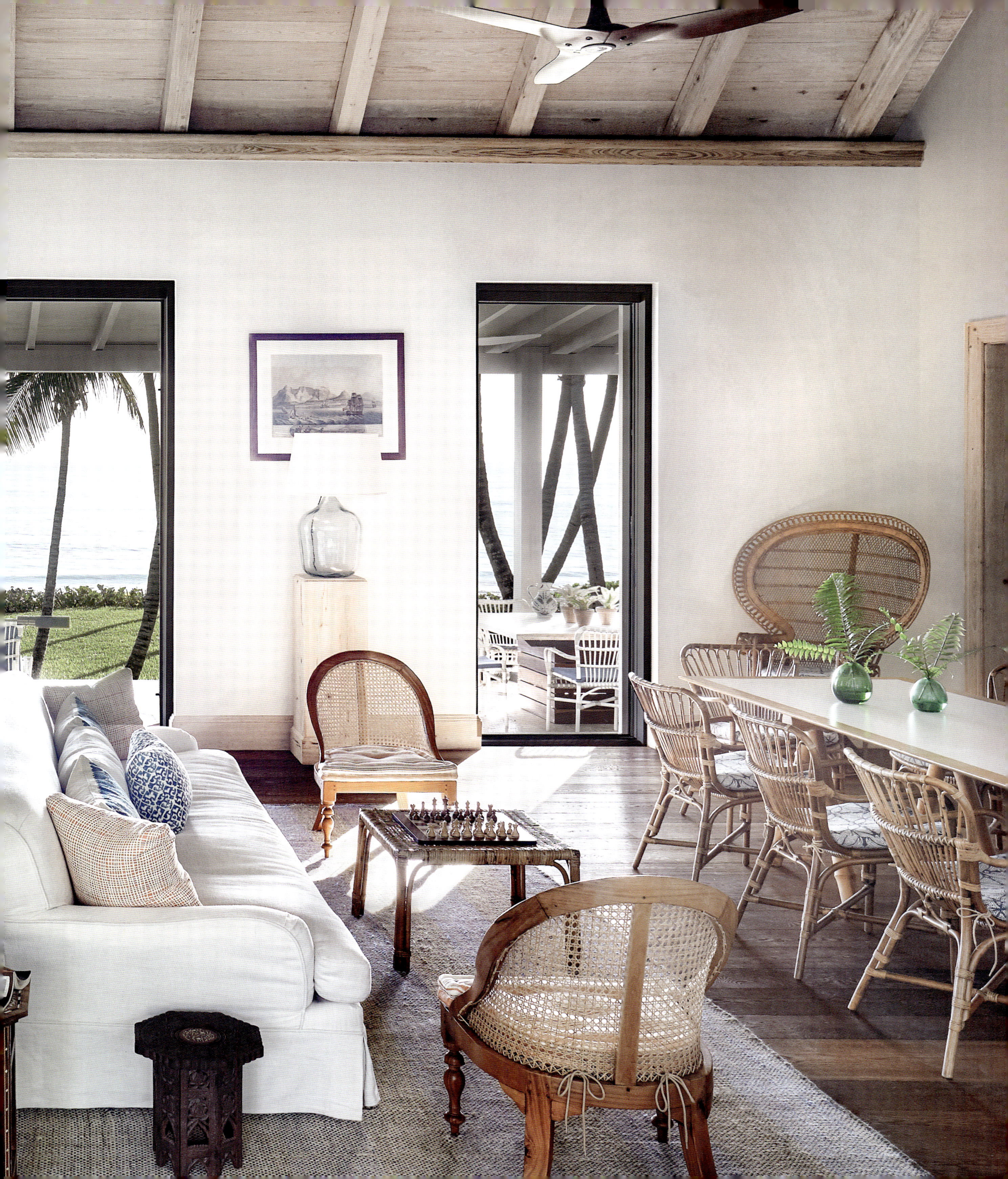

ABOVE The jaunty pattern of blue, brown, and white Cuban tiles "papering" the walls in the kitchen reprises the color scheme of adjacent living areas. The steel range hood, painted white to match the woodwork, quiets the visual "noise." Lazy Lucy outdoor dining chairs are equally at home at the veranda and kitchen tables. They are moved back and forth, depending on the crowd. **OPPOSITE** The enormous, low-silled window slides entirely into the wall and creates an arresting picture frame for the palm-dotted view of the ocean.

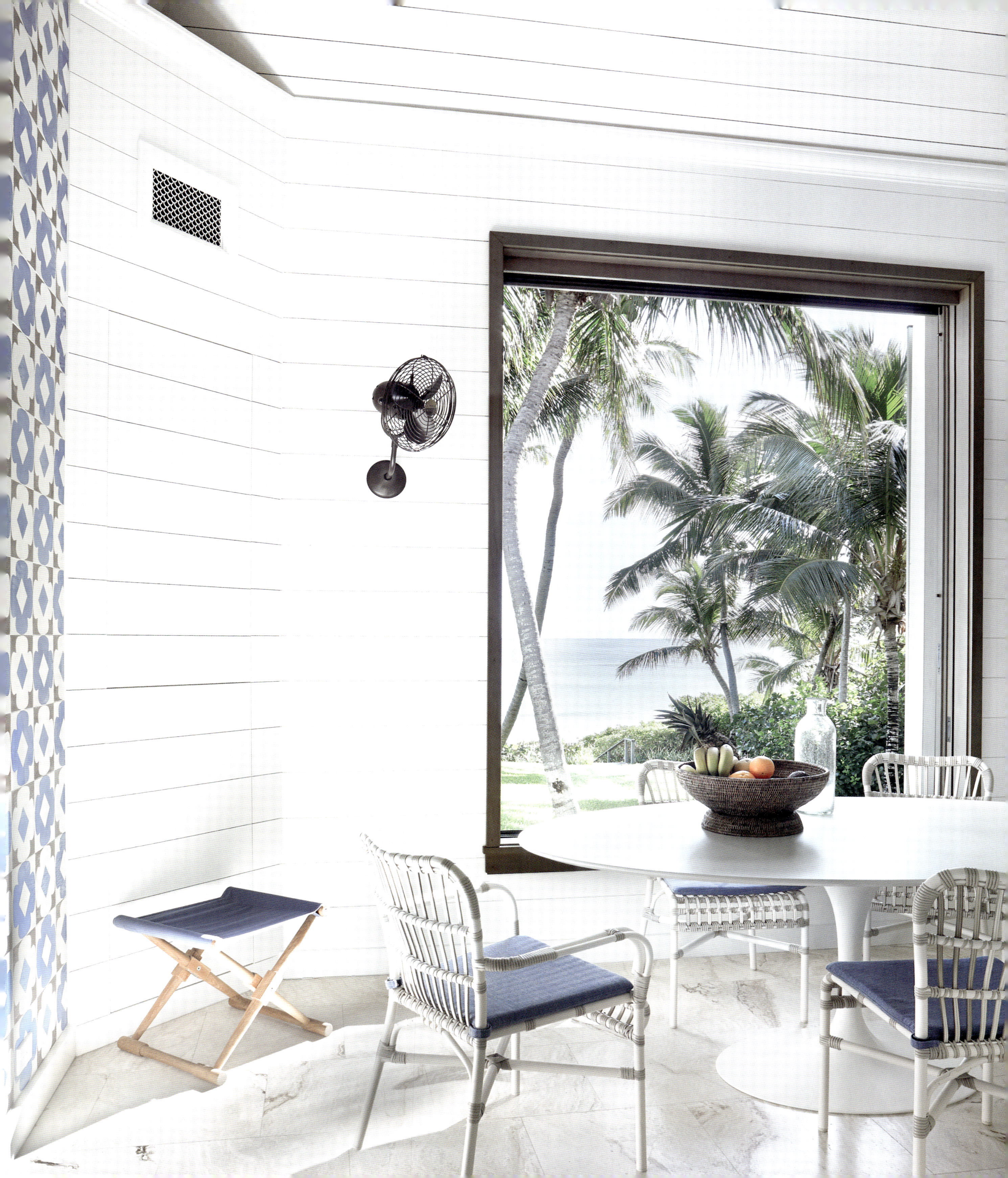

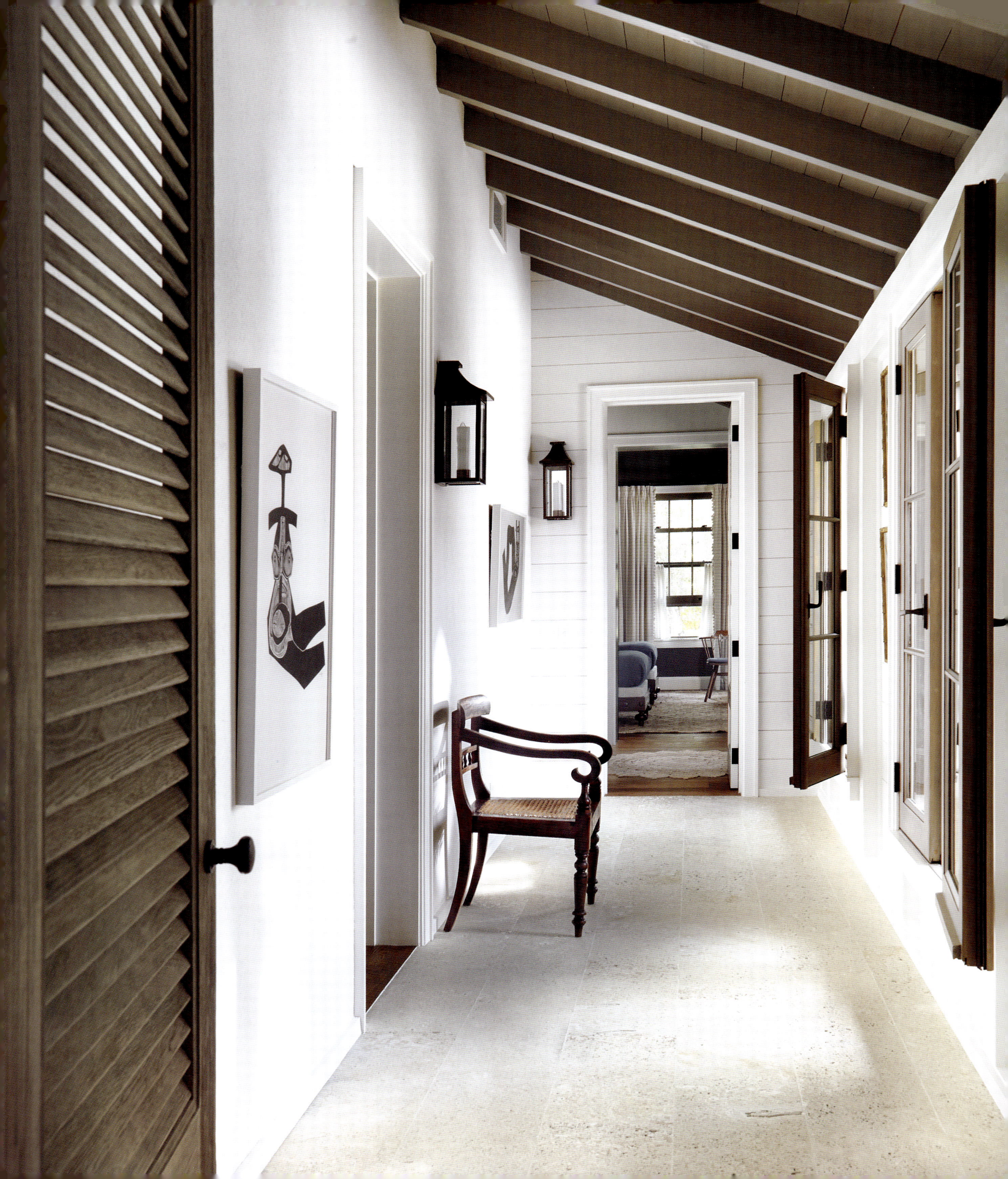

OPPOSITE The courtyard is bracketed by bedroom halls, which are designed to resemble enclosed verandas. They terminate in hip-roofed one-room pavilions. ABOVE The salient feature of the boys' room is an embroidered reproduction of a 1789 map of Africa made in India by Ranjana Khan Home. The actual map appears over the bar next to the living room. The bedside table marries two vintage rattan night tables with a mahogany base and a tray made by the Raj Company. They can be separated if the beds need to be pushed together. OVERLEAF Another embroidered hanging from Ranjana Khan Home hangs in the master bedroom behind the pickled-teak and cane bed. A fussy dust skirt was eschewed here and wherever else possible. The facing chairs from Bielecky may have the most advantageous spot in the house. The clients joke that this is where they have their *House of Cards* moments.

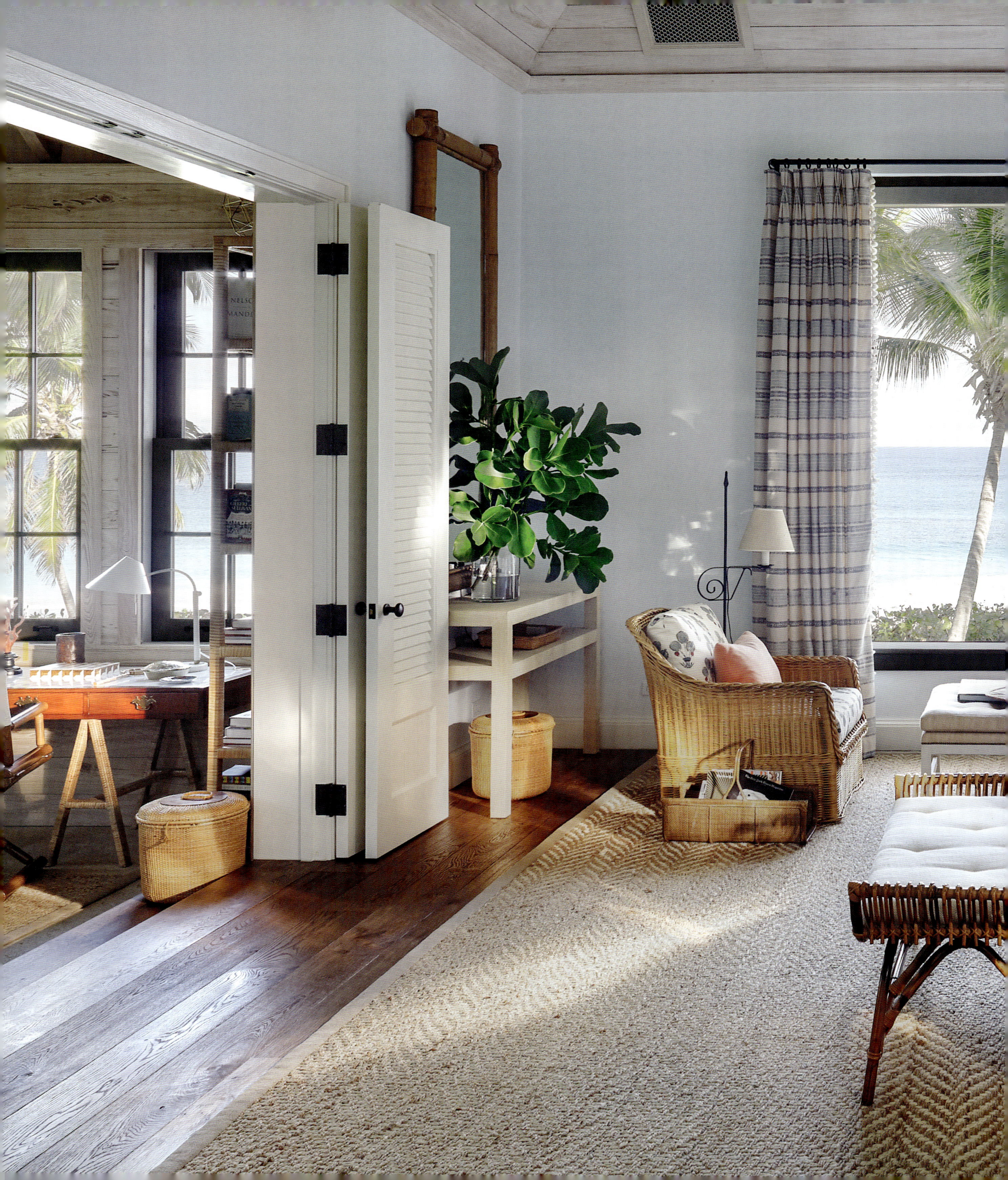

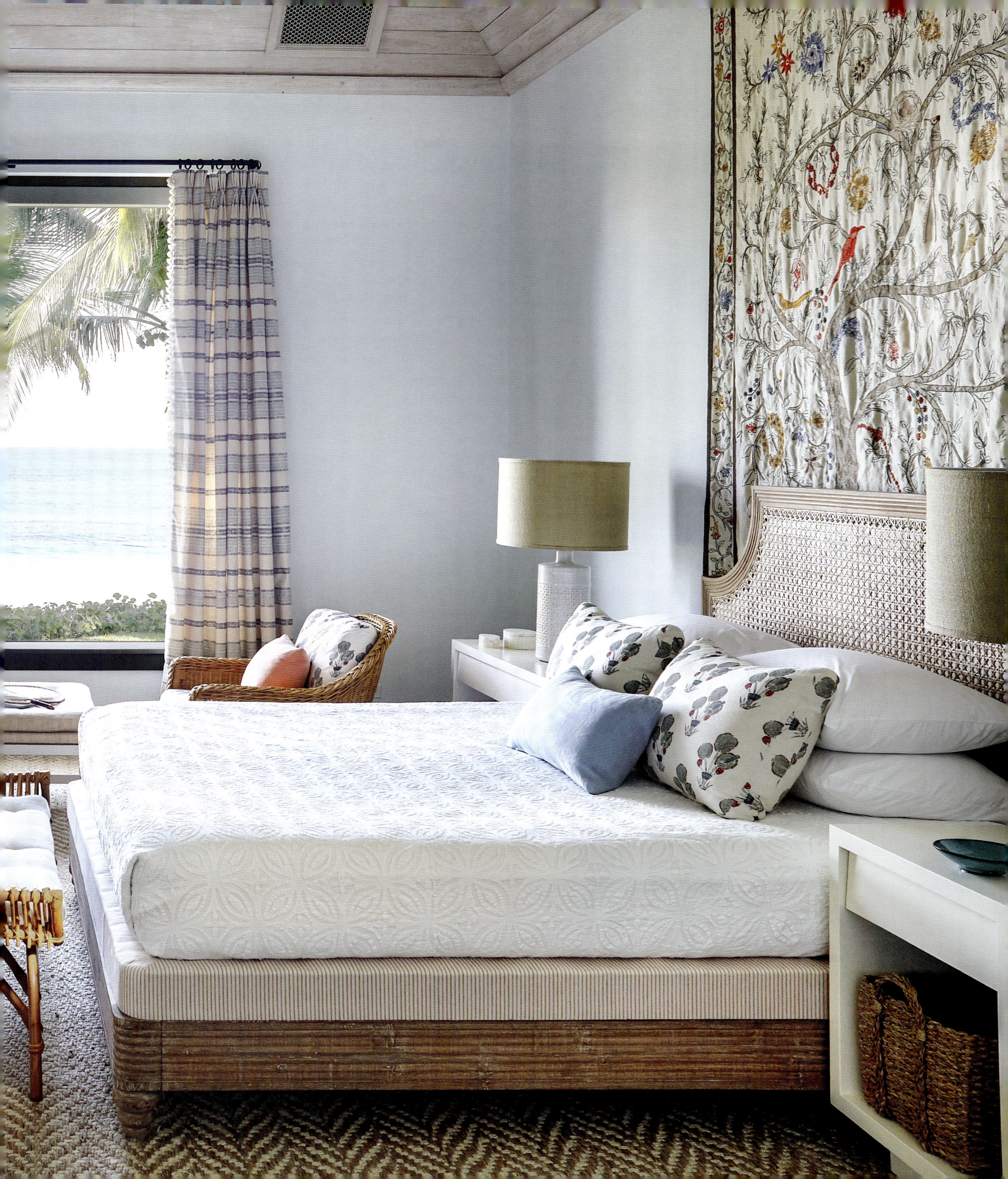

ABOVE The cypress-lined study has the air of a captain's bridge. It features a 270-degree view of the garden. The ocean lies "dead ahead" from the extra-long campaign-style desk, which was made for the room. **OPPOSITE** The comfort of various tub shapes was debated, but in the end we went with Waterworks' Candide model for its sublime silhouette against the protective and decorative panel of Cuban tile.

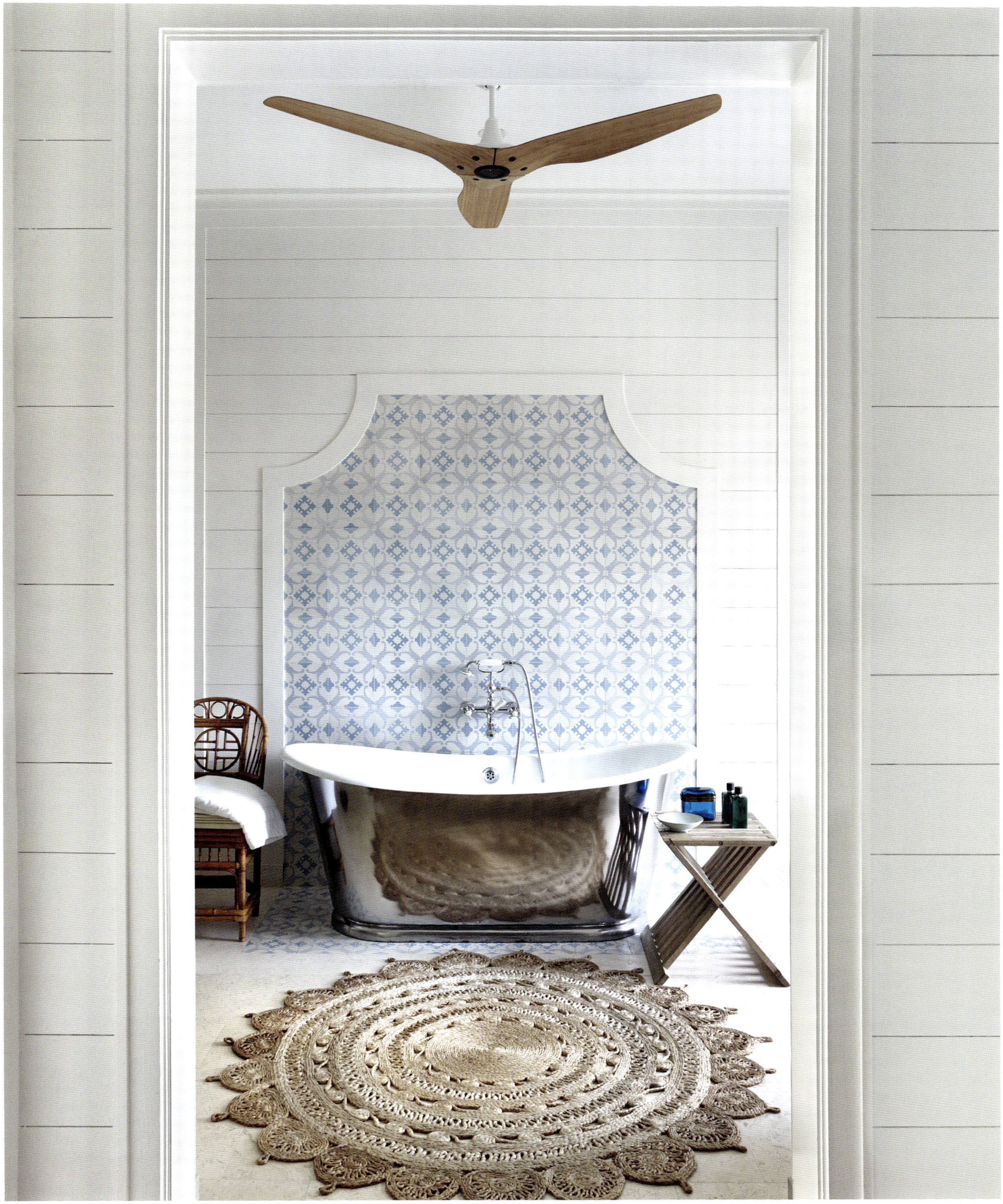

ABOVE LEFT An anachronistic but useful boudoir is adjacent to the master bedroom. It's decorated with a set of antique fan frames, most likely from Indochina. The intricate silhouettes tell entire Kara Walker–like stories. **ABOVE RIGHT** The baths were all "color coded" with unique tonal combinations in the same patterned tile. **BELOW AND OPPOSITE** Another wing contains a feminine suite of rooms for the girls in the family. The twin beds were painted white and, in a divergence from the Indian theme, the mirrors are Mexican tinwork studded with turquoise stones.

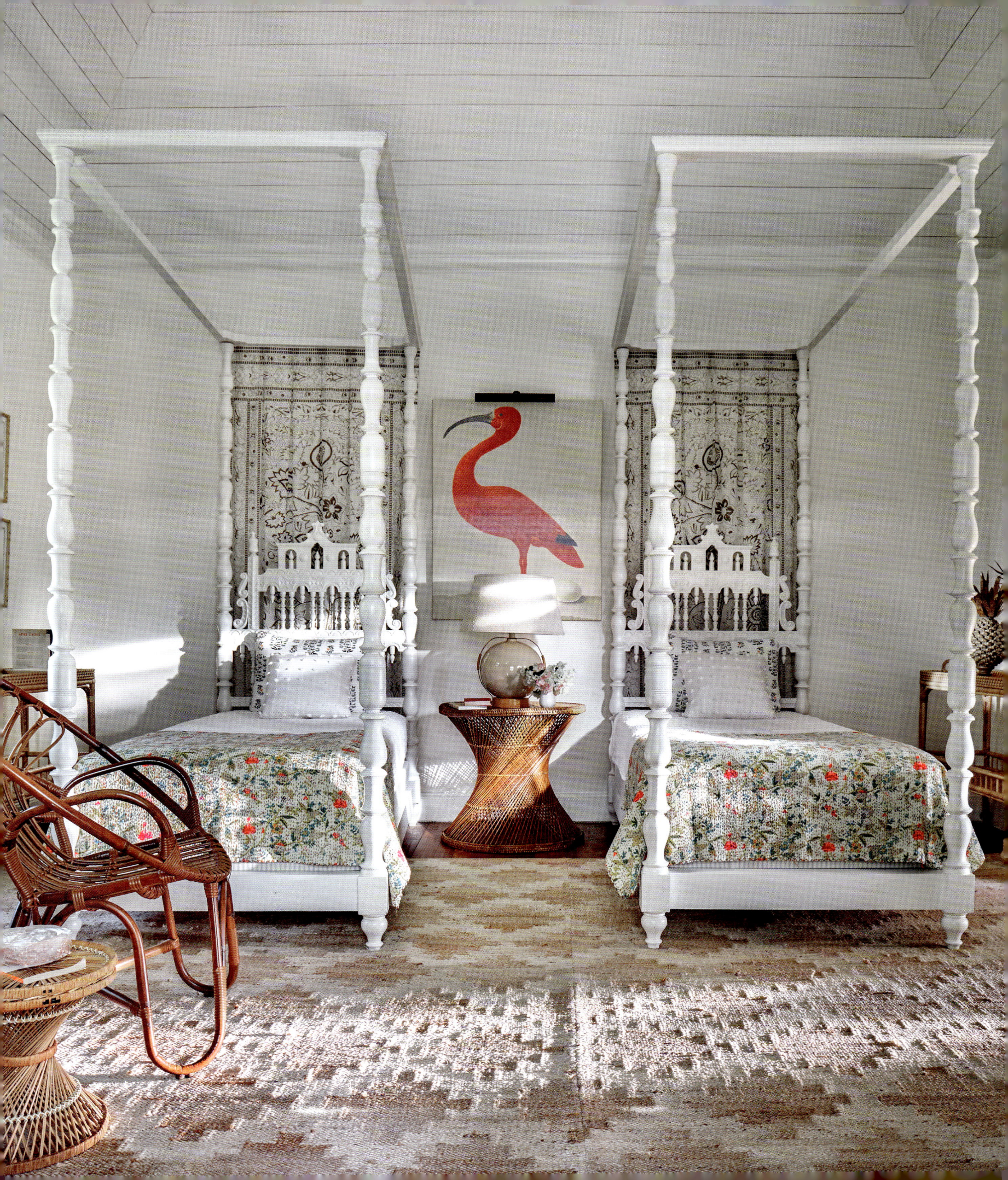

ABOVE The "little house" facing the bay at the western end of the property serves as a guesthouse. A swimming pool and a dock populated with boats for fishing and other watersports compete with the lovely prospect of *dolce far niente*. **OPPOSITE** Masonry banquettes fitted with cushions bring a hint of Cape Dutch style to the terrace.

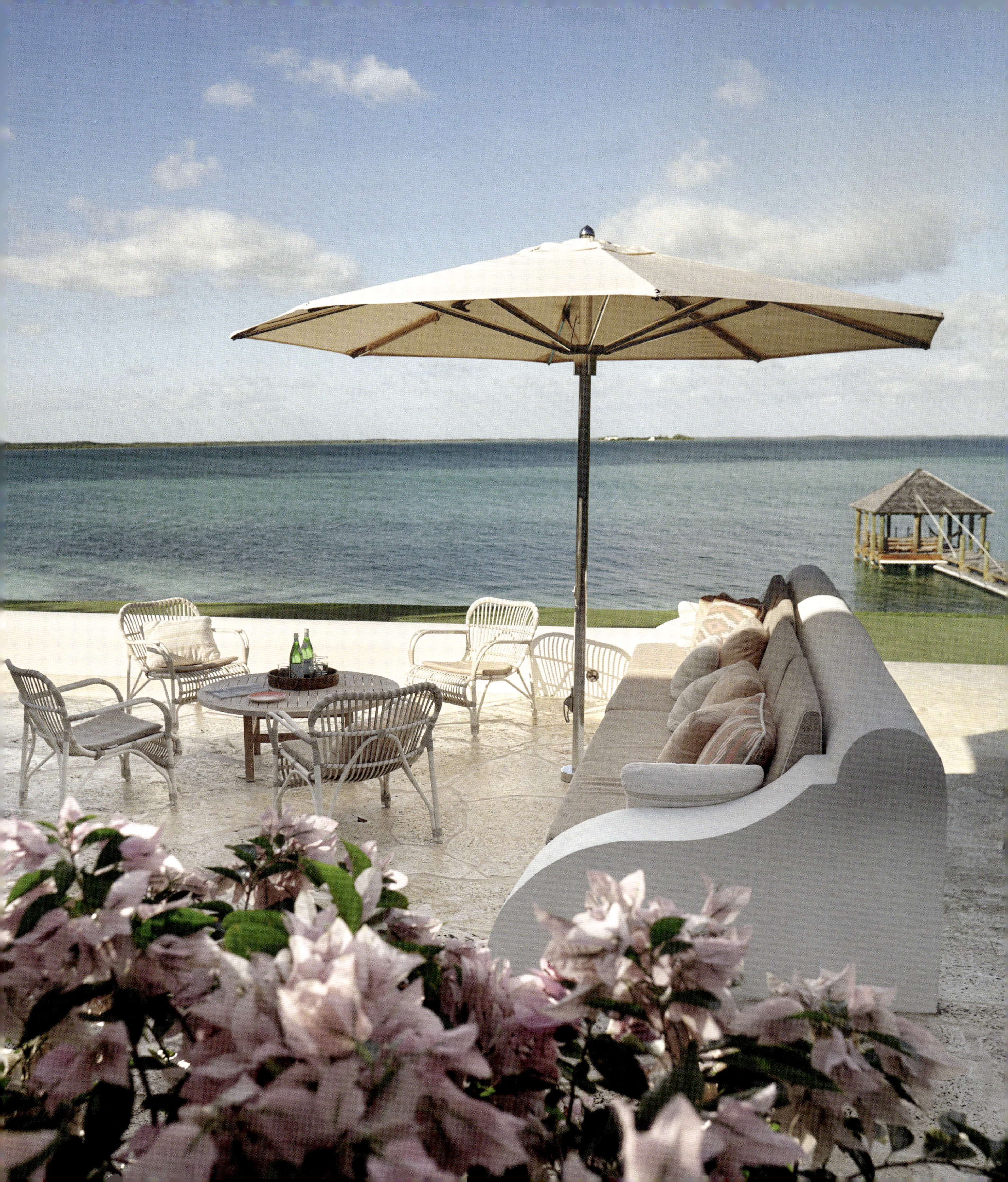

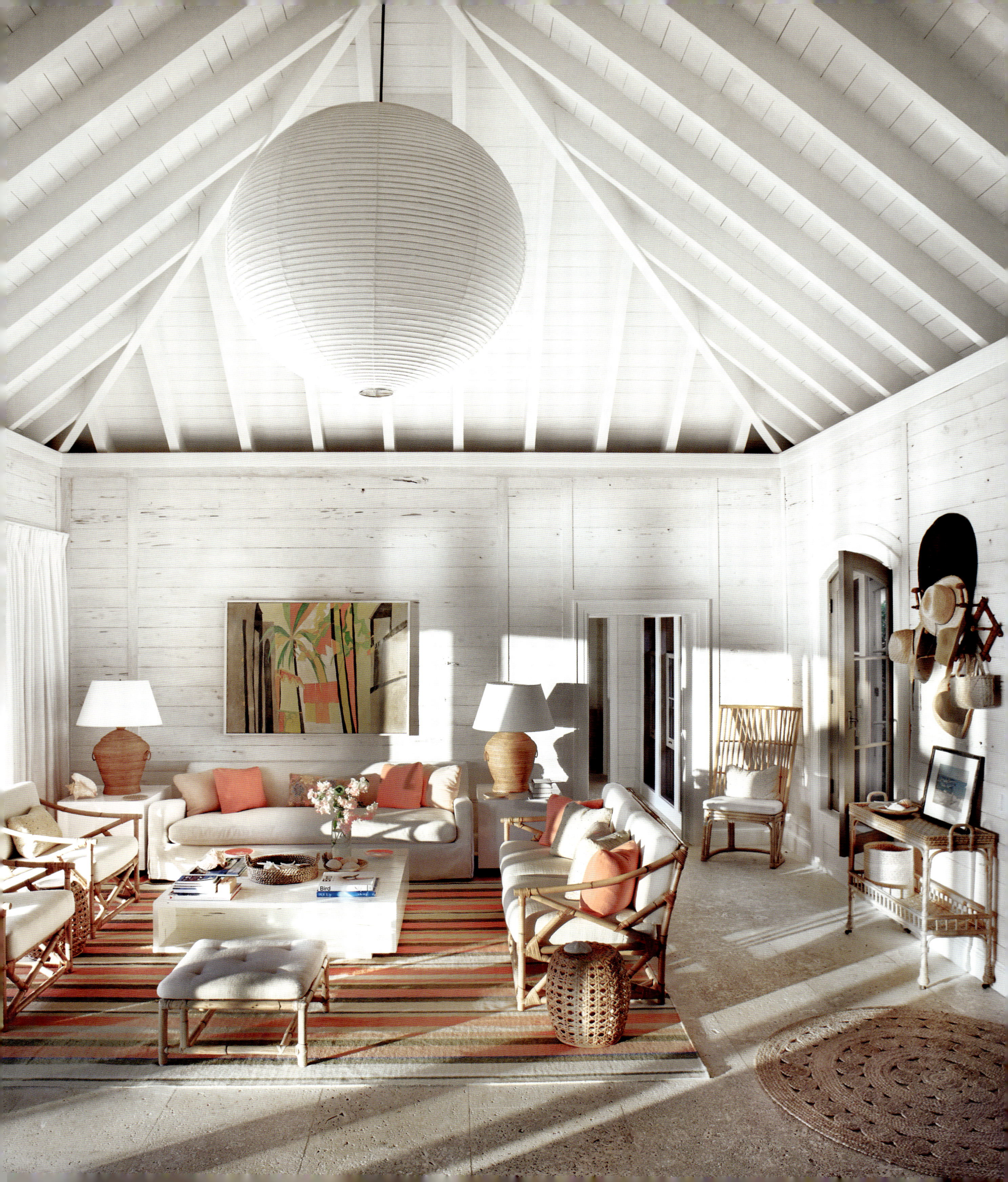
Bird

OPPOSITE Paneled in textural whitewashed pecky cypress, the central room has a beachy "soul." The sunny color scheme purposefully diverges from that of the big house to set a palpably different tone. The large and colorful encaustic painting over the sofa was serendipitously found in a Palm Beach shop when the scheme had already been determined. ABOVE The room is full of surprises. The white-lacquered tabletop conceals a full-size billiards surface, and the four-part map of the Bahamas folds back to reveal a television.

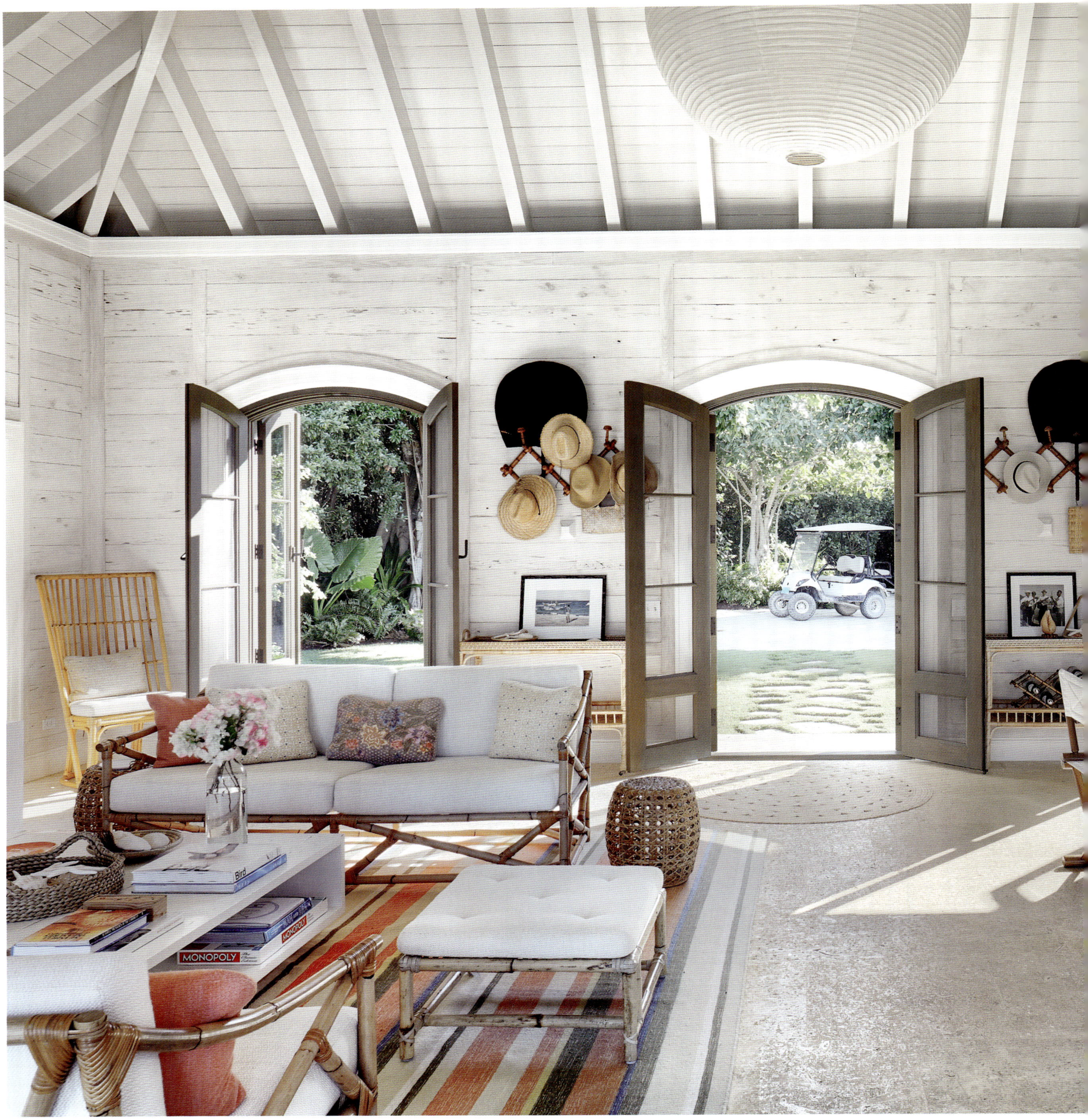
Bird
MONOPOLY

LEFT Golf carts arrive from the big house and park under transplanted banyans shipped from Florida. Also from Florida came the suite of custom-designed rattan furniture fitted with cushions covered in Perennials' Linen, which can be scrubbed clean with soap and water. The striped rug of wool interwoven with tough jute fiber has the look of a multicolored and beach-appropriate sisal. **ABOVE** The tile pattern in the kitchen is the same as the one in the big house but in a different color combination. The endearing, white-enameled Big Chill refrigerator is set in a niche like the old-fashioned fridge it is not. **OVERLEAF** Hallways in symmetrical flanking wings lead to the guest rooms.

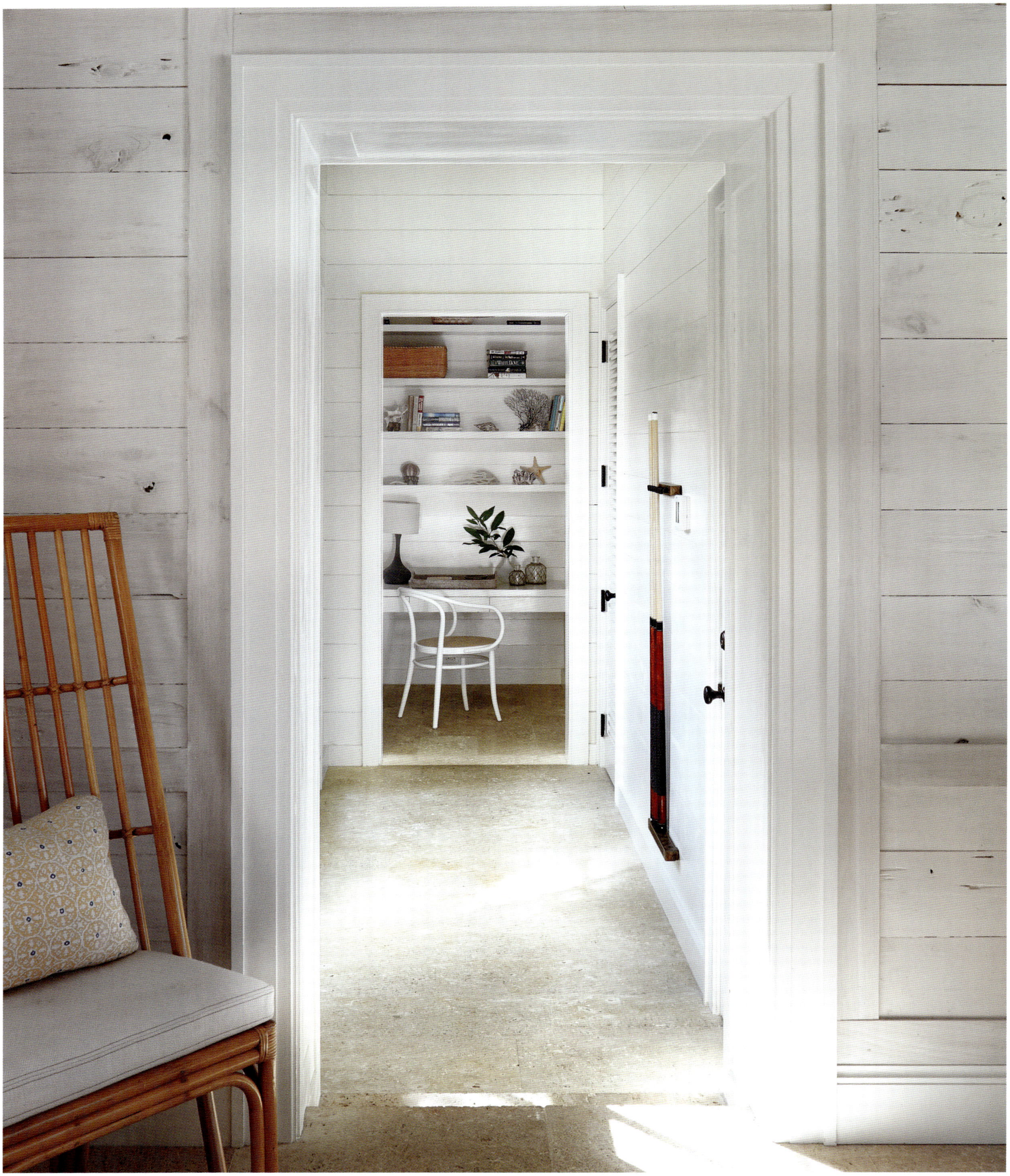

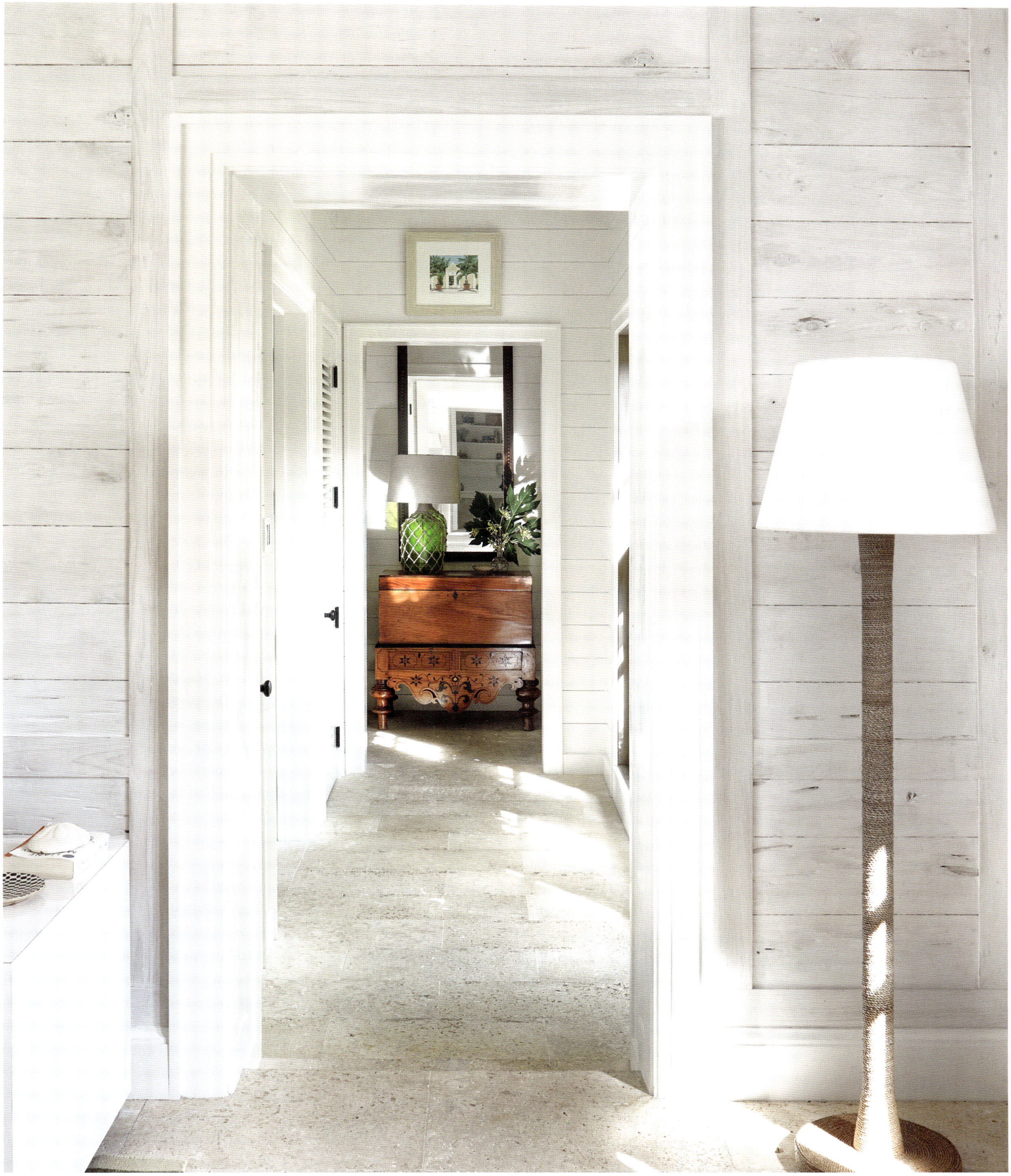

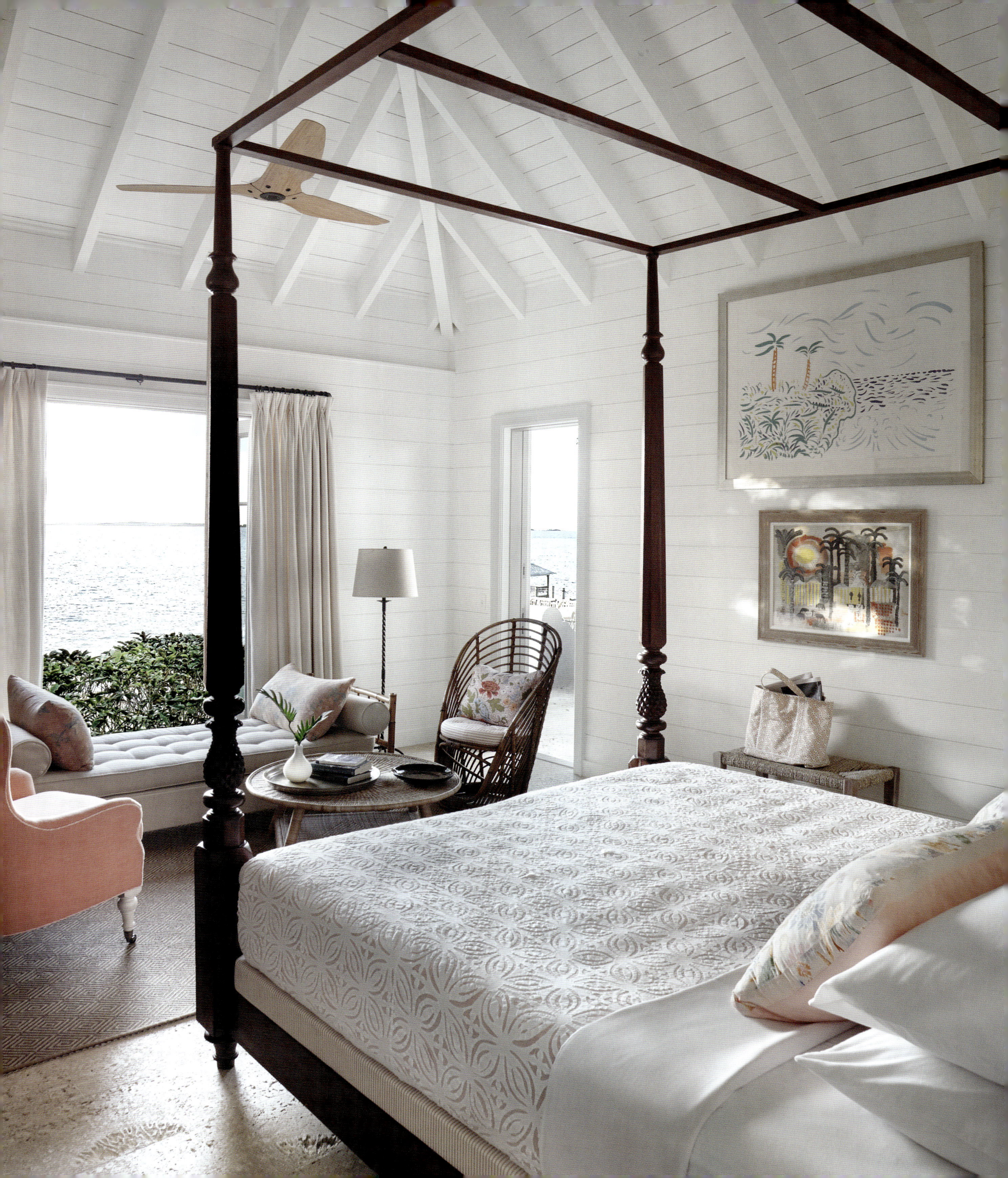

OPPOSITE In a guest room, the window folds out of sight, and an insect screen can be rolled down at night. The low-slung bamboo-and-brass daybed is a rare model by Jacques Adnet. ABOVE These twin beds share a single, wall-mounted headboard. The multi-hued striped fabric from Lee Jofa furthers the nautical atmosphere established by framed charts of the surrounding waters. The dock is only steps away. OVERLEAF Sunsets here rarely fail to take the breath away.

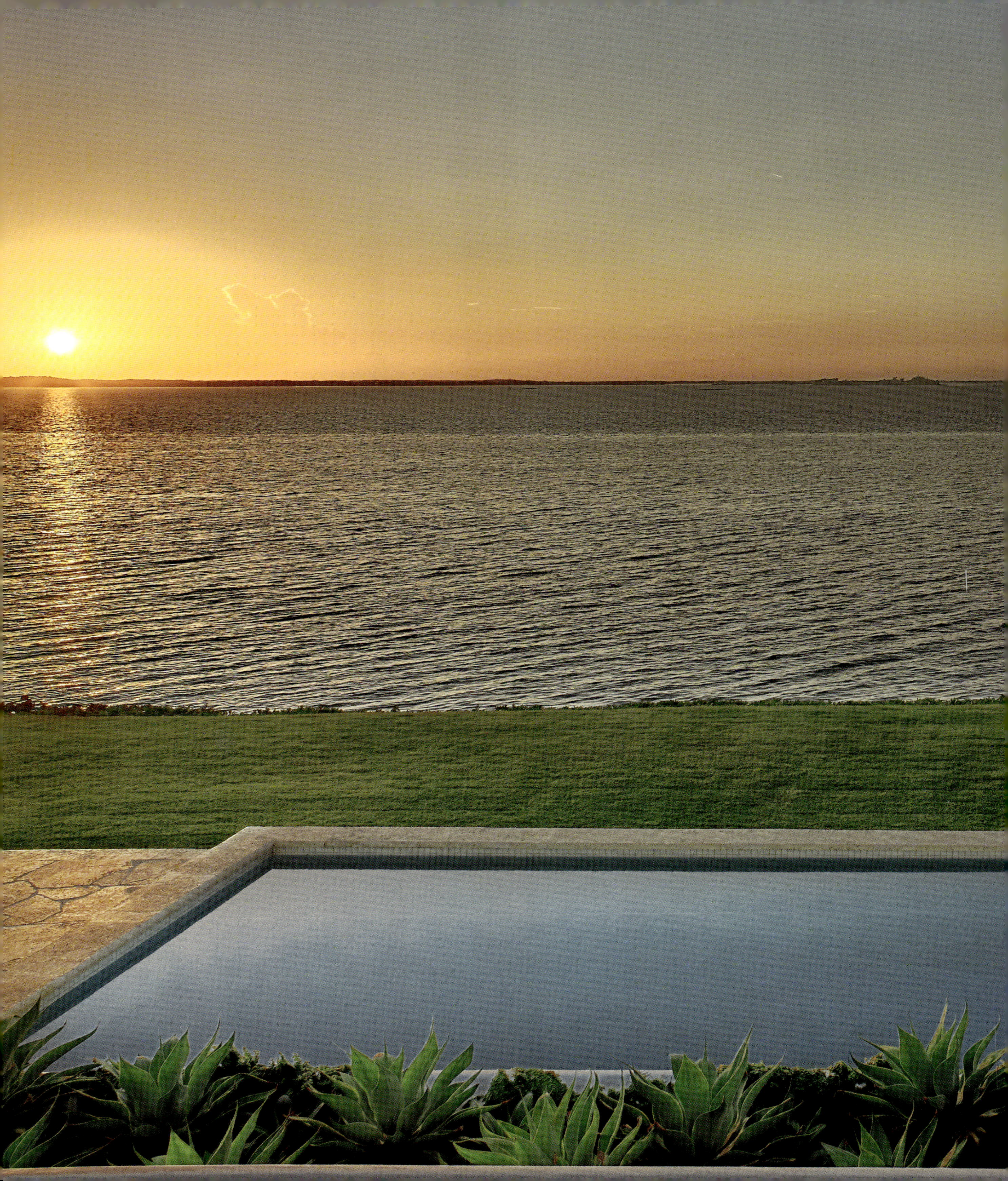

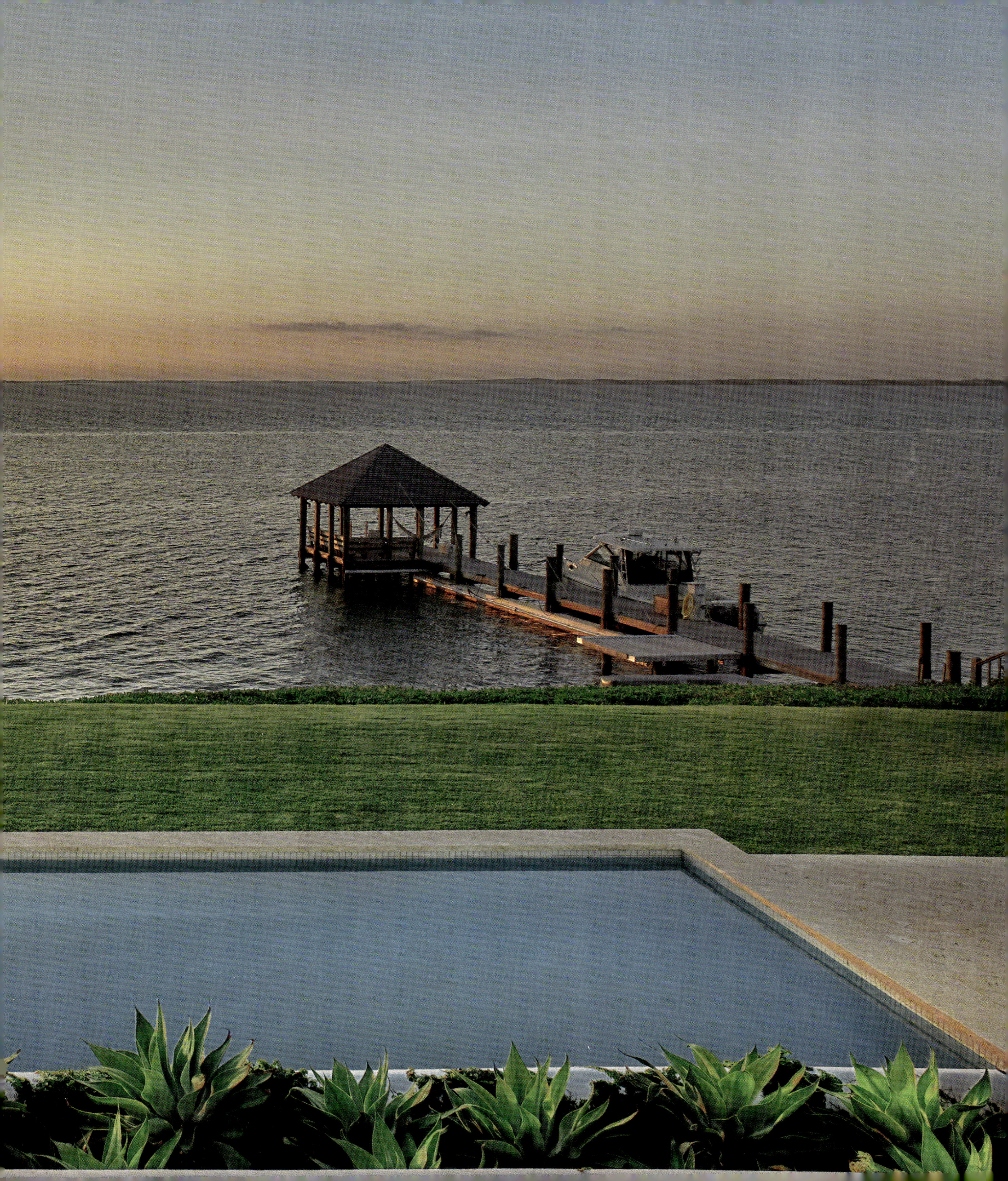

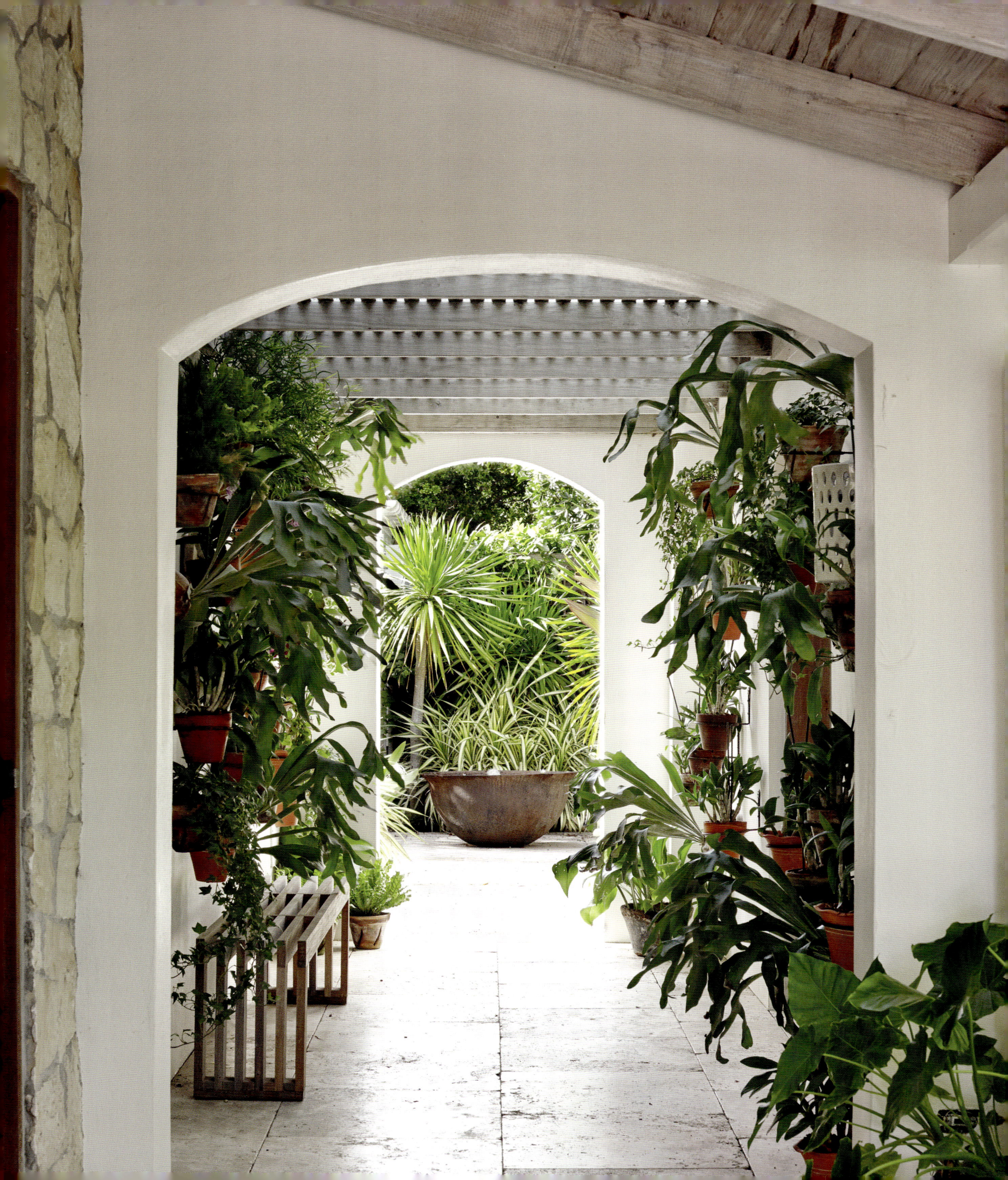

French Leave

SOMETIMES CONFUSED WITH THE SUBTLE snicker of an "English good-bye," the expression "French Leave" makes a fitting name for this holiday house in the West Indies. In this case, it denotes not a shirking party guest but a charmed life that allows stealing away from a madding crowd without the need to make an excuse. And not for an assignation (as the French would have it) but more for one's own particular pleasures.

The property is located in an Anglo-American enclave where the houses are well spaced and independent of one another. Many are perched dramatically on the hills and precipices overlooking scalloped bays, exposed to the elements, and offering dramatic views of the sea. But French Leave is veritably *pieds dans l'eau*, tucked in at one end of a long, reef-protected crescent of beach and shielded only by low mounds of sea lettuce and sea grape. The hills rise gently behind it, further sheltering the site—now entirely transformed into an idyllic world.

A long drive meanders through the once coarse indigenous "bush," now an artful and lush jungle. The drive culminates in a graveled clearing under a high canopy of old trees. There, an arched stone gateway opens to a path that side-winds along the base of a steep slope dense with tropical foliage.

The path leads to a stone-paved and tree-pierced "piazza" in the center of a precinct of various low-eaved pavilions and outdoor passages, some with bedrooms windowed and louvered for privacy, some entirely open air with deep overhangs, and some with openings fitted out with wind-breaking sliding glass and views through them to the Caribbean.

The most salient landscape feature is a narrow yet monumental coral-stone stair leading up the hill. On axis with the living room of the principal pavilion, it's the garden designer's masterstroke. At the top of the stair is a simple platform that overlooks the roofs of French Leave and the sea. There's a plan afoot to erect something more substantial up there, but for now the stair serves as a bold and thought-provoking question mark. Elsewhere, old and wonderfully sculptural trees were preserved by designing the terraces and veranda roofs around them.

A passage was transformed into a lattice-roofed orchid house that skirts the dining room and leads to one of several guest quarters. This one, the single wooden building on the site, is a charming antique vestige and the most sought after guest room.

Dinner is most often served in the leeward and open-air dining pavilion. At one end, a new, arched opening was cut to frame a deliberately orchestrated tableau. It features a stone water basin in the foreground, behind which a stone and gravel path recedes through a layered thicket of tropical planting.

Breakfast and lunch are taken close to the water's edge in a sun-shaded and vivid green alcove of contrasting coastal planting. Bare feet luxuriate in the sand, which camouflages stone pavers that are cleverly set just under the surface to keep the table and chairs from wobbling.

It's probably not a good idea for the decorator to downplay his own work, but here he is happy to play second fiddle. At French Leave, the landscape tells the most important part of the story.

OPPOSITE An open-air passage skims by the dining room. It's a shaded and lushly tropical microclimate, perfect for the orchids that cover the walls.

ABOVE The site was transformed by the masterful landscape design of Chicago-based Doug Hoerr of Hoerr Schaudt Landscape Architects. In addition to entirely new plantings, he introduced gates, pathways, terraces, and the intriguing stone staircase. OPPOSITE Eight-foot-high sliding doors were installed in three of the living room's walls. An old and magnificently gnarled tree forms a shading canopy. All-weather chaises longues from Casa Mobel face the Caribbean across low-trimmed sea grape. OVERLEAF The chic vintage wicker tub chairs and matching settee came with the 1960s house, and the living room was decorated around them. The caterpillar fringe on the new St. Thomas sofa is an all-weather version, as are all the fabrics except for the Quadrille Island Floral batik.

252 . THE TROPICS

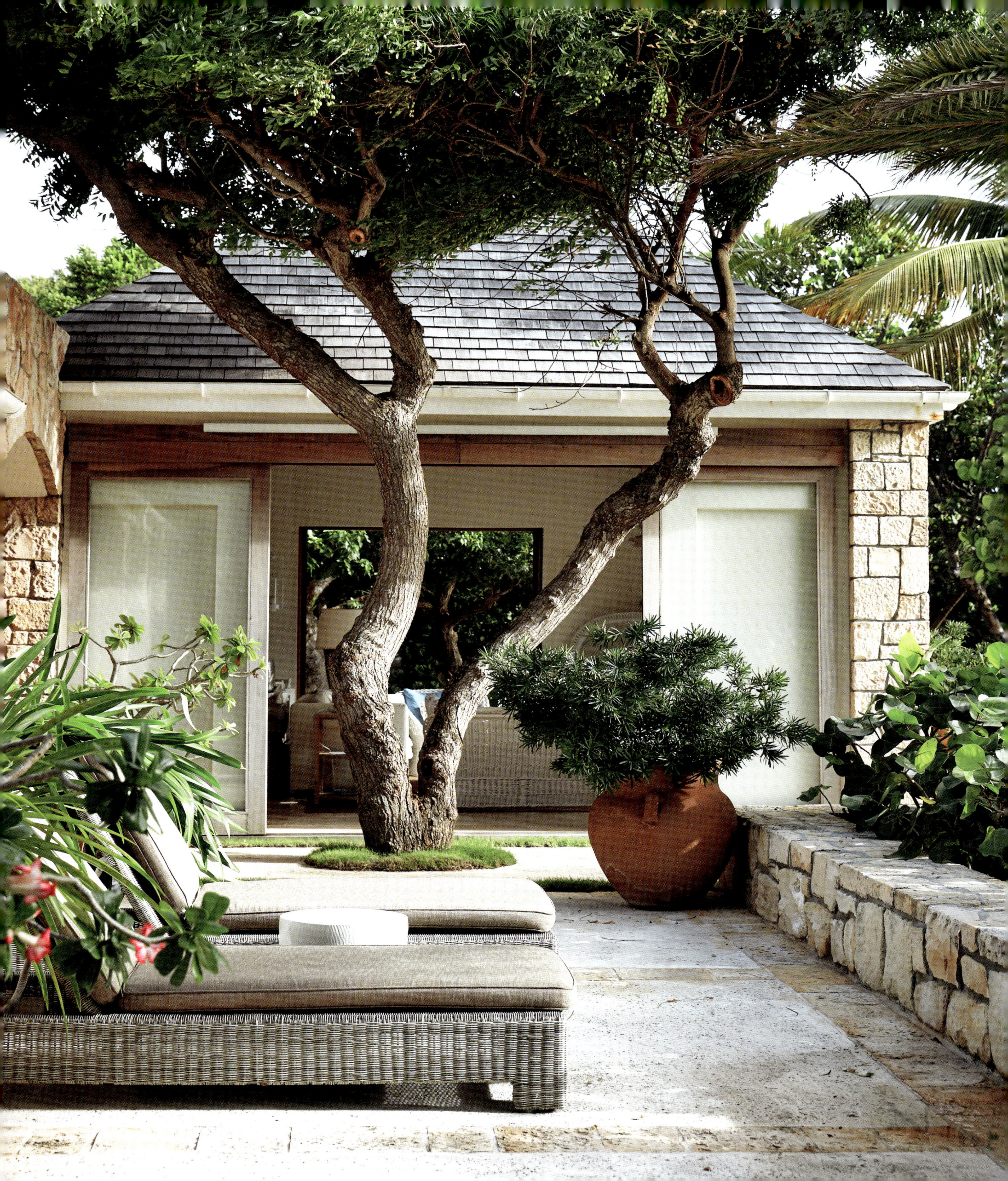

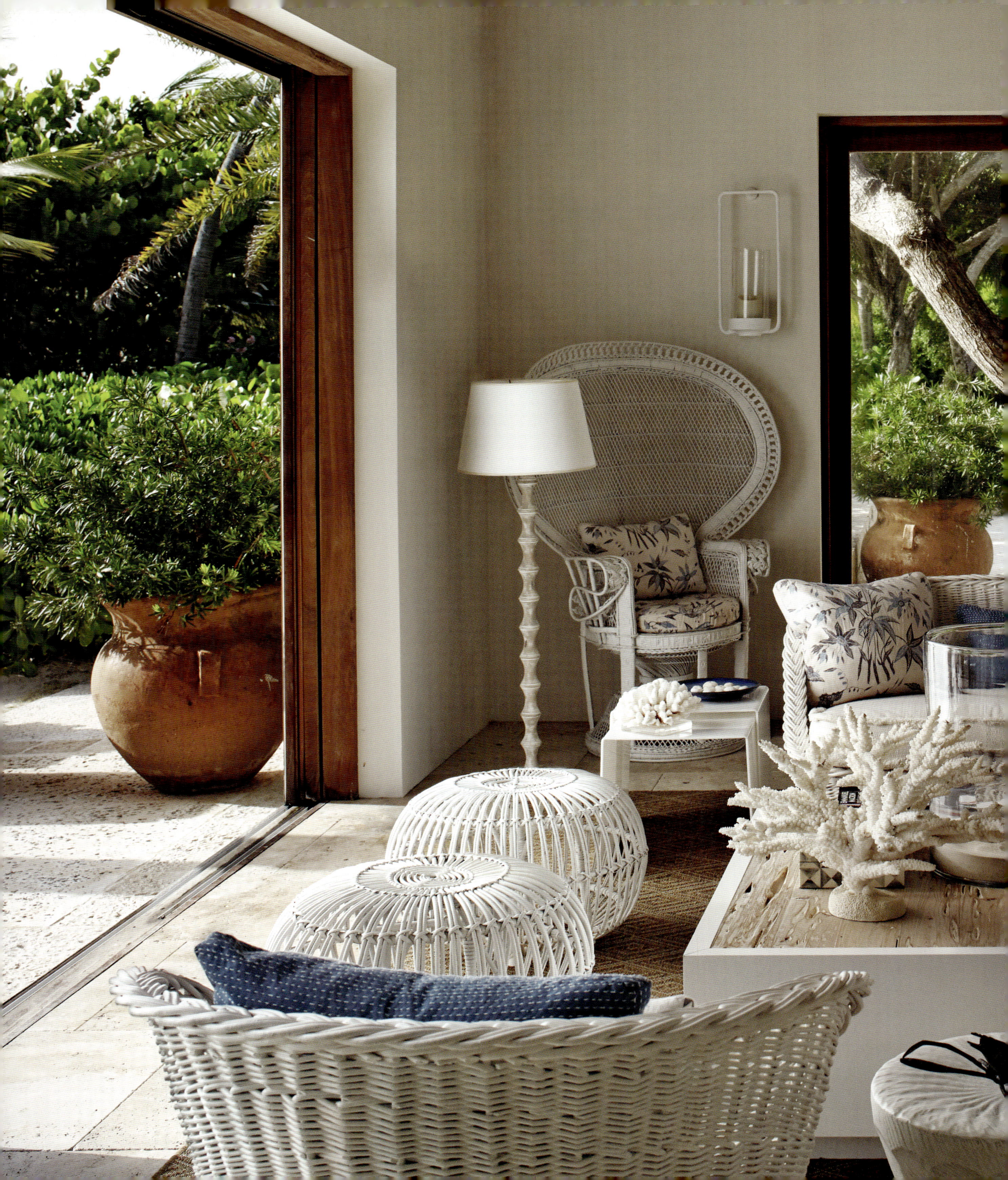

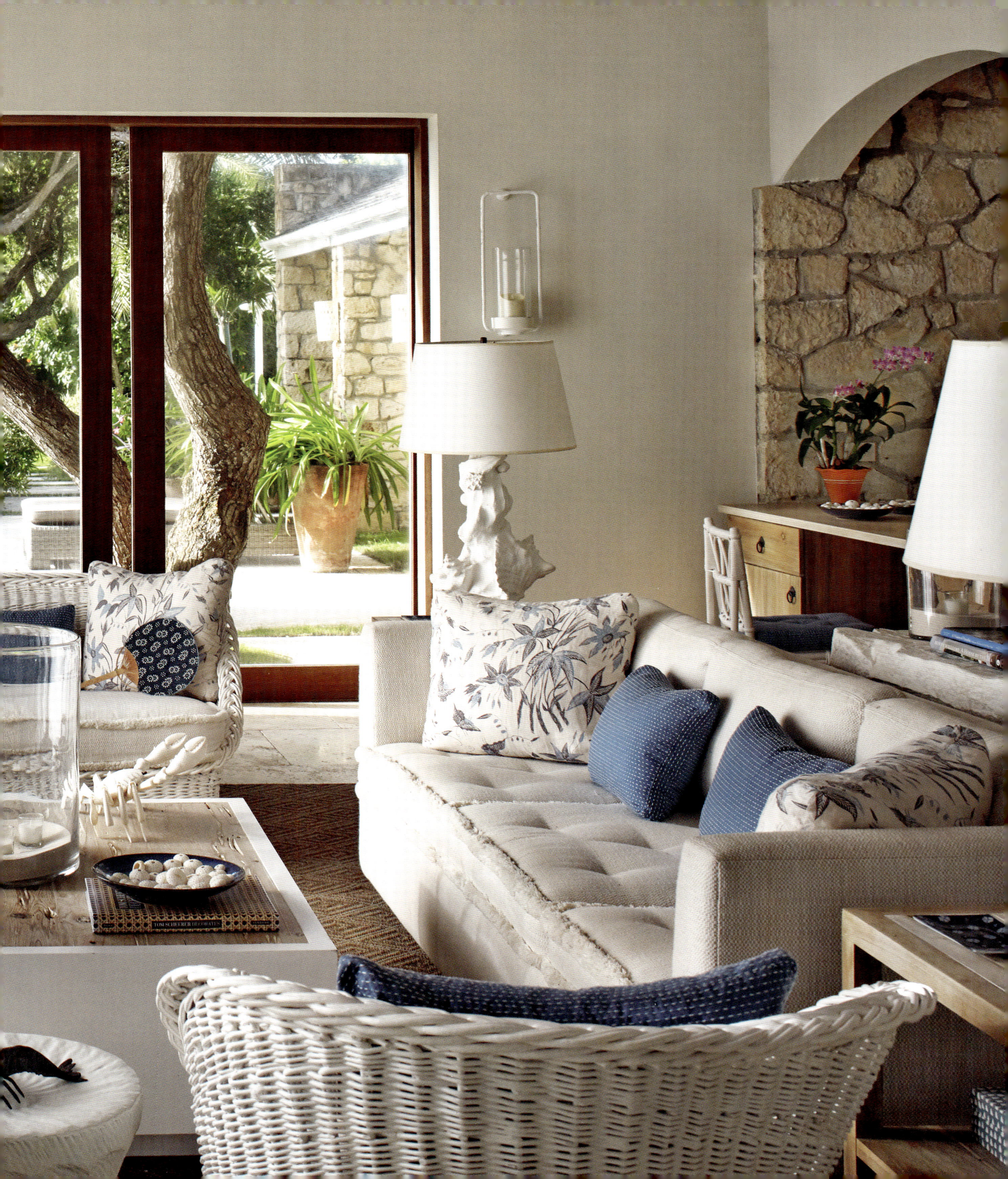

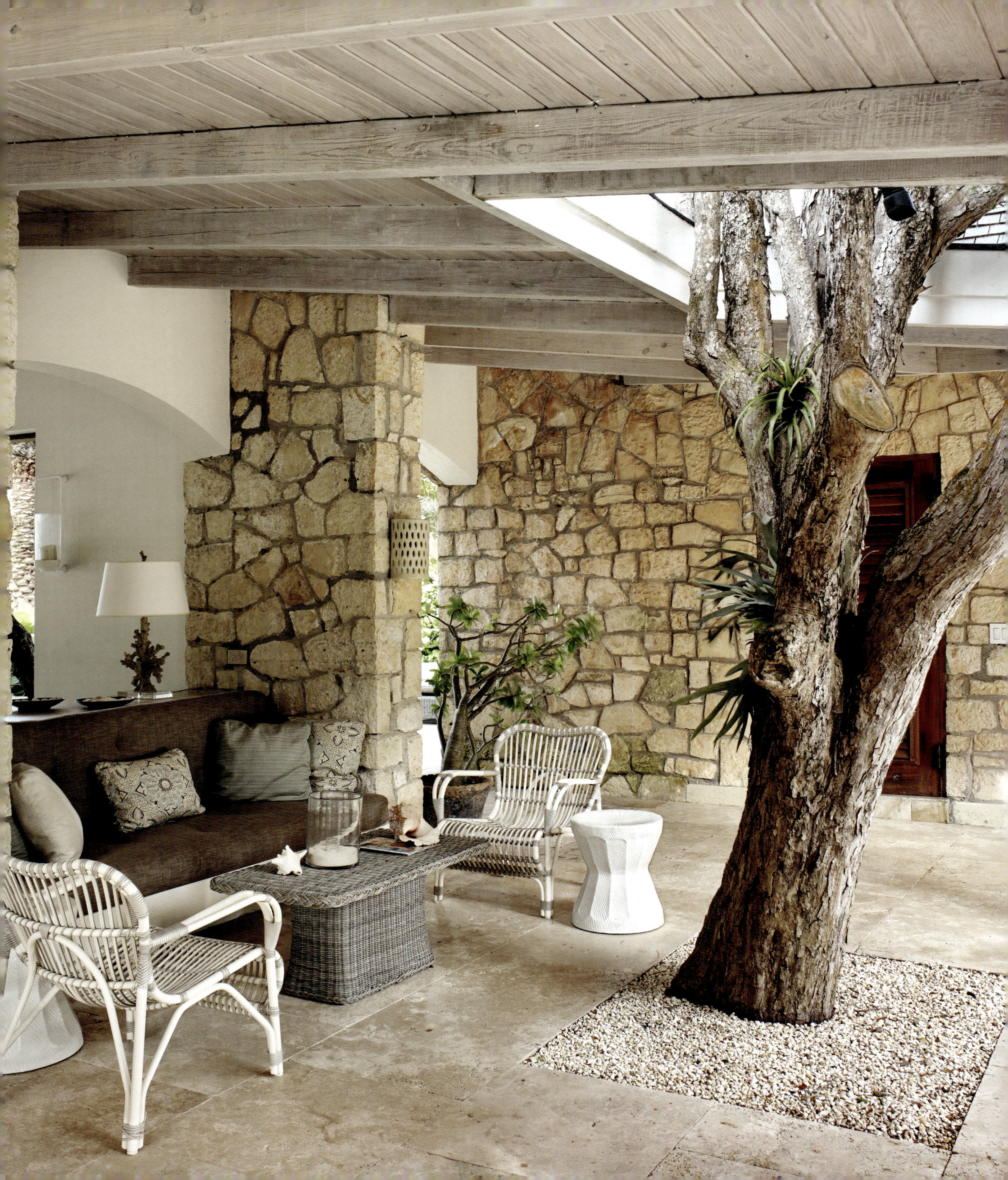

OPPOSITE The veranda's extended roof was carefully built around another old tree. The cushioned banquette faces low-slung "cocktail" chairs from Janus et Cie and a resin wicker table from Casa Mobel. **ABOVE** An arched opening was cut into one end of the veranda. With shutters folded back, it frames the landscaped view. The old-fashioned painted rattan chairs came with the house but were partially culled to make way for more modern and snappy Italian-made director's chairs.

ABOVE An enticing collection of Caribbean rums announces that it might be "that time." The bar shelf and the cabinets are trimmed in split rattan, a not-too-veiled reference to this Anglo-American crowd's fond memories of Trader Vic and his rum drinks. **OPPOSITE** The coloring of the Cuban tile was inspired by the tropical fruits that abound on the island, a sampling of which is seen on the butcher-block island. This is a working kitchen only. Meals are served in a variety of shaded and covered oases around the property. **OVERLEAF LEFT** A guest room's twin tester beds are extra-wide, extra-long, and extra-high. The louvered windows and doors are screened to permit free-flowing night air. The mosquito nets are optional. **OVERLEAF RIGHT** Green-glazed pineapples "stand guard" in an outdoor passage to the guest rooms. A universal symbol of hospitality, these particular ones are a craft tradition of the Mexican state Michoacán.

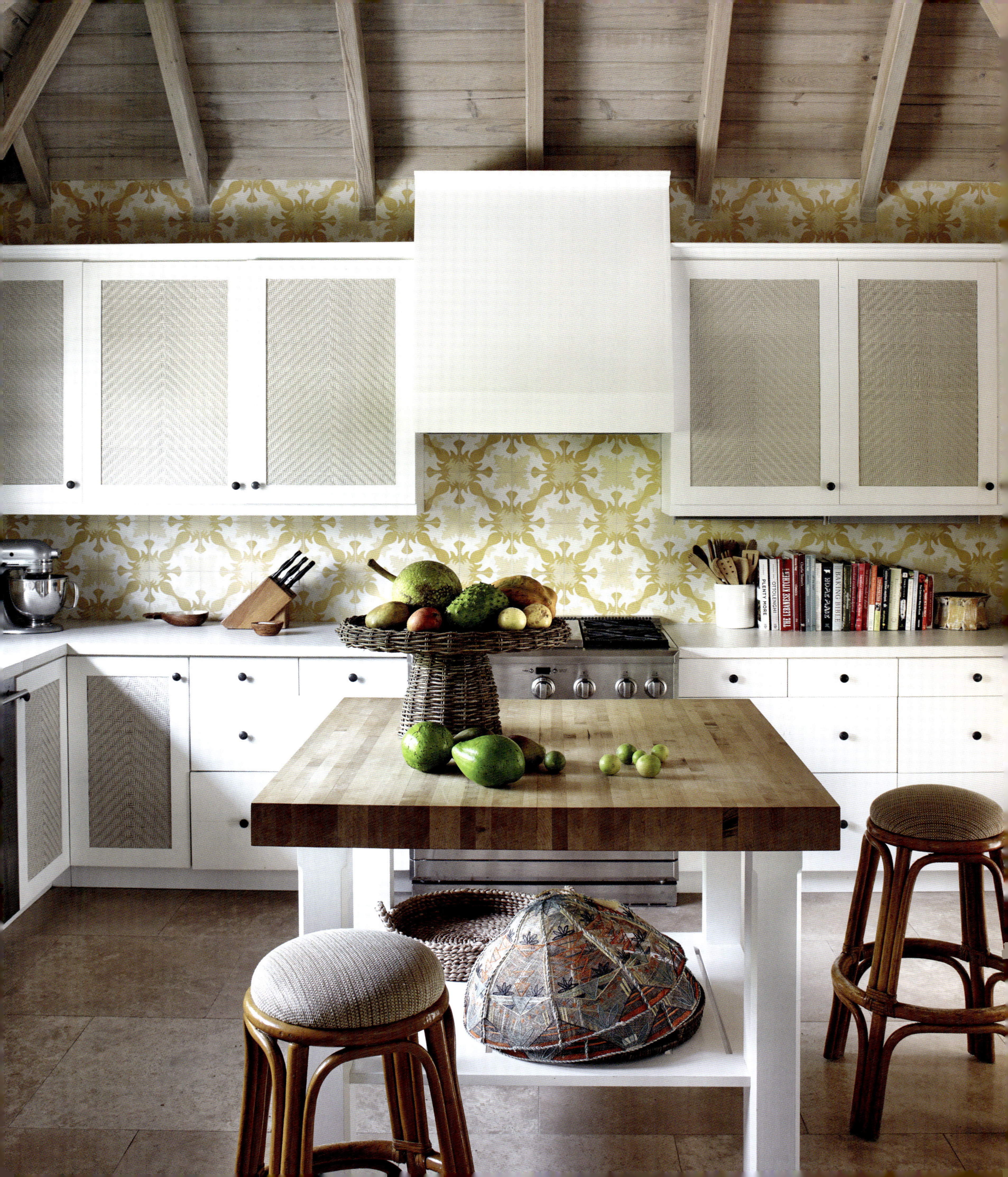

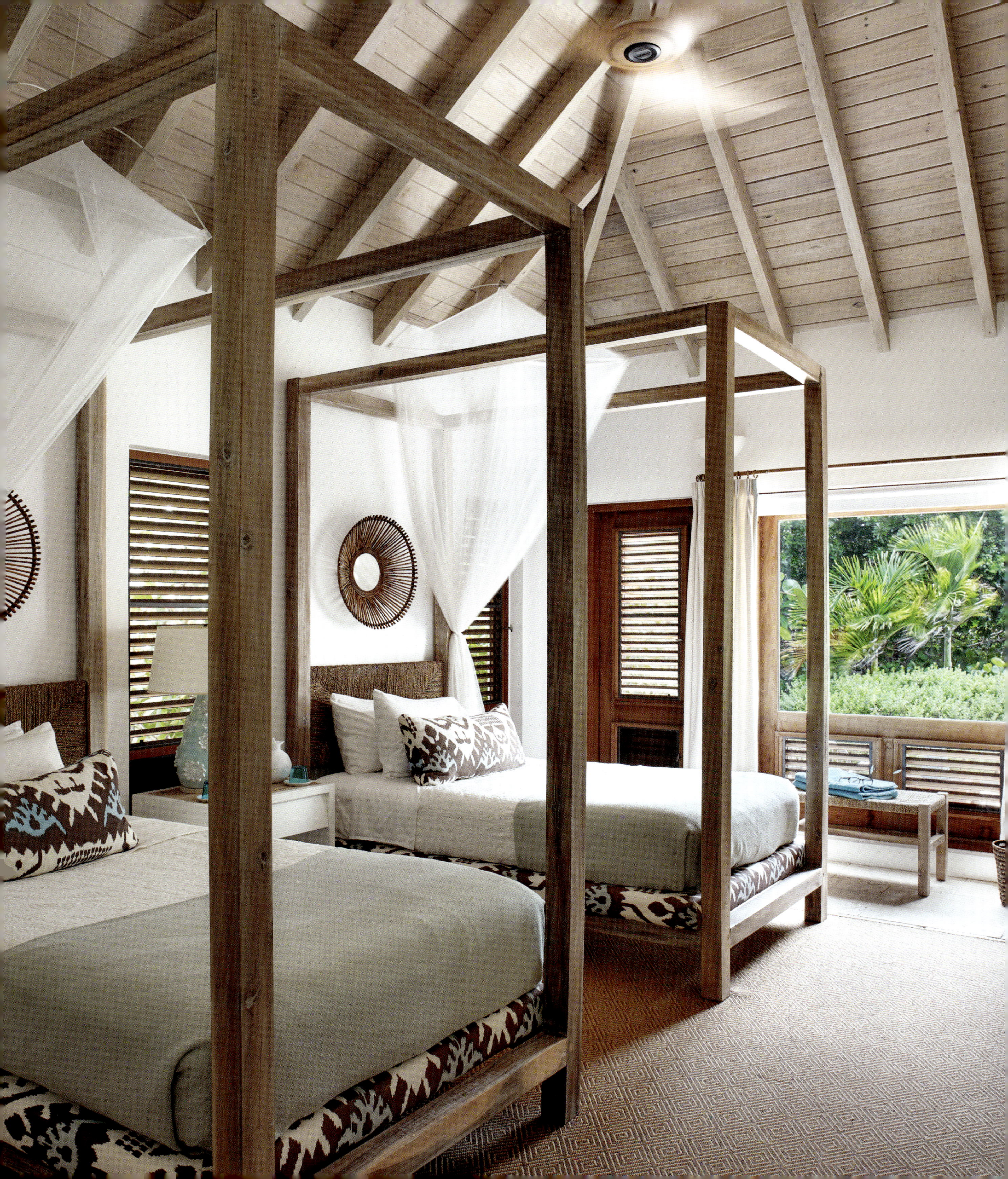

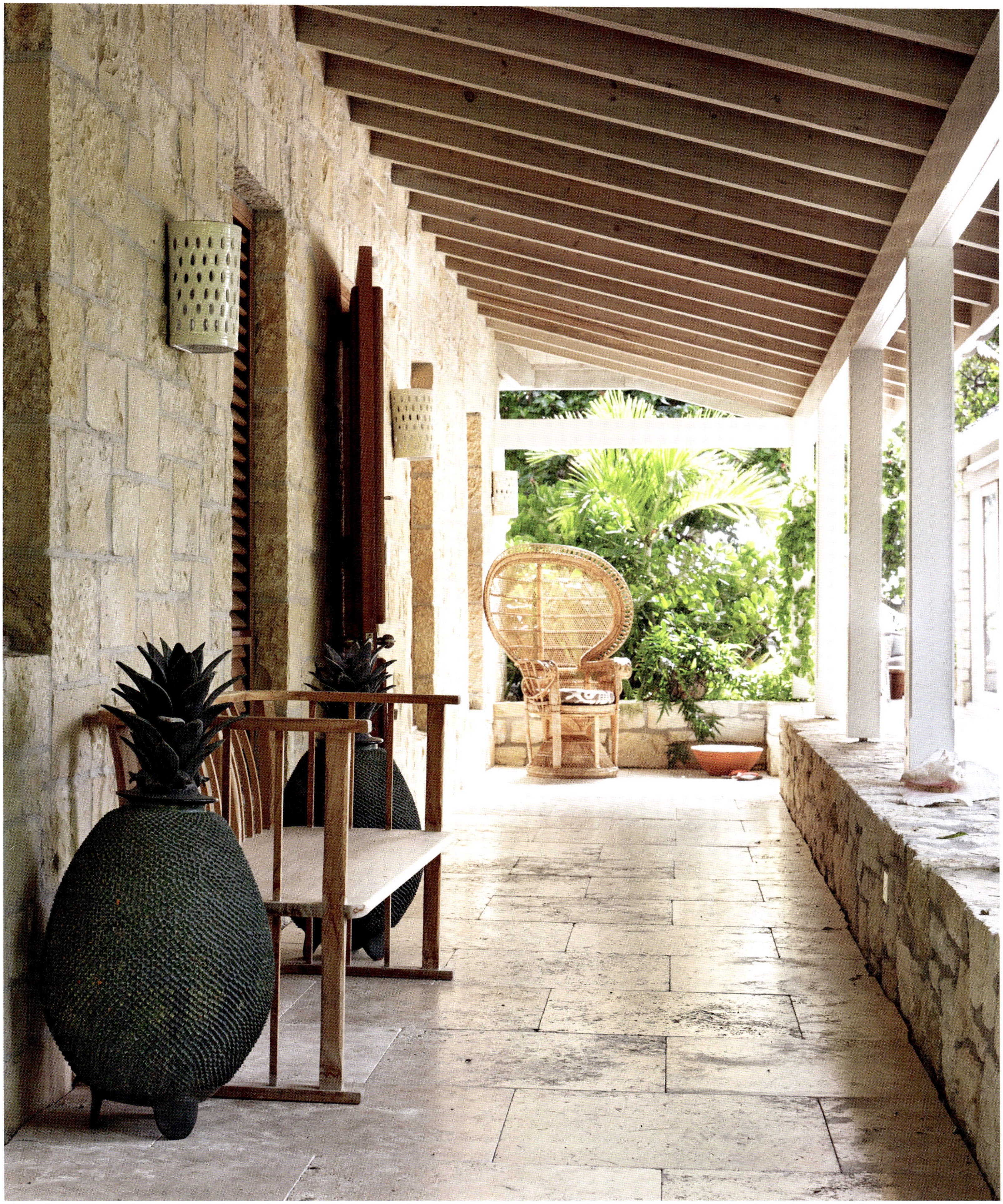

ABOVE Schumacher's Katsugi printed cotton was the starting point for the decoration of the master bedroom. Its yellow and purple coloring comes as a refreshing surprise in the tropics.
OPPOSITE Mama Bear and Papa Bear white wicker chairs face each other in front of the bed. The room's one un-windowed and imposing stone wall called for a very large secretary desk. A dark mahogany behemoth was located in Hudson, New York. It was pickled to approximate the color of the room's cypress paneling before immigrating to the West Indies.

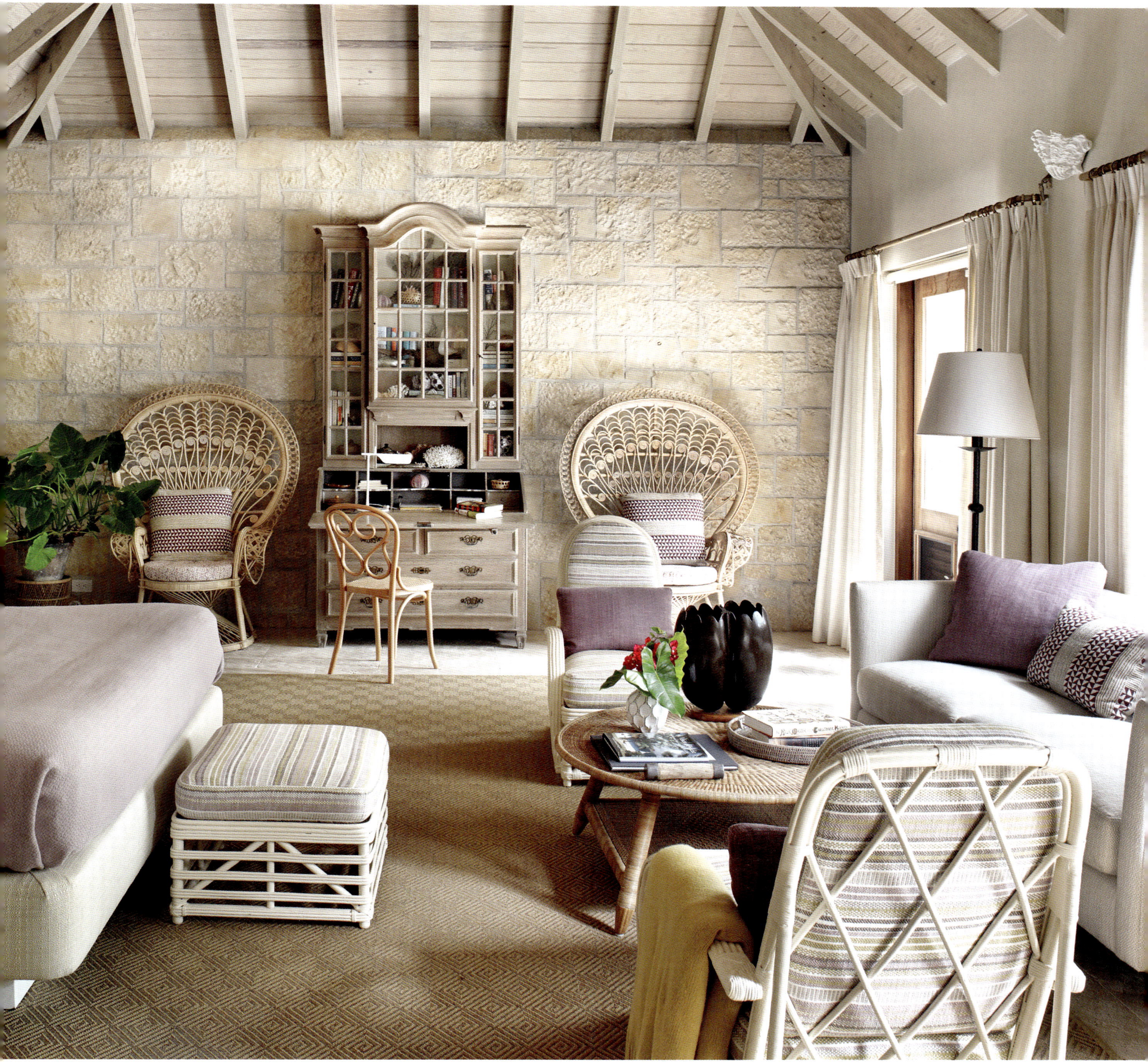

ABOVE In addition to a bit of "retro chic" tropical furniture, French Leave came with this rustic, antique, and typically West Indian one-room cottage. It's a favored guest accommodation. **OPPOSITE** The Jamaican-style bed was made in India by the Raj Company, as were the cane-paneled cupboard doors. The cotton curtain and bed hanging fabrics are from Les Indiennes.

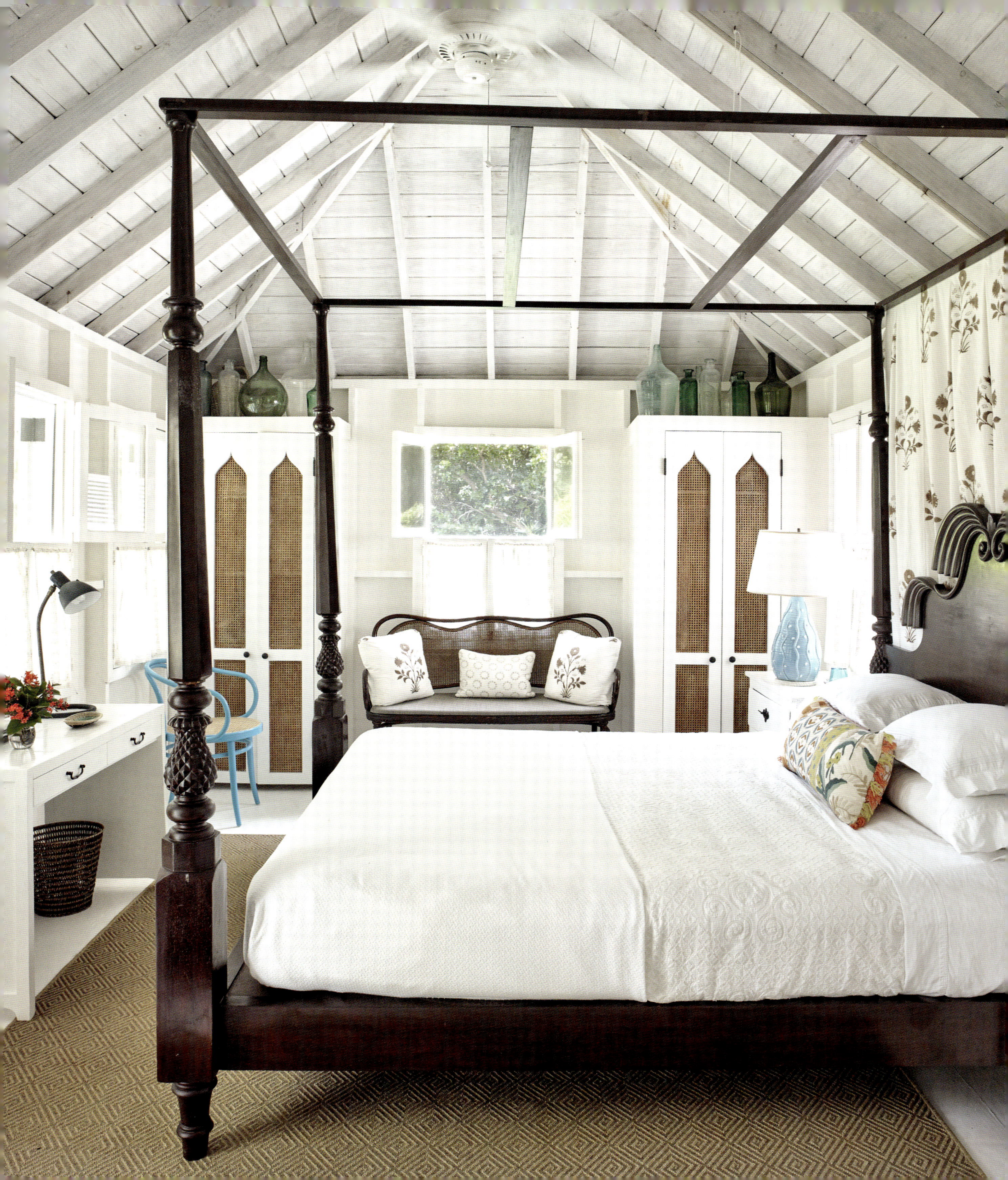

ABOVE Outdoor furniture styles and materials are carefully modulated and repeated throughout the property. Muted colors keep visual clutter to a minimum, allowing the eye to travel to the landscape and the sea. **OPPOSITE** Doug Hoerr's landscaping tour de force is the monumental stair in local stone. Though full of possibility, for now it rises to "nowhere."

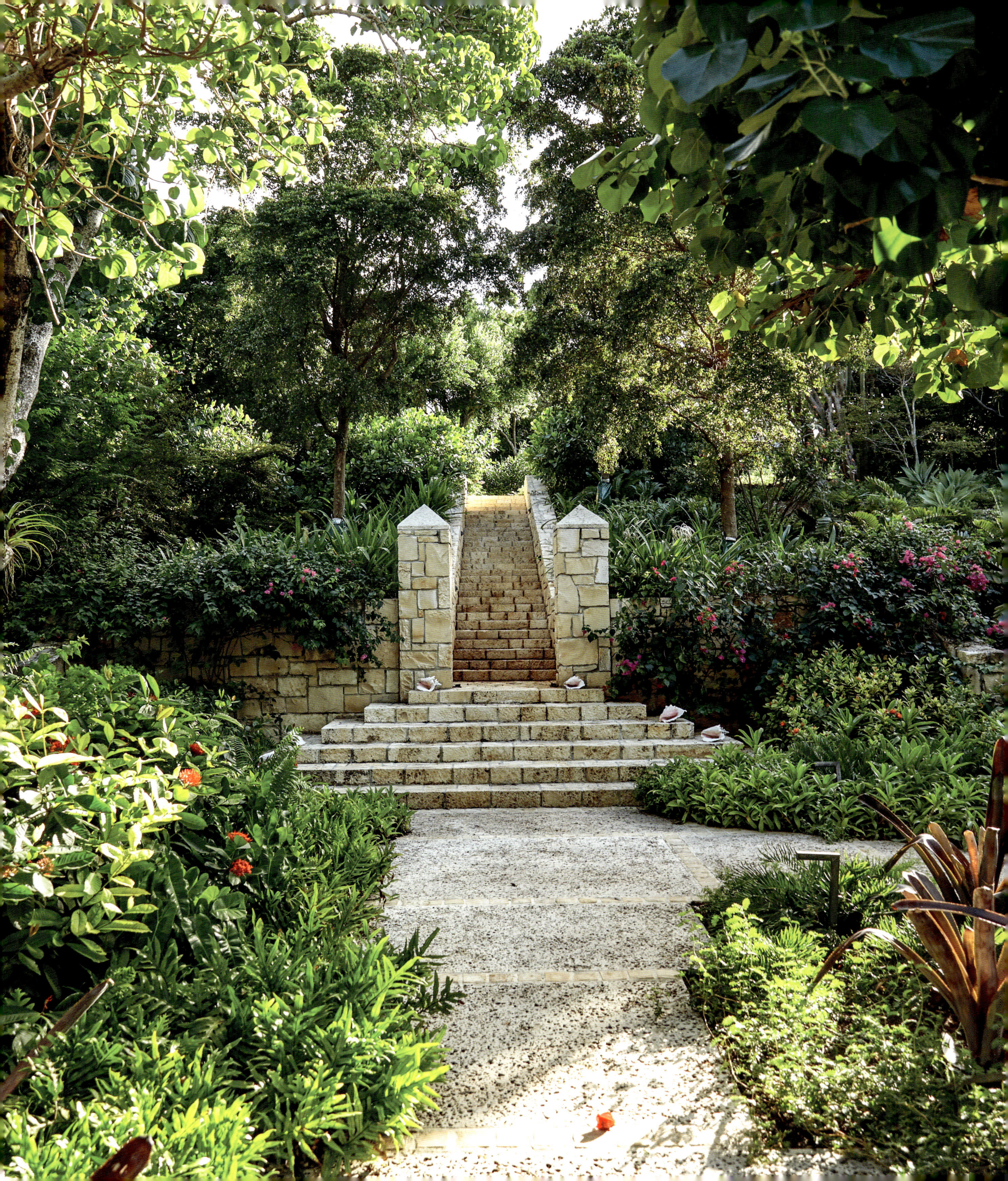

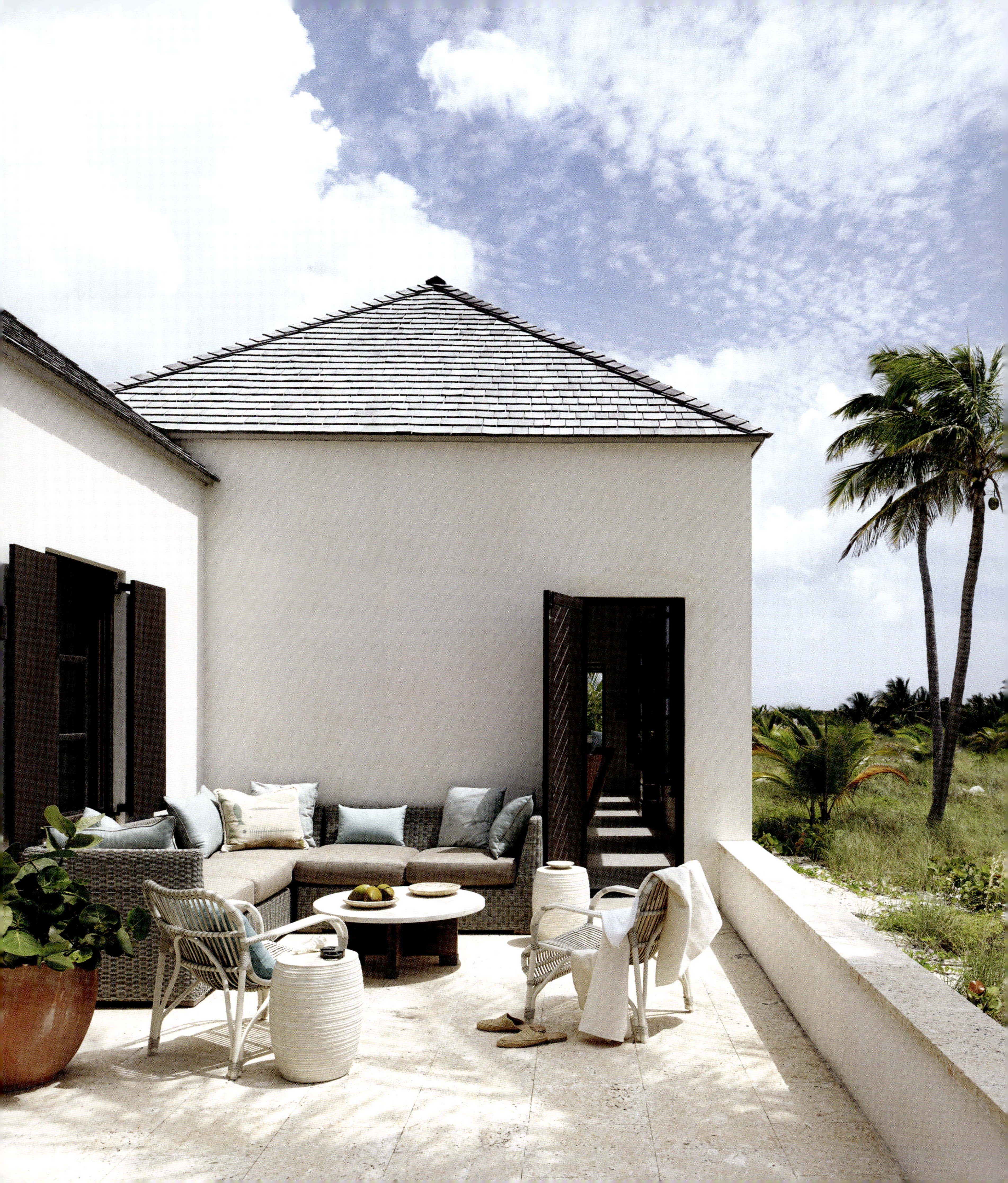

Zanzibar

Choosing a name for one's house is bound to be fraught with either cutesy-ness or pretension. No doubt there are books for the loo written on the possibilities. I opted for the latter. This Zanzibar is merely 182 miles east of Palm Beach, nestled on a narrow isthmus of rock and scrub between the all-but-uninhabited pine barren expanses of North and South Abaco. I liked the word's graphic and alliterative qualities—the swashbuckle of the double Zs, as my inner wanderer/rusticator is drawn to the remote, the exotic, and the coastally wild. "Bagging" the trophy-mounted kudu and oryx horns in a Sag Harbor antique shop was the ultimate deciding factor. Zanzibar. Of course.

The compound of buildings is inspired by the sturdy red-roofed, pavilioned houses of St. Barts and also by a trip to palm tree–rife Kerala, where the plantation houses are stuccoed, brown trimmed, and formed around sheltered courtyards. Despite the far-flung and romanticized source material (I haven't been to the real Zanzibar), the result is utterly Bahamian, resembling the coral-stone cottages and hermitages found, mostly in ruin, throughout the archipelago.

The house is compact, yet the effect is large. With four bedrooms, a 15-by-30-foot living room, and a garage, the interior is only 1,800 square feet, and the house's entire footprint, including several terraces and courtyards, is 5,000 square feet. The principal room, under the largest of the hipped cedar roofs, stands in for a more predictable and Bahama-ubiquitous "living" veranda. It has four large windows facing the ocean and doors on either end. The leeward side is entirely open to the cloistered courtyard; its heavy barn doors need to be closed only during the hurricane season.

The teak windows and doors are "in the vernacular" to the extreme. They are stripped down to atavistic simplicity—no special hardware mechanisms, weather stripping, or complicated profiles. No one in the first world would deign to produce such low-tech, sensible stuff, so it was commissioned in India. The units (doors and casements, jambs and storm shutters, all hinges and latches) came in crates to be unpacked, assembled, and placed in the thick, poured-concrete openings precisely sized for them. The logic of the building system astounded the Bahamians, who installed each in a matter of minutes. The panes keep in the rarely needed air conditioning in the bedrooms; in the living room they break the wind, but all are almost always flung wide open.

The floors are either coral stone or (for variety) roughly polished shell- and stone-impregnated cement, a crude form of terrazzo. Both do well to obscure the sand inevitably brought in from the beach. In the storm season (when we are elsewhere), there is no fear of the shuttered windows leaking and damaging the floors. And we usually remember to roll up the rugs.

So Zanzibar is a manifesto of sorts—it's the antidote to the often complicated challenges I'm given as a working decorator. Only one color of paint was used inside and out—white. And one brown wood stain. Simplicity, rusticity, and time- and space-saving economies are generally not high on my clients' wish lists.

There's no need for square-foot-hungry walk-in closets here; luggage is discouraged, flip-flops and bathing suits are perfectly fine, even at dinnertime. The outdoor showers (there are two) are well used, and the weather is welcomed inside. There's a prime seating area in the courtyard under the spreading sea grape that catches both the sunrise (through the living room windows) and the sunset. The house is elemental in many ways deliberate and in other ways happily accidental.

OPPOSITE The West Indies and the Abaco Islands are far from each other, but the same outdoor furniture works well in both. At Zanzibar, the rattan suite outside the master bedroom softens the stark geometric forms.

The swimming pool, used for a freshwater dip after an ocean swim, is an admitted and modern indulgence. I'll also confess to a large television set and Bahamian-ly intermittent Wi-Fi.

However, the fireplace (an extinct fixture in new Bahamian houses) is central to the way we live at Zanzibar. It's used all winter, when the weather ranges between pleasantly hot and pleasantly cool. At night there can be a slight chill in the air, but it rarely warrants shutting the windows. The local casuarina wood is plentiful and burns hot and long. It smudges the air with piney perfume. Candles are always lit in any case. The big room glows, its four tall and open windows look out eagerly to the next sunrise.

OPPOSITE TOP, LEFT TO RIGHT Straw, caning, rattan, and bamboo are all beach house basic necessities. Zanzibar is prudently and protectively set back from the beach behind a wide dune. The house was christened in absentia and the driftwood sign was painted on a summer day in Maine long before the house was complete. **BELOW** The 100-by-50-foot plot contains four bedrooms, four baths, an ample kitchen, and a small garage. Additionally, there's a swimming pool and several terraces, verandas, and courtyards.
ABOVE, LEFT TO RIGHT A wall of one kind or another forms the precisely rectangular perimeter of the 5,000 square foot footprint. Here it's in the form of a sitting wall. The chimney stands as a sentinel and is the only element that can be seen peeking over the dune. The windows arrived from India in crates with frame, sill, sash, screen, and shutter all in one integral unit. They popped right into the anticipating masonry openings.

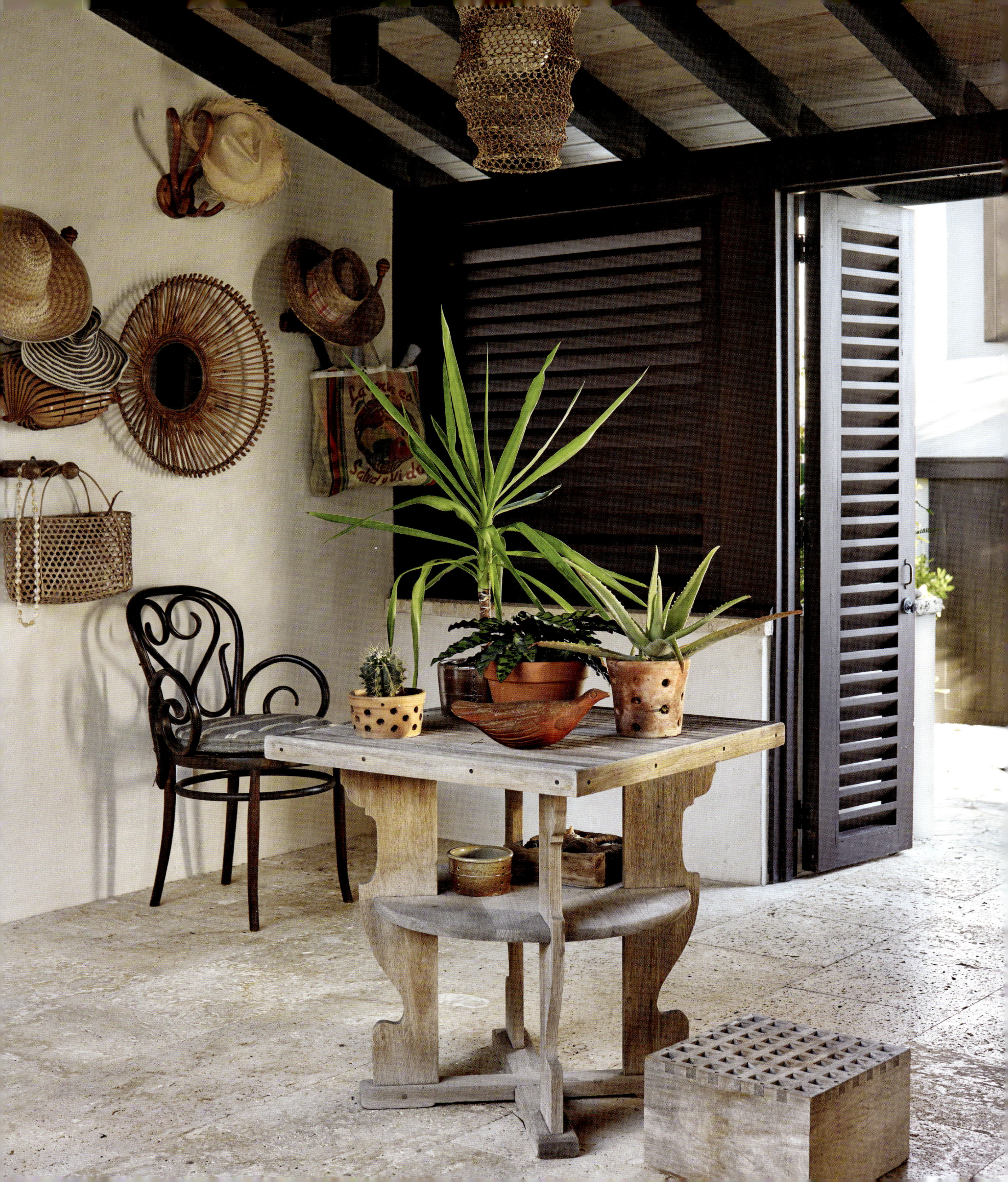
Salud y Vida

OPPOSITE The house is entered from a small parking court, golf carts only. The clever English garden table was evidently built to endure. Already a certified antique when it was bought from Cove Landing in New York, it has now been outdoors full-time in the Bahamas for twenty years. ABOVE A rustic peristyle connects three of the bedrooms. The India-made pickled-teak louver doors are screened, and on occasion the solid outer doors are employed to keep in the air conditioning. The Nevelson-esque found object on the wall is a wooden machinery mold left unpainted to the mercy of the elements.

ABOVE Duplicate sets of white duck slipcovers were ordered from Room & Board for the facing pair of Jasper sofas. **BELOW** The bifurcation of the main room into living and dining areas is broadcast by a pyramidal stack of antique boxes that came from India in the crates with the windows and doors. Pottery Barn wall sconces with battery-operated flicker candles turn on automatically at dusk. Elsewhere the candles are real and often citronella—the living room is mostly unscreened. **OPPOSITE** A pair of zoomorphic woven rattan "rockers" may have their backs to the view, but they face the pretty courtyard and the oryx horns–crowned television.

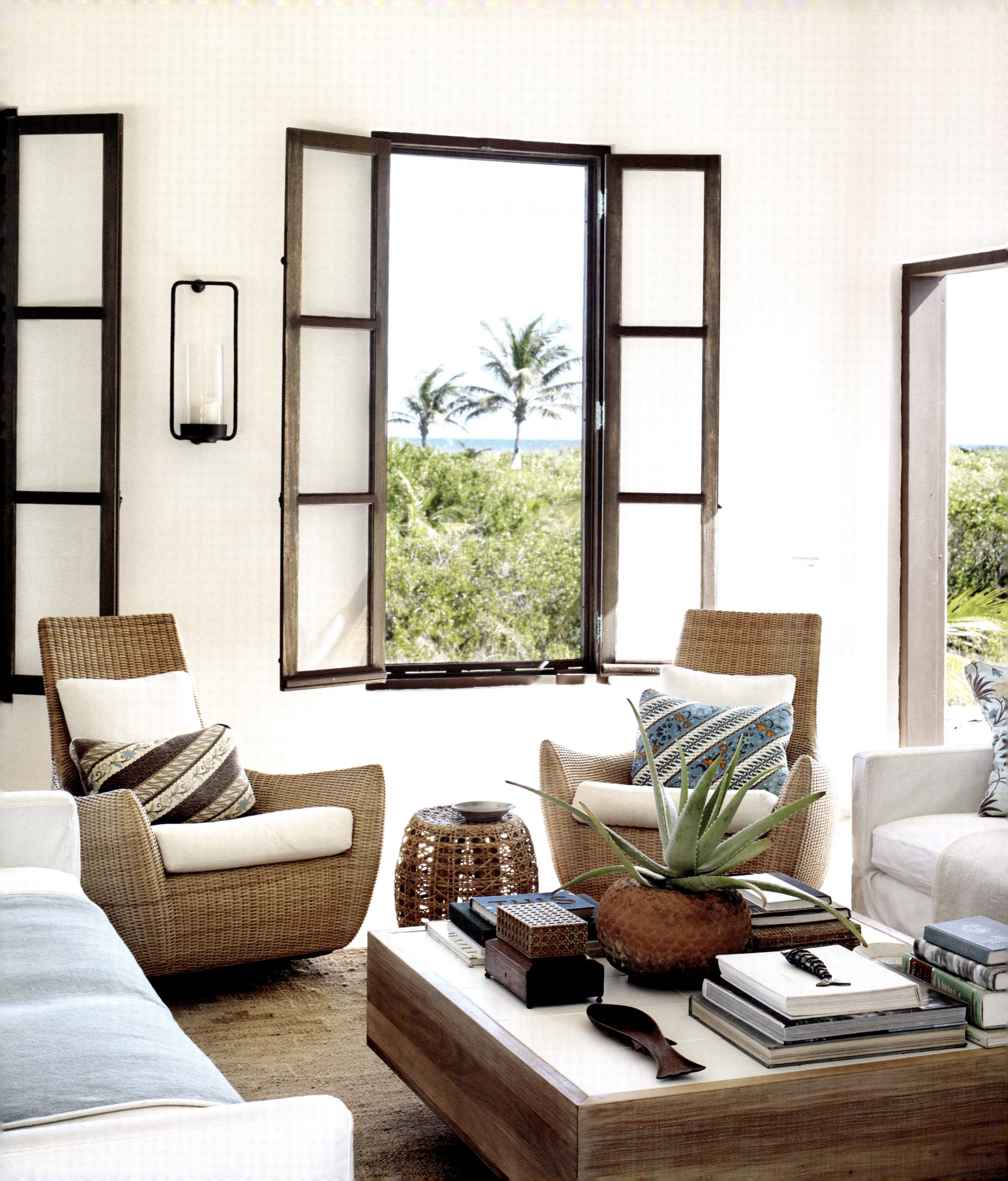

ABOVE The weather is always welcome inside, so a protective cabinet of curiosities was installed. Family memorabilia, beach finds, and natural wonders, delicate and otherwise, are periodically augmented, edited, and rearranged. OPPOSITE The enormous and boldly graphic kudu horns are antique and were bought at Sage Street Antiques in Sag Harbor. Like the framed Noguchi "bull's-eye" lantern that faces it across the room, the trophy is a weather-durable wall decoration. But more certainly, it helped to justify the Zanzibar sobriquet. Behind a beaded curtain to the left of the hearth is the kitchen and bar, which open onto the pergola-shaded dining terrace.

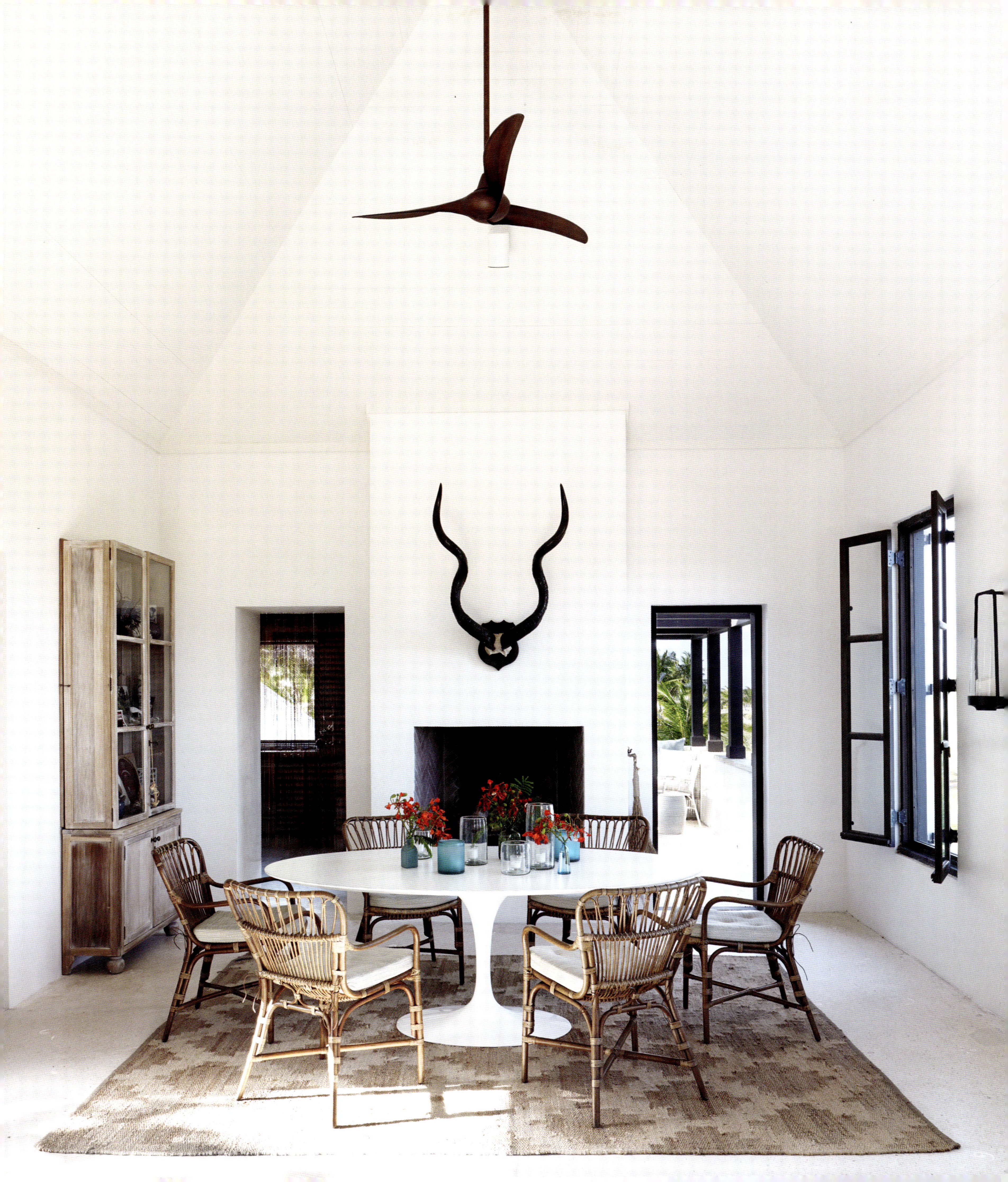

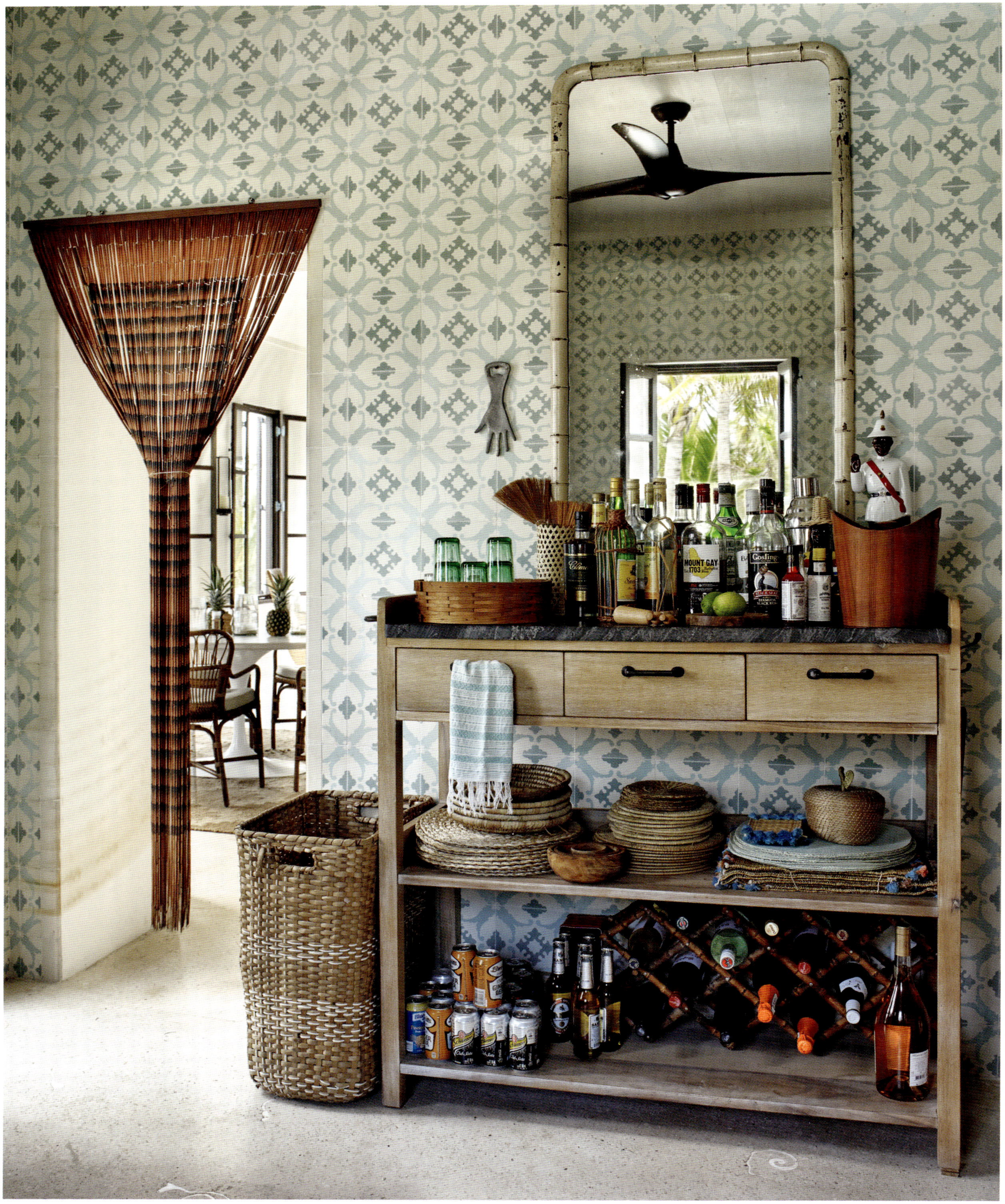
MOUNT GAY
1703
Gosling

OPPOSITE The shelves below the bar contain sets of straw placemats collected on travels to Burma, Morocco, Colombia, and the Hicksville, New York, Ikea. The surrealist Italian bottle opener "waving" from the tile is one of the decorator's long-held and favorite possessions.
ABOVE The geographical proximity to Cuba explains the longstanding Bahamian tradition of covering kitchens in the island's eponymous cement tiles. Alas, they are no longer exported from Cuba, if they are still being made there. These came from Mexico, where the technique is the same but the attitude toward capitalism is stronger.

ABOVE In the master bedroom, unlined curtains made from striped Turkish *foutas* hang at the doors to the terrace. A niche was sized to fit the vintage yellow-lacquered desk. The house parts came in crates from India and new furniture in a container from Florida, but the artwork, many books, and personalizing accessories came via speedboat from the decorator's former house on Harbour Island, fifty-five miles to the south. OPPOSITE On the floor next to the bed is a vintage Winslow Homer print. It was accepted as a going-away gift from a Harbour Islander who had no inkling. Homer's 1898 palm tree and horizon, weather and light, could not be more like Zanzibar's.

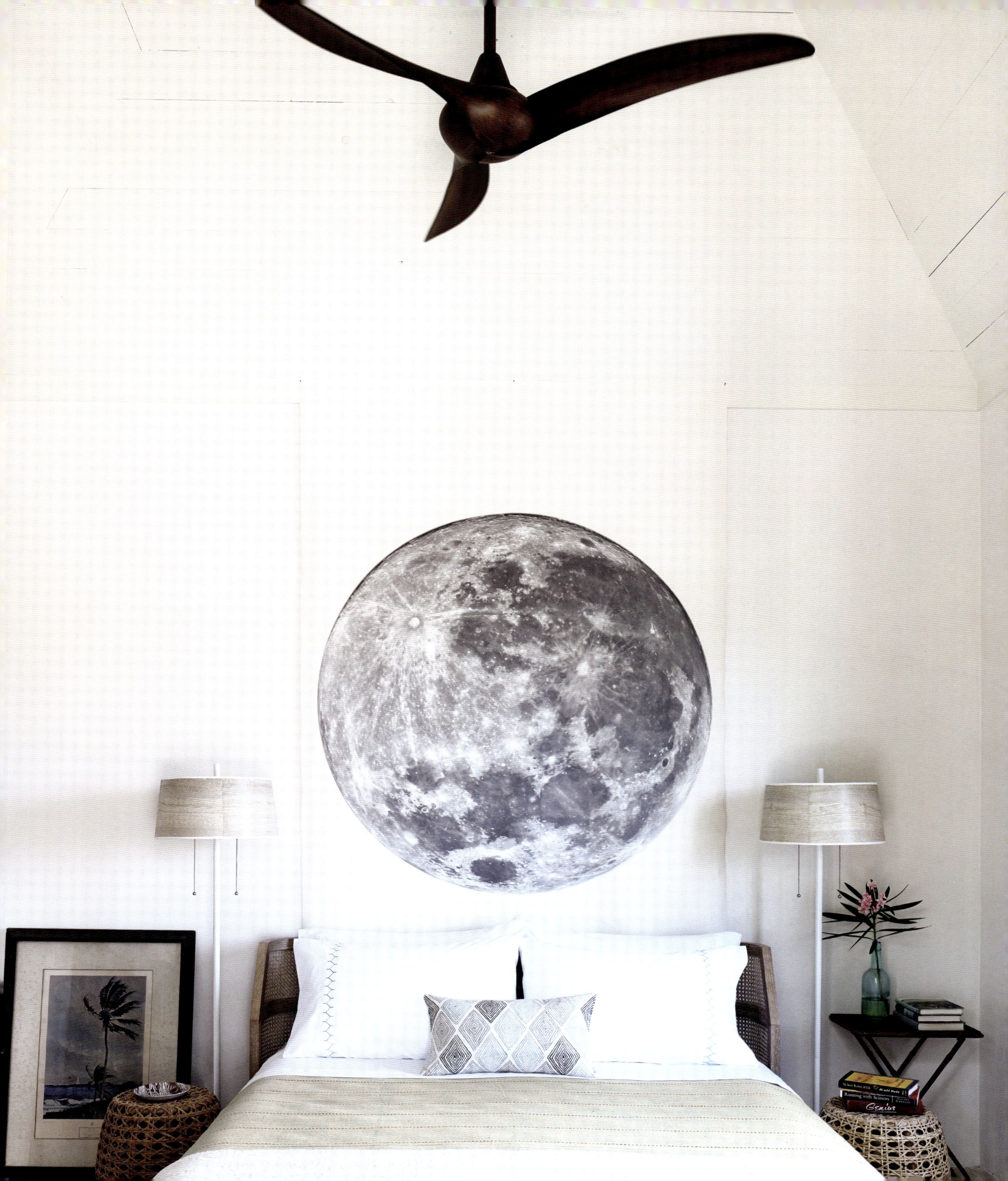
Running with Scissors
Genius

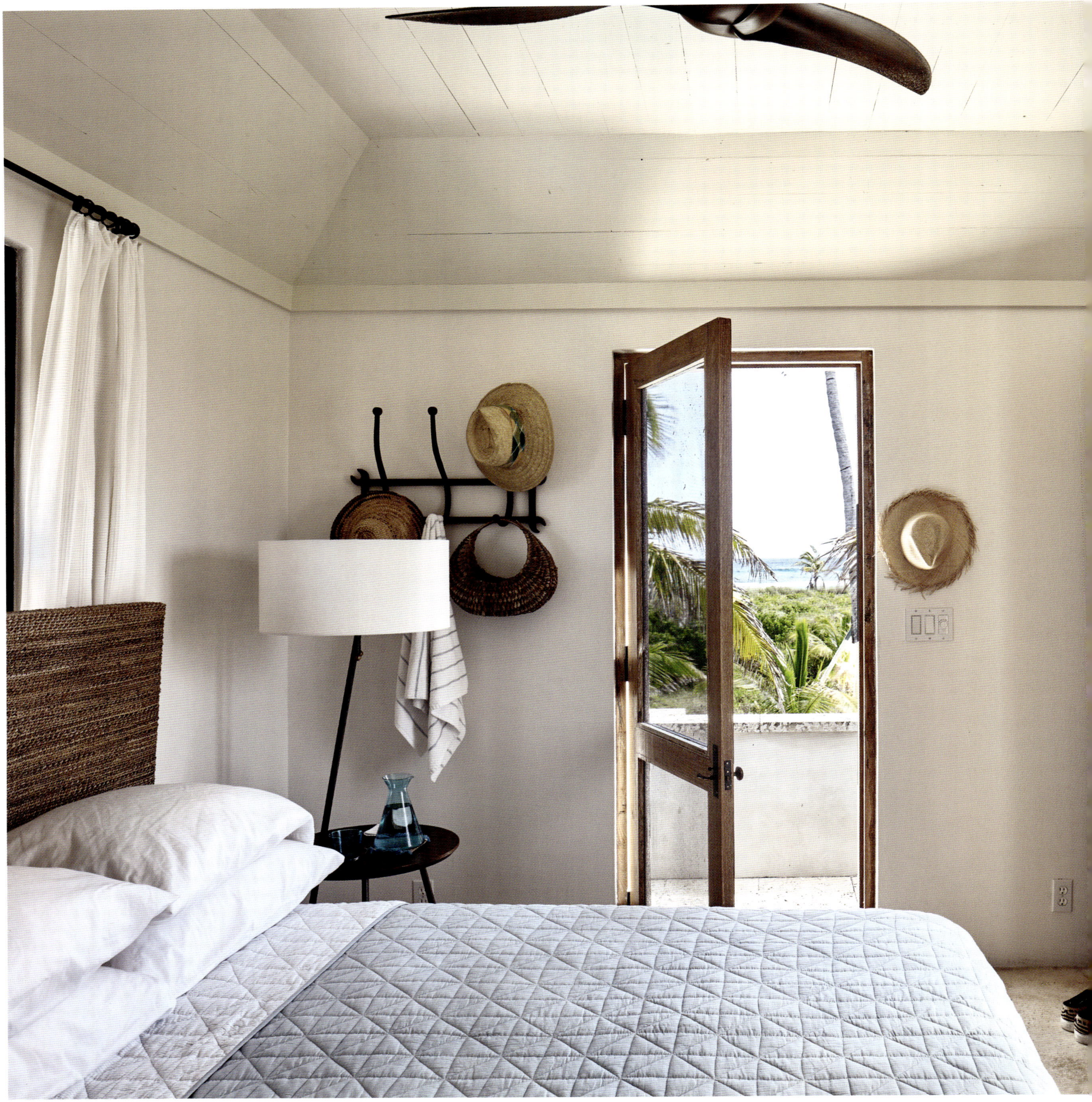

OPPOSITE The "tower" guest room looks over the pool toward the open Atlantic. Its small volume is mitigated by floating wardrobes and openings on three sides.
ABOVE In another guest room, the same wardrobes flank a writing table that overlooks a filigreed sea grape. At night the tree is romantically up-lit.
OVERLEAF LEFT The queen-size tester bed was designed to profit from this guest room's high ceiling. The textured lampshades are made from Nobilis's driftwood-like wallpaper. **OVERLEAF RIGHT** A sliding "barn door" makes the smallest of the bathrooms work. The tropical "Cousin Itt" hula skirt camouflages the works under the wall-hung sink.

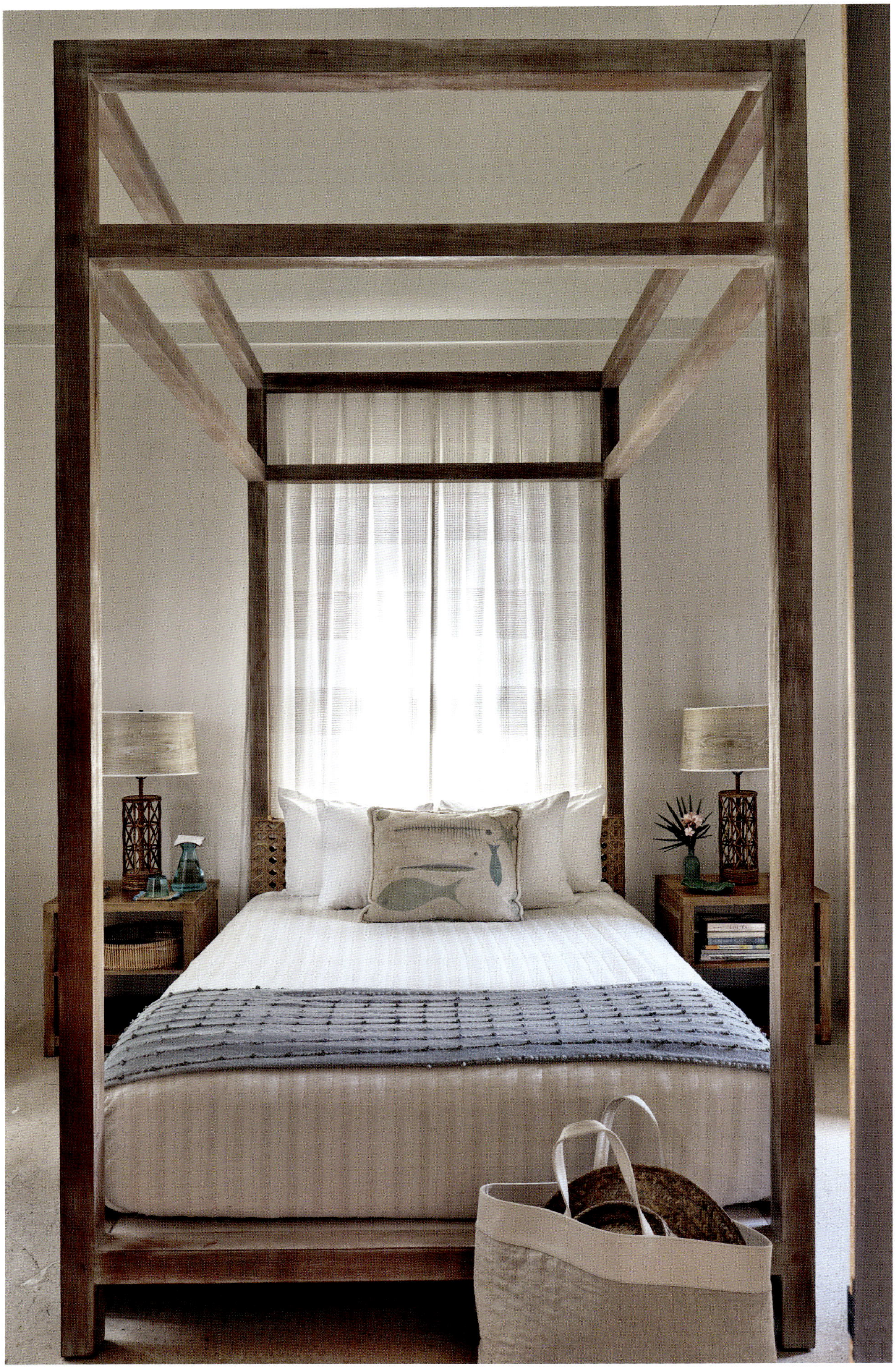

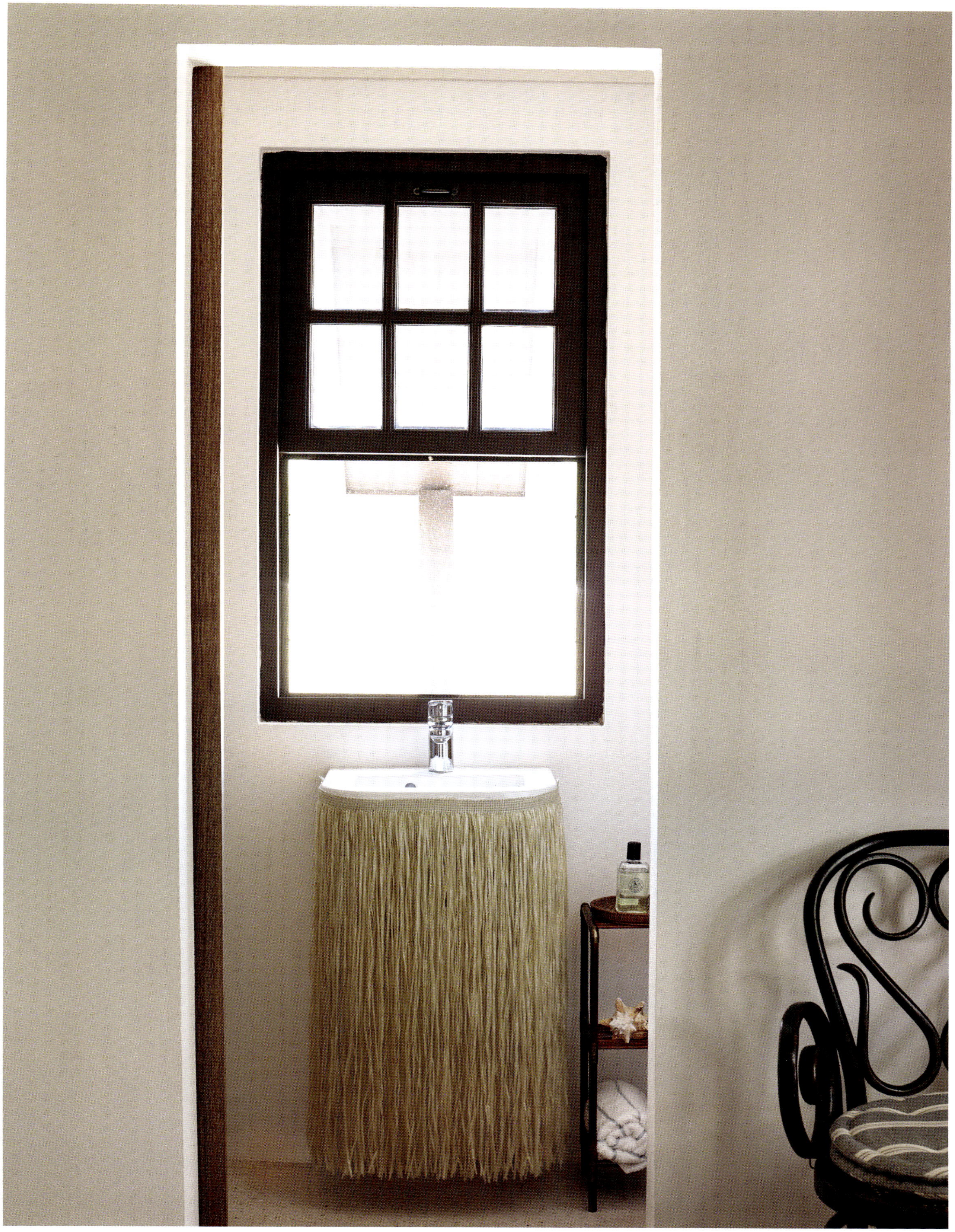

ABOVE Under the shade of bamboo matting, the table is set for an informal meal. The all-weather wicker banquette, ordered long before the house was finished, fit within a sixteenth of an inch. **OPPOSITE** As seen from the balcony of the tower guest room, the steps from the dining terrace and kitchen continue right to the bottom of the pool.

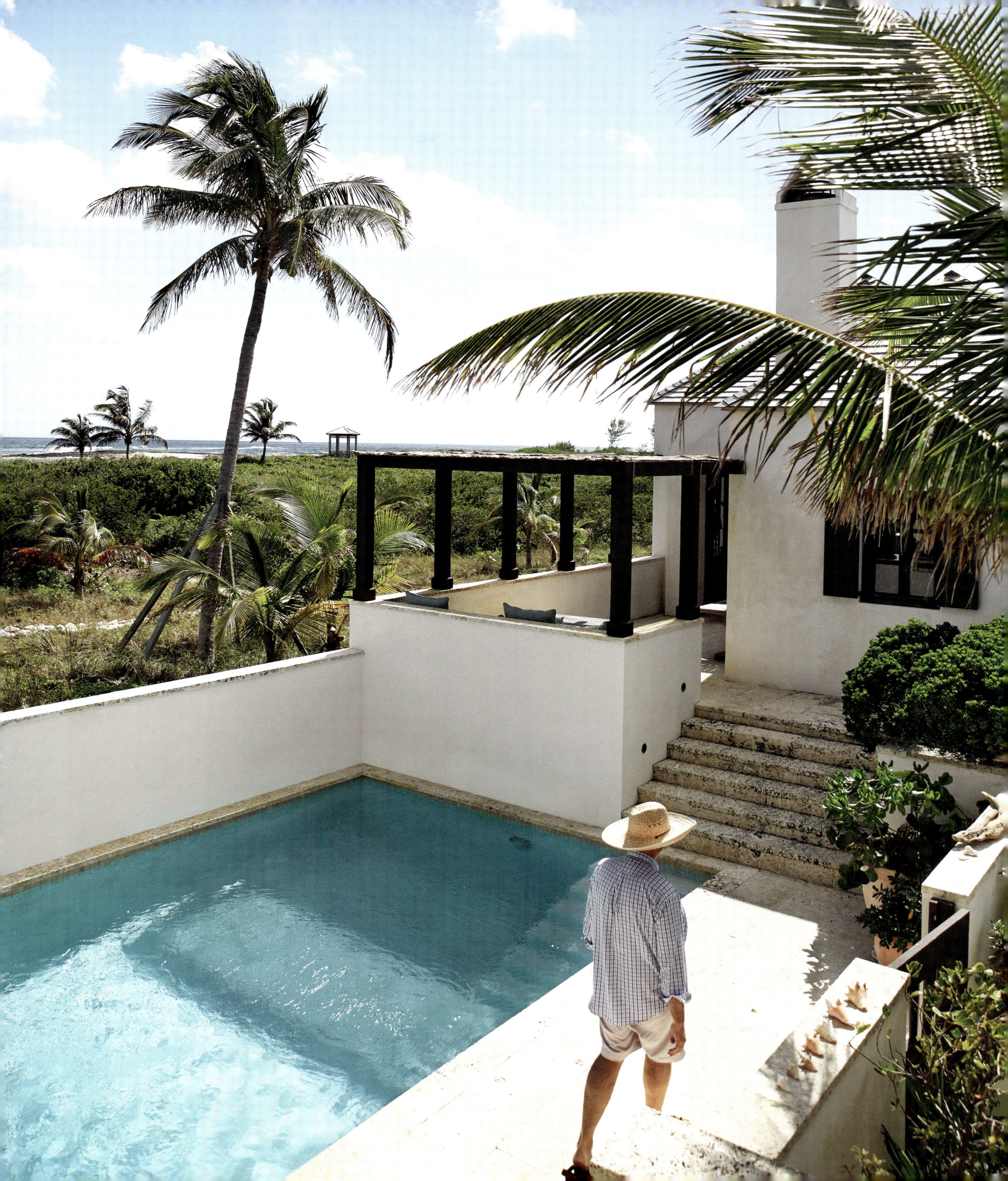

ABOVE The out-of-the-wind courtyard is furnished with a vintage Maguire daybed fitted with a mattress-style cushion in a Perennials all-weather stripe. It is used at all times except high noon, when shade is available elsewhere. The vintage batik pillows are interchangeable with those inside, as are the Palecek dining chairs. Housekeeping is as simplified as possible. OPPOSITE The kitchen door, seen here on the far side of the courtyard, is conveniently located adjacent to the principal entry, rather than at the back of the house. OVERLEAF The remains of the day at Zanzibar.

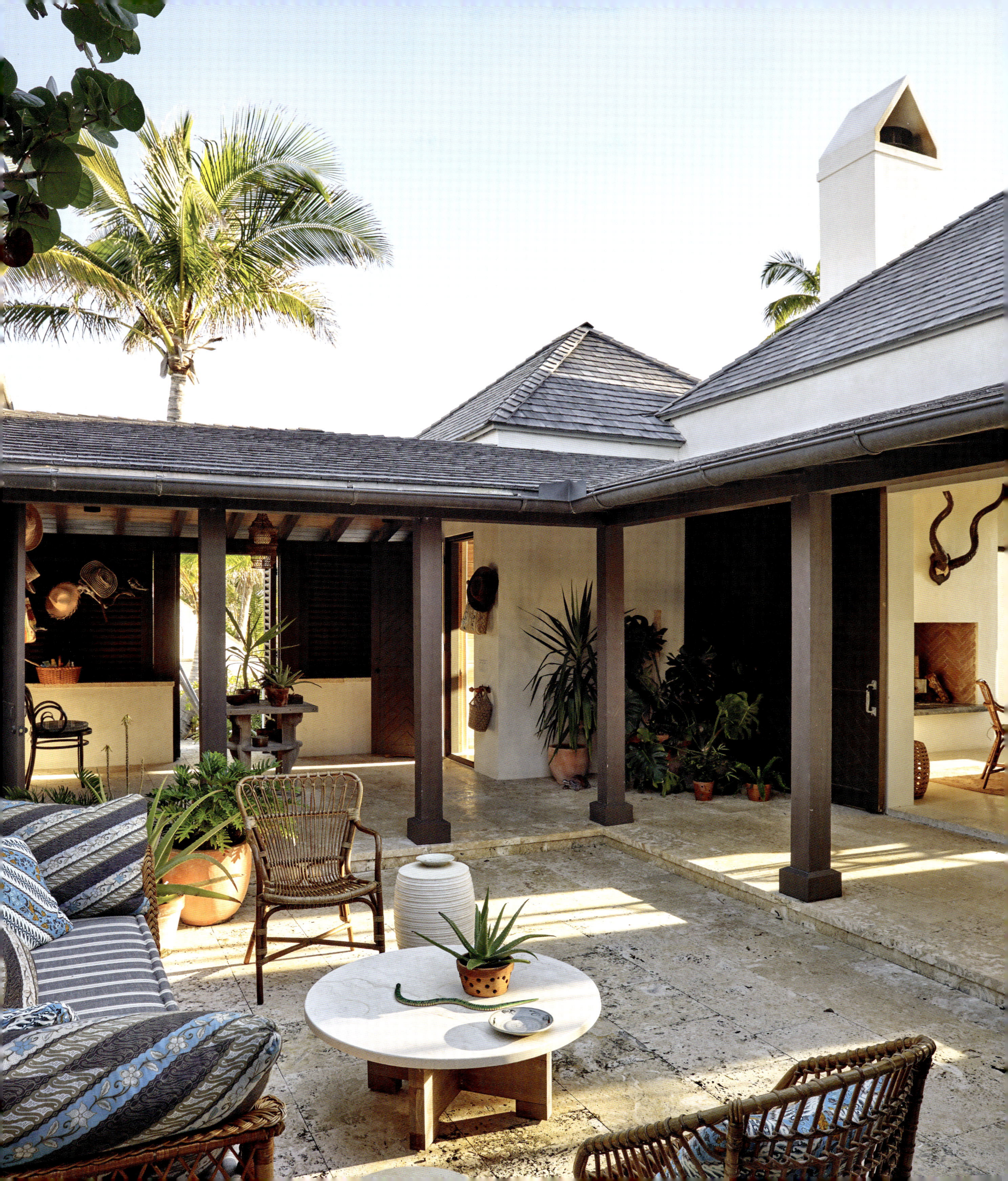

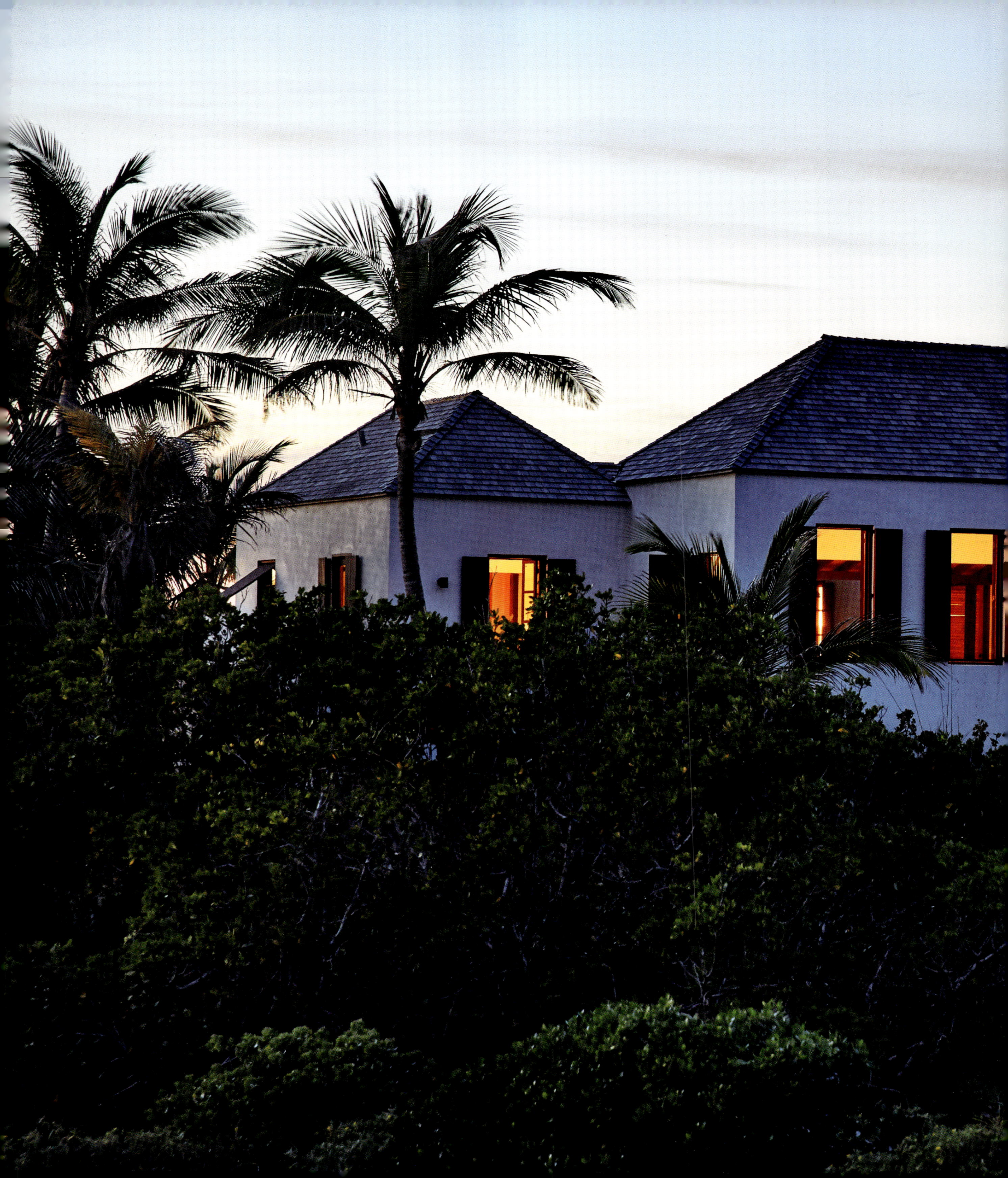

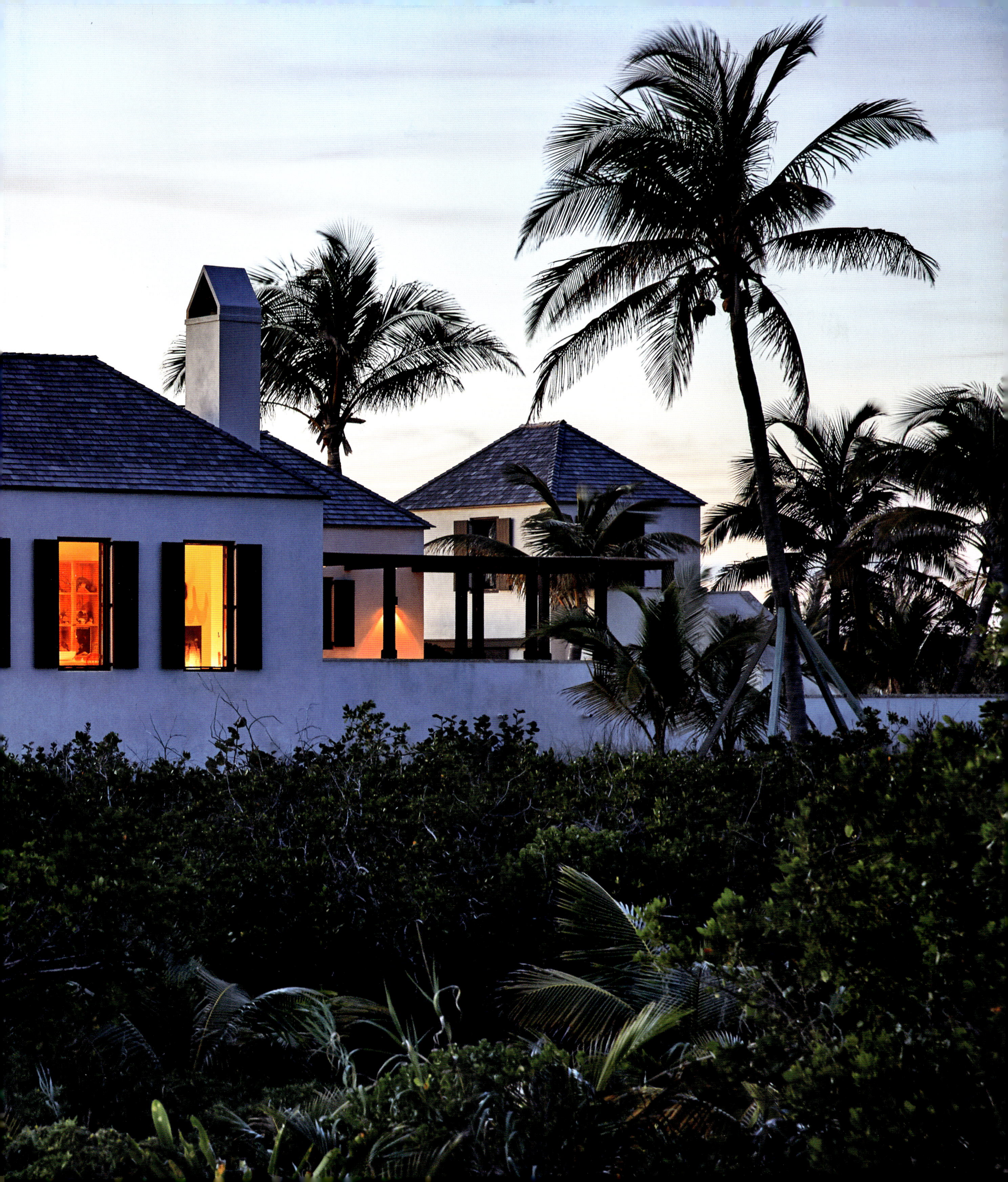

Sources

ANTIQUES
Corner House Antiques
americanantiquewicker.com

Cove Landing
(212) 288-7597

Gerald Bland
geraldblandinc.com

Jonathan Burden
jonathanburden.com

Modernity
modernity.se

Naga Antiques
nagaantiques.com

Neo Studio
(631) 725-5632

R. E. Steele
(631) 324-7812

Sage Street Antiques
(631) 725-4036

ARCHITECTS
de la Guardia Victoria Architects & Urbanists
dlgvarchitects.com

Merrill, Pastor & Colgan Architects
merrillpastor.com

Samuel G. White, PBDW Architects
pbdw.com

ARTISTS AND ART GALLERIES
Christopher Brooks
christopherbrooks101.com

Dryden Gallery & Framing
drydengalleryframing.com

Gill & Lagodich
gill-lagodich.com

Idoline Duke
idolineduke.com

Jane Parkes
arcfineartllc.com

Marcus Leatherdale
marcusleatherdale.com

Sears-Peyton Gallery
searspeyton.com

Simon Parkes
simonparkes.com

Trunk Archive
trunkarchive.com

CARPETS AND RUGS
Beauvais Carpets
beauvaiscarpets.com

Shyam Ahuja
shyamahuja.com

Studio Four NYC
studiofournyc.com

DECORATIVE PAINTERS
Brian Leaver
brianleaver.com

Frank Reijnen
(212) 794-1610

FABRICS
Bramalta
bramalta.com

Brunschwig & Fils
brunschwig.com

Carolina Irving Textiles
carolinairvingtextiles.com

Clarence House
clarencehouse.com

Holland & Sherry
interiors.hollandandsherry.com

John Robshaw Textiles
johnrobshaw.com

John Rosselli & Associates
johnrosselli.com

Katie Leede & Company
katieleede.com

Kravet
kravet.com

Lee Jofa
leejofa.com

Les Indiennes
lesindiennes.com

Lisa Fine Textiles
lisafinetextiles.com

Loro Piana
loropiana.com

Muriel Brandolini
murielbrandolini.com

Penny Morrison
pennymorrison.com

Perennials Fabrics
perennialsfabric.com

Peter Dunham Textiles
peterdunhamtextiles.com

Quadrille
quadrillefabrics.com

Ranjana Khan Home
info@ranjanakhan.com

Raoul Textiles
raoultextiles.com

Travers
zimmer-rohde.com

TylerGraphic
tylergraphic.com

FURNITURE
Bamboo & Rattan
vintagebamboorattan.com

Bauhaus 2 Your House
bauhaus2yourhouse.com

BenchSmith
benchsmith.com

Bielecky Brothers, Inc.
bieleckybrothers.com

Bonacina 1889
bonacina1889.it

Casa Mobel
casamobel.com

CB2
cb2.com

Crate & Barrel
crateandbarrel.com

Design Within Reach
dwr.com

Frontgate
frontgate.com

Homeward Furniture
homewardfurniture.com

Ikea
ikea.com

Janus et Cie
janusetcie.com

John Derian
johnderian.com

Leonards Antiques
leonardsantiques.com

Luther Quintana Upholstery, Inc.
lqupholstery.com

Palecek
palecek.com

Pottery Barn
potterybarn.com

The Raj Company
therajcompany.com

Room & Board
roomandboard.com

Rose Tarlow
rosetarlow.com

Sika Design
sika-design.com

Tucker Robbins
tuckerrobbins.com

Walters Wicker
walterswicker.com

West Elm
westelm.com

Wolf Hill Furniture
(978) 949-1150

HARDWARE
Morgik Metal Designs
morgik.com

Waterworks
waterworks.com

LANDSCAPE DESIGN AND ARCHITECTURE
Cecilia de Grelle
(305) 361-0110

David Hruska
hruskadavid@yahoo.com

Hoerr Schaudt Landscape Architects
hoerrschaudt.com

LIGHTING
Akari Associates
shop.noguchi.org

Ann-Morris
annmorrislighting.com

Blanche P. Field
blanchefield.com

Galerie des Lampes
galeriedeslampes.com

Lumfardo
lumfardo.com

O'Lampia Studio
olampia.com

Rose Uniacke
roseuniacke.com

Stephen Antonson
stephenantonson.com

The Urban Electric Co.
urbanelectricco.com

Vaughan
vaughandesigns.com

WALL COVERINGS
Adelphi Paper Hangings
adelphipaperhangings.com

Caba Company
barkskin.com

The Detroit Wallpaper Co.
detroitwallpaper.com

Nobilis
nobilis.fr

Peter Fasano
peterfasano.com

Phillip Jeffries
phillipjeffries.com

Twigs Fabrics & Wallpaper
twigswallpaperandfabric.com

Villa Lagoon Tile
villalagoontile.com

Zuber
zuber.fr

WINDOW SHADES
Conrad
conradshades.com

The Shade Store
theshadestore.com

Acknowledgments

DECORATORS CAN BE A TOUGH BUNCH. SOME of us have a good laugh about one of our often supercilious rank. He claims that his rooms are so good they "photograph themselves." They do not, nor do mine. Even the very best rooms require the photographer's discerning and editing eye to appear as good in print as in real life. Each photograph is a work of art and craft—the genuine labor cannot be underestimated.

Not every last photograph in this book is his, but I am most indebted to Francesco Lagnese. His talent, work, and steady friendship shaped this book.

Thanks to Simon Upton, Björn Wallander, and Lizzie Himmel for providing photographs from past magazine work, and to Pieter Estersohn for our photo safari to the Bahamas, which resulted in the chapter "Sunrise and Sunset."

I thank my staff at Union Square for making it fun to go to work. Still. They are the producers and deserve much credit for the work shown in this book. Particularly my factotum and friend Nancy "When She Quits, I Quit" Tripptree, who never imagined she would be around thirty years later. Her innate feel for cash flow continues to astound. She makes the unnerving business end of things worry free.

Long ago, a style-acute editor friend and accidental mentor would periodically excoriate me: "Ah! Rip Van With-It." Thank you, D.D., I'm still at your knee. Luckily, there are younger editors, too, who find my work newsworthy even when it's a bit "old fashioned." It's just decorating the way I do it. Thank you to Amy Astley, Sophie Dow Donelson, Whitney Robinson, Stellene Volandes, Carolina Irving, and Howard Christian. You have all kept me going. I also thank Jennifer Boles and Stephen Drucker, the very best authorities, who placed me in their pantheon, however undeservedly. And a shout-out to Instagram for my fan base and inspiration for the layout of this book.

Thanks to the clients who have allowed their houses to be included in this book and to the many others who also turned over a part of their lives to the decorator. I've made a career out of your trust, and hope I got it right—the houses and the commentary.

I'm thankful for the collegial round-table meetings (a Saarinen, of course) with the Vendome family. Mark and Nina Magowan, my publishers, who continue to keep me engaged as a decorator, a friend, and now as an author. Celia Fuller, the preternaturally able and talented book designer. The cadence of the photographs and design of the pages were revealed to us as if by magic. Adjustments came almost without asking. But special thanks to Jackie Decter—her punctuation and syntactical revisions are a sow's-ear-to-silk-purse miracle. Somehow Jackie knew I'd embrace an alien and daunting task and would be adequately able. It's been enriching, but I'm going back to decorating.

My family went unthanked in *Tom Scheerer Decorates* but will not here: Mike Baldridge, who expands life beyond my career in many ways—part time in Paris and a full-time life of fun all over. My sisters, a triumvirate of extraordinary talents and individual graces. They keep us all close to home in spirit when we can't be there in body. My father (who "left the room" over ten years ago). He kvelled (WASPs do this too) at my accomplishments and foresaw the favorable "earnings report" where I did not. The two books would have made him additionally proud.

Mothers must be somewhere near the heart of all decorating—domestic divas and glamorous doyennes are the driving forces, whether real or fantasized. Mine, however, has a life well beyond houses, clothes, and "style"; in fact, she's more often a bemused bystander. She's a realist—self-deprecating and no-nonsense practical, while managing to be a generous host and a loving friend and parent. At eighty-seven she is fearless—still making friends while keeping up with her old and dear ones. My friends are her friends. She's the most fun and funniest and has been one of my life's main calling cards. Always curious about the telling details of life, she casts her gimlet eye and her loving gaze with equal measure. She is the standard by which I judge all things, all people, and myself.

Tom Scheerer: More Decorating
First published in 2019 by The Vendome Press
Vendome is a registered trademark of The Vendome Press, LLC

NEW YORK
Suite 2043
244 Fifth Avenue
New York, NY 10001

LONDON
63 Edith Grove
London,
SW10 0LB, UK

www.vendomepress.com

Copyright © 2019 The Vendome Press
Text copyright © 2019 Tom Scheerer
Photographs copyright © 2019 Francesco Lagnese

All rights reserved. No part of the contents of this book may be reproduced in whole or in part without prior written permission from the publisher.

Distributed in North America by Abrams Books
Distributed in the United Kingdom, and the rest of the world, by Thames & Hudson

ISBN 978-0-86565-363-4

PUBLISHERS: Beatrice Vincenzini, Mark Magowan, and Francesco Venturi
EDITOR: Jacqueline Decter
PRODUCTION DIRECTOR: Jim Spivey
PREPRESS COLOR MANAGER: Dana Cole
DESIGNER: Celia Fuller

Library of Congress Cataloging-in-Publication Data
available upon request

PRINTED AND BOUND IN CHINA BY 1010 PRINTING INTERNATIONAL LTD.
FIRST PRINTING

All photos by Francesco Lagnese, with the exception of the following:
Lizzie Himmel, pp. 14–15
Pieter Estersohn, pp. 16, 216–49
Simon Upton, pp. 142–67
Björn Wallander, pp. 268, 277, 280–81

PAGE 1 An entrance hall in the Bahamas lined in pickled pecky cypress.
PAGES 2–3 The veranda of a Harbour Island house overlooks the island's famous pink sand beach.
PAGES 4–5 Travels on the Subcontinent inspired this Île Saint-Louis bedroom.
PAGES 6–7 A Long Island summer living room features wicker furniture with cushions upholstered in glazed chintz.
PAGES 8–9 My living room in the Bahamas mixes custom and ready-made furniture, vintage batiks, and island-style printed cottons from Quadrille Fabrics.

GEONOMA BREVISPATHA
A. SCHEELEA QUADRISPERMA
B. GUILLIELMA MATTOGROSSENSIS
BACTRIS VULGARIS
COCOS PICROPHYLLA
BACTRIS GASTONIANA
A. SCHEELEA CORUMBAENSIS
B. SCHEELEA ANISITSII
C. SCHEELEA PRINCEPS
TAB. 53
A. EUTERPE YATAPUENSIS
B. EUTERPE BADIOCARPA
C. EUTERPE CONTROVERSA
D. EUTERPE OLERACEA
E. EUTERPE EDULIS